Born on 29 August 1632. Entered Christ Church, Oxford, in 1652, where he received his M.A. in 1658. At Christ Church he was elected Student in 1658, Lecturer in Greek in 1660, Lecturer in Rhetoric in 1662, and Censor of Moral Philosophy, 1664. Physician and Secretary to Anthony Ashley Cooper (later Earl of Shaftesbury), 1667–81. Elected Fellow of the Royal Society, 1668. Secretary to the Lords Proprietors of Carolina, 1668–75. Secretary to the Council of Trade and Plantations, 1673–5. Deprived of his appointment to Christ Church by royal decree, 1684. Voluntary exile in Holland, 1683–9. Commissioner on the Board of Trade, 1696–1700. Died on 28 October 1704.

JOHN LOCKE

An Essay Concerning Human Understanding

Abridged and edited with an introduction by
John W. Yolton
Dean of Rutgers College and Professor of Philosophy at Rutgers
University, New Brunswick

Dent: London and Melbourne
EVERYMAN'S LIBRARY

© Editing, J. M. Dent & Sons Ltd, 1961
© Selection and introduction, J. M. Dent & Sons Ltd, 1977
All rights reserved

Made in Great Britain by
Guernsey Press Co. Ltd, Guernsey, C.I. for
J. M. Dent & Sons Ltd
Aldine House, 33 Welbeck Street, London W1M 8LX

First abridged edition included in
Everyman's Library in 1947
Complete two-volume edition first published 1961
New edition, abridged, 1976
Last reprinted 1985

No. 1332 Paperback ISBN 0 460 11332 1

CONTENTS

[SQUARE BRACKETS INDICATE OMITTED MATERIAL]

BOOK I

OF INNATE NOTIONS

BOOK II

OF IDEAS

v

BOOK III

Of Words

BOOK IV

Of Knowledge and Opinion

INTRODUCTION

In 1671 Locke began to write what became his *Essay concerning Human Understanding*, first published in 1690. During those intervening years the *Essay* went through many drafts, many starts and stops. In letters to friends he discussed some of the problems he confronted during its composition. He himself describes the work as having been 'written by incoherent parcels' ('Epistle to the Reader'). He recognized that what he referred to as, 'This discontinued way of writing may have occasioned, besides others, two faults, viz. that too little and too much be said in it'. He admits that 'possibly it might be reduced to a narrower compass than it is, and that some parts of it might be contracted: the ways it has been writ in, by catches and many long intervals of interruption, being apt to cause some repetitions'. He claimed, however, that he was 'now too lazy, or too busy, to make it shorter'.

When John Wynne, an Oxford tutor, wrote to Locke in 1694 about an abridgment he had begun for his own students, Locke replied in the tones of these remarks from the 'Epistle to the Reader'. He agreed with Wynne that perhaps a shortened version might help to overcome some of the adverse reactions the *Essay* had received. Wynne's published abridgment was essentially a précis, for the most part in Wynne's own words, of what Locke said on various topics and in the different chapters. There were, in the eighteenth and early nineteenth centuries, a number of other abridgments, outlines, synopses of Locke's *Essay*, usually, like Wynne's, designed for the use of students. One interesting book, not purporting to be an abridgment of Locke but one which does come close to being a detailed paraphrase (in many places an almost verbatim reproduction) of Locke's *Essay*, was William Duncan's *The Elements of Logic* (1748). This logic had several reprintings in the century: it was widely read and used.

Duncan's logic, one of a number of indigenous British logics in the eighteenth century, indicates the strength of Locke's influence in that century. These Lockean logics, together with the *Essay* itself, were used by students at Oxford. Jeremy Bentham read Locke while at Oxford. Later, writing to John Lind, Bentham remarked: 'Without Locke I could have known nothing. But I think I could now take Locke's Essay and write

it over again, so as to make it much more precise and appre-
hensible in half the compass.'[1] Bentham's reaction is probably
typical of many readers of Locke.

The abridgment which follows is not a rewriting of Locke: it
is Locke's text, not rearranged, but condensed into one volume.
It is more like the French abridgment or extract Locke published
just prior to the appearance of the first English edition.[2] There is,
within the *Essay* itself, a kind of abridgment, an outline or over-
view. Book I of that work has usually been known for its polemic
against innate ideas and principles. But, in fact, that book contains more comment on and appeals to Locke's own positive
doctrines than it does negative attacks against innatism. It is a
rather cogent foreshadowing of the main doctrines elaborated in
the three following books. An examination of those doctrines in
the context of Book I can serve as an effective introduction to the
study of Locke. Concentrating on what Book I reveals about
Locke's views has one other advantage: by placing his own
views in the context of those he rejected, we may escape some of
the preconceived notions about what he says, which so many of
his subsequent readers have brought to their study of Locke.[3] It
is often useful, when we seek an understanding of a philosophic
text, to pay attention to the doctrines which the author attacks or
rejects. What he writes against may be more informative of his
own doctrines than are his statements of the alternatives. The
first book of Locke's *Essay* is important for just this reason.

1   LOCKE AND INNATISM

While a certain aspect of the theory of innateness has recently
been revived by Chomsky, lending perhaps more timeliness to
Locke's polemic against innateness in Book I, the doctrine
Locke opposed seems to us too naïve to take seriously.[4] The

[1] Letter of 5 October 1774, in vol. I of *The Correspondence of Jeremy
Bentham*, ed. by T. L. S. Sprigge (1968), p. 205.

[2] Printed as 'Extrait d'un Livre Anglois qui n'est pas encore publié,
intitulé *Essai Philosophique* concernant *L'Entendement*', in *Bibliothèque
Universelle et Historique de l'Année* 1688, t. VIII, pp. 49–142.

[3] There is another interesting feature of Book I: between it and the final
chapter of the fourth book, there is a symmetry. The first chapter of Book I
is an Introduction to the whole of the *Essay*. Each of the three remaining
chapters of that book deals in order with Locke's views on logic and know-
edge, on action and morality, and on the nature of ideas. This threefold
discussion is not unlike the threefold division of the sciences at the very end
of the *Essay*: the science of nature, of action, and of signs.

[4] See N. Chomsky, *Cartesian Linguistics* (1966). The central claim of
Chomsky's linguistic theory is 'that the general features of grammatical
structure are common to all languages and reflect certain fundamental
properties of the mind' (p. 59). These grammatical universals set the conditions for language learning; they are not learned themselves but 'provide

'established opinion amongst some men' in seventeenth-century Britain was, Locke tells us, 'that there are in the *understanding* certain *innate principles*, some primary notions, κοιναὶ ἔννοιαι, characters, as it were, stamped upon the mind of man, which the soul receives in its very first being and brings into the world with it' (1.2.1).[1] Metaphors of 'red letters emblazoned on the heart', of marks on the soul, were, for many of Locke's contemporaries, devices for articulating non-conventional, non-relative moral standards.[2] These metaphors were also ways of referring to maxims from which certain knowledge could be derived. Locke took these metaphors seriously, he pushed the defenders of innatism to justify their claims (e.g. by showing that in fact there are principles universally accepted). He insisted that they clarify whether or not they meant that no experience or reason is necessary for the recognition of the truth of such principles. Locke produced sociological and anthropological evidence to reject the claims of universal acceptance.[3] If the holders of this doctrine of innateness claimed that the principles said to be innate were accepted only after reason or experience had intervened, then, Locke pointed out, a great number—in fact, an indefinite number—of principles and maxims could claim to be innate: all the truths of mathematics, for example. Locke offered a stronger objection still to innatism, an objection which reveals an important psychological principle of his own. 'To say a notion is imprinted on the mind, and yet at the same time to say that the mind is ignorant of it and never yet took notice of it, is to make this impression nothing' (1.2.5). This psychological truth is almost a conceptual truth: 'it seeming to me near a contradiction to say that there are truths imprinted on the soul which it perceives or understands not'.

This principle, that what is in my mind must be conscious to me, underlies Locke's accounts of awareness and of the nature of ideas. I shall return to it later. It is important here to note that

---

the organizing principles that make language learning possible, that must exist if data are to lead to knowledge' (pp. 59–60). There are many problems surrounding Chomsky's theory. For two useful recent discussions, in the light of the seventeenth-century doctrine of innateness, see R. Edgley's 'Innate Ideas', in *Knowledge and Necessity*, vol. 3, Royal Institute of Philosophy Lectures, ed. by G. N. A. Vesey (1970), and Jonathan Barnes, 'Mr. Locke's Darling Notion', in *The Philosophical Quarterly*, 22 (1972), pp. 193–214.

[1] All references to Locke are to the Everyman text and are given by these numbers, the numbers representing in order the book, the chapter and the section.

[2] For a detailed discussion of the holders of this doctrine of innateness, see my *John Locke and the Way of Ideas*, Chapter 2 (1956).

[3] See, e.g., *Essay*, 1.3.9–12.

this principle is announced and used in the first book of the *Essay*. By seeing against which alternative account of ideas it is invoked, we can gain some appreciation of the doctrine of ideas in Locke's theory of knowledge. But there are two other aspects of the polemic against innateness which we must examine first.

The particular version of innateness to which Locke objects is of less importance for understanding his own doctrines than are the specific uses to which appeals to innateness were made. There were two specific uses: the one was to provide a basis for morality, in truths common to all mankind; the other was to provide certain primitive notions, basic truths (those Locke called 'speculative principles') which were said to be necessary in accounting for the possibility or actuality of knowledge. To this second use Locke insisted that knowledge is derived from experience, rather than principles.

2   PRINCIPLES OF KNOWLEDGE

Locke was of course aware that in challenging this latter use of innateness he was going against a widely held belief. The way to knowledge was thought to be by means of demonstration from self-evident maxims. The principles Locke mentions (those 'magnified principles of demonstration') are, 'Whatsoever is, is'; 'it is impossible for the same thing to be and not to be'; 'the same is not different'. There were writers who claimed [1] that any identity proposition had to be derived from the general principle of identity, that to know and accept a proposition that, for example (these are Locke's examples), 'green is not red' or that the nurse 'is neither the *cat* it [the child] plays with nor the *blackamoor* it is afraid of', or 'mustard is not an apple', the child must know the general principle that 'it is impossible for the same thing to be and not to be' (1.2.25). We do not acquire our knowledge of the world by working from such general principles. They are 'the language and business of the schools and academies of learned nations, accustomed to that sort of conversation or learning, where disputes are frequent, these maxims being suited to artificial argumentation and useful for conviction, but not much conducing to the discovery of truth or advancement of knowledge' (1.2.27).

In Locke's view, we learn all such general propositions after we have acquired specific ideas and understood the meanings of words. As the child acquires his stock of ideas, he learns,

---

[1] John Sergeant is a good example. See his *Method to Science* (1696). I have a discussion of Locke's method in my *Locke and the Compass of Human Understanding*, Chapter 3 (1970).

without of course formulating it thus, that each idea is what it is and not another idea (1.2.23). Whenever we consider any proposition, 'so as to perceive the two *ideas* signified by the terms and affirmed or denied one of the other, to be the same or different', we are 'presently and infallibly certain of the truth of such a proposition, and this equally whether these propositions be in terms standing for more general *ideas*, or such as are less so, v.g. whether the general *idea* of *being* be affirmed of itself, as in this proposition, *Whatsoever is, is*; or a more particular *idea* be affirmed of itself, as *A man is a man*' (4.7.4). It is the difference of the ideas which, 'as soon as the terms are understood, makes the truth of the proposition presently visible'. The whole of Chapters VII and VIII of Book IV constitutes an extended attack on the scholastic maxim that, 'All reasonings are *ex praecognitis et praeconcessis*' (4.7.8). These chapters are also attacks upon the method of disputation used in the Examination Schools at Oxford, in which syllogisms were freely constructed using general maxims about whole and part, same and difference. No one who is unaware of the pervasive use of this scholastic method of arguing, and of the disdain many people such as Locke had for the frivolity of the disputations at Oxford, can fully appreciate the vehemence of Locke's rejection of the syllogism and such maxims. Knowledge is not, he insisted, acquired by reasoning from general principles, nor is the syllogism a logic of discovery. Against the appeal to maxims, Locke offered his account of the acquisition and understanding of ideas. Against the use of the syllogism, he offered his notion of demonstration as conceptual clarification. His polemic in Book I against innate speculative principles is thus closely related to important doctrines of his own about the nature of knowledge: acquisition of ideas through experience stands in stark opposition to derivation of knowledge from innate (or merely accepted) general principles.

3 MORAL ACTION AND RULES

The other use made of the doctrine of innateness was as a claim for universal moral truths. Locke has an easy time establishing that societies vary in what they accept as moral rules or practices. But a more important objection to innate practical principles is that such principles are not, as are speculative ones, self-evident. Moral principles 'require reasoning and discourse, and some exercise of the mind' (1.3.1). We can always justifiably demand a reason for any moral rule (1.3.4). The truth of moral rules 'plainly depends upon some other, antecedent to them and from

which they must be deduced'. The sort of reasoning and discourse required for moral rules may be demonstration; it is at
least a form of conceptual analysis. Before we look more closely
at Locke's view of moral reasoning, we need to consider several
other aspects of his discussion of innate practical principles.

First of all, we should note that, in one sense of 'practical',
Locke recognizes some innate, non-learned principles. A desire
for happiness and an aversion to misery are 'innate practical
principles which (as practical principles ought) do continue
constantly to operate and influence all our actions' (1.3.3). It is
'Nature' that has put into all men these principles, these 'natural
tendencies'.[1] Locke even borrows from the innatist's vocabulary
and speaks of these tendencies being 'imprinted on the minds of
men'. What Locke rejects are 'characters on the mind, which
are to be the principles of knowledge, regulating our practice'.
The desire for happiness and the aversion to misery are 'principles of action . . . lodged in our appetites'. Not only are they
not innate rules, they are not even moral. If 'left to their full
swing, they would carry men to the over-turning of all morality'
(1.3.13). The function of moral laws is to curb and restrain
'these exorbitant desires'.

For Locke, moral action must be rule-following, at least rule-
conforming. He makes an important distinction between the
description of an action as, for example, drunkenness, and the
appraisal of that action as good, bad, or indifferent. For appraisal,
we must refer the description to a rule (2.28.15). Locke recognized that we frequently combine these features (the descriptive
or positive feature with the evaluative feature), using the same
word to 'express both the mode or action and its moral rectitude
or obliquity' (2.28.16). There are three different types of rules to
which men refer their actions for appraisal: the divine law, civil
law, and the law of opinion or reputation (what he sometimes
calls the 'law of fashion or private censure') (2.28.7, 13). He
knew that 'virtue' is most commonly taken 'for those actions
which according to the different opinions of several countries are
accustomed laudable' (1.3.18). Custom is, in fact, 'a greater
power than nature' (1.3.25), the principles or rules acquired in
our childhood from 'the superstition of a nurse or the authority
of an old woman' stay with us and, unless we later become self-
critical, these principles become accepted as the standards for
action (1.3.22). The force of custom and our fear of discovering

---

[1] His *Some Thoughts concerning Education* (1693) spoke of tendencies,
character traits which children have and which the tutor must recognize.
(See sects. 66, 102, 139, 216.)

that rules we have always taken as sound may have an origin in superstition, lead us to follow the received opinion of our country or party (1.3.25).[1] The difficulties of being critical about rules for our actions are greatly increased if we mistakenly believe our rules to be 'the standard set up by God'.

In these passages of Book I, Locke indicates how it is that 'it comes to pass that *men* worship the idols that have been set up in their minds' (1.3.26). Locke was concerned not only that we mistake as innate, rules which are not innate, but also that we mistake as God's rules those which only have the force of custom behind them. The true ground of morality 'can only be the will and law of a god, who sees men in the dark, has in his hand rewards and punishments, and power enough to call to account the proudest offender' (1.3.6). '*To do as one would be done to*' is 'the great principle of morality' (1.3.7). The principle is described as 'that most unshaken rule of morality and foundation of all social virtue' (1.3.4). Locke makes the general point that 'what duty is cannot be understood without a law, nor a law be known or supposed without a law maker, or without reward and punishment'. It is clear, from numerous passages in Book I and later, that for Locke, the law-maker is God, the reward and punishment is eternal damnation or happiness, and the law against which we should measure all our actions is God's law (see, e.g., 1.3.12, 13). God's law—which he also refers to as the law of nature—is not innate or 'imprinted on our minds in their very originals'. The law of nature is 'something that we, being ignorant of, may attain to the knowledge of, by the use and due application of our natural faculties' (1.3.13).

How can we use our natural faculties to attain the true rule for moral action? In those essays written while Locke was Moral Censor at Christ Church in 1664 (the *Essays on the Law of Nature*) he argues that we at least can, by experience and reason, arrive at 'the notion of the maker of nature'. Once we have this notion, 'the notion of a universal law of nature binding on all men necessarily emerges' (p. 133). The arguments for a god to which Locke makes reference in these early *Essays* are obviously a variation of the argument from design, an argument derived, as he there says, 'from the matter, motion, and the visible structure and arrangement of this world' (p. 135). It is, he says, 'surely undisputed that' the beauty, order, and structure of the world 'could not have come together casually and by chance into so regular and in every respect so perfect and ingeniously pre-

[1] For similar remarks on the force of custom, see Locke's *Essays on the Law of Nature*, ed. by W. von Leyden (1954) p. 135.

pared a structure' (p. 153).[1] We reach the second of the above
conclusions—that there is a universal law binding on all men—
by an appeal to teleology: God has not created the world 'for
nothing and without purpose' (p. 157).[2]

So far, Locke has produced arguments showing how we can
reach by reason the conclusion that there is a law-maker who
'intends man to do something'. Can he show, by reason and
discourse, how we can discover what it is God intends us to do?
Locke's answers are not exactly evasive in these early *Essays*, but
he does not produce any specific rules. He thinks, for example,
that 'from the end in view for all things', we can discover that,
since God is gracious, wise, and perfect, he intends us to glorify
God (p. 157). Since man 'is neither made without design nor
endowed to no purpose with these faculties . . . his functions
appear to be that which nature has prepared him to perform',
that is, to contemplate God's works and his wisdom. Man also
'feels himself not only to be impelled by life's experience and
pressing needs to procure and preserve a life in society with
other men, but also to enter into society by a certain
propensity of nature, and to be prepared for the maintenance of
society by the gift of speech' (p. 157). He makes a few other
claims for the law of nature, for example, that it forbids 'us to
offend or injure without cause any private person' (p. 163); but
he makes no attempt to reason to such specific conclusions.
There are many anticipations in these *Essays* of claims and
arguments advanced in his later published works, especially in
the *Essay* and *Two Treatises*. On the basis of these early *Essays*,
the best we can do to establish the nature of moral reasoning is
to say, if we accept the argument from design, that reason provides us with what Locke later called the true ground of morality,
that is, God as a universal law-maker, who can reward and
punish, etc.

There are, in the published works of Locke, various specific
rules cited as laws of nature; but his defence of these as laws of
nature, not just laws of custom, is not really any stronger than
the innatist's defence of his principles. I think that Locke did not
much disagree with the sort of moral rules cited by the innatists.
What he wanted to do was to attack their claim that these rules
are innate. He claimed that the precepts of natural religion are

---

[1] Cf. *Essay*, 1.4.9: 'For the visible marks of extraordinary wisdom and
power appear so plainly in all the works of the creation that a rational
creature who will but seriously reflect on them cannot miss the discovery of
a *deity* . . .'
[2] For other expressions of his belief in a purposive universe, see *Essay*,
2.1.15.

'plain and very intelligible to all mankind' and that they are seldom controverted (3.9.23), but his claim that we should be able to derive the true measure of right and wrong by going from self-evident propositions to necessary consequences (4.3.18) was never exemplified. It is not entirely clear what he understood by the notion of a demonstrative morality. Did he intend a proper formal deduction of specific rules from some general premise, perhaps from the premise that there is a God? If so, he attempted no such demonstration. He may have thought that such a derivation of moral rules could be made, but perhaps his notion of demonstration would take a different form. There is good evidence in the *Essay* that, by 'demonstrative', Locke (like Descartes) understood a movement of thought much more informal and intuitive.[1] He speaks of ideas placed in an order permitting us to compare them and reach new ideas (1.4.23), of the understanding seeing the agreement or disagreement of ideas when they are so ordered (4.8.3), of the juxtaposition of ideas (4.13.1); and he has a sustained and forceful attack on the formal logic of his day, the syllogism (see, e.g., 4.17.4). If all reasoning proceeds by the understanding's seeing the relation between ideas and then moving through a series, the moral reasoning which he thought essential for all moral rules may have been a species of conceptual analysis, an exposition of the inter-relations of our moral concepts. If he was so convinced of what the specific laws of nature were, no other demonstration would have been required.

4 THE DISCOVERY OF TRUTH

We have seen thus far how Locke uses his attack against the innatists as a means of introducing his own alternative claims. Not only are there no innate speculative maxims, knowledge cannot proceed by invoking the standard logical principles of identity and contradiction, or by any other self-evident principle. Knowledge is a product of experience and observation, aided by reason. There are no innate moral rules, moral rules are not self-evident, they can only be reached by reason. There *are* universal rules of action, but they are not universally accepted or acted upon. God is the author of these rules, but he has not stamped them on our minds: he has rather given us the faculties for dis-covering them. In a parallel fashion, the final chapter of Book I is an attack against the notion of innate *ideas* (the constituents of

[1] For Descartes' attack on the syllogism, and his less formal notion of demonstration, see his *Regulae*, rules 3, 10, 12, and 13. I have developed the case for an informal logic in Locke, in my *Locke and the Compass of Human Understanding*, pp. 92–103.

principles), but it also provides Locke with a forum for some important groundwork on the nature and origin of ideas.

There may be something of the Puritan work ethic in Locke's repeated assurances that God not only intends us to act, but he intends us to use our faculties to discover truth and attain knowledge. He did not have the confidence of a Descartes in the unlimited knowledge available to us. He was convinced that our knowledge is limited, but we can learn all we need for this life. Just as we should not be enticed by the sceptic into giving up the search for knowledge,[1] so we should not seek the easy way by looking for innate knowledge, for which we need expend no energy. Our faculties of knowledge and understanding are more than ample, once we discover where are the limits to human knowledge, and duly apply ourselves to discovering truth. Even the idea of God, the one idea we might think was imprinted on our souls, must be acquired by experience and reason. God has fitted us with faculties to attain this and other ideas; 'it is want of industry and consideration in us and not of bounty in him if we' do not acquire those ideas within our capabilities (1.4.17). His repeated assertion is that '*knowledge depends upon the right use of those powers nature hath bestowed on us*'; knowledge does not depend upon innate principles.

How should we employ our faculties in the attainment of truth? Locke's firm answer is: we must not trust authority, even in the area of geometrical truth. We must ourselves examine the demonstrations, we must understand how the conclusion follows from the definitions, axioms, and prior demonstrations. For other truths, truths of the world, we must seek them 'in the fountain, *in the consideration of things themselves*' (1.4.24. Cf. 1.4.21). Each of us must make truth and knowledge his own. Especially in the sciences, 'everyone has so much as he really knows and comprehends: what he believes only and takes upon trust are but shreds; which, however well in the whole piece, make no considerable addition to his stock who gathers them. Such borrowed wealth, like fairy-money, though it were gold in the hand from which he received it, will be but leaves and dust when it comes to use' (1.4.24). Locke was not so much concerned with the details of methods in science, as he was interested in urging men to attend to and to consider 'the being of things themselves' (1.4.25). He was also concerned (and this was the

---

[1] See his comment on scepticism in 1.1.5: 'If we will disbelieve everything, because we cannot certainly know all things, we shall do much what as wisely as he who would not use his legs, but sit still and perish because he had no wings to fly.'

task he set himself as an under-labourer to the great scientists) to lay the foundations for an account of scientific knowledge. Convinced that there are no innate principles or propositions, it follows that there are no innate ideas, ideas being the constituents of propositions. He had, then, to show how we acquire ideas, and how we form propositions true of the world. He used Descartes' term, 'adventitious truths', to contrast with 'innate' (1.4.23). Book II contains his programme of the acquisition of ideas, but in Book I we find some outlines of that programme. In particular, we find a discussion of the origin of ideas in children: Locke works with a rudimentary genetic psychology.

New-born children do not, Locke thinks, 'bring many *ideas* into the world with them' (1.4.2). They do very likely have experience of hunger, thirst, warmth and perhaps pain in the womb, resulting from their experiences there. Subsequently, other ideas arise from experience and observation. As the range of things with which the child comes into contact increases, so his stock of ideas is enlarged (1.4.13). By retaining ideas in their memories, by learning to 'compound and enlarge them, and several ways put them together', children extend their thoughts.[1] Locke was particularly anxious to point out that the ideas of impossibility and identity are late acquisitions (even some grown men lack them), for these are the ideas necessary for those speculative principles the innatists cited. Moreover, the child learns to distinguish its mother from a stranger well before it learns principles of identity or contradiction (1.4.3). To have an idea of identity would enable us to solve, at least to formulate, some of those puzzles about the sameness of a man which trouble Locke in his long chapter on identity and diversity (2.27). Here, in Book I, he cites some of those puzzles (1.4.4. Cf.2.1.12). At least, if the identity of the same was innate, we would have a clear understanding of how identity is affected if the same soul can inhabit two bodies, and of what would constitute the same man at the resurrection (1.4.5). The idea of identity, then, is not innate or early and easily acquired.[2]

[1] For other accounts of the genesis of ideas in children, see 2.1.6, 8, 21, 22; 2.9.5–7. I have given a more detailed account of Locke's genetic psychology in my *John Locke and Education* (1971), Chapter 3.

[2] One idea Locke thinks it would have been useful to have innate is the idea of substance, for this is an important idea but one which is not acquired by experience or reason, 'by *sensation* or *reflection*' (1.4.19). This is an idea, like that of identity, which occupies much of Locke's attention in the rest of the *Essay*. His inclusion of a brief remark about it in Book I can only be understood as part of his expository strategy: in attacking the innatists, he includes as many references as possible to ideas and issues to be discussed in the later books, especially those that constitute some of his more important claims.

5   TWO CONCEPTS OF IDEAS

One of the more pervasive concepts in the whole of the *Essay* is
that of *idea*. Locke was careful to include in Book I several statements about ideas which were most important for his use of that
term. These statements were written with the innatist in mind,
who worked with a different notion of idea. I have already
referred to Locke's remark, in 1.2.5, that to have an idea in the
mind but not to be conscious of that idea is impossible. He
reverts to this claim in 1.4.2. There, he says that the only way in
which there could be ideas in the mind 'which the mind does not
actually think on' is if those ideas are in the memory. He formu-
lates his general principle about ideas and awareness as follows:
'Whatever *idea* is in the mind is either an actual perception or
else, having been an actual perception, is so in the mind that by
the memory it can be made an actual perception again.' This
principle, that 'what is not either actually in view, or in the
memory, is in the mind no way at all', had for Locke a direct
bearing upon a question which the innatists thought important:
what is the nature of ideas? The innatists' only possible answer
to this question is that ideas are either substances or modes; if
substances, then either material or spiritual. One of the earliest
attacks against Locke's polemic was written by John Norris, an
English follower of the Cartesian Malebranche. For Norris,
ideas are real beings, spiritual entities.[1] Locke penned a reply to
Norris, the first draft of which has recently been published.[2] In
that draft, Locke complains that, 'If you once mention ideas you
must be presently called to an account *what kind of things you
make these same ideas to be* though perhaps you have no design
to consider them any further than as *the immediate objects of
perception* or if you have you find they are a sort of sullen things
which will only show them what but will not tell you whence
they came nor whither they go nor what they are made of.'[3]
Two points are worth noting in this remark. First, that Locke
only wanted to consider ideas as epistemic objects; secondly,
that the ontological consideration of ideas tells us nothing about
the important features of ideas: their origin, their make-up,
their role in knowledge. Locke's concern was with the second of
these points; for that, the consideration of ideas as epistemic
objects was sufficient. But there is a more important issue

---

[1] John Norris, *Cursory Reflections upon a Book Call'd, An Essay concerning Human Understanding* (1690).
[2] Published by R. Ackworth, in *The Locke Newsletter*, 2 (1971), pp. 7–11.
[3] *Ibid.*, pp. 10–11, unpunctuated, following the manuscript.

embedded in Locke's remark to Norris: a definite view of the nature of ideas, echoed in many passages in his remarks on Malebranche, in a later draft of his reply to Norris, and in many passages in the *Essay*. This view was commented upon in an important tract, published anonymously in 1705, *A Philosophick Essay concerning Ideas*.

The author of this tract said that 'Thought and Idea are the same thing', and showed how this account of ideas can be derived from a few definitions, the main two being (1) the definition of 'idea' as 'the Representation of something in the mind' and (2) 'a Representation of something in the mind, and to frame such a Representation of an Object, is to Think'. This author notes that Locke sometimes speaks of ideas as the *objects* of thought, as if ideas are something different from thought; but he takes as Locke's considered statement the passage in 2.1.9, that to have ideas and to perceive are the same. In that passage, Locke gives as the answer, to the question 'at what time does a man first have any ideas?', 'when he begins to perceive; having *ideas* and perception being the same thing'. In 2.1.5, the ideas of sensible qualities are described as 'all those different perceptions' external objects produce in us. In 2.10.2, he speaks of 'our *ideas* being nothing but actual perceptions in the mind'. The author of this tract considers the definition of ideas as the representation of something to the mind to be a neutral position between the two views of ideas: ideas as 'a Modification of the Mind' or as 'a Distinct Being, or Substance United to the Mind'. The more common view is, he says, the former: ideas 'are not *Real Beings*, but only *Modes of Thinking* upon the several objects presented to the Mind; or if you please, it is the Mind itself operating after *such* and *such* a Manner, just as the Roundness of a Body, and its Motion are nothing but the Body itself figur'd and translated after such and such a Sort'.

This author's recognition of Locke's attempt to use ideas in his theory of knowledge without making them into entities is an indication that he viewed Locke working amid a running battle of some of the Cartesians over the nature of ideas. The insistence that ideas are acts of thought, that to have an idea and to be conscious are the same, was a position taken by Arnauld in his dispute with Malebranche.[1] For Malebranche, ideas were

[1] Malebranche published his *De la Recherche de la Vérité* in 1674. Arnauld attacked him in *Des Vraies et des Fausses Idées* (1683). A series of exchanges then followed for many years between the two. Monte Cook has recently given a brief but lucid account of Arnauld's doctrine, in his 'Arnauld's Alleged Representationalism', *Journal of the History of Philosophy*, XII (1974), pp. 53–62.

entities in the mind of God. When we perceive, God puts the
appropriate ideas into our minds. In some remarks he wrote on
Malebranche,[1] Locke reponded as he did to Norris. When told
by Malebranche that we perceive all things in the mind of God
(by God's placing in our minds the idea-entities), Locke says:
'I am no more instructed in their [ideas'] nature, than when I
am told, they are perceptions, such as I find them.'[2] In the later
draft of his reply to Norris, Locke stresses the same point. He
asks Norris and Malebranche to explain to him 'what the
alteration in the mind is [when we perceive], besides saying, as
we vulgar do, it is having a perception'.[3] He professes ignorance
as to what ideas are, 'any further than as they are perceptions we
experiment [i.e. experience] in ourselves'.[4]

   Once again, to understand Locke's doctrines, it is necessary to
know what he was opposing. Locke read the many exchanges
between Arnauld and Malebranche; he was in fact reading them
as they appeared, during the years when he was putting the
finishing touches to the *Essay*. The term 'idea' in his *Essay* has
perplexed many readers. Locke tells us early in his book that he
uses it as 'that term which, I think, serves best to stand for
whatsoever is the object of the understanding when a man
thinks' (1.1.8). This very generality of the term has contributed
to the difficulties of interpretation. There are many apparently
different uses of that term in the course of the *Essay*. I do not
claim that the various difficulties can all be resolved if we follow
Locke's lead in the passages I have cited, but it would seem a
good place to begin, by recognizing these passages, seeing in
them clear echoes of Arnauld's reading of Descartes against
Malebranche. The view of ideas which Locke rejected, the one
linked with the claim for innate ideas, was that of ideas as real
beings. I shall shortly consider some of the ways in which, with
this fact in mind, we can correct at least one interpretation of
Locke's account of perception. We may also be able to avoid
some misunderstandings of his account of idea-genesis in
Book II.

6   MENTAL FACULTIES AND THE CAUSAL THEORY
OF PERCEPTION

One misunderstanding we can avoid is that of allowing Locke's
remarks about the passivity of the mind in the acquisition of

---

[1] 'An Examination of P. Malebranche's Opinion', in *Works* (1823), IX,
pp. 211–56.
[2] *Ibid.*, sect. 18, p. 220.
[3] Published in *Works* (1823), vol. X, sect. 2, pp. 248–9.
[4] *Ibid.*, sect. 18.

some ideas to cloud the fact that, as the anonymous pamphleteer of 1705 said, ideas as modes of thinking just are the mind itself operating after such and such a manner. The account in Book II of how ideas arise is equally an account of what the mind does under such and such situations, with particular physical stimuli affecting the sense organs. If ideas are entities, to talk of how they arise or get into the mind would be to talk as the Epicureans did, of images coming from objects and entering the mind; or it would be to talk of sensible species being conveyed to the brain where the 'Common Sense' extracts from those species an intelligible species fit for mind; or it would be to talk (however mysteriously) of God implanting ideas in the mind, either at birth or upon the occasion of specific experiences. Locke tells us that he does not accept the Epicurean account.[1] His remarks on Norris and Malebranche make it clear that he rejects this latter, occasionalist account. While 1.1.8 of the *Essay* extends the generality of 'idea' to the scholastic terms 'phantasm, notion, species', there is no indication in the *Essay* that he accepted this scholastic version either.[2] He does accept some causal links between objects and perceptions, although he always denied that we can understand how perceptions result from physical causation. When he says that '*our senses*, conversant about particular sensible objects, do *convey into the mind* several distinct *perceptions* of things, according to those various ways wherein those objects do affect them', he explains that by 'convey into the mind', he means that the senses 'from external objects convey into the mind what produces there those *perceptions*' (2.1.3). We know something of the causal process from objects to brain, for Locke accepted the current corpuscular theory. This theory said that bodies operate by impulse, that varying degrees and modes of motion of particles in objects cause motion of the animal spirits in our nerves, and the motion of the animal spirits in the nerves is carried to the brain. It is at the brain that the animal spirits 'produce in *our minds the particular* ideas' we have of the external objects (2.8.4, 12. Cf. 2.1.23).[3] Locke was content to accept the fact that God annexed 'such *ideas* [as blue or sweet] to such motions', even though this sort of ideas bears no resemblance to qualities of the object. Even in

[1] See his *Examination of Malebranche*, op. cit., sect. 14, p. 218.
[2] There are however a number of similarities between the scholastic theory and that of Locke (and Descartes). For some elaboration of this, see my 'Ideas and Knowledge in Seventeenth-Century Philosophy', in *Journal of the History of Philosophy*, XIII (1975), pp. 145–65.
[3] In 2.3.1, the nerves are described as 'the conduits' for conveying sensible qualities from objects to 'the brain, the mind's presence-room'.

the case of ideas which are resemblances of qualities, for example, size, figure, solidity, he did not think this physiological account explained how perceptions arise out of the motion of animal spirits.[1] He took over the physiology of animal spirits from Descartes and Malebranche, who had given it a detailed analysis. Animal spirits were useful intermediaries between mind and body, for they were less material than solid corpuscles. By means of these spirits we were also thought to move our limbs, although no writer, including Locke, who employed this physiology, professed to understand how we could activate the animal spirits in the brain.

Even though Malebranche used this physiology of animal spirits, he made God the efficient cause of the motion of objects and of our perceptions. Man and external objects are the passive, occasional causes of perceptions: when certain physical motions occur, we have perceptions of a specific sort. Locke believed there was a causal connection between objects and perceptions, just as he believed we have causal power to move our bodies. Thus, when he says that 'the objects of our senses do, many of them, obtrude their particular *ideas* upon our minds whether we will or no', and that the mind in these circumstances 'is merely passive' (2.1.25), he does not mean to make the mind passive in Malebranche's sense, unconnected causally with objects. He used the metaphor of the mind as 'white paper, void of all characters' (2.1.2) as a way of stressing his alternative to innateness. The innate theory located the causal relation between God and our mind, not between objects and our mind. For Locke, we are born into a world 'surrounded with bodies that perpetually and diversely affect' us (2.1.6). Whether 'care be taken about it or no', a variety of ideas 'are imprinted on the minds of children'. Without the relevant sense-object, ideas will not arise; for example, we cannot *fancy* a taste which our palate has never had, nor 'frame the *idea* of a scent' we have never smelt (2.2.2).

In general, then, sense experience provides the necessary conditions for perceptions or ideas. A child's acquisition of more and more ideas is compared with his becoming awake (2.1.22). Once the child has a stock of ideas, he begins to enlarge, compound, and abstract his ideas, and to reason about them. Perception, remembering, considering, reasoning, abstracting, enlarging are just a few of the activities the mind engages in while extending its range of ideas. The mental faculties are a most important ingredient in the metaphorical white paper; waiting for the characters to be imprinted, these faculties soon rush ahead and

[1] Cf. *Essay*, 2.8.13 and *Remarks on Norris*, *Works*, X, sect. 15, pp. 254–5.

extend the mind's ideas. Experience for Locke is also internal, in the sense of being directed towards the sensory ideas, as well as the operations of the mind. By attending to our perceiving, recalling, reasoning, we acquire ideas of these activities. By means of some of these operations the mind also acquires more sophisticated ideas, such as those of solidity, space, existence, unity, power, cause. The derivation programme for ideas laid out in Book II is complex and involved, far different from the rather mechanical adding and abstracting which Locke's talk of simple and complex ideas seems to suggest. We should not be misled by his talk of white paper, passivity, imprinting, enlarging.

Locke's account of the formation of the idea of power is not atypical of his derivation programme. In that account, the idea of power emerges after the mind has *taken notice* of the way some things and events cease to be and others begin; has *reflected* on its own change of ideas; has *concluded* that 'like changes will for the future be made in the same things, by like agents, and by the like ways'; and has *considered* 'in one thing the possibility of having any of its simple *ideas* changed, and in another the possibility of making that change' (2.21.1). These mental operations of considering, concluding, reflecting themselves cloak some fundamental assumptions about change and the course of nature, but the account they enable Locke to give of the origin of the idea of power is hardly amenable to the compositionalism frequently credited to Locke, or to the notion of a passive mind commentators sometimes attribute to him.

7 QUALITIES, POWERS AND PARTICLES

In our examination of some of the doctrines of the *Essay*, as they are foreshadowed in Book I, we have come across a number of metaphysical beliefs Locke used: the existence of God; laws of nature established by God for moral action; an orderly, purposive universe; the workings of a specific physiology with its causal antecedents in objects and events; a world around us which activates our perceptual processes (both physiological and psychological). Locke's account of the workings of the mind was based upon what he discovered when he reflected upon his own experience. Convinced that the innatist's account of how the mind discovers moral rules was wrong, that that account was also wrong on how knowledge is or should be obtained, and that the innatist's notion of the contents of the mind as entities was misleading and unnecessary, Locke's alternative account of knowledge and understanding was not divorced from fundamental metaphysical beliefs. He thought that some of these beliefs, for example, of a god, of a purposive universe, of laws of nature, could be reached by reason and experience. Thus, some at least of these beliefs would conform to his general programme for the derivation of ideas. Some other beliefs, for example, in the corpuscular account of matter and in the physiology of perception, he recognized as hypothetical. He very likely thought that Boyle's work in chemistry supported the corpuscular theory of matter.[1] That theory also had general acceptance in the seventeenth century.

The corpuscular theory viewed matter as consisting of insensible particles. The qualities of matter—both in aggregate, sensible states and in particulate, insensible states—were solidity, extension, figure, motion or rest, and number (2.8.9). On this theory, matter also had *powers*, the power to affect and change the constitution of corpuscles in other bits of matter, as fire melts wax or clay, and the power to produce changes in our nerves and brain which in turn give rise to ideas or perceptions (2.8.10). Matter is not, on this theory, coloured, hot, or odoriferous. Some of what we take to be properties of objects—colour, taste, sound, smell—are in fact not properties of objects: they are the result of the powers objects possess to affect our sense organs in specific ways, by the diverse 'motion and figure, bulk and number' of their particles. Locke is not very clear on the status of the powers of matter, but he does talk of powers *belonging* to matter.[2] Presumably, matter has these powers even when it is not manifesting them. Thus, in the absence of sensation, there will be no light or sound, no tastes or smells; but the particular bulk, figure, and motion of the parts of matter would still have the power to cause these sensations in a perceiver (2.8.17). Heat and cold, for example, are 'nothing but the increase or diminution of the motion of the minute parts of our bodies' (the animal spirits); but the difference between the powers of matter and its extension, figure, or motion is that these latter are always present and manifested in matter, while the powers are actualized only when a perceiver is affected by the particles, or when one body is affected by another (2.8.22). Locke's list of the qualities of body (2.8.23) contains both kinds

[1] See in particular Boyle's *The Origine of Forms and Qualities* (1666). For a good account of Boyle's use of the corpuscular theory, and its distinction between two kinds of qualities, see F. J. O'Toole, 'Qualities and Powers in the Corpuscular Philosophy of Robert Boyle', *Journal of the History of Philosophy*, XII (1974), pp. 295–315.

[2] That he considered powers an important aspect of matter is evidenced by the attention he gives to them when discussing our idea of things in his chapter on substance (2.23.7–10).

of qualities: those that are always present (the occurrent qualities) and the powers (the dispositional qualities—Locke calls them 'potentialities' in 2.23.7).

The specification of qualities of body to include powers, as well as bulk, figure, number, motion, etc., is meant by Locke as an indication of the nature of matter. He also offers it in the context of his distinction between *qualities* of objects and *ideas* we have of the qualities of objects. We have two sorts of ideas of qualities. The one sort is of the powers of objects. In this case, we normally think our ideas are of qualities, not of powers. That is, we normally think this desk is brown, that cherry sweet. We also of course take the desk to be rectangular and solid, the cherry to be spherical. We have, in short, ideas or perceptions of those qualities which the corpuscular theory says belong to matter always and actually, and those which this theory tells us are only the powers matter has in virtue of the action of its extended, movable, solid particles. Both these sorts of ideas are caused by the same corpuscular and physiological processes. Both kinds of qualities compose the objects around us. Gold, for example, is yellow, but it is also malleable, fusible in fire, and soluble in *aqua regia* (3.6.2). Iron has a certain colour but also the power (in this case, a passive power) of being drawn by a loadstone (2.23.7). Any particular piece of gold or iron of course has also a specific shape and extension; but when we are talking about gold or iron as a *kind* of metal, shape or extension is not relevant at the observable level. The occurrent qualities of gold as gold apply at the insensible level, to the particles composing the micro-structure, the internal constitution of that kind of substance. To identify gold or iron (or any kind of thing), it is the powers of that kind which we use, what Locke calls the secondary qualities (2.23.8. See also the whole of 2.8). The colour we perceive, the solubility or fusibility which occur, are powers of the object, powers of the internal constitution of gold acting on our sense organs and powers of the internal constitution of gold responding to the internal constitution of *aqua regia* and fire. We should guard against considering the secondary qualities as merely colours, sounds, tastes, etc. For Locke, they include as well dispositional properties such as fusibility, malleability, etc. His point is that these latter do not differ from colour, sound, etc., in being powers in the object. Both sorts are powers. That is why he can say that most of the qualities of objects available to us are powers. Not *all* are powers, of course, for we also observe extension, figure, and motion, although not of the particles.

8 THINGS AND KINDS

Locke recognized that our concept of *a* thing is of a collection of properties united together in one substance; but he points out (in Book I) the ambiguity (indeed, the vacuity) of the substance part of this concept. The only content we can give to this notion of a thing, besides the observable qualities, is that of something which supports or is the subject of the qualities. We cannot imagine what the substance is to which the qualities belong (2.21.1–4). We 'cannot conceive how' the qualities which we observe as coexisting 'should subsist alone, nor in one another', so 'we suppose them existing in and supported by some common subject' (2.23.4). As usual, Locke has in mind a specific attempt to supply some content to this notion of a substance or support for qualities. *Substantial forms* were frequently said to be what underlies observed qualities. A form was a kind of matrix, a real type which constitutes gold as gold, iron as iron. But when pressed to explain this notion of a substantial form, all the defenders could say was that it was what made opium soporific, or gold malleable. The attempted explanation merely repeated the qualities for which the substantial form was the supposed cause. Against this traditional way of talking about *a thing* which has specific qualities, Locke insisted first that the 'thing' stood for nothing; secondly, that our ideas of a man, horse, gold, water, etc., were just of coexisting qualities observed and experienced together. Thirdly and most importantly, against the talk of substantial forms, Locke insisted that the corpuscular theory supplies a coherent concept for the internal constitution from which it is supposed the observed qualities flow (2.23.3). Observed qualities (the two sorts of powers) are, as we have seen, a product of the insensible particles of matter.

Substantial forms were supposed to be real kinds in nature, a limited number of types of things that could be. Locke objects to this notion also, on two grounds. First, he did not think there were sharp boundaries in nature, but rather a gradual shading of one type into another. There are no gaps or chasms in the chain of being (3.6.12). Secondly, Locke was convinced that our knowledge did not (and very likely could not) extend to the internal constitution of particles.[1] Nevertheless, the corpuscular theory of matter provided Locke with a theoretic basis to

---

[1] The reasons here are complex. He did consider the possibility that the new microscopes might yield some knowledge of the insensible particles, but until we could understand cohesion—why the least particle did not fly apart —he thought we would be unable to understand why and how the observed qualities were caused by the particles (2.23.27).

replace the vague one of substantial forms. His philosophy of nature accepted that part of the substantial-form doctrine which saw the forms as the causal basis for observed phenomena. He insisted that what we can *know* is only the coexisting group of qualities which careful observation and experimentation disclose. It is on this observable basis alone that we can classify things and refine our knowledge of nature. Locke uses the term 'nominal essence' to designate the coexisting group of qualities for each kind of thing, as distinguished by us. The 'real essence' 'is the constitution of the insensible parts of that body, on which those qualities and all the other properties of gold depend' (3.6.2).

9 KNOWLEDGE OF THINGS

Were we able to know the real essence, we would have a quite different knowledge of nature from that we in fact have, or are capable of having. In the absence of a knowledge of the internal constitution of matter, our science of nature can only be observational, 'the want of *ideas* of their real *essences* sends us from our own thoughts to the things themselves as they exist. *Experience here must teach me* what reason cannot' (4.12.9. Cf. 4.12.10–13). When, in Book IV, Locke defines knowledge as '*the perception of the connexion and agreement, or disagreement and repugnancy, of any of our ideas*' (4.1.1), he explicitly includes among his list of types of agreement that of *coexistence*. Noting, by observation but also by experimentation, what qualities go with what other qualities was for him, and for many of his fellow members of the Royal Society, the proper task of a scientist. It was an activity which in the seventeenth century was called the making of natural histories of phenomena.

Convinced that God had given us faculties for discovering truths about ourselves and the world, Locke tried to elaborate, in a vocabulary inherited from Cartesian philosophers and from contemporary science, an account of our knowledge of the world. To the extent that we can discover such truths by careful observation and experimentation, Locke accepted the corpuscular account of matter and of perception. Insisting that each one of us must, if we are to avoid borrowed opinions, see truths for ourselves, like Descartes, he placed intuition (cognitive 'seeing', grasping, apprehending) at the head of his list of methods to knowledge. What we intuit are relations between our ideas. That the knowledge relations are features of ideas, not things, is not due to any belief Locke held about the impossibility of knowledge of things. He believed he could precisely specify what we could and could not know about the external world: nominal but not real essence. His definition of knowledge in terms of relations of ideas was a result of (1) the account of the nature of matter which he accepted and (2) his recognition that knowledge relations are not object relations. This account of the nature of matter led him to the conclusion that what we perceive of bodies is for the most part the result of powers that bodies have as matter, not their occurrent qualities. Some of the powers of body are manifested whether we observe them or not; sun melts wax, the loadstone draws iron, one substance dissolves another. Our perception of any of these processes in nature occurs by means of the other sort of powers of bodies, their powers to affect our sense organs and animal spirits, which powers result in ideas and perceptions. We cannot sense or perceive bodies without sensing or perceiving. But perceiving is a cognitive or psychological process. Our awareness of anything is and must be in terms of ideas and perceptions. Otherwise, awareness would not be awareness, would not occur. From this point of view, Locke's definition of knowledge is a truism. The only way we can learn about the world is in terms of awareness. To be aware is to perceive or to have ideas or thoughts.

If ideas are taken as some sort of things, entities (cf. the innatists and Malebranche), then the contents of awareness are turned into objects, the problems of scepticism begin to affect the theory of knowledge. According to Malebranche's theory, Locke observed, 'we see nothing but God and ideas; and it is impossible for us to know that there is anything else in the universe'.[1] Malebranche had equivocated on the word 'see', restricting the French 'voir' to seeing (that is, apprehending) ideas in the mind of God, and using 'sentiment' and 'apercevoir' for sensation and sensing. But the scepticism Locke notes is inherent in Malebranche's theory of ideas as real beings in the mind of God. Locke, as we have seen, firmly rejected this account of ideas. There has been a long tradition of interpretations of Locke which has found indirectness in his account of knowledge of nature. His talk of some ideas resembling some qualities of body, his frequent talk of ideas as _objects_ of the mind when it thinks, even his causal theory of perception have led many readers of Locke to credit him with a representative theory, where ideas as the representatives of things or their qualities stand, as it were, between things and the perceiver. Scepticism is soon discovered at the heart of Locke's account. The very possibility he raised and dismissed in 4.4.3–5 is said to

[1] _Examination of P. Malebranche's Opinion, Works_, IX, sect. 43, p. 239.

be inescapable. 'If it be true that all knowledge lies only in the perception of the agreement or disagreement of our own *ideas*, the visions of an enthusiast and the reasonings of a sober man will be equally certain. It is no matter how things are: so a man observe but the agreement of his own imaginations and talk conformably, it is all truth, all certainty. Such castles in the air will be as strongholds of truth as the demonstrations of *Euclid*' (4.4.1).

In this Introduction, I cannot extend my suggestion that those who read Locke in this way misread him by overlooking the important distinction between the two concepts of idea which the author of that 1705 tract saw so clearly. I have attempted some elaboration of my suggestion elsewhere,[1] but what is still lacking is a detailed account of the history of the term 'idea' from Descartes to Locke and beyond. What is needed especially is to place Locke in the context of the debate Arnauld had with Malebranche over the nature of ideas, representation, and cognition. Getting clear about these questions of the knowledge of body in Locke will clarify the very nature of his enterprise, for his *Essay* was an attempt at cognitive psychology.

CONCLUSION

Locke's *Essay* is more than an inquiry into the 'original, certainty, and extent of human knowledge, together with the grounds and degrees of belief, opinion, and assent' (1.1.2). There are long discussions of space, time, and infinity (pivotal concepts in the new science); of personal identity and the power of persons in action; of the nature and use of language, especially of the abuse of language through the misuse of words, or the use of words without real meaning. The *Essay* is in fact a mine of concepts, issues, and problems in science, philosophy, ethics, linguistics, psychology, logic, theology. I hope that by working from the contents of Book I, I have succeeded in showing some of those issues and concepts, together with the direction in which Locke approached them.

[1] In Chapter 5 of my *Locke and the Compass of Human Understanding*, and more recently in 'Ideas and Knowledge in Seventeenth-Century Philosophy', loc. cit.

NOTE ON THIS EDITION

This Everyman abridgment is designed to give the reader samples (some more extensive than others) from all the topics and disciplines which appear in Locke's *Essay*. The same text used in the two-volume complete edition in Everyman's Library (Nos. 332, 984) has been reproduced here: that is, the fifth, 1706 edition, the last one corrected by Locke before his death in 1704, the one he himself gave to the Bodleian Library at Oxford. I would of course not claim (as I did not claim for the complete Everyman edition) that the text here printed is the final text of the *Essay* as authenticated and established by a proper comparison of all five editions, the French abridgment, the first French translation, the various drafts of the *Essay*, remarks in letters, etc. As I noted in the Introduction to the two-volume edition, 'spelling and punctuation have been modernized throughout, although the italicization has been retained'. For this abridged edition, I have for reasons of space also left out the detailed analytic contents. I have retained the general contents, indicating for each chapter where omissions have been made.

A number of readers have been helpful in recording textual misprints in the Everyman Locke, especially Professors Nidditch and Woozley.[1] In acknowledging their help, I would like to cite a few remarks of mine, made in response to their lists as printed in *The Locke Newsletter*. First of all, I pointed out that Professor Nidditch's corrigenda for pp. 30, 46–7, and 51 of Volume 1 in the Everyman Locke (relating to 1.3.9, 1.4.8, and 1.4.15) criticized my filling out of footnote references, or references to books in Locke's text, of books not readily identifiable by the present-day reader. Secondly, a number of other entries in Professor Nidditch's and in Professor Woozley's lists consisted of noting where I had corrected for the Everyman edition some mis-numberings of sections, omissions of section numbers, and some discrepancies in numbering between contents page and the chapter or section in the text. Some of the other differences between my text and these lists of corrigenda resulted from the modernization of spelling or from punctuation which I inserted to help the reader with Locke's text. All other genuine errors in the Everyman text we have tried to incorporate into recent reprintings and of course in this abridgment.

Professor Nidditch has now given us the first volume of 'a

---

[1] See *The Locke Newsletter*, 2 (1971), pp. 21–30; 3 (1972), pp. 34–9.

comprehensive critical edition of the *Essay*'.[1] That edition will be invaluable for the scholar and, as a reference, for the student of Locke. The Everyman Locke remains the more easily accessible text, especially for the student and general reader. By issuing an abridgment of the Everyman text, we hope to extend the range of its use.

York University, Toronto, 1976   JOHN W. YOLTON

[1] *An Essay concerning Human Understanding*, edited with an Introduction, Critical Apparatus and Glossary. Oxford, Clarendon Press, 1975.

SELECT BIBLIOGRAPHY

Note: For a complete list of Locke's works, as well as the known manuscripts, other contemporary books on Locke, and recent studies in his philosophy, see the bibliographies in Aaron, Long, Polin, and Yolton given below.

1663   *Essays on the Law of Nature.*   The Latin text with a translation, edited by W. von Leyden, Oxford, 1954.

1675–9 *Locke's Travels in France, As Related in his Journals, Correspondence, and Other Papers.* Edited by John Lough, Cambridge, 1953.

1686   'Methode Nouvelle de Dresser des Recueils.' In Jean LeClerc's *Bibliothèque Universelle et Historique*, July, p. 315. (Reprinted in English in the *Posthumous Works*, 1706).

1689   *Epistola de Tolerantia*, Gouda. (Translated as *A Letter concerning Toleration*, by W. Popple, and published in 1689.)

1690   *A Second Letter concerning Toleration.*

1690   *Two Treatises of Government* (2nd edition, 1694; 3rd edition, 1698). (For a critical edition with introduction and notes, see Laslett's *Locke's Two Treatises of Government*, Cambridge, 1960.)

1690   *An Essay Concerning Human Understanding.* (2nd edition, 1694; 3rd edition, 1695; 4th edition, 1700; 5th edition, 1706.)

1692   *A Third Letter for Toleration.*

1692   *Some Considerations of the Consequences of the Lowering of Interest and the Raising of the Value of Money.*

1693   *Some Thoughts Concerning Education.*

1695   *Short Observations on a Printed Paper Intituled For Encouraging the Coinage of Silver Money in England.*

1695   *The Reasonableness of Christianity, As Delivered in the Scriptures.*

1695   *A Vindication of the Reasonableness of Christianity, etc. from Mr. Edwards' Reflections.*

1697   *A Letter to the Right Rev. Edward Lord Bishop of Worcester, concerning Some Passages Relating to Mr. Locke's Essay of Human Understanding.* (Locke's replies to the Bishop's replies appeared in 1697 and 1699.)

1705–7 *Paraphrases of the Epistles of St. Paul.*

1714   *Works of John Locke*, 3 vols. (2nd edition, 1722; 3rd edition, 1727).

BIOGRAPHY AND CRITICISM

Aaron, R. I. *John Locke*, 2nd edition. Oxford, 1955.

Cranston, M. *John Locke: A Biography.* London, 1957.

Gibson, J. *Locke's Theory of Knowledge.* Cambridge, 1917.

Hall, R. and Woolhouse, R. 'Forty Years of Work on John Locke', *Philosophical Quarterly*, July 1970. (Addenda in *P.Q.*, October 1970, and in *The Locke Newsletter*, 1, 1970; 3, 1972; 4, 1973; 6, 1973.)

James, D. G. *The Life of Reason: Hobbes, Locke and Bolingbroke.* London, 1949.

Klemnt, A. *John Locke: Theorestische Philosophie.* Meisenheim/Glan, 1952.

Lamprecht, S. *The Moral and Political Philosophy of John Locke.* New York, 1918.

Long, P. *A Summary Catalogue of the Lovelace Collection of Papers of John Locke* in the Bodleian Library. Oxford, 1959.

MacLachlan, H. *The Religious Opinions of Milton, Locke, and Newton.* London, 1941.

MacLean, K. *John Locke and English Literature of the Eighteenth Century.* New Haven, Conn., 1936.

O'Connor, D. L. *John Locke.* London (Pelican), 1952.

Polin, R. *La Politique Morale de John Locke.* Paris, 1960.

Yolton, J. W. *John Locke and the Way of Ideas.* Oxford, 1956.

Yolton, J. W. *Locke and the Compass of Human Understanding.* Cambridge, 1970.

Yolton, J. W. *John Locke and Education.* New York, 1971.

AN
ESSAY
CONCERNING
𝕳𝖚𝖒𝖆𝖓𝖊 𝖀𝖓𝖉𝖊𝖗𝖘𝖙𝖆𝖓𝖉𝖎𝖓𝖌.

In Four BOOKS.

Written by *JOHN LOCKE*, Gent.

The Fifth Edition, with large Additions.

ECCLES. XI. 5.

*As thou knowest not what is the Way of the Spirit, nor how the
Bones do grow in the Womb of her that is with Child : Even
so thou knowest not the Works of God, who maketh all things.*

*Quam bellum est velle confiteri potius nescire quod nescias, quam
ista effutientem nauseare, atque ipsum sibi displicere !* Cic. de
Natur. Deor. *l.* 1.

LONDON:

Printed for *Awnsham* and *John Churchill*, at the *Black Swan* in
Pater-Noster-Row ; and *Samuel Manship*, at the *Ship* in *Corn-
hill*, near the *Royal Exchange*, M DCC VI.

THE EPISTLE TO THE READER

I here put into thy hands what has been the diversion of some of my idle and heavy hours. If it has the good luck to prove so of any of thine, and thou hast but half so much pleasure in reading as I had in writing it, thou wilt as little think thy money, as I do my pains, ill bestowed. Mistake not this for a commendation of my work; nor conclude, because I was pleased with the doing of it, that therefore I am fondly taken with it now it is done. He that hawks at larks and sparrows has no less sport, though a much less considerable quarry, than he that flies at nobler game; and he is little acquainted with the subject of this treatise, the UNDERSTANDING, who does not know that, as it is the most elevated faculty of the soul, so it is employed with a greater and more constant delight than any of the other. Its searches after truth are a sort of hawking and hunting, wherein the very pursuit makes a great part of the pleasure. Every step the mind takes in its progress towards knowledge makes some discovery, which is not only new, but the best too, for the time at least.

For the understanding, like the eye, judging of objects only by its own sight, cannot but be pleased with what it discovers, having less regret for what has escaped it, because it is unknown. Thus he who has raised himself above the alms-basket, and, not content to live lazily on scraps of begged opinions, sets his own thoughts on work, to find and follow truth, will (whatever he lights on) not miss the hunter's satisfaction; every moment of his pursuit will reward his pains with some delight; and he will have reason to think his time not ill spent, even when he cannot much boast of any great acquisition.

This, Reader, is the entertainment of those who let loose their own thoughts, and follow them in writing; which thou oughtest not to envy them, since they afford thee an opportunity of the like diversion, if thou wilt make use of thy own thoughts in reading. It is to them, if they are thy own, that I refer myself; but if they are taken upon trust from others, it is no great matter what they are, they not following truth, but some meaner consideration; and it is not worth while to be concerned what he says or thinks who says or thinks only as he is directed by another. If thou judgest for thyself I know thou wilt judge candidly, and then I shall not be harmed or offended, whatever be thy censure. For though it be certain that there is nothing in this treatise of the truth whereof I am not fully persuaded, yet I consider myself as liable to mistakes as I can think thee, and know that this book must stand or fall with thee, not by any opinion I have of it, but thy own. If thou findest little in it new or instructive to thee, thou art not to blame me for it. It was not meant for those that had already mastered this subject, and made a thorough acquaintance with their own understandings; but for my own information, and the satisfaction of a few friends, who acknowledged themselves not to have sufficiently considered it. Were it fit to trouble thee with the history of this *Essay*, I should tell thee that five or six friends, meeting at my chamber and discoursing on a subject very remote from this, found themselves quickly at a stand, by the difficulties that rose on every side. After we had awhile puzzled ourselves, without coming any nearer a resolution of those doubts which perplexed us, it came into my thoughts that we took a wrong course; and that before we set ourselves upon inquiries of that nature, it was necessary to examine our own abilities and see what objects our understandings were, or were not, fitted to deal with. This I proposed to the company, who all readily assented; and thereupon it was agreed that this should be our first inquiry. Some hasty and undigested thoughts, on a subject I had never before considered, which I set down against our next meeting, gave the first entrance into this discourse; which having been thus begun by chance, was continued by entreaty; written by incoherent parcels; and after long intervals of neglect, resumed again, as my humour or occasions permitted; and at last, in a retirement where an attendance on my health gave me leisure, it was brought into that order thou now seest it.

This discontinued way of writing may have occasioned, besides others, two contrary faults, viz. that too little and too much may be said in it. If thou findest anything wanting, I shall be glad that what I have writ gives thee any desire that I should have gone further. If it seems too much to thee, thou must blame the subject; for when I first put pen to paper, I thought all I should have to say on this matter would have been contained in one sheet of paper; but the further I went the larger prospect I had; new discoveries led me still on, and so it grew insensibly to the bulk it now appears in. I will not deny but possibly it might be reduced to a narrower compass than it is, and that some parts of it might be contracted: the way it has been writ in, by catches and many long intervals of interruption, being apt to cause some repetitions. But to confess the truth, I am now too lazy, or too busy, to make it shorter.

I am not ignorant how little I herein consult my own reputation, when I knowingly let it go with a fault, so apt to disgust the most judicious, who are always the nicest readers. But they who know sloth is apt to content itself with any excuse, will pardon me if mine has prevailed on me, where I think I have a very good one. I will not therefore allege in my defence that the same notion, having different respects, may be convenient or necessary to prove or illustrate several parts of the same discourse, and that so it has happened in many parts of this; but waiving that, I shall frankly avow that I have sometimes dwelt long upon the same argument, and expressed it different ways, with a quite different design. I pretend not to publish this *Essay* for the information of men of large thoughts and quick apprehensions; to such masters of knowledge I profess myself a scholar, and therefore warn them beforehand not to expect anything here but what, being spun out of my own coarse thoughts, is fitted to men of my own size, to whom, perhaps, it will not be unacceptable that I have taken some pains to make plain and familiar to their thoughts some truths which established prejudice, or the abstractness of the *ideas* themselves, might render difficult. Some objects had need be turned on every side; and when the notion is new, as I confess some of these are to me, or out of the ordinary road, as I suspect they will appear to others, it is not one simple view of it that will gain it admittance into every understanding or fix it there with a clear and lasting impression. There are few, I believe, who have not observed in themselves or others, that what in one way of proposing was very obscure, another way of expressing it has made very clear and intelligible, though afterward the mind found little difference in the phrases and wondered why one failed to be understood more than the other. But everything does not hit alike upon every man's imagination. We have our understandings no less different than our palates; and he that thinks the same truth shall be equally relished by everyone in the same dress, may as well hope to feast everyone with the same sort of cookery: the meat may be the same, and the nourishment good, yet everyone not be able to receive it with that seasoning; and it must be dressed another way, if you will have it go down with some, even of strong constitutions. The truth is, those who advised me to publish it, advised me, for this reason, to publish it as it is; and since I have been brought to let it go abroad, I desire it should be understood by whoever gives himself the pains to read it. I have so little affection to be in print that, if I were not flattered this *Essay* might be of some use to others, as I think it has been to me, I should have confined it to the view of some friends, who gave the first occasion to it. My appearing therefore in print being on purpose to be as useful as I may, I think it necessary to make what I have to say as easy and intelligible to all sorts of readers as I can. And I had much rather the speculative and quick-sighted should complain of my being in some parts tedious than that anyone, not accustomed to abstract speculations, or prepossessed with different notions, should mistake or not comprehend my meaning.

It will possibly be censured as a great piece of vanity or insolence in me, to pretend to instruct this our knowing age: it amounting to little less, when I own that I publish this *Essay* with hopes it may be useful to others. But, if it may be permitted to speak freely of those who with a feigned modesty condemn as useless what they themselves write, methinks it savours much more of vanity or insolence to publish a book for any other end; and he fails very much of that respect he owes the public, who prints and consequently expects men should read that wherein he intends not they should meet with anything of use to themselves or others; and should nothing else be found allowable in this treatise, yet my design will not cease to be so; and the goodness of my intention ought to be some excuse for the worthlessness of my present. It is that chiefly which secures me from the fear of censure, which I expect not to escape more than better writers. Men's principles, notions, and relishes are so different, that it is hard to find a book which pleases or displeases all men. I acknowledge the age we live in is not the least knowing, and therefore not the most easy to be satisfied. If I have not the good luck to please, yet nobody ought to be offended with me. I plainly tell all my readers, except half a dozen, this treatise was not at first intended for them; and therefore they need not be at the trouble to be of that number. But yet if anyone thinks fit to be angry and rail at it, he may do it securely, for I shall find some better way of spending my time than in such kind of conversation. I shall always have the satisfaction to have aimed sincerely at truth and usefulness, though in one of the meanest ways. The commonwealth of learning is not at this time without master-builders, whose mighty designs, in advancing the sciences, will leave lasting monuments to the admiration of posterity; but everyone must not hope to be a *Boyle* or a *Sydenham*; and in an age that produces such masters as the great *Huygenius* and the incomparable Mr. *Newton*, with some others of that strain, it is ambition enough to be employed as an underlabourer in clearing ground a little, and removing some of the rubbish that lies in the way to knowledge; which certainly had been very much more advanced in the world, if the endeavours of ingenious and industrious men had not been much cumbered with the learned but frivolous use of uncouth, affected, or unintelligible terms, introduced into the sciences, and there made an art of, to that degree that philosophy, which is nothing but the true knowledge of things, was thought unfit or incapable to be brought into well-bred company and polite conversation. Vague and insignificant forms of speech and abuse of language have so long passed for mysteries of science; and hard or misapplied words, with little or no meaning, have, by prescription, such a right to be mistaken for deep learning and height of speculation, that it will not be easy to persuade either those who speak or those who hear them that they are but the covers of ignorance and hindrance of true knowledge. To break in upon the sanctuary of vanity and ignorance will be, I suppose, some service to human understanding: though so few are apt to think t' ey deceive or are deceived in the use of words, or that the language of the sect they are of has any faults in it which ought to be examined or corrected, that I hope I shall be pardoned if I have in the Third Book dwelt long on this subject and endeavoured to make it so plain that neither the inveterateness of the mischief nor the prevalency of the fashion shall be any excuse for those who will not take care about the meaning of their own words, and will not suffer the significancy of their expressions to be inquired into.

I have been told that a short epitome of this treatise, which was printed in 1688, was by some condemned without reading, because innate *ideas* were denied in it: they too hastily concluding that, if innate *ideas* were not supposed, there would be little left either of the notion or proof of spirits. If anyone take the like offence at the entrance of this treatise, I shall desire him to read it through; and then I hope he will be convinced that the taking away false foundations is not to the prejudice but advantage of truth, which is never injured or endangered so much as when mixed with, or built on, falsehood. In the Second Edition, I added as followeth:

The bookseller will not forgive me if I say nothing of this Second Edition, which he has promised, by the correctness of it, shall make amends for the many faults committed in the former. He desires, too, that it should be known that it has one whole new chapter concerning *Identity*, and many additions and amendments in other places. These I must inform my reader are not all new matter, but most of them either further confirmation of what I had said, or explications to prevent others being mistaken in the sense of what was formerly printed, and not any variation in me from it. I must only except the alterations I have made in Book 2, Chap. 21.

What I had there writ concerning *Liberty* and the *Will*, I thought deserved as accurate a review as I was capable of: those subjects having in all ages exercised the learned part of the world with questions and difficulties, that have not a little perplexed morality and divinity, those parts of knowledge that men are most concerned to be clear in. Upon a closer inspection into the working of men's minds, and a stricter examination of those motives and views they are turned by, I have found reason somewhat to alter the thoughts I formerly had concerning that which gives the last determination to the *Will* in all voluntary actions. This I cannot forbear to acknowledge to the world with as much freedom and readiness as I at first published what then seemed to me to be right, thinking myself more concerned to quit and renounce any opinion of my own, than oppose that of another, when truth appears against it. For it is truth alone I seek, and that will always be welcome to me, when or from whencesoever it comes.

But what forwardness soever I have to resign any opinion I have, or to recede from anything I have writ, upon the first evidence of any error in it: yet this I must own, that I have not had the good luck to receive any light from those exceptions I have met with in print against any part of my book, nor have, from anything that has been urged against it, found reason to alter my sense in any of the points that have been questioned. Whether the subject I have in hand requires often more thought and attention than cursory readers, at least such as are prepossessed, are willing to allow; or whether any obscurity in my expressions casts a cloud over it, and these notions are made difficult to others' apprehension in my way of treating them: so it is that my meaning, I find, is often mistaken, and I have not the good luck to be everywhere rightly understood. There are so many instances of this, that I think it justice to my reader and myself to conclude that either my book is plainly enough written to be rightly understood by those who peruse it with that attention and indifferency which everyone who will give himself the pains to read ought to employ in reading, or else that I have writ mine so obscurely that it is in vain to go about to mend it. Whichever of these be that truth, it is myself only am affected thereby; and therefore I shall be far from troubling my reader with what I think might be said in answer to those several objections I have met with, to passages here and there of my book: since I persuade myself that he who thinks them of moment enough to be concerned whether they are true or false, will be able to see that what is said is either not well founded, or else not contrary to my doctrine, when I and my opposer come both to be well understood.

If any, careful that none of their good thoughts should be lost, have published their censures of my *Essay*, with this honour done to it, that they will not suffer it to be an *Essay*, I leave it to the public to value the obligation they have to their critical pens, and shall not waste my reader's time in so idle or ill-natured an employment of mine, as to lessen the satisfaction anyone has in himself, or gives to others in so hasty a confutation of what I have written.

The booksellers preparing for the Fourth Edition of my *Essay*, gave me notice of it that I might, if I had leisure, make any additions or alterations I should think fit. Whereupon I thought it convenient to advertise the reader that, besides several corrections I had made here and there, there was one alteration which it was necessary to mention, because it ran through the whole book, and is of consequence to be rightly understood. What I thereupon said was this:

Clear and distinct ideas are terms which, though familiar and frequent in men's mouths, I have reason to think everyone who uses does not perfectly understand. And possibly it is but here and there one who gives himself the trouble to consider them so far as to know what he himself or others precisely mean by them. I have therefore in most places chosen to put *determinate* or *determined*, instead of *clear* and *distinct*, as more likely to direct men's thoughts to my meaning in this matter. By those denominations, I mean some object in the mind, and consequently *determined*, i.e. such as it is there seen and perceived to be. This, I think, may fitly be called a *determinate* or *determined* idea, when, such as it is at any time objectively in the mind and so *determined* there, it is annexed and without variation *determined* to a name or articulate sound, which is to be steadily the sign of that very same object of the mind, or *determinate* idea.

To explain this a little more particularly. By *determinate*, when applied to a simple idea, I mean that simple appearance which the mind has in its view, or perceives in itself, when that idea is said to be in it; by *determined*, when applied to a *complex idea*, I mean such an one as consists of a determinate number of certain simple or less complex ideas, joined in such a proportion and situation as the mind has before its view and sees in itself, when that idea is present in it or should be present in it, when a man gives a name to it. I say *should* be, because it is not every-one, nor perhaps anyone, who is so careful of his language as to use no word till he views in his mind the precise *determined* idea which he resolves to make it the sign of. The want of this is the cause of no small obscurity and confusion in men's thoughts and discourses.

I know there are not words enough in any language to answer all the variety of ideas that enter into men's discourses and reasonings. But this hinders not but that when anyone uses any term, he may have in his mind a *determined* idea, which he makes it the sign of, and to which he should keep it steadily annexed during that present discourse. Where he does not or cannot do this, he in vain pretends to *clear* or *distinct ideas*: it is plain his are not so; and therefore there can be expected nothing but obscurity and confusion, where such terms are made use of which have not such a precise determination.

Upon this ground I have thought *determined* ideas a way of speaking less liable to mistake, than *clear* and *distinct*; and where men have got such *determined* ideas of all that they reason, inquire, or argue about, they will find a great part of their doubts and disputes at an end: the greatest part of the questions and controversies that perplex mankind depending on the doubtful and uncertain use of words or (which is the same) *indetermined ideas*, which they are made to stand for. I have made choice of these terms to signify (1) some immediate object of the mind, which it perceives and has before it, distinct from the sound it uses as a sign of it; (2) that this idea, thus *determined*, i.e. which the mind has in itself and knows and sees there, be *determined* without any change to that name, and that name *determined* to that precise idea. If men had such *determined* ideas in their inquiries and discourses, they would both discern how far their own inquiries and discourses went, and avoid the greatest part of the disputes and wranglings they have with others.

Besides this, the bookseller will think it necessary I should advertise the reader that there is an addition of two chapters wholly new, the one *of the association of ideas*, the other *of enthusiasm*. These, with some other larger additions never before printed, he has engaged to print by themselves after the same manner, and for the same purpose as was done when this *Essay* had the Second Impression.

In this Fifth Edition, there is very little added or altered. The greatest part of what is new is contained in the 21st chapter of the Second Book, which anyone, if he thinks it worth the while, may, with a very little labour, transcribe into the margin of the former edition.

BOOK I

OF INNATE NOTIONS

CHAPTER I

INTRODUCTION

1. SINCE it is the *understanding* that sets man above the rest of sensible beings, and gives him all the advantage and dominion which he has over them, it is certainly a subject, even for its nobleness, worth our labour to inquire into. The understanding, like the eye, whilst it makes us see and perceive all other things, takes no notice of itself; and it requires art and pains to set it at a distance and make it its own object. But whatever be the difficulties that lie in the way of this inquiry, whatever it be that keeps us so much in the dark to ourselves, sure I am that all the light we can let in upon our own minds, all the acquaintance we can make with our own understandings, will not only be very pleasant, but bring us great advantage, in directing our thoughts in the search of other things.

2. This, therefore, being my *purpose*, to inquire into the original, certainty, and extent of human knowledge, together with the grounds and degrees of belief, opinion, and assent: I shall not at present meddle with the physical consideration of the mind; or trouble myself to examine wherein its essence consists; or by what motions of our spirits or alterations of our bodies we come to have any sensation by our organs, or any *ideas* in our understandings; and whether those *ideas* do in their formation, any or all of them, depend on matter or no. These are speculations which, however curious and entertaining, I shall decline, as lying out of my way in the design I am now upon. It shall suffice to my present purpose to consider the discerning faculties of a man, as they are employed about the objects which they have to do with. And I shall imagine I have not wholly misemployed myself in the thoughts I shall have on this occasion, if, in this historical, plain method, I can give any account of the ways whereby our understandings come to attain those notions of things we have, and can set down any measures of the certainty of our knowledge, or the grounds of those persuasions which are to be found amongst men, so various, different, and wholly con-

tradictory; and yet asserted somewhere or other with such assurance and confidence that he that shall take a view of the opinions of mankind, observe their opposition, and at the same time consider the fondness and devotion wherewith they are embraced, the resolution and eagerness wherewith they are maintained, may perhaps have reason to suspect that either there is no such thing as truth at all, or that mankind hath no sufficient means to attain a certain knowledge of it.

3. It is therefore worth while to search out the *bounds* between opinion and knowledge, and examine by what measures, in things whereof we have no certain knowledge, we ought to regulate our assent and moderate our persuasions. In order whereunto I shall pursue this following method:

First, I shall inquire into the *original* of those *ideas*, notions, or whatever else you please to call them, which a man observes and is conscious to himself he has in his mind; and the ways whereby the understanding comes to be furnished with them.

Secondly, I shall endeavour to show what *knowledge* the understanding hath by those *ideas*, and the certainty, evidence, and extent of it.

Thirdly, I shall make some inquiry into the nature and grounds of *faith* or *opinion*: whereby I mean that assent which we give to any proposition as true, of whose truth yet we have no certain knowledge. And here we shall have occasion to examine the reasons and degrees of *assent*.

4. If by this inquiry into the nature of the understanding, I can discover the powers thereof: *how far* they reach; to what things they are in any degree proportionate; and where they fail us, I suppose it may be of use to prevail with the busy mind of man to be more cautious in meddling with things exceeding its comprehension; to stop when it is at the utmost extent of its tether; and to sit down in a quiet ignorance of those things which upon examination are found to be beyond the reach of our capacities. We should not then perhaps be so forward, out of an affectation of an universal knowledge, to raise questions and perplex ourselves and others with disputes about things to which our understandings are not suited, and of which we cannot frame in our minds any clear or distinct perceptions, or whereof (as it has perhaps too often happened) we have not any notions at all. If we can find out how far the understanding can extend its view, how far it has faculties to attain certainty, and in what cases it can only judge and guess, we may learn to content ourselves with what is attainable by us in this state.

5. For though the *comprehension* of our understandings comes

exceeding short of the vast extent of things, yet we shall have cause enough to magnify the bountiful Author of our being, for that portion and degree of knowledge he has bestowed on us, so far above all the rest of the inhabitants of this our mansion. Men have reason to be well satisfied with what God hath thought fit for them, since he has given them (as St. *Peter* says) πάντα πρὸς ζωὴν καὶ εὐσέβειαν, whatsoever is necessary for the conveniences of life and information of virtue; and has put within the reach of their discovery, the comfortable provision for this life and the way that leads to a better. How short soever their knowledge may come of an universal or perfect comprehension of whatsoever is, it yet secures their great concernments, that they have light enough to lead them to the knowledge of their Maker and the sight of their own duties. Men may find matter sufficient to busy their heads and employ their hands with variety, delight, and satisfaction, if they will not boldly quarrel with their own constitution and throw away the blessings their hands are filled with, because they are not big enough to grasp everything. We shall not have much reason to complain of the narrowness of our minds, if we will but employ them about what may be of use to us; for of that they are very capable. And it will be an unpardonable as well as childish peevishness, if we undervalue the advantages of our knowledge and neglect to improve it to the ends for which it was given us, because there are some things that are set out of the reach of it. It will be no excuse to an idle and untoward servant, who would not attend his business by candle light, to plead that he had not broad sunshine. The candle that is set up in us shines bright enough for all our purposes. The discoveries we can make with this ought to satisfy us; and we shall then use our understandings right, when we entertain all objects in that way and proportion that they are suited to our faculties, and upon those grounds they are capable of being proposed to us; and not peremptorily or intemperately require demonstration and demand certainty, where probability only is to be had, and which is sufficient to govern all our concernments. If we will disbelieve everything, because we cannot certainly know all things, we shall do much what as wisely as he who would not use his legs, but sit still and perish because he had no wings to fly.

6. When we know our own *strength*, we shall the better know what to undertake with hopes of success; and when we have well surveyed the *powers* of our own minds, and made some estimate what we may expect from them, we shall not be inclined either to sit still and not set our thoughts on work at all, in despair of

knowing anything, nor, on the other side, question everything
and disclaim all knowledge, because some things are not to be
understood. It is of great use to the sailor to know the length
of his line, though he cannot with it fathom all the depths of the
ocean. It is well he knows that it is long enough to reach the
bottom, at such places as are necessary to direct his voyage, and
caution him against running upon shoals that may ruin him.
Our business here is not to know all things, but those which concern our conduct. If we can find out those measures whereby
a rational creature, put in that state in which man is in this
world, may and ought to govern his opinions and actions depending thereon, we need not be troubled that some other
things escape our knowledge.

7. This was that which gave the first *rise* to this *Essay* concerning the *understanding*. For I thought that the first step
towards satisfying several inquiries the mind of man was very
apt to run into was to take a survey of our own understandings,
examine our own powers, and see to what things they were
adapted. Till that was done I suspected we began at the wrong
end and in vain sought for satisfaction in a quiet and sure possession of truths that most concerned us, whilst we let loose our
thoughts into the vast ocean of *Being*, as if all that boundless
extent were the natural and undoubted possession of our understandings, wherein there was nothing exempt from its decisions
or that escaped its comprehension. Thus men, extending their
inquiries beyond their capacities, and letting their thoughts
wander into those depths where they can find no sure footing, it
is no wonder that they raise questions and multiply disputes,
which, never coming to any clear resolution, are proper only to
continue and increase their doubts and to confirm them at last
in perfect scepticism. Whereas, were the capacities of our understandings well considered, the extent of our knowledge once
discovered, and the horizon found which sets the bounds
between the enlightened and dark parts of things, between
what is and what is not comprehensible by us, men would perhaps with less scruple acquiesce in the avowed ignorance of the
one, and employ their thoughts and discourse with more
advantage and satisfaction in the other.

8. Thus much I thought necessary to say concerning the
occasion of this inquiry into human understanding. But, before
I proceed on to what I have thought on this subject, I must here
in the entrance beg pardon of my reader for the frequent use of
the word *idea*, which he will find in the following treatise. It
being that term which, I think, serves best to stand for whatso-

ever is the object of the understanding when a man thinks, I
have used it to express whatever is meant by *phantasm, notion,
species,* or whatever it is which the mind can be employed about
in thinking; and I could not avoid frequently using it.

I presume it will be easily granted me that there are such *ideas*
in men's minds: everyone is conscious of them in himself, and
men's words and actions will satisfy him that they are in others.

Our first inquiry then shall be how they come into the mind.

CHAPTER II

NO INNATE PRINCIPLES IN THE MIND

1. IT is an established opinion amongst some men that there
are in the *understanding* certain *innate principles,* some primary
notions, κοιναὶ ἔννοιαι, characters, as it were, stamped upon
the mind of man, which the soul receives in its very first being
and brings into the world with it. It would be sufficient to convince unprejudiced readers of the falseness of this supposition,
if I should only show (as I hope I shall in the following parts of
this discourse) how men, barely by the use of their natural
faculties, may attain to all the knowledge they have, without the
help of any innate impressions, and may arrive at certainty
without any such original notions or principles. For I imagine
anyone will easily grant that it would be impertinent to suppose
the *ideas* of colours innate in a creature to whom God has given
sight, and a power to receive them by the eyes, from external
objects; and no less unreasonable would it be to attribute several
truths to the impressions of nature and innate characters, when
we may observe in ourselves faculties, fit to attain as easy and
certain knowledge of them, as if they were originally imprinted
on the mind.

But because a man is not permitted without censure to follow
his own thoughts in the search of truth, when they lead him ever
so little out of the common road, I shall set down the reasons
that made me doubt of the truth of that opinion, as an excuse
for my mistake, if I be in one; which I leave to be considered by
those who, with me, dispose themselves to embrace truth,
wherever they find it.

2. There is nothing more commonly taken for granted than
that there are certain principles, both *speculative* and *practical*
(for they speak of both), universally agreed upon by all man-

kind: which therefore, they argue, must needs be constant impressions which the souls of men receive in their first beings, and which they bring into the world with them, as necessarily and really as they do any of their inherent faculties.

3. This argument, drawn from *universal consent*, has this misfortune in it, that if it were true in matter of fact that there were certain truths wherein all mankind agreed, it would not prove them innate, if there can be any other way shown how men may come to that universal agreement, in the things they do consent in, which I presume may be done.

4. But, which is worse, this argument of universal consent, which is made use of to prove innate principles, seems to me a demonstration that there are none such: because there are none to which all mankind give an universal assent. I shall begin with the speculative, and instance in those magnified principles of demonstration, *Whatsoever is, is* and *It is impossible for the same thing to be and not to be*, which of all others I think have the most allowed title to innate. These have so settled a reputation of maxims universally received that it will, no doubt, be thought strange if anyone should seem to question it. But yet I take liberty to say that these propositions are so far from having an universal assent, that there are a great part of mankind to whom they are not so much as known.

5. For, first, it is evident that all *children* and *idiots* have not the least apprehension or thought of them. And the want of that is enough to destroy that universal assent which must needs be the necessary concomitant of all innate truths: it seeming to me near a contradiction to say that there are truths imprinted on the soul which it perceives or understands not: imprinting, if it signify anything, being nothing else but the making certain truths to be perceived. For to imprint anything on the mind, without the mind's perceiving it, seems to me hardly intelligible. If therefore *children* and *idiots* have souls, have minds, with those impressions upon them, they must unavoidably perceive them, and necessarily know and assent to these truths; which since they do not, it is evident that there are no such impressions. For if they are not notions naturally imprinted, how can they be innate? And if they are notions imprinted, how can they be unknown? To say a notion is imprinted on the mind, and yet at the same time to say that the mind is ignorant of it, and never yet took notice of it, is to make this impression nothing. No proposition can be said to be in the mind, which it never yet knew, which it was never yet conscious of. For if any one may, then by the same reason all propositions that are true and the

mind is capable ever of assenting to, may be said to be in the
mind and to be imprinted: since, if any one can be said to be in
the mind which it never yet knew, it must be only because it is
capable of knowing it; and so the mind is of all truths it ever
shall know. Nay, thus truths may be imprinted on the mind
which it never did nor ever shall know; for a man may live long,
and die at last in ignorance of many truths which his mind was
capable of knowing, and that with certainty. So that if the
capacity of knowing be the natural impression contended for,
all the truths a man ever comes to know will, by this account, be
every one of them innate; and this great point will amount to no
more, but only to a very improper way of speaking; which,
whilst it pretends to assert the contrary, says nothing different
from those who deny innate principles. For nobody, I think,
ever denied that the mind was capable of knowing several truths.
The capacity they say is innate, the knowledge acquired. But
then to what end such contest for certain innate maxims? If
truths can be imprinted on the understanding without being
perceived, I can see no difference there can be between any
truths the mind is capable of knowing, in respect of their
original: they must all be innate, or all adventitious. In vain
shall a man go about to distinguish them. He therefore that
talks of innate notions in the understanding, cannot (if he intend
thereby any distinct sort of truths) mean such truths to be in the
understanding as it never perceived, and is yet wholly ignorant
of. For if these words (*to be in the understanding*) have any
propriety, they signify to be understood. So that to be in the
understanding and not to be understood, to be in the mind and
never to be perceived, is all one as to say: anything is and is not
in the mind or understanding. If therefore these two propositions, *Whatsoever is, is* and *It is impossible for the same thing to
be and not to be*, are by nature imprinted, children cannot be
ignorant of them; infants, and all that have souls, must necessarily have them in their understandings, know the truth of
them, and assent to it.

6. To avoid this, it is usually answered that all men know and
assent to them, *when they come to the use of reason*; and this is
enough to prove them innate. I answer:

7. Doubtful expressions, that have scarce any signification, go
for clear reasons to those who, being prepossessed, take not the
pains to examine even what they themselves say. For, to apply
this answer with any tolerable sense to our present purpose, it
must signify one of these two things: either, that as soon as men
come to the use of reason these supposed native inscriptions

come to be known and observed by them; or else, that the use and exercise of men's reason assists them in the discovery of these principles, and certainly makes them known to them.

8.   If they mean that by the *use of reason* men may discover these principles, and that this is sufficient to prove them innate, their way of arguing will stand thus: viz. that whatever truths reason can certainly discover to us and make us firmly assent to, those are all naturally imprinted on the mind, since that universal assent, which is made the mark of them, amounts to no more but this: that by the use of reason we are capable to come to a certain knowledge of and assent to them; and, by this means, there will be no difference between the maxims of the mathematicians and theorems they deduce from them: all must be equally allowed innate, they being all discoveries made by the use of reason, and truths that a rational creature may certainly come to know, if he apply his thoughts rightly that way.

9.   But how can these men think the *use of reason* necessary to discover principles that are supposed innate, when reason (if we may believe them) is nothing else but the faculty of deducing unknown truths from principles or propositions that are already known? That certainly can never be thought innate which we have need of reason to discover, unless, as I have said, we will have all the certain truths that reason ever teaches us to be innate. We may as well think the use of reason necessary to make our eyes discover visible objects, as that there should be need of reason, or the exercise thereof, to make the understanding see what is originally engraven in it, and cannot be in the understanding before it be perceived by it. So that to make reason discover those truths thus imprinted is to say that the use of reason discovers to a man what he knew before; and if men have those innate, impressed truths originally, and before the use of reason, and yet are always ignorant of them till they come to the use of reason, it is in effect to say that men know and know them not at the same time.

10.   It will here perhaps be said that mathematical demonstrations and other truths that are not innate, are not assented to as soon as proposed, wherein they are distinguished from these maxims and other innate truths.   I shall have occasion to speak of assent upon the first proposing, more particularly by and by. I shall here only, and that very readily, allow that these maxims and mathematical demonstrations are in this different: that the one has need of reason, using of proofs, to make them out and to gain our assent; but the other, as soon as understood, are, without any the least reasoning, embraced and assented to. But I

withal beg leave to observe that it lays open the weakness of this subterfuge which requires the *use of reason* for the discovery of these general truths, since it must be confessed that in their discovery there is no use made of reasoning at all. And I think those who give this answer will not be forward to affirm that the knowledge of this maxim, *That it is impossible for the same thing to be, and not to be,* is a deduction of our reason. For this would be to destroy that bounty of nature they seem so fond of, whilst they make the knowledge of those principles to depend on the labour of our thoughts. For all reasoning is search and casting about and requires pains and application. And how can it with any tolerable sense be supposed that what was imprinted by nature, as the foundation and guide of our reason, should need the use of reason to discover it?

11. Those who will take the pains to reflect with a little attention on the operations of the understanding will find that this ready assent of the mind to some truths depends not either on native inscription or the *use of reason,* but on a faculty of the mind quite distinct from both of them, as we shall see hereafter. Reason, therefore, having nothing to do in procuring our assent to these maxims, if by saying that *men know and assent to them when they come to the use of reason* be meant that the use of reason assists us in the knowledge of these maxims, it is utterly false; and were it true, would prove them not to be innate.

12. If by knowing and assenting to them *when we come to the use of reason* be meant that this is the time when they come to be taken notice of by the mind; and that as soon as children come to the use of reason, they come also to know and assent to these maxims: this also is false and frivolous. *First,* it is false. Because it is evident these maxims are not in the mind so early as the use of reason; and therefore the coming to the use of reason is falsely assigned as the time of their discovery. How many instances of the use of reason may we observe in children a long time before they have any knowledge of this maxim, *That it is impossible for the same thing to be, and not to be?* And a great part of illiterate people and savages pass many years, even of their rational age, without ever thinking on this, and the like general propositions. I grant men come not to the knowledge of these general and more abstract truths, which are thought innate, till they come to the use of reason; and I add, nor then neither. Which is so, because, till after they come to the use of reason, those general abstract *ideas* are not framed in the mind, about which those general maxims are which are mistaken for innate principles, but are indeed discoveries made and verities

introduced and brought into the mind by the same way and discovered by the same steps as several other propositions, which nobody was ever so extravagant as to suppose innate. This I hope to make plain in the sequel of this discourse. I allow therefore a necessity that men should come to the use of reason before they get the knowledge of those general truths, but deny that men's coming to the use of reason is the time of their discovery.

13. In the meantime, it is observable that this saying, that men know and assent to these maxims *when they come to the use of reason*, amounts in reality of fact to no more but this, that they are never known nor taken notice of before the use of reason, but may possibly be assented to sometime after, during a man's life; but when, is uncertain. And so may all other knowable truths, as well as these which therefore have no advantage nor distinction from others, by this note of being known when we come to the use of reason; nor are thereby proved to be innate, but quite the contrary.

14. But, *Secondly*, were it true that the precise time of their being known and assented to were when men come to the *use of reason*, neither would that prove them innate. This way of arguing is so frivolous as the supposition of itself is false. For, by what kind of logic will it appear that any notion is originally by nature imprinted in the mind in its first constitution, because it comes first to be observed and assented to when a faculty of the mind, which has quite a distinct province, begins to exert itself? And therefore the coming to the use of speech, if it were supposed the time that these maxims are first assented to (which it may be with as much truth as the time when men come to the use of reason), would be as good a proof that they were innate, as to say they are innate because men assent to them when they come to the use of reason. I agree then with these men of innate principles that there is no knowledge of these general and self-evident maxims in the mind till it comes to the exercise of reason; but I deny that the coming to the use of reason is the precise time when they are first taken notice of; and if that were the precise time, I deny that it would prove them innate. All that can with any truth be meant by this proposition, that men *assent to them when they come to the use of reason*, is no more but this: that the making of general abstract *ideas* and the understanding of general names being a concomitant of the rational faculty and growing up with it, children commonly get not those general *ideas* nor learn the names that stand for them, till having for a good while exercised their reason about familiar

and more particular *ideas*, they are by their ordinary discourse and actions with others acknowledged to be capable of rational conversation. If assenting to these maxims, when men come to the use of reason, can be true in any other sense, I desire it may be shown; or at least, how in this or any other sense it proves them innate.

15. The senses at first let in particular *ideas* and furnish the yet empty cabinet; and the mind by degrees growing familiar with some of them, they are lodged in the memory, and names got to them. Afterwards the mind, proceeding further, abstracts them, and by degrees learns the use of general names. In this manner the mind comes to be furnished with *ideas* and language, the materials about which to exercise its discursive faculty. And the use of reason becomes daily more visible, as these materials that give it employment increase. But though the having of general *ideas* and the use of general words and reason usually grow together, yet I see not how this any way proves them innate. The knowledge of some truths, I confess, is very early in the mind, but in a way that shows them not to be innate. For, if we will observe, we shall find it still to be about *ideas*, not innate, but acquired: it being about those first which are imprinted by external things, with which infants have earliest to do, which make the most frequent impressions on their senses. In *ideas* thus got, the mind discovers that some agree and others differ, probably as soon as it has any use of memory, as soon as it is able to retain and receive distinct *ideas*. But whether it be then or no, this is certain: it does so long before it has the use of words, or comes to that which we commonly call the *use of reason*. For a child knows as certainly, before it can speak, the difference between the *ideas* of sweet and bitter (i.e. that sweet is not bitter) as it knows afterwards (when it comes to speak) that wormwood and sugar-plums are not the same thing.

16. A child knows not that three and four are equal to seven till he comes to be able to count to seven, and has got the name and *idea* of equality; and then upon explaining those words, he presently assents to, or rather perceives the truth of that proposition. But neither does he then readily assent, because it is an innate truth, nor was his assent wanting till then because he wanted the *use of reason*; but the truth of it appears to him as soon as he has settled in his mind the clear and distinct *ideas* that these names stand for. And then he knows the truth of that proposition upon the same grounds and by the same means that he knew before that a rod and cherry are not the same

thing, and upon the same grounds also that he may come to know afterwards that *It is impossible for the same thing to be, and not to be,* as shall be more fully shown hereafter. So that the later it is before anyone comes to have those general *ideas* about which those maxims are, or to know the signification of those general terms that stand for them, or to put together in his mind the *ideas* they stand for, the later also will it be before he comes to assent to those maxims; whose terms, with the *ideas* they stand for, being no more innate than those of a cat or a weasel, he must stay till time and observation have acquainted him with them; and then he will be in a capacity to know the truth of these maxims, upon the first occasion that shall make him put together those *ideas* in his mind and observe whether they agree or disagree, according as is expressed in those propositions. And therefore it is that a man knows that eighteen and nineteen are equal to thirty-seven, by the same self-evidence that he knows one and two to be equal to three; yet a child knows this not so soon as the other, not for want of the use of reason, but because the *ideas* the words eighteen, nineteen, and thirty-seven stand for are not so soon got as those which are signified by one, two, and three.

17.   This evasion therefore of general assent when men come to the use of reason failing as it does, and leaving no difference between those supposed innate and other truths that are afterwards acquired and learnt, men have endeavoured to secure an universal assent to those they call maxims by saying they are generally *assented to, as soon as proposed,* and the terms they are proposed in understood; seeing all men, even children, as soon as they hear and understand the terms, assent to these propositions, they think it is sufficient to prove them innate. For since men never fail, after they have once understood the words, to acknowledge them for undoubted truths, they would infer that certainly these propositions were first lodged in the understanding which, without any teaching, the mind at very first proposal immediately closes with and assents to, and after that never doubts again.

18.   In answer to this, I demand whether ready *assent* given to a proposition, *upon first hearing* and understanding the terms, be a certain mark of an innate principle? If it be not, such a general assent is in vain urged as a proof of them; if it be said that it is a mark of innate, they must then allow all such propositions to be innate which are generally assented to as soon as heard, whereby they will find themselves plentifully stored with innate principles. For upon the same ground, viz. of assent at

first hearing and understanding the terms, that men would have those maxims pass for innate, they must also admit several propositions about numbers to be innate; and thus, that *One and two are equal to three*, that *Two and two are equal to four*, and a multitude of other the like propositions in numbers that everybody assents to at first hearing and understanding the terms, must have a place amongst these innate axioms. Nor is this the prerogative of numbers alone, and propositions made about several of them; but even natural philosophy and all the other sciences afford propositions which are sure to meet with assent as soon as they are understood. That *Two bodies cannot be in the same place* is a truth that nobody any more sticks at than at these maxims that *It is impossible for the same thing to be and not to be*, that *White is not black*, that *A square is not a circle*, that *Yellowness is not sweetness*. These and a million of other such propositions, as many at least as we have distinct *ideas*, every man in his wits, at first hearing and knowing what the names stand for, must necessarily assent to. If these men will be true to their own rule and have *assent at first hearing and understanding the terms* to be a mark of innate, they must allow not only as many innate propositions as men have distinct *ideas*, but as many as men can make propositions wherein different *ideas* are denied one of another. Since every proposition wherein one different *idea* is denied of another will as certainly find assent at first hearing and understanding the terms as this general one, *It is impossible for the same to be, and not to be*, or that which is the foundation of it and is the easier understood of the two, *The same is not different*: by which account they will have legions of innate propositions of this one sort, without mentioning any other. But since no proposition can be innate unless the *ideas* about which it is be innate, this will be to suppose all our *ideas* of colours, sounds, tastes, figure, etc., innate, than which there cannot be anything more opposite to reason and experience. Universal and ready assent upon hearing and understanding the terms is (I grant) a mark of self-evidence; but self-evidence, depending not on innate impressions but on something else (as we shall show hereafter), belongs to several propositions, which nobody was yet so extravagant as to pretend to be innate.

19. Nor let it be said that those more particular self-evident propositions which are assented to at first hearing, as that *One and two are equal to three*, that *Green is not red*, etc., are received as the consequences of those more universal propositions which are looked on as innate principles, since anyone who will but take the pains to observe what passes in the understanding will

certainly find that these and the like less general propositions
are certainly known and firmly assented to by those who are
utterly ignorant of those more general maxims, and so, being
earlier in the mind than those (as they are called) first principles,
cannot owe to them the assent wherewith they are received at
first hearing.

20.   If it be said that these propositions, viz., *Two and two are
equal to four*, *Red is not blue*, etc., are not general maxims nor of
any great use, I answer that makes nothing to the argument of
universal assent upon hearing and understanding. For, if that
be the certain mark of innate, whatever proposition can be
found that receives general assent as soon as heard and understood, that must be admitted for an innate proposition, as well
as this maxim, that *It is impossible for the same thing to be, and
not to be*, they being upon this ground equal. And as to the
difference of being more general, that makes this maxim more
remote from being innate, those general and abstract *ideas*
being more strangers to our first apprehensions than those of
more particular self-evident propositions, and therefore it is
longer before they are admitted and assented to by the growing
understanding. And as to the usefulness of these magnified
maxims, that perhaps will not be found so great as is generally
conceived when it comes to its due place to be more fully
considered.

21.   But we have not yet done with *assenting to propositions at
first hearing and understanding their terms*. It is fit we first take
notice that this, instead of being a mark that they are innate, is
a proof of the contrary, since it supposes that several, who
understand and know other things, are ignorant of these principles till they are proposed to them, and that one may be
unacquainted with these truths till he hears them from others.
For if they were innate, what need they be proposed in order to
gaining assent, when, by being in the understanding, by a
natural and original impression (if there were any such) they
could not but be known before? Or doth the proposing them
print them clearer in the mind than nature did? If so, then the
consequence will be that a man knows them better after he has
been thus taught them than he did before. Whence it will
follow that these principles may be made more evident to us by
others' teaching than nature has made them by impression:
which will ill agree with the opinion of innate principles, and
give but little authority to them, but on the contrary makes
them unfit to be the foundations of all our other knowledge, as
they are pretended to be. This cannot be denied: that men

grow first acquainted with many of these self-evident truths upon their being proposed; but it is clear that whosoever does so finds in himself that he then begins to know a proposition which he knew not before, and which from thenceforth he never questions, not because it was innate, but because the consideration of the nature of the things contained in those words would not suffer him to think otherwise, how or whensoever he is brought to reflect on them. And if whatever is assented to at first hearing and understanding the terms must pass for an innate principle, every well-grounded observation drawn from particulars into a general rule must be innate. When yet it is certain that not all but only sagacious heads light at first on these observations and reduce them into general propositions, not innate but collected from a preceding acquaintance and reflection on particular instances. These, when observing men have made them, unobserving men, when they are proposed to them, cannot refuse their assent to.

22. If it be said the understanding hath an *implicit knowledge* of these principles, but not an explicit, before this first hearing (as they must who will say that they are in the understanding before they are known), it will be hard to conceive what is meant by a principle imprinted on the understanding implicitly, unless it be this, that the mind is capable of understanding and assenting firmly to such propositions. And thus all mathematical demonstrations, as well as first principles, must be received as native impressions on the mind; which I fear they will scarce allow them to be, who find it harder to demonstrate a proposition than assent to it when demonstrated. And few mathematicians will be forward to believe that all the diagrams they have drawn were but copies of those innate characters which nature had engraven upon their minds.

23. There is, I fear, this further weakness in the foregoing argument, which would persuade us that therefore those maxims are to be thought innate which men *admit at first hearing,* because they assent to propositions which they are not taught nor do receive from the force of any argument or demonstration, but a bare explication or understanding of the terms. Under which there seems to me to lie this fallacy, that men are supposed not to be *taught* nor to *learn* anything *de novo,* when, in truth, they are taught and do learn something they were ignorant of before. For, first, it is evident they have learned the terms and their signification, neither of which was born with them. But this is not all the acquired knowledge in the case: the *ideas* themselves, about which the proposition is, are not born with

them, no more than their names, but got afterwards. So that
in all propositions that are assented to at first hearing: the terms
of the proposition, their standing for such *ideas*, and the *ideas*
themselves that they stand for being neither of them innate,
I would fain know what there is remaining in such propositions
that is innate. For I would gladly have anyone name that proposition whose terms or *ideas* were either of them innate. We
by degrees get *ideas* and names, and learn their appropriated
connection one with another; and then to propositions made in
such terms, whose signification we have learnt, and wherein the
agreement or disagreement we can perceive in our *ideas* when
put together is expressed, we at first hearing assent; though to
other propositions, in themselves as certain and evident, but
which are concerning *ideas* not so soon or so easily got, we are at
the same time no way capable of assenting. For though a child
quickly assent to this proposition, that *An apple is not fire*, when
by familiar acquaintance he has got the *ideas* of those two different things distinctly imprinted on his mind, and has learnt that
the names *apple* and *fire* stand for them: yet it will be some years
after, perhaps, before the same child will assent to this proposition, that *It is impossible for the same thing to be, and not to be*.
Because, though perhaps the words are as easy to be learnt,
yet the signification of them, being more large, comprehensive,
and abstract than of the names annexed to those sensible things
the child hath to do with, it is longer before he learns their
precise meaning, and it requires more time plainly to form in his
mind those general *ideas* they stand for. Till that be done, you
will in vain endeavour to make any child assent to a proposition
made up of such general terms; but as soon as ever he has got
those *ideas* and learned their names, he forwardly closes with
the one as well as the other of the fore-mentioned propositions,
and with both for the same reason, viz. because he finds the
ideas he has in his mind to agree or disagree, according as the
words standing for them are affirmed or denied one of another
in the proposition. But if propositions be brought to him in
words which stand for *ideas* he has not yet in his mind, to such
propositions, however evidently true or false in themselves, he
affords neither assent nor dissent but is ignorant. For words
being but empty sounds, any further than they are signs of our
ideas we cannot but assent to them as they correspond to those
ideas we have, but no further than that. But the showing by
what steps and ways knowledge comes into our minds, and the
grounds of several degrees of assent, being the business of the
following discourse, it may suffice to have only touched on it

here, as one reason that made me doubt of those innate principles.
24. To conclude this argument of *universal consent*, I agree
with these defenders of innate principles that if they are *innate*
they must needs *have universal assent*. For that a truth should
be innate and yet not assented to is to me as unintelligible as for
a man to know a truth and be ignorant of it at the same time.
But then, by these men's own confession, they cannot be innate,
since they are not assented to by those who understand not the
terms; nor by a great part of those who do understand them, but
have yet never heard nor thought of those propositions; which
I think, is at least one-half of mankind. But were the number
far less, it would be enough to destroy *universal assent*, and
thereby show these propositions not to be innate, if children
alone were ignorant of them.

CHAPTER III

NO INNATE PRACTICAL PRINCIPLES

1. IF those speculative maxims, whereof we discoursed in the
foregoing chapter, have not an actual universal assent from all
mankind, as we there proved, it is much more visible concerning
practical principles that they *come short of an universal reception*;
and I think it will be hard to instance any one moral rule which
can pretend to so general and ready an assent as *What is*, *is*, or
to be so manifest a truth as this, that *It is impossible for the
same thing to be and not to be*. Whereby it is evident that they
are further removed from a title to be innate, and the doubt of
their being native impressions on the mind is stronger against
these moral principles than the others. Not that it brings their
truth at all in question. They are equally true, though not
equally evident. Those speculative maxims carry their own
evidence with them; but moral principles require reasoning and
discourse, and some exercise of the mind, to discover the
certainty of their truth. They lie not open as natural characters
engraven on the mind; which if any such were, they must needs
be visible by themselves, and by their own light be certain and
known to everybody. But this is no derogation to their truth
and certainty, no more than it is to the truth or certainty of the
three angles of a triangle being equal to two right ones: because
it is not so evident as *The whole is bigger than a part*, nor so apt
to be assented to at first hearing. It may suffice that these moral
rules are capable of demonstration, and therefore it is our own

faults if we come not to a certain knowledge of them. But the ignorance wherein many men are of them, and the slowness of assent wherewith others receive them, are manifest proofs that they are not innate and such as offer themselves to their view without searching.

2.   Whether there be any such moral principles wherein all men do agree, I appeal to any who have been but moderately conversant in the history of mankind, and looked abroad beyond the smoke of their own chimneys. Where is that practical truth that is universally received, without doubt or question, as it must be if innate? *Justice*, and keeping of contracts, is that which *most men seem to agree in*. This is a principle which is thought to extend itself to the dens of thieves, and the confederacies of the greatest villains; and they who have gone furthest towards the putting off of humanity itself, keep faith and rules of justice one with another. I grant that outlaws themselves do this one amongst another, but it is without receiving these as the innate laws of nature. They practise them as rules of convenience within their own communities; but it is impossible to conceive that he embraces justice as a practical principle, who acts fairly with his fellow highwaymen and at the same time plunders or kills the next honest man he meets with. Justice and truth are the common ties of society; and therefore even outlaws and robbers, who break with all the world besides, must keep faith and rules of equity amongst themselves, or else they cannot hold together. But will anyone say that those that live by fraud and rapine have innate principles of truth and justice which they allow and assent to?

3.   Perhaps it will be urged that the *tacit assent of their minds agrees to what their practice contradicts*. I answer, *first*, I have always thought the actions of men the best interpreters of their thoughts. But, since it is certain that most men's practice, and some men's open professions have either questioned or denied these principles, it is impossible to establish an universal consent (though we should look for it only amongst grown men), without which it is impossible to conclude them innate. *Secondly*, it is very strange and unreasonable to suppose innate practical principles that terminate only in contemplation. Practical principles, derived from nature, are there for operation, and must produce conformity of action, not barely speculative assent to their truth, or else they are in vain distinguished from speculative maxims. Nature, I confess, has put into man a desire of happiness and an aversion to misery: these indeed are innate practical principles which (as practical principles ought) do continue con-

stantly to operate and influence all our actions without ceasing; these may be observed in all persons and all ages, steady and universal; but these are inclinations of the appetite to good, not impressions of truth on the understanding. I deny not that there are natural tendencies imprinted on the minds of men, and that from the very first instances of sense and perception, there are some things that are grateful and others unwelcome to them, some things that they incline to, and others that they fly: but this makes nothing for innate characters on the mind, which are to be the principles of knowledge, regulating our practice. Such natural impressions on the understanding are so far from being confirmed hereby, that this is an argument against them, since, if there were certain characters imprinted by nature on the understanding, as the principles of knowledge, we could not but perceive them constantly operate in us and influence our knowledge, as we do those others on the will and appetite; which never cease to be the constant springs and motives of all our actions to which we perpetually feel them strongly impelling us.

4. Another reason that makes me doubt of any innate practical principles is that I think *there cannot any one moral rule be proposed whereof a man may not justly demand a reason*: which would be perfectly ridiculous and absurd if they were innate, or so much as self-evident, which every innate principle must needs be, and not need any proof to ascertain its truth, nor want any reason to gain it approbation. He would be thought void of common sense who asked on the one side, or on the other side went to give a reason *why it is impossible for the same thing to be and not to be*. It carries its own light and evidence with it, and needs no other proof: he that understands the terms assents to it for its own sake, or else nothing will ever be able to prevail with him to do it. But should that most unshaken rule of morality and foundation of all social virtue, that *One should do as he would be done unto*, be proposed to one who never heard it before, but yet is of capacity to understand its meaning, might he not without any absurdity ask a reason why? And were not he that proposed it bound to make out the truth and reasonableness of it to him? Which plainly shows it not to be innate; for if it were it could neither want nor receive any proof, but must needs (at least as soon as heard and understood) be received and assented to as an unquestionable truth, which a man can by no means doubt of. So that the truth of all these moral rules plainly depends upon some other, antecedent to them and from which they must be deduced: which could not be if either they were

innate or so much as self-evident.

5.   That men should keep their compacts is certainly a great and undeniable rule in morality.   But yet, if a Christian, who has the view of happiness and misery in another life, be asked why a man must keep his word, he will *give* this as a *reason*: because God, who has the power of eternal life and death, requires it of us.   But if an *Hobbist* be asked why, he will answer: because the public requires it, and the *Leviathan* will punish you if you do not.   And if one of the old *heathen* philosophers had been asked, he would have answered: because it was dishonest, below the dignity of a man, and opposite to virtue, the highest perfection of human nature, to do otherwise.

6.   Hence naturally flows the great variety of opinions concerning moral rules which are to be found amongst men, according to the different sorts of happiness they have a prospect of, or propose to themselves; which could not be if practical principles were innate and imprinted in our minds immediately by the hand of God.   I grant the existence of God is so many ways manifest, and the obedience we owe him so congruous to the light of reason, that a great part of mankind give testimony to the law of nature: but yet I think it must be allowed that several moral rules may receive from mankind a very general approbation, without either knowing or admitting the true ground of morality; which can only be the will and law of a god, who sees men in the dark, has in his hand rewards and punishments, and power enough to call to account the proudest offender.   For, God having, by an inseparable connexion, joined *virtue* and *public happiness* together, and made the practice thereof necessary to the preservation of society, and visibly *beneficial* to all with whom the virtuous man has to do, it is no wonder that everyone should not only allow, but recommend and magnify those rules to others, from whose observance of them he is sure to reap advantage to himself.   He may, out of interest as well as conviction, cry up that for sacred, which if once trampled on and profaned, he himself cannot be safe nor secure.   This, though it takes nothing from the moral and eternal obligation which these rules evidently have, yet it shows that the outward acknowledgment men pay to them in their words proves not that they are innate principles.   Nay, it proves not so much as that men assent to them inwardly in their own minds as the inviolable rules of their own practice, since we find that self-interest and the conveniences of this life make many men own an outward profession and approbation of them, whose actions sufficiently prove that they very little consider the

Law-giver that prescribed these rules, nor the hell he has ordained for the punishment of those that transgress them.

7. For, if we will not in civility allow too much sincerity to the professions of most *men*, but think their actions to be the inter-preters of their thoughts, we shall find that they have *no* such internal veneration for these rules, nor so *full a persuasion of their certainty* and obligation. The great principle of morality, *To do as one would be done to*, is more commended than practised. But the breach of this rule cannot be a greater vice than to teach others that it is no moral rule, nor obligatory, would be thought madness and contrary to that interest men sacrifice to when they break it themselves. Perhaps *conscience* will be urged as check-ing us for such breaches, and so the internal obligation and establishment of the rule be preserved.

8. To which I answer that I doubt not but without being written on their hearts, many men may, by the same way that they come to the knowledge of other things, come to assent to several moral rules and be convinced of their obligation. Others also may come to be of the same mind, from their education, company, and customs of their country; which *persuasion, how-ever got, will serve to set conscience on work*, which is nothing else but our own opinion or judgment of the moral rectitude or pravity of our own actions. And if conscience be a proof of innate principles, contraries may be innate principles: since some men, with the same bent of conscience, prosecute what others avoid.

12. The breaking of a rule, say you, is no argument that it is unknown. I grant it: but the *generally allowed breach of it any-where*, I say, *is a proof that it is not innate*. For example, let us take any of these rules, which, being the most obvious deduc-tions of human reason and conformable to the natural inclina-tion of the greatest part of men, fewest people have had the impudence to deny or inconsideration to doubt of. If any can be thought to be naturally imprinted, none, I think, can have a fairer pretence to be innate than this: *Parents, preserve and cherish your children.* When therefore you say that this is an innate rule, what do you mean? Either that it is an innate prin-ciple which upon all occasions excites and directs the actions of all men, or else that it is a truth which all men have imprinted on their minds and which therefore they know and assent to. But in neither of these senses is it innate. *First*, that it is not a principle which influences all men's actions is what I have proved by the examples before cited; nor need we seek so far as *Mingrelia* or *Peru* to find instances of such as neglect, abuse,

nay and destroy their children, or look on it only as the more than brutality of some savage and barbarous nations, when we remember that it was a familiar and uncondemned practice amongst the *Greeks* and *Romans* to expose without pity or remorse their innocent infants. *Secondly*, that it is an innate truth, known to all men, is also false. For *Parents, preserve your children* is so far from an innate truth that it is no truth at all, it being a command and not a proposition, and so not capable of truth or falsehood. To make it capable of being assented to as true, it must be reduced to some such proposition as this: *It is the duty of parents to preserve their children.* But what duty is cannot be understood without a law, nor a law be known or supposed without a law-maker, or without reward and punishment; so that it is impossible that this or any other practical principle should be innate, i.e. be imprinted on the mind as a duty, without supposing the *ideas* of God, of law, of obligation, of punishment, of a life after this innate. For, that punishment follows not in this life the breach of this rule, and consequently that it has not the force of a law in countries where the generally allowed practice runs counter to it, is in itself evident. But these *ideas* (which must be all of them innate, if anything as a duty be so) are so far from being innate that it is not every studious or thinking man, much less everyone that is born, in whom they are to be found clear and distinct; and that one of them, which of all others seems most likely to be innate, is not so (I mean the *idea* of God), I think, in the next chapter will appear very evident to any considering man.

13. From what has been said, I think we may safely conclude that *whatever practical rule is in any place generally and with allowance broken, cannot be supposed innate*, it being impossible that men should, without shame or fear, confidently and serenely, break a rule which they could not but evidently know that God had set up, and would certainly punish the breach of (which they must, if it were innate), to a degree to make it a very ill bargain to the transgressor. Without such a knowledge as this, a man can never be certain that anything is his duty. Ignorance or doubt of the law, hopes to escape the knowledge or power of the law-maker, or the like may make men give way to a present appetite; but let anyone see the fault, and the rod by it, and with the transgression, a fire ready to punish it: a pleasure tempting, and the hand of the Almighty visibly held up and prepared to take vengeance (for this must be the case where any duty is imprinted on the mind), and then tell me whether it be possible for people with such a prospect, such a certain know-

ledge as this, wantonly and without scruple, to offend against a law which they carry about them in indelible characters, and that stares them in the face whilst they are breaking it? Whether men at the same time that they feel in themselves the imprinted edicts of an omnipotent law-maker can, with assurance and gaiety, slight and trample under foot his most sacred injunctions? And lastly, whether it be possible that, whilst a man thus openly bids defiance to this innate law and supreme law-giver, all the bystanders, yea, even the governors and rulers of the people, full of the same sense both of the law and law-maker, should silently connive without testifying their dislike or laying the least blame on it? Principles of actions indeed there are lodged in men's appetites, but these are so far from being innate moral principles that, if they were left to their full swing, they would carry men to the over-turning of all morality. Moral laws are set as a curb and restraint to these exorbitant desires, which they cannot be but by rewards and punishments that will over-balance the satisfaction anyone shall propose to himself in the breach of the law. If therefore anything be imprinted on the mind of all men as a law, all men must have a certain and unavoidable knowledge that certain and unavoidable punishment will attend the breach of it. For if men can be ignorant or doubtful of what is innate, innate principles are insisted on and urged to no purpose: truth and certainty (the things pretended) are not at all secured by them; but men are in the same uncertain, floating estate with as without them. An evident indubitable knowledge of unavoidable punishment, great enough to make the transgression very ineligible, must accompany an innate law, unless with an innate law they can suppose an innate gospel too. I would not be here mistaken as if, because I deny an innate law, I thought there were none but positive laws. There is a great deal of difference between an innate law and a law of nature, between something imprinted on our minds in their very original, and something that we, being ignorant of, may attain to the knowledge of, by the use and due application of our natural faculties. And I think they equally forsake the truth who, running into the contrary extremes, either affirm an innate law, or deny that there is a law knowable by the light of nature, i.e. without the help of positive revelation.

CHAPTER IV

OTHER CONSIDERATIONS CONCERNING INNATE PRINCIPLES,
BOTH SPECULATIVE AND PRACTICAL

1. HAD those who would persuade us that there are innate principles not taken them together in gross, but considered separately the parts out of which those propositions are made, they would not, perhaps, have been so forward to believe they were innate: since, if the *ideas* which made up those truths were not, it was impossible that the propositions made up of them should be innate or our knowledge of them be born with us. For if the *ideas* be not *innate*, there was a time when the mind was without those principles; and then they will not be innate, but be derived from some other original. For, where the *ideas* themselves are not, there can be no knowledge, no assent, no mental or verbal propositions about them.

2. If we will attentively consider new-born *children*, we shall have little reason to think that they bring many *ideas* into the world with them. For, bating perhaps some faint *ideas* of hunger, and thirst, and warmth, and some pains which they may *have* felt in the womb, there is *not* the least appearance of any settled *ideas* at all in them, especially of *ideas answering the terms which make up those universal propositions* that are esteemed innate principles. One may perceive how, by degrees, afterwards, *ideas* come into their minds, and that they get no more nor no other than what experience and the observation of things that come in their way furnish them with: which might be enough to satisfy us that they are not original characters stamped on the mind.

3. *It is impossible for the same thing to be and not to be* is certainly (if there be any such) an innate principle. But can anyone think, or will anyone say that *impossibility* and *identity* are two innate *ideas*? Are they such as all mankind have and bring into the world with them? And are they those that are the first in children and antecedent to all acquired ones? If they are innate, they must needs be so. Hath a child an *idea* of *impossibility* and *identity* before it has of *white* or *black*, *sweet* or *bitter*? And is it from the knowledge of this principle that it concludes that wormwood rubbed on the nipple hath not the same taste that it used to receive from thence? Is it the actual knowledge of *impossibile est idem esse et non esse* that makes a child distinguish between its mother and a stranger, or that makes it fond of the one and fly the other? Or does the mind

regulate itself and its assent by *ideas* that it never yet had? Or the understanding draw conclusions from principles which it never yet knew or understood? The names *impossibility* and *identity* stand for two *ideas* so *far from being innate* or born with us that I think it requires great care and attention to form them right in our understandings. They are so far from being brought into the world with us, so remote from the thoughts of infancy and childhood that, I believe, upon examination it will be found that many grown men want them.

4. If *identity* (to instance in that alone) be a native impression, and consequently so clear and obvious to us that we must needs know it even from our cradles, I would gladly be resolved by one of seven or seventy years old, whether a man, being a creature consisting of soul and body, be the same man when his body is changed? Whether *Euphorbus* and *Pythagoras*, having had the same soul, were the same man though they lived several ages asunder? Nay, whether the cock too, which had the same soul, were not the same with both of them? Whereby, perhaps, it will appear that our *idea of sameness* is *not* so settled and clear as to deserve to be thought *innate* in us. For if those innate *ideas* are not clear and distinct so as to be universally known and naturally agreed on, they cannot be subjects of universal and undoubted truths, but will be the unavoidable occasion of perpetual uncertainty. For, I suppose, everyone's *idea* of *identity* will not be the same, that *Pythagoras* and thousands others of his followers have. And which then shall be the true? Which innate? Or are there two different *ideas* of *identity*, both innate?

5. Nor let anyone think that the questions I have here proposed about the *identity* of man are bare, empty speculations; which, if they were, would be enough to show that there was in the understandings of men *no innate* idea *of* identity. He that shall, with a little attention, reflect on the Resurrection and consider that divine justice shall bring to judgment, at the last day, the very same persons to be happy or miserable in the other who did well or ill in this life, will find it perhaps not easy to resolve with himself what makes the same man or wherein *identity* consists, and will not be forward to think he and everyone, even children themselves, have naturally a clear *idea* of it.

6. Let us examine that principle of mathematics, viz. that *The whole is bigger than a part*. This, I take it, is reckoned amongst innate principles. I am sure it has as good a title as any to be thought so; which yet nobody can think it to be, when he considers the *ideas* it comprehends in it, *whole* and *part*, are

perfectly relative; but the positive *ideas* to which they properly
and immediately belong are extension and number, of which
alone *whole* and *part* are relations. So that if *whole* and *part* are
innate *ideas*, extension and number must be so too: it being
impossible to have an *idea* of a relation, without having any at all
of the thing to which it belongs, and in which it is founded.
Now, whether the minds of men have naturally imprinted on
them the *ideas* of extension and number, I leave to be considered
by those who are the patrons of innate principles.

7. That *God is to be worshipped* is, without doubt, as great a
truth as any can enter into the mind of man and deserves the
first place amongst all practical principles. But yet, it can by no
means be thought innate, unless the *ideas* of *God* and *worship*
are innate. That the *idea* the term *worship* stands for is not in
the understanding of children and a character stamped on the
mind in its first original, I think will be easily granted by anyone that considers how few there be amongst grown men who
have a clear and distinct notion of it. And, I suppose, there
cannot be anything more ridiculous than to say that children
have this practical principle innate, *that God is to be worshipped*,
and yet that they know not what that worship of God is which is
their duty. But to pass by this.

8. If any *idea* can be imagined *innate*, the *idea of God* may, of
all others, for many reasons be thought so, since it is hard to
conceive how there should be innate moral principles without
an innate *idea* of a *deity*. Without a notion of a law-maker, it is
impossible to have a notion of a law and an obligation to observe
it. Besides the atheists taken notice of amongst the ancients and
left branded upon the records of history, hath not navigation
discovered, in these latter ages, whole nations, at the bay of
Saldanha[1], in *Brazil*[2], in *Boranday*[3], and the *Caribbee* islands,
etc. amongst whom there was to be found no notion of a god, no
religion. Nicholaus del Techo, *In literis, ex Paraquaria de
Caaiguarum conversione* has these words[4]: *Reperi eam gentem
nullum nomen habere, quod Deum, et Hominis animam significet,
nulla sacra habet, nulla idola.* These are instances of nations
where uncultivated nature has been left to itself, without the
help of letters and discipline and the improvements of arts and
sciences. But there are others to be found who have enjoyed

[1]Roe *in* Thévenot, t. i, pt. i, p. 2.
[2]Léry, ch. 16.
[3]La Martiniére, P. M. de. *Voyages des pays septentrionaux.* 1676. p. 201. Terry,
E. *A Voyage to East-India.* 1655. p. 17. Ovington, J. *A Voyage to the Suratt.*
1696. p. 489.
[4]In *Relatio triplex de rebus Indicis Caaiguarum*, 1654. p. 43.

these in a very great measure who yet, for want of a due application of their thoughts this way, want the *idea* and knowledge of
God. It will I doubt not be a surprise to others, as it was to me,
to find the *Siamites* of this number. But for this, let them consult the King of *France's* late envoy thither[5] who gives no better
account of the *Chinese* themselves[6]. And if we will not believe
La Loubère, the missionaries of *China*, even the Jesuits themselves, the great encomiasts of the *Chinese*, do all to a man agree
and will convince us that the sect of the *litterati* or *learned*,
keeping to the old religion of *China* and the ruling party there,
are all of them *atheists*. *Vide* D. Fernandez Navarrete's 'An
Account of the Empire of China' in vol. I of A. & J. Churchill's
A Collection of voyages and travels (1704) and *Historia Cultus
Sinensium* (1700). And, perhaps, if we should with attention
mind the lives and discourses of people not so far off, we should
have too much reason to fear that many in more civilized
countries have no very strong and clear impressions of a deity
upon their minds, and that the complaints of atheism made from
the pulpit are not without reason. And though only some profli-
gate wretches own it too bare-facedly now, yet perhaps we should
hear, more than we do, of it from others, did not the fear of the
magistrate's sword or their neighbour's censure tie up people's
tongues; which, were the apprehensions of punishment or shame
taken away, would as openly proclaim their *atheism* as their
lives do.

21. To which let me add: if there be any innate *ideas*, any
ideas in the mind which the mind does not actually think on,
they must be lodged in the memory and from thence must be
brought into view by remembrance, i.e. must be known when
they are remembered to have been perceptions in the mind
before, unless remembrance can be without remembrance. For
to remember is to perceive anything with memory, or with a
consciousness, that it was known or perceived before; without
this, whatever *idea* comes into the mind is new and not remembered: this consciousness of its having been in the mind before
being that which distinguishes remembering from all other ways
of thinking. Whatever *idea* was never perceived by the mind
was never in the mind. Whatever *idea* is in the mind is either an
actual perception or else, having been an actual perception, is so
in the mind that by the memory it can be made an actual perception again. Whenever there is the actual perception of an *idea*

[5] La Loubère, S. de. *Du royaume de Siam.* 1691. t. i, ch. 9, §15 et seq.; ch. 20,
§22; ch. 22, §6.
[6] *Ibid.*, t. i, ch. 20, §4; ch. 23.

without memory, the *idea* appears perfectly new and unknown before to the understanding. Whenever the memory brings any *idea* into actual view, it is with a consciousness that it had been there before and was not wholly a stranger to the mind. Whether this be not so, I appeal to everyone's observation. And then I desire an instance of an *idea* pretended to be innate which (before any impression of it by ways hereafter to be mentioned) anyone could revive and remember as an *idea* he had formerly known: without which consciousness of a former perception there is no remembrance; and whatever *idea* comes into the mind without that consciousness is not remembered, or comes not out of the memory, nor can be said to be in the mind before that appearance. For what is not either actually in view, or in the memory, is in the mind no way at all, and is all one as if it never had been there. Suppose a child had the use of his eyes till he knows and distinguishes colours; but then cataracts shut the windows and he is forty or fifty years perfectly in the dark; and in that time perfectly loses all memory of the *ideas* of colours he once had. This was the case of a blind man I once talked with, who lost his sight by the smallpox when he was a child and had no more notion of colours than one born blind. I ask whether anyone can say this man had then any *ideas* of colours in his mind, any more than one born blind? And I think nobody will say that either of them had in his mind any *idea* of colours at all. His cataracts are couched and then he has the *ideas* (which he remembers not) of colours, *de novo*, by his restored sight conveyed to his mind, and that without any consciousness of a former acquaintance. And these now he can revive and call to mind in the dark. In this case all these *ideas* of colours, which when out of view can be revived with a consciousness of a former acquaintance, being thus in the memory, are said to be in the mind. The use I make of this is that whatever *idea*, being not actually in view, is in the mind is there only by being in the memory; and if it be not in the memory, it is not in the mind; and if it be in the memory, it cannot by the memory be brought into actual view without a perception that it comes out of the memory: which is this, that it had been known before and is now remembered. If therefore there be any innate *ideas*, they must be in the memory or else nowhere in the mind; and if they be in the memory, they can be revived without any impression from without; and whenever they are brought into the mind, they are remembered, i.e. they bring with them a perception of their not being wholly new to it. This being a constant and distinguishing difference between what is and what is not in the

memory, or in the mind: that what is not in the memory, whenever it appears there, appears perfectly new and unknown before;
and what is in the memory or in the mind, whenever it is suggested by the memory, appears not to be new, but the mind
finds it in itself and knows it was there before. By this it may
be tried whether there be any innate *ideas* in the mind before
impression from *sensation* or *reflection*. I would fain meet with
the man who, when he came to the use of reason or at any other
time, remembered any of them, and to whom, after he was born,
they were never new. If anyone will say there are *ideas* in the
mind that are not in the memory, I desire him to explain himself
and make what he says intelligible.

23. To conclude: some *ideas* forwardly offer themselves to all
men's understanding; some sorts of truths result from any
ideas, as soon as the mind puts them into propositions; other
truths require a train of *ideas* placed in order, a due comparing
of them, and deductions made with attention, before they can be
discovered and assented to. Some of the first sort, because of
their general and easy reception, have been mistaken for innate;
but the truth is, *ideas* and notions are no more born with us than
arts and sciences, though some of them indeed offer themselves
to our faculties more readily than others and therefore are more
generally received, though that too be according as the organs of
our bodies and powers of our minds happen to be employed:
*God having fitted men with faculties and means to discover,
receive, and retain truths, accordingly as they are employed.* The
great difference that is to be found in the notions of mankind is
from the different use they put their faculties to; whilst some
(and those the most), taking things upon trust, misemploy their
power of assent, by lazily enslaving their minds to the dictates
and dominion of others, in doctrines which it is their duty carefully to examine and not blindly, with an implicit faith, to
swallow; others, employing their thoughts only about some few
things, grow acquainted sufficiently with them, attain great
degrees of knowledge in them, and are ignorant of all other,
having never let their thoughts loose in the search of other
inquiries. Thus, that the three angles of a triangle are equal to
two right ones is a truth as certain as anything can be, and I
think more evident than many of those propositions that go for
principles; and yet there are millions, however expert in other
things, who know not this at all because they never set their
thoughts on work about such angles; and he that certainly
knows this proposition may yet be utterly ignorant of the truth
of other propositions in mathematics itself, which are as clear

and evident as this, because, in his search of those mathematical truths, he stopped his thoughts short and went not so far. The same may happen concerning the notions we have of the being of a deity. For, though there be no truth which a man may more evidently make out to himself than the existence of a god, yet he that shall content himself with things as he finds them in this world, as they minister to his pleasures and passions, and not make inquiry a little further into their causes, ends, and admirable contrivances, and pursue the thoughts thereof with diligence and attention, may live long without any notion of such a being. And if any person hath, by talk, put such a notion into his head, he may, perhaps, believe it; but if he hath never *examined* it, his knowledge of it will be no perfecter than his who, having been told that the three angles of a triangle are equal to two right ones, takes it upon trust without examining the demonstration, and may yield his assent as a probable opinion but hath no knowledge of the truth of it; which yet his faculties, if carefully employed, were able to make clear and evident to him. But this only by the by, to show how much our *knowledge depends upon the right use of those powers nature hath bestowed upon us,* and how little upon such innate principles as are in vain supposed to be in all mankind for their direction; which all men could not but know if they were there, or else they would be there to no purpose; and which, since all men do not know, nor can distinguish from other adventitious truths, we may well conclude there are no such.

26. *To show how the understanding proceeds herein is the design of the following discourse*; which I shall proceed to, when I have first premised that hitherto, to clear my way to those foundations which I conceive are the only true ones whereon to establish those notions we can have of our own knowledge, it hath been necessary for me to give an account of the reasons I had to doubt of innate principles. And since the arguments which are against them do some of them rise from common received opinions, I have been forced to take several things for granted, which is hardly avoidable to anyone whose task it is to show the falsehood or improbability of any tenet: it happening in controversial discourses, as it does in assaulting of towns, where, if the ground be but firm whereon the batteries are erected, there is no further inquiry of whom it is borrowed nor whom it belongs to, so it affords but a fit rise for the present purpose. But in the future part of this discourse, designing to raise an edifice uniform and consistent with itself, as far as my own experience and observation will assist me, I hope to erect it on

such a basis that I shall not need to shore it up with props and buttresses, leaning on borrowed or begged foundations; or at least if mine prove a castle in the air, I will endeavour it shall be all of a piece and hang together. Wherein I warn the reader not to expect undeniable cogent demonstrations, unless I may be allowed the privilege, not seldom assumed by others, to take my principles for granted; and then, I doubt not but I can demonstrate too. All that I shall say for the principles I proceed on is that I can only *appeal* to men's own unprejudiced *experience* and observation whether they be true or no; and this is enough for a man who professes no more than to lay down candidly and freely his own conjectures concerning a subject lying somewhat in the dark, without any other design than an unbiased inquiry after truth.

BOOK II

OF IDEAS

CHAPTER I

OF IDEAS IN GENERAL, AND THEIR ORIGINAL

1. Every man being conscious to himself that he thinks, and that which his mind is applied about whilst thinking being the *ideas* that are there, it is past doubt that men have in their minds several *ideas* such as are those expressed by the words *whiteness, hardness, sweetness, thinking, motion, man, elephant, army, drunkenness* and others: it is in the first place then to be inquired, how he comes by them? I know it is a received doctrine that men have native *ideas* and original characters stamped upon their minds in their very first being. This opinion I have at large examined already; and, I suppose, what I have said in the foregoing book will be much more easily admitted when I have shown whence the understanding may get all the *ideas* it has, and by what ways and degrees they may come into the mind; for which I shall appeal to everyone's own observation and experience.

2. Let us then suppose the mind to be, as we say, white paper void of all characters, without any *ideas*. How comes it to be furnished? Whence comes it by that vast store which the busy and boundless fancy of man has painted on it with an almost endless variety? Whence has it all the materials of reason and knowledge? To this I answer, in one word, from *experience*; in that all our knowledge is founded, and from that it ultimately derives itself. Our observation, employed either about *external sensible objects, or about the internal operations of our minds perceived and reflected on by ourselves, is that which supplies our understandings with all the materials of thinking*. These two are the fountains of knowledge, from whence all the *ideas* we have, or can naturally have, do spring.

3. First, *our senses*, conversant about particular sensible objects, do *convey into the mind* several distinct *perceptions* of things, according to those various ways wherein those objects do affect them. And thus we come by those *ideas* we have of *yellow, white, heat, cold, soft, hard, bitter, sweet,* and all those

33

which we call sensible qualities; which when I say the senses convey into the mind, I mean, they from external objects convey into the mind what produces there those *perceptions*. This great source of most of the *ideas* we have, depending wholly upon our senses, and derived by them to the understanding, I call SENSATION.

4.   Secondly, the other fountain from which experience furnisheth the understanding with *ideas* is the *perception of the operations of our own minds* within us, as it is employed about the *ideas* it has got; which operations, when the soul comes to reflect on and consider, do furnish the understanding with another set of *ideas*, which could not be had from things without. And such are *perception, thinking, doubting, believing, reasoning, knowing, willing*, and all the different actings of our own minds; which we, being conscious of and observing in ourselves, do from these receive into our understandings as distinct *ideas* as we do from bodies affecting our senses. This source of *ideas* every man has wholly in himself; and though it be not sense, as having nothing to do with external objects, yet it is very like it, and might properly enough be called internal sense. But as I call the other *sensation*, so I call this REFLECTION, the *ideas* it affords being such only as the mind gets by reflecting on its own operations within itself. By REFLECTION then, in the following part of this discourse, I would be understood to mean that notice which the mind takes of its own operations, and the manner of them, by reason whereof there come to be *ideas* of these operations in the understanding. These two, I say, viz. external material things as the objects of SENSATION, and the operations of our own minds within as the objects of REFLECTION, are to me the only originals from whence all our *ideas* take their beginnings. The term *operations* here I use in a large sense, as comprehending not barely the actions of the mind about its *ideas*, but some sort of passions arising sometimes from them, such as is the satisfaction or uneasiness arising from any thought.

5.   The understanding seems to me not to have the least glimmering of any *ideas* which it doth not receive from one of these two. *External objects furnish the mind with the* ideas *of sensible qualities*, which are all those different perceptions they produce in us; and the *mind furnishes the understanding with* ideas *of its own operations*.

These, when we have taken a full survey of them and their several modes, combinations, and relations, we shall find to contain all our whole stock of *ideas*, and that we have nothing in our minds which did not come in one of these two ways. Let anyone examine his own thoughts and thoroughly search into his understanding and then let him tell me whether all the original *ideas* he has there are any other than of the objects of his *senses*, or of the operations of his mind, considered as objects of his *reflection*. And how great a mass of knowledge soever he imagines to be lodged there, he will, upon taking a strict view, see that he has *not any* idea *in his mind but what one of these two have imprinted*, though perhaps, with infinite variety compounded and enlarged by the understanding, as we shall see hereafter.

6. He that attentively considers the state of a *child*, at his first coming into the world, will have little reason to think him stored with plenty of *ideas*, that are to be the matter of his future knowledge. It is by degrees he comes to be furnished with them. And though the *ideas* of obvious and familiar qualities imprint themselves before the memory begins to keep a register of time and order, yet it is often so late before some unusual qualities come in the way, that there are few men that cannot recollect the beginning of their acquaintance with them. And if it were worthwhile, no doubt a child might be so ordered as to have but a very few, even of the ordinary *ideas*, till he were grown up to a man. But all that are born into the world being surrounded with bodies that perpetually and diversely affect them, variety of *ideas*, whether care be taken about it or no, are imprinted on the minds of children. *Light* and *colours* are busy at hand everywhere when the eye is but open; *sounds* and some *tangible qualities* fail not to solicit their proper senses and force an entrance to the mind; but yet, I think it will be granted easily that, if a child were kept in a place where he never saw any other but black and white till he were a man, he would have no more *ideas* of scarlet or green than he that from his childhood never tasted an oyster or a pineapple has of those particular relishes.

7. Men then come to be furnished with fewer or more simple *ideas* from without, according as the *objects* they converse with afford greater or less variety; and from the operation of their minds within, according as they more or less *reflect* on them. For, though he that contemplates the operations of his mind cannot but have plain and clear *ideas* of them: yet, unless he turn his thoughts that way and consider them *attentively*, he will no more have clear and distinct *ideas* of all the *operations of his mind*, and all that may be observed therein, than he will have all the particular *ideas* of any landscape, or of the parts and motions of a clock, who will not turn his eyes to it and with

attention heed all the parts of it. The picture or clock may be so placed that they may come in his way every day, but yet he will have but a confused *idea* of all the parts they are made up of, till he *applies himself with attention* to consider them each in particular.

8. And hence we see the reason why it is pretty late before most children get *ideas* of the operations of their own minds; and some have not any very clear or perfect *ideas* of the greatest part of them all their lives. Because, though they pass there continually, yet, like floating visions, they make not deep impressions enough to leave in the mind clear, distinct, lasting *ideas*, till the understanding turns inwards upon itself, *reflects* on its own *operations*, and makes them the object of its own contemplation. Children, when they come first into it, are surrounded with a world of new things which, by a constant solicitation of their senses, draw the mind constantly to them, forward to take notice of new and apt to be delighted with the variety of changing objects. Thus the first years are usually employed and diverted in looking abroad. Men's business in them is to acquaint themselves with what is to be found without; and so growing up in a constant attention to outward sensations, seldom make any considerable reflection on what passes within them, till they come to be of riper years; and some scarce ever at all.

9. To ask *at what time a man has first any* ideas is to ask when he begins to perceive: having *ideas* and perception being the same thing. I know it is an opinion that the soul always thinks, and that it has the actual perception of *ideas* in itself constantly, as long as it exists; and that actual thinking is as inseparable from the soul as actual extension is from the body; which if true, to inquire after the beginning of a man's *ideas* is the same as to inquire after the beginning of his soul. For, by this account, soul and its *ideas*, as body and its extension, will begin to exist both at the same time.

10. But whether the soul be supposed to exist antecedent to, or coeval with, or some time after, the first rudiments of organization, or the beginnings of life in the body, I leave to be disputed by those who have better thought of that matter. I confess myself to have one of those dull souls, that doth not perceive itself always to contemplate *ideas*; nor can conceive it any more necessary for the *soul always to think*, than for the body always to move: the perception of *ideas* being (as I conceive) to the soul what motion is to the body: not its essence, but one of its operations. And therefore, though thinking be supposed

never so much the proper action of the soul, yet it is not necessary to suppose that it should be always thinking, always in action. That, perhaps, is the privilege of the infinite Author and Preserver of things, *who never slumbers nor sleeps*; but is not competent to any finite being, at least not to the soul of man. We know certainly, by experience, that we sometimes think; and thence draw this infallible consequence, that there is something in us that has a power to think. But whether that substance perpetually thinks or no, we can be no further assured than experience informs us. For to say that actual thinking is essential to the soul and inseparable from it is to beg what is in question and not to prove it by reason; which is necessary to be done, if it be not a self-evident proposition. But whether this, *that the soul always thinks*, be a self-evident proposition that everybody assents to at first hearing, I appeal to mankind. It is doubted whether I thought all last night or no; the question being about a matter of fact, it is begging it to bring as a proof for it an hypothesis which is the very thing in dispute: by which way one may prove anything, and it is but supposing that all watches, whilst the balance beats, think, and it is sufficiently proved and past doubt that my watch thought all last night. But he that would not deceive himself ought to build his hypothesis on matter of fact and make it out by sensible experience and not presume on matter of fact because of his hypothesis, that is, because he supposes it to be so; which way of proving amounts to this, that I must necessarily think all last night because another supposes I always think, though I myself cannot perceive that I always do so.

But men in love with their opinions may not only suppose what is in question, but allege wrong matter of fact. How else could anyone make it an *inference* of mine *that a thing is not because we are not sensible of it in our sleep*? I do not say there is no soul in a man, because he is not sensible of it in his sleep; but I do say he cannot think at any time waking or sleeping without being sensible of it. Our being sensible of it is not necessary to anything but to our thoughts; and to them it is and to them it will always be necessary, until we can think without being conscious of it.

11. I grant that the soul, in a waking man, is never without thought, because it is the condition of being awake. But whether sleeping without dreaming be not an affection of the whole man, mind as well as body, may be worth a waking man's consideration: it being hard to conceive that anything should think and not be conscious of it. If the *soul* doth *think in a sleeping man*

without being conscious of it, I ask whether, during such thinking, it has any pleasure or pain, or be capable of happiness or
misery? I am sure the man is not, no more than the bed or
earth he lies on. For to be happy or miserable without being
conscious of it seems to me utterly inconsistent and impossible.
Or if it be possible that the soul can, whilst the body is sleeping,
have its thinking, enjoyments, and concerns, its pleasure or
pain, apart, which the man is not conscious of nor partakes in,
it is certain that *Socrates* asleep and *Socrates* awake is not the
same person; but his soul, when he sleeps, and *Socrates* the
man consisting of body and soul, when he is waking, are two
persons, since waking *Socrates* has no knowledge of or concernment for that happiness or misery of his soul which it enjoys
alone by itself whilst he sleeps, without perceiving anything of
it, no more than he has for the happiness or misery of a man in
the *Indies*, whom he knows not. For, if we take wholly away all
consciousness of our actions and sensations, especially of
pleasure and pain, and the concernment that accompanies it, it
will be hard to know wherein to place personal identity.

12. The soul, during sound sleep, thinks, say these men.
Whilst it thinks and perceives, it is capable certainly of those of
delight or trouble, as well as any other perceptions; and *it must
necessarily be conscious of its own perceptions.* But it has all this
apart: the sleeping man, it is plain, is conscious of nothing of all
this. Let us suppose, then, the soul of *Castor*, whilst he is sleeping, retired from his body; which is no impossible supposition
for the men I have here to do with, who so liberally allow life
without a thinking soul to all other animals. These men cannot
then judge it impossible or a contradiction that the body should
live without the soul; nor that the soul should subsist and think,
or have perception, even perception of happiness or misery,
without the body. Let us then, as I say, suppose the soul of
Castor separated during his sleep from his body, to think apart.
Let us suppose, too, that it chooses for its scene of thinking the
body of another man, e.g. *Pollux*, who is sleeping without a
soul. For, if *Castor's* soul can think whilst *Castor* is asleep,
what *Castor* is never conscious of, it is no matter what place it
chooses to think in. We have here, then, the bodies of two men
with only one soul between them, which we will suppose to
sleep and wake by turns; and the soul still thinking in the
waking man, whereof the sleeping man is never conscious, has
never the least perception. I ask, then, whether *Castor* and
Pollux, thus with only one soul between them which thinks and
perceives in one what the other is never conscious of nor is con-

cerned for, are not two as distinct persons as *Castor* and *Hercules*, or as *Socrates* and *Plato* were? And whether one of them might not be very happy, and the other very miserable? Just by the same reason, they make the soul and the man two persons, who make the soul think apart what the man is not conscious of. For, I suppose, nobody will make identity of persons to consist in the soul's being united to the very same numerical particles of matter. For if that be necessary to identity, it will be impossible, in that constant flux of the particles of our bodies, that any man should be the same person two days, or two moments, together.

13. Thus, methinks, every drowsy nod shakes their doctrine, who teach that the soul is always thinking. Those, at least, who do at any time *sleep without dreaming* can never be convinced that their thoughts are sometimes for four hours busy without their knowing of it; and if they are taken in the very act, waked in the middle of that sleeping contemplation, can give no manner of account of it.

14. It will perhaps be said that the *soul thinks* even *in* the soundest *sleep, but the memory retains it not.* That the soul in a sleeping man should be this moment busy a-thinking, and the next moment in a waking man not remember nor be able to recollect one jot of all those thoughts, is very hard to be conceived and would need some better proof than bare assertion to make it be believed. For who can, without any more ado, but being barely told so, imagine that the greatest part of men do, during all their lives, for several hours every day, think of something, which if they were asked, even in the middle of these thoughts, they could remember nothing at all of?

Most men, I think, pass a great part of their sleep without dreaming. I once knew a man that was bred a scholar and had no bad memory who told me he had never dreamed in his life till he had that fever he was then newly recovered of, which was about the five or six and twentieth year of his age. I suppose the world affords more such instances: at least everyone's acquaintance will furnish him with examples enough of such as pass most of their nights without dreaming.

15. *To think often and never to retain it so much as one moment is a very useless sort of thinking*; and the soul in such a state of thinking does very little if at all excel that of a looking-glass, which constantly receives variety of images or *ideas* but retains none: they disappear and vanish and there remain no footsteps of them; the looking-glass is never the better for such *ideas*, nor the soul for such thoughts. Perhaps it will be said that in a

waking man the materials of the body are employed and made use of in thinking, and that the memory of thoughts is retained by the impressions that are made on the brain, and the traces there left after such thinking; but that in the *thinking of the soul*, which is not perceived *in a sleeping man*, there the soul thinks apart, and *making no use* of the organs of *the body, leaves no impressions on it, and consequently no memory* of such thoughts. Not to mention again the absurdity of two distinct persons which follows from this supposition, I answer further that whatever *ideas* the mind can receive and contemplate without the help of the body, it is reasonable to conclude it can retain without the help of the body too, or else the soul or any separate spirit will have but little advantage by thinking. If it has no memory of its own thoughts; if it cannot lay up them for its use and be able to recall them upon occasion; if it cannot reflect upon what is past and make use of its former experiences, reasonings, and contemplations, to what purpose does it think? They, who make the soul a thinking thing, at this rate will not make it a much more noble being than those do whom they condemn for allowing it to be nothing but the subtlest parts of matter. Characters drawn on dust that the first breath of wind effaces, or impressions made on a heap of atoms or animal spirits are altogether as useful and render the subject as noble as the thoughts of a soul that perish in thinking, that once out of sight are gone for ever and leave no memory of themselves behind them. Nature never makes excellent things for mean or no uses; and it is hardly to be conceived that our infinitely wise Creator should make so admirable a faculty as the power of thinking, that faculty which comes nearest the excellency of his own incomprehensible being, to be so idly and uselessly employed, at least one-fourth part of its time here, as to think constantly without remembering any of those thoughts, without doing any good to itself or others or being any way useful to any other part of the creation. If we will examine it, we shall not find, I suppose, the motion of dull and senseless matter anywhere in the universe made so little use of and so wholly thrown away.

16.   It is true, we have sometimes instances of perception whilst we are *asleep*, and retain the memory of those *thoughts*: but how *extravagant* and incoherent for the most part they are, how little conformable to the perfection and order of a rational being, those who are acquainted with dreams need not be told. This I would willingly be satisfied in: whether the soul, when it thinks thus apart and as it were separate from the body, acts less rationally than when conjointly with it, or no. If its separate thoughts be

less rational, then these men must say that the soul owes the perfection of rational thinking to the body; if it does not, it is a wonder that our dreams should be, for the most part, so frivolous and irrational, and that the soul should retain none of its more rational soliloquies and meditations.

17. Those who so confidently tell us that the soul always actually thinks, I would they would also tell us what those *ideas* are that are in the soul of a child before or just at the union with the body, before it hath received any by *sensation*. The *dreams* of sleeping men *are*, as I take it, all *made up of the waking man's* ideas, though for the most part oddly put together. It is strange, if the soul has *ideas* of its own that it derived not from *sensation* or *reflection* (as it must have, if it thought before it received any impressions from the body), that it should never in its private thinking (so private that the man himself perceives it not) retain any of them the very moment it wakes out of them and then make the man glad with new discoveries. Who can find it reasonable that the soul should, in its retirement during sleep, have so many hours' thoughts and yet never light on any of those *ideas* it borrowed not from *sensation* or *reflection*; or at least preserve the memory of none but such, which being occasioned from the body, must needs be less natural to a spirit? It is strange the soul should never once in a man's whole life recall over any of its pure, native thoughts and those *ideas* it had before it borrowed anything from the body, never bring into the waking man's view any other *ideas* but what have a tang of the cask and manifestly derive their original from that union. If it always thinks and so had *ideas* before it was united or before it received any from the body, it is not to be supposed but that during sleep it recollects its native *ideas*; and during that retirement from communicating with the body, whilst it thinks by itself, the *ideas* it is busied about should be, sometimes at least, those more natural and congenial ones which it had in itself, underived from the body or its own operations about them: which since the waking man never remembers, we must from this hypothesis conclude either that the soul remembers something that the man does not, or else that memory belongs only to such *ideas* as are derived from the body or the mind's operations about them.

18. I would be glad also to learn from these men who so confidently pronounce that the human soul or, which is all one, that a man always thinks, how they come to know it; nay, *how they come to know that they themselves think, when they themselves do not perceive it*. This, I am afraid, is to be sure without proofs, and to know without perceiving; it is, I suspect, a con-

fused notion, taken up to serve an hypothesis, and none of those clear truths that either their own evidence forces us to admit or common experience makes it impudence to deny. For the most that can be said of it is that it is possible the soul may always think, but not always retain it in memory. And I say, it is as possible that the soul may not always think, and much more probable that it should sometimes not think, than that it should often think, and that a long while together, and not be conscious to itself, the next moment after, that it had thought.

19. To suppose the soul to think, and the man not to perceive it is, as has been said, to make two persons in one man. And if one considers well these men's way of speaking, one should be led into a suspicion that they do so. For they who tell us that the soul always thinks do never, that I remember, say that a man always thinks. Can the soul think and not the man? Or a man think and not be conscious of it? This perhaps would be suspected of *jargon* in others. If they say the man thinks always but is not always conscious of it, they may as well say his body is extended without having parts. For it is altogether as intelligible to say that a body is extended without parts, as that anything *thinks without being conscious of it* or perceiving that it does so. They who talk thus may, with as much reason, if it be necessary to their hypothesis, say that a man is always hungry but that he does not always feel it; whereas hunger consists in that very sensation, as thinking consists in being conscious that one thinks. If they say that a man is always conscious to himself of thinking, I ask how they know it? Consciousness is the perception of what passes in a man's own mind. Can another man perceive that I am conscious of anything when I perceive it not myself? No man's knowledge here can go beyond his experience. Wake a man out of a sound sleep, and ask him what he was that moment thinking on. If he himself be conscious of nothing he then thought on, he must be a notable diviner of thoughts that can assure him that he was thinking. May he not, with more reason, assure him he was not asleep? This is something beyond philosophy, and it cannot be less than revelation that discovers to another thoughts in my mind, when I can find none there myself. And they must needs have a penetrating sight who can certainly see that I think when I cannot perceive it myself and when I declare that I do not, and yet can see that dogs or elephants do not think, when they give all the demonstration of it imaginable, except only telling us that they do so. This some may suspect to be a step beyond the *Rosicrucians*: it seeming easier to make one's self invisible to others than to make

another's thoughts visible to me, which are not visible to himself. But it is but defining the soul to be a substance that always thinks, and the business is done. If such definition be of any authority, I know not what it can serve for but to make many men suspect that they have no souls at all, since they find a good part of their lives pass away without thinking. For no definitions that I know, no suppositions of any sect, are of force enough to destroy constant experience; and perhaps, it is the affectation of knowing beyond what we perceive that makes so much useless dispute and noise in the world.

20. I see no reason therefore to believe that the *soul thinks before the senses have furnished it with ideas* to think on; and as those are increased and retained, so it comes by exercise to improve its faculty of thinking in the several parts of it; as well as, afterwards, by compounding those *ideas* and reflecting on its own operations, it increases its stock as well as facility in remembering, imagining, reasoning, and other modes of thinking.

21. He that will suffer himself to be informed by observation and experience, and not make his own hypothesis the rule of nature, will find few signs of a soul accustomed to much thinking in a new-born child and much fewer of any reasoning at all. And yet it is hard to imagine that the rational soul should think so much and not reason at all. And he that will consider that infants newly come into the world spend the greatest part of their time in sleep and are seldom awake but when either hunger calls for the teat or some pain (the most importunate of all sensations) or some other violent impression on the body forces the mind to perceive and attend to it. He, I say, who considers this will perhaps find reason to imagine that a *foetus in the mother's womb differs not much from the state of a vegetable*, but passes the greatest part of its time without perception or thought, doing very little but sleep in a place where it needs not seek for food, and is surrounded with liquor, always equally soft, and near of the same temper, where the eyes have no light and the ears, so shut up, are not very susceptible of sounds, and where there is little or no variety or change of objects to move the senses.

22. Follow a *child* from its birth and observe the alterations that time makes, and you shall find, as the mind by the senses comes more and more to be furnished with *ideas*, it comes to be more and more awake; thinks more, the more it has matter to think on. After some time it begins to know the objects which, being most familiar with it, have made lasting impressions. Thus it comes by degrees to know the persons it daily converses with,

and distinguish them from strangers; which are instances and effects of its coming to retain and distinguish the *ideas* the senses convey to it. And so we may observe how the mind, *by degrees,* improves in these, and *advances* to the exercise of those other faculties of *enlarging, compounding,* and *abstracting* its *ideas,* and of reasoning about them, and reflecting upon all these, of which I shall have occasion to speak more hereafter.

23.   If it shall be demanded then *when a man begins to have any ideas,* I think the true answer is, when he first has any *sensation.* For, since there appear not to be any *ideas* in the mind before the senses have conveyed any in, I conceive that *ideas* in the understanding are coeval with *sensation;* which is such an impression or motion made in some part of the body, as produces some perception in the understanding. It is about these impressions made on our senses by outward objects that the mind seems first to employ itself in such operations as we call *perception, remembering, consideration, reasoning,* etc.

24.   In time, the mind comes to reflect on its own *operations* about the *ideas* got by *sensation* and thereby stores itself with a new set of *ideas,* which I call *ideas* of *reflection.* These are the *impressions* that are made on our *senses* by outward objects that are extrinsical to the mind; and *its own operations,* proceeding from powers intrinsical and proper to itself, which when reflected on by itself become also objects of its contemplation, are, as I have said, *the original of all knowledge.* Thus the first capacity of human intellect is that the mind is fitted to receive the impressions made on it either through the *senses* by outward objects, or by its own operations when it *reflects* on them. This is the first step a man makes towards the discovery of anything and the ground-work whereon to build all those notions which ever he shall have naturally in this world. All those sublime thoughts, which tower above the clouds and reach as high as heaven itself, take their rise and footing here: in all that great extent wherein the mind wanders, in those remote speculations it may seem to be elevated with, it stirs not one jot beyond those *ideas* which *sense* or *reflection* have offered for its contemplation.

25.   In this part the *understanding* is merely *passive;* and whether or no it will have these beginnings and, as it were, materials of knowledge, is not in its own power. For the objects of our senses do, many of them, obtrude their particular *ideas* upon our minds whether we will or no; and the operations of our minds will not let us be without, at least, some obscure notions of them. No man can be wholly ignorant of what he does when he thinks. These *simple ideas,* when offered

to the mind, *the understanding can* no more refuse to have, nor alter when they are imprinted, nor blot them out and make new ones itself, than a mirror can refuse, alter, or obliterate the images or *ideas* which the objects set before it do therein produce. As the bodies that surround us do diversely affect our organs, the mind is forced to receive the impressions; and cannot avoid the perception of those *ideas* that are annexed to them.

CHAPTER II

OF SIMPLE IDEAS

1. THE better to understand the nature, manner, and extent of our knowledge, one thing is carefully to be observed concerning the *ideas* we have, and that is that *some* of them are *simple* and *some complex*.

Though the qualities that affect our senses are, in the things themselves, so united and blended that there is no separation, no distance between them, yet it is plain the *ideas* they produce in the mind enter by the senses simple and unmixed. For, though the sight and touch often take in from the same object, at the same time, different *ideas*, as a man sees at once motion and colour, the hand feels softness and warmth in the same piece of wax: yet the simple *ideas* thus united in the same subject are as perfectly distinct as those that come in by different senses. The coldness and hardness which a man feels in a piece of *ice* being as distinct *ideas* in the mind as the smell and whiteness of a lily, or as the taste of sugar, and smell of a rose; and there is nothing can be plainer to a man than the clear and distinct perception he has of those simple *ideas*; which, being each in itself uncompounded, contains in it nothing but *one uniform appearance* or conception in the mind, and is not distinguishable into different *ideas*.

2. These simple *ideas*, the materials of all our knowledge, are suggested and furnished to the mind only by those two ways above mentioned, viz. *sensation* and *reflection*. When the understanding is once stored with these simple *ideas*, it has the power to repeat, compare, and unite them, even to an almost infinite variety, and so can make at pleasure new complex *ideas*. But it is not in the power of the most exalted wit or enlarged understanding, by any quickness or variety of thought, to *invent or*

frame one new simple idea in the mind, not taken in by the ways before mentioned; nor can any force of the understanding *destroy* those that are there, the dominion of man in this little world of his own understanding being much what the same as it is in the great world of visible things; wherein his power, however managed by art and skill, reaches no further than to compound and divide the materials that are made to his hand, but can do nothing towards the making the least particle of new matter, or destroying one atom of what is already in being. The same inability will everyone find in himself, who shall go about to fashion in his understanding any simple *idea*, not received in by his senses from external objects, or by reflection from the operations of his own mind about them. I would have anyone try to fancy any taste which had never affected his palate, or frame the *idea* of a scent he had never smelt; and when he can do this, I will also conclude that a blind man hath *ideas* of colours and a deaf man true distinct notions of sounds.

3. This is the reason why, though we cannot believe it impossible to God to make a creature with other organs and more ways to convey into the understanding the notice of corporeal things than those five, as they are usually counted, which he has given to man: yet I think it is *not possible* for anyone *to imagine* any other *qualities* in bodies, howsoever constituted, whereby they can be taken notice of besides sounds, tastes, smells, visible and tangible qualities. And had mankind been made with but four senses, the qualities then which are the object of the fifth sense had been as far from our notice, imagination, and conception as now any *belonging to a sixth, seventh, or eighth sense* can possibly be; which, whether yet some other creatures in some other parts of this vast and stupendous universe may not have, will be a great presumption to deny. He that will not set himself proudly at the top of all things, but will consider the immensity of this fabric and the great variety that is to be found in this little and inconsiderable part of it which he has to do with, may be apt to think that in other mansions of it there may be other and different intelligent beings of whose faculties he has as little knowledge or apprehension as a worm shut up in one drawer of a cabinet hath of the senses or understanding of a man, such variety and excellency being suitable to the wisdom and power of the Maker. I have here followed the common opinion of man's having but five senses, though perhaps there may be justly counted more; but either supposition serves equally to my present purpose.

CHAPTER III

OF IDEAS OF ONE SENSE

1. THE better to conceive the *ideas* we receive from sensation, it may not be amiss for us to consider them in reference to the different ways whereby they make their approaches to our minds and make themselves perceivable by us.

First, then, There are some which come into our minds *by one sense* only.

Secondly, There are others that convey themselves into the mind *by more senses than one*.

Thirdly, Others that are had from *reflection* only.

Fourthly, There are some that make themselves way and are suggested to the mind *by all the ways of sensation and reflection*. We shall consider them apart under these several heads.

First, There are *some* ideas *which have admittance only through one sense*, which is peculiarly adapted to receive them. Thus light and colours, as white, red, yellow, blue, with their several degrees or shades and mixtures, as green, scarlet, purple, sea-green, and the rest, come in only by the eyes. All kinds of noises, sounds, and tones, only by the ears. The several tastes and smells, by the nose and palate. And if these organs or the nerves which are the conduits to convey them from without to their audience in the brain, the mind's presence-room (as I may so call it), are any of them so disordered as not to perform their functions, they have no postern to be admitted by, no other way to bring themselves into view and be perceived by the understanding.

The most considerable of those belonging to the touch are heat and cold, and solidity; all the rest—consisting almost wholly in the sensible configuration, as smooth and rough; or else, more or less firm adhesion of the parts, as hard and soft, tough and brittle—are obvious enough.

2. I think it will be needless to enumerate all the particular *simple ideas* belonging to each sense. Nor indeed is it possible if we would, there being a great many *more* of them belonging to most of the senses *than we have names for*. The variety of smells, which are as many almost, if not more, than species of bodies in the world, do most of them want names. *Sweet* and

stinking commonly serve our turn for these *ideas*, which in effect is little more than to call them pleasing or displeasing; though the smell of a rose and violet, both sweet, are certainly very distinct *ideas*. Nor are the different tastes, that by our palates we receive *ideas* of, much better provided with names. Sweet, bitter, sour, harsh, and salt are almost all the epithets we have to denominate that numberless variety of relishes which are to be found distinct, not only in almost every sort of creatures, but in the different parts of the same plant, fruit, or animal. The same may be said of colours and sounds. I shall, therefore, in the account of simple *ideas* I am here giving, content myself to set down only such as are most material to our present purpose, or are in themselves less apt to be taken notice of, though they are very frequently the ingredients of our complex *ideas*; amongst which, I think, I may well account solidity, which therefore I shall treat of in the next chapter.

CHAPTER IV

OF SOLIDITY

1. THE *idea* of *solidity* we receive by our touch; and it arises from the resistance which we find in body to the entrance of any other body into the place it possesses, till it has left it. There is no *idea* which we receive more constantly from sensation than *solidity*. Whether we move or rest, in what posture soever we are, we always feel something under us that supports us and hinders our further sinking downwards; and the bodies which we daily handle make us perceive that, whilst they remain between them, they do, by an insurmountable force, hinder the approach of the parts of our hands that press them. That which thus hinders the approach of two bodies, when they are moving one towards another, I call *solidity*. I will not dispute whether this acceptation of the word *solid* be nearer to its original signification than that which mathematicians use it in: it suffices that I think the common notion of solidity will allow, if not justify this use of it; but if anyone think it better to call it *impenetrability*, he has my consent. Only I have thought the term *solidity* the more proper to express this *idea*, not only because of its vulgar use in that sense, but also because it carries something more of positive in it than *impenetrability*; which is negative, and is perhaps more a consequence of *solidity*, than *solidity* itself. This, of all others, seems the *idea* most intimately connected with and essential to body, so as nowhere else to be found or imagined, but only in matter. And though our senses take no notice of it, but in masses of matter, of a bulk sufficient to cause a sensation in us: yet the mind, having once got this *idea* from such grosser sensible bodies, traces it further and considers it, as well as figure, in the minutest particle of matter that can exist, and finds it inseparably inherent in body, wherever or however modified.

2. This is the *idea* which belongs to body, whereby we conceive it *to fill space*. The *idea* of which filling of space is that, where we imagine any space taken up by a solid substance, we conceive it so to possess it that it excludes all other solid substances, and will for ever hinder any two other bodies, that move towards one another in a straight line, from coming to touch one another, unless it removes from between them in a line not parallel to that which they move in. This *idea* of it, the bodies which we ordinarily handle sufficiently furnish us with.

3. This resistance, whereby it keeps other bodies out of the space which it possesses, is so great that no force, how great soever, can surmount it. All the bodies in the world, pressing a drop of water on all sides, will never be able to overcome the resistance which it will make, as soft as it is, to their approaching one another, till it be removed out of their way: whereby our *idea* of *solidity* is *distinguished* both *from pure space*, which is capable neither of resistance nor motion, and from the ordinary *idea* of *hardness*. For a man may conceive two bodies at a distance so as they may approach one another without touching or displacing any solid thing till their superficies come to meet; whereby, I think, we have the clear *idea* of space without *solidity*. For (not to go so far as annihilation of any particular body) I ask whether a man cannot have the *idea* of the motion of one single body alone, without any other succeeding immediately into its place? I think it is evident he can: the *idea* of motion in one body no more including the *idea* of motion in another, than the *idea* of a square figure in one body includes the *idea* of a square figure in another. I do not ask whether bodies do so exist that the motion of one body cannot really be without the motion of another. To determine this either way is to beg the question for or against a *vacuum*. But my question is whether one cannot have the *idea* of one body moved, whilst others are at rest. And I think this no one will deny. If so, then the place it deserted gives us the *idea* of pure space without solidity,

whereinto another body may enter without either resistance or protrusion of anything. When the sucker in a pump is drawn, the space it filled in the tube is certainly the same, whether another body follows the motion of the sucker or no; nor does it imply a contradiction that, upon the motion of one body, another that is only contiguous to it should not follow it. The necessity of such a motion is built only on the supposition that the world is full; but not on the distinct *ideas* of space and solidity, which are as different as resistance and not resistance, protrusion and not protrusion. And that men have *ideas* of space without body, their very disputes about a *vacuum* plainly demonstrate, as is shown in another place.

4. *Solidity* is hereby also *differenced from hardness*, in that solidity consists in repletion, and so an utter exclusion of other bodies out of the space it possesses: but hardness, in a firm cohesion of the parts of matter making up masses of a sensible bulk, so that the whole does not easily change its figure. And indeed, hard and soft are names that we give to things only in relation to the constitutions of our own bodies: that being generally called hard by us which will put us to pain sooner than change figure by the pressure of any part of our bodies; and that, on the contrary, soft, which changes the situation of its parts upon an easy and unpainful touch.

But this difficulty of changing the situation of the sensible parts amongst themselves, or of the figure of the whole, gives no more solidity to the hardest body in the world than to the softest; nor is an adamant one jot more solid than water. For, though the two flat sides of two pieces of marble will more easily approach each other, between which there is nothing but water or air, than if there be a diamond between them: yet it is not that the parts of the diamond are more solid than those of water or resist more, but because, the parts of water being more easily separable from each other, they will, by a side motion, be more easily removed and give way to the approach of the two pieces of marble. But if they could be kept from making place by that side motion, they would eternally hinder the approach of these two pieces of marble, as much as the diamond; and it would be as impossible by any force to surmount their resistance, as to surmount the resistance of the parts of a diamond. The softest body in the world will as invincibly resist the coming together of any two other bodies, if it be not put out of the way but remain between them, as the hardest that can be found or imagined. He that shall fill a yielding soft body well with air or water will quickly find its resistance. And he that thinks that nothing but bodies that are hard can keep his hands from approaching one another, may be pleased to make a trial with the air enclosed in a football. The experiment I have been told was made at *Florence* with a hollow globe of gold, filled with water and exactly closed, further shows the solidity of so soft a body as water. For the golden globe thus filled being put into a press, which was driven by the extreme force of screws, the water made itself way through the pores of that very close metal and, finding no room for a nearer approach of its particles within, got to the outside where it rose like a dew and so fell in drops before the sides of the globe could be made to yield to the violent compression of the engine that squeezed it.

5. By this *idea* of solidity is the extension of body distinguished from the extension of space: the extension of body being nothing but the cohesion or continuity of solid, separable, moveable parts; and the extension of space, the continuity of unsolid, inseparable, and immoveable parts. *Upon the solidity of bodies* also *depend their mutual impulse, resistance, and protrusion.* Of pure space then and solidity, there are several (amongst which I confess myself one) who persuade themselves they have clear and distinct *ideas*, and that they can think on space without anything in it that resists or is protruded by body. This is the *idea* of pure space which they think they have as clear as any *idea* they can have of the extension of body: the *idea* of the distance between the opposite parts of a concave superficies being equally as clear without, as with the *idea* of any solid parts between; and on the other side they persuade themselves that they have, distinct from that of pure space, the *idea* of something that fills space, that can be protruded by the impulse of other bodies or resist their motion. If there be others that have not these two *ideas* distinct, but confound them and make but one of them, I know not how men who have the same *idea* under different names, or different *ideas* under the same name, can in that case talk with one another: any more than a man who, not being blind or deaf, has distinct *ideas* of the colour of scarlet and the sound of a trumpet, could discourse concerning scarlet-colour with the blind man I mention in another place, who fancied that the *idea* of scarlet was like the sound of a trumpet.

6. If anyone asks me *what this solidity is*, I send him to his senses to inform him. Let him put a flint or a football between his hands and then endeavour to join them, and he will know. If he thinks this not a sufficient explication of solidity, what it is

and wherein it consists, I promise to tell him what it is and wherein it consists when he tells me what thinking is or wherein it consists, or explains to me what extension or motion is, which perhaps seems much easier. The simple *ideas* we have are such as experience teaches them us; but if, beyond that, we endeavour by words to make them clearer in the mind, we shall succeed no better than if we went about to clear up the darkness of a blind man's mind by talking, and to discourse into him the *ideas* of light and colours. The reason of this I shall show in another place.

CHAPTER VI

OF SIMPLE IDEAS OF REFLECTION

1.   THE mind, receiving the *ideas* mentioned in the foregoing chapters from without, when it turns its view inward upon itself and observes its own actions about those *ideas* it has, takes from thence other *ideas*, which are as capable to be the objects of its contemplation as any of those it received from foreign things.
2.   The two great and principal actions of the mind, which are most frequently considered, and which are so frequent that everyone that pleases may take notice of them in himself, are these two:

> *Perception*, or *Thinking*; and
> *Volition*, or *Willing*.

The power of thinking is called the *understanding* and the power of volition is called the *will*, and these two powers or abilities in the mind are denominated *faculties*. Of some of the modes of these simple *ideas* of reflection, such as are *remembrance, discerning, reasoning, judging, knowledge, faith,* etc., I shall have occasion to speak hereafter.

CHAPTER VII

OF SIMPLE IDEAS OF BOTH SENSATION AND REFLECTION

1.   THERE be other simple *ideas* which convey themselves into

the mind by all the ways of sensation and reflection, viz:

> *Pleasure* or *Delight*, and its opposite.
> *Pain*, or *Uneasiness*.
> *Power*.
> *Existence*.
> *Unity.*

2.   *Delight* or *uneasiness*, one or other of them, join themselves
to almost all our *ideas* both of sensation and reflection: and there
is scarce any affection of our senses from without, any retired
thought of our mind within, which is not able to produce in us
pleasure or *pain*. By *pleasure* and *pain* I would be understood
to signify whatsoever delights or molests us, whether it arises
from the thoughts of our minds, or anything operating on our
bodies. For, whether we call it satisfaction, delight, pleasure,
happiness, etc., on the one side, or uneasiness, trouble, pain,
torment, anguish, misery, etc., on the other, they are still but
different degrees of the same thing, and belong to the *ideas* of
pleasure and *pain*, delight or uneasiness; which are the names
I shall most commonly use for those two sorts of *ideas*.
3.   The infinite wise Author of our being, having given us the
power over several parts of our bodies to move or keep them at
rest as we think fit; and also, by the motion of them, to move ourselves and other contiguous bodies, in which consists all the
actions of our body; having also given a power to our minds, in
several instances, to choose, amongst its *ideas*, which it will think
on, and to pursue the inquiry of this or that subject with consideration and attention: to excite us to these actions of thinking
and motion that we are capable of, has been pleased to join to
several thoughts and several sensations a *perception* of *delight*.
If this were wholly separated from all our outward sensations and
inward thoughts, we should have no reason to prefer one thought
or action to another, negligence to attention, or motion to rest.
And so we should neither stir our bodies, nor employ our minds,
but let our thoughts (if I may so call it) run adrift, without any
direction or design, and suffer the *ideas* of our minds, like unregarded shadows, to make their appearances there, as it happened, without attending to them. In which state man, however
furnished with the faculties of understanding and will, would be
a very idle, inactive creature, and pass his time only in a lazy,
lethargic dream. It has therefore pleased our wise Creator to
annex to several objects and to the *ideas* which we receive from
them, as also to several of our thoughts, a concomitant pleasure,
and that in several objects, to several degrees: that those faculties

which he had endowed us with might not remain wholly idle and unemployed by us.

4. *Pain* has the same efficacy and use to set us on work that pleasure has, we being as ready to employ our faculties to avoid that as to pursue this; only this is worth our consideration: that *pain is often produced by the same objects and* ideas *that produce pleasure* in us. This their near conjunction, which makes us often feel pain in the sensations where we expected pleasure, gives us new occasion of admiring the wisdom and goodness of our Maker, who, designing the preservation of our being, has annexed pain to the application of many things to our bodies, to warn us of the harm that they will do, and as advices to withdraw from them. But he, not designing our preservation barely, but the preservation of every part and organ in its perfection, hath in many cases annexed pain to those very *ideas* which delight us. Thus heat, that is very agreeable to us in one degree, by a little greater increase of it proves no ordinary torment; and the most pleasant of all sensible objects, light itself, if there be too much of it, if increased beyond a due proportion to our eyes, causes a very painful sensation. Which is wisely and favourably so ordered by nature that, when any object does by the vehemency of its operation disorder the instruments of sensation, whose structures cannot but be very nice and delicate, we might, by the pain, be warned to withdraw, before the organ be quite put out of order, and so be unfitted for its proper functions for the future. The consideration of those objects that produce it may well persuade us that this is the end or use of pain. For though great light be insufferable to our eyes, yet the highest degree of darkness does not at all disease them; because that, causing no disorderly motion in it, leaves that curious organ unharmed in its natural state. But yet excess of cold as well as heat pains us: because it is equally destructive to that temper which is necessary to the preservation of life and the exercise of the several functions of the body, and which consists in a moderate degree of warmth or, if you please, a motion of the insensible parts of our bodies confined within certain bounds.

5. Beyond all this, we may find another reason *why* God hath scattered up and down *several degrees of pleasure and pain in all the things that environ and affect us* and blended them together in almost all that our thoughts and senses have to do with, that we, finding imperfection, dissatisfaction, and want of complete happiness in all the enjoyments which the creatures can afford us, might be led to seek it in the enjoyment of Him, *with whom there is fullness of joy and at whose right hand are pleasures for*

evermore.

6. Though what I have here said may not, perhaps, make the *ideas of pleasure and pain* clearer to us than our own experience does, which is the only way that we are capable of having them: yet the consideration of the reason why they are annexed to so many other *ideas*, serving to give us due sentiments of the wisdom and goodness of the Sovereign Disposer of all things, may not be unsuitable to the main end of these inquiries: the knowledge and veneration of Him being the chief end of all our thoughts, and the proper business of all understandings.

7. *Existence* and *unity* are two other *ideas* that are suggested to the understanding by every object without, and every *idea* within. When *ideas* are in our minds, we consider them as being actually there, as well as we consider things to be actually without us; which is, that they exist or have *existence*. And whatever we can consider as one thing, whether a real being or *idea*, suggests to the understanding the *idea* of *unity*.

8. *Power* also is another of those simple *ideas* which we receive from *sensation and reflection*. For, observing in ourselves that we can at pleasure move several parts of our bodies which were at rest; the effects, also, that natural bodies are able to produce in one another occurring every moment to our senses, we both these ways get the *idea* of *power*.

9. Besides these there is another *idea*, which, though suggested by our senses, yet is more constantly offered us by what passes in our own minds, and that is the *idea* of *succession*. For if we look immediately into ourselves, and reflect on what is observable there, we shall find our *ideas* always, whilst we are awake or have any thought, passing in train, one going and another coming, without intermission.

10. These, if they are not all, are at least (as I think) the most considerable of those *simple ideas* which the mind has, and out of which is made all its other knowledge, all which it receives only by the two forementioned ways of *sensation* and *reflection*.

Nor let anyone think these too narrow bounds for the capacious mind of man to expatiate in, which takes its flight further than the stars and cannot be confined by the limits of the world, that extends its thoughts often even beyond the utmost expansion of matter, and makes excursions into that incomprehensible *inane*. I grant all this, but desire anyone to assign any *simple idea* which is not *received from* one of *those inlets* before mentioned, or any *complex idea* not *made out of those simple ones*. Nor will it be so strange to think these few simple *ideas* sufficient to employ the quickest thought or largest capacity, and to furnish the materials of all that various knowledge and more various fancies and opinions of all mankind, if we consider how many words may be made out of the various composition of twenty-four letters; or if, going one step further, we will but reflect on the variety of combinations that may be made with barely one of the above-mentioned *ideas*, viz. number, whose stock is inexhaustible and truly infinite; and what a large and immense field doth extension alone afford the mathematicians!

CHAPTER VIII

SOME FURTHER CONSIDERATIONS CONCERNING OUR SIMPLE IDEAS

1.   CONCERNING the simple *ideas* of sensation, it is to be considered that whatsoever is so constituted in nature as to be able, by affecting our senses, to cause any perception in the mind, doth thereby produce in the understanding a simple *idea*; which, whatever be the external cause of it, when it comes to be taken notice of by our discerning faculty, it is by the mind looked on and considered there to be a real *positive idea* in the understanding, as much as any other whatsoever, though perhaps the cause of it be but a privation in the subject.

2.   Thus the *ideas* of heat and cold, light and darkness, white and black, motion and rest, are equally clear and *positive ideas* in the mind, though perhaps some of *the causes* which produce them are barely *privations* in those subjects from whence our senses derive those *ideas*. These the understanding, in its view of them, considers all as distinct positive *ideas*, without taking notice of the causes that produce them: which is an inquiry not belonging to the *idea*, as it is in the understanding, but to the nature of the things existing without us. These are two very different things, and carefully to be distinguished: it being one thing to perceive and know the *idea* of white or black, and quite another to examine what kind of particles they must be and how ranged in the superficies, to make any object appear white or black.

3.   A painter or dyer who never inquired into their causes hath the *ideas* of white and black, and other colours, as clearly, perfectly, and distinctly in his understanding, and perhaps more distinctly, than the philosopher who hath busied himself in considering their natures and thinks he knows how far either of

them is, in its cause, positive or privative; and the *idea of black* is no less *positive* in his mind than that of white, *however the cause* of that colour in the external object may *be only a privation*.

4.   If it were the design of my present undertaking to inquire into the natural causes and manner of perception, I should offer this as a reason *why a privative cause might*, in some cases at least, *produce a positive idea*, viz. that all sensation being produced in us only by different degrees and modes of motion in our animal spirits, variously agitated by external objects, the abatement of any former motion must as necessarily produce a new sensation as the variation or increase of it, and so introduce a new *idea*, which depends only on a different motion of the animal spirits in that organ.

5.   But whether this be so or no, I will not here determine but appeal to everyone's own experience whether the shadow of a man, though it consists of nothing but the absence of light (and the more the absence of light is, the more discernible is the shadow) does not, when a man looks on it, cause as clear and positive an *idea* in his mind as a man himself, though covered over with clear sunshine? And the picture of a shadow is a positive thing. Indeed, we have *negative names* which stand not directly for positive *ideas* but for their absence, such as *insipid, silence, nihil*, etc., which words denote positive *ideas*, v.g., *taste, sound, being* with a signification of their absence.

6.   And thus one may truly be said to see darkness. For supposing a hole perfectly dark, from whence no light is reflected, it is certain one may see the figure of it, or it may be painted; or, whether the ink I write with makes any other *idea* is a question. The privative causes I have here assigned of positive *ideas* are according to the common opinion; but in truth it will be hard to determine whether there be really any *ideas* from a privative cause, till it be determined *whether rest be any more a privation than motion*.

7.   To discover the nature of our *ideas* the better, and to discourse of them intelligibly, it will be convenient to distinguish them as they are *ideas* or perceptions in our minds, and as they are modifications of matter in the bodies that cause such perceptions in us: that so we *may not* think (as perhaps usually is done) that they are exactly the images and *resemblances* of something inherent in the subject: most of those of sensation being in the mind no more the likeness of something existing without us, than the names that stand for them are the likeness of our *ideas*, which yet upon hearing they are apt to excite in us.

8.   Whatsoever the mind perceives in itself, or is the immediate

object of perception, thought, or understanding, that I call *idea*; and the power to produce any *idea* in our mind, I call *quality* of the subject wherein that power is. Thus a snowball having the power to produce in us the *ideas* of *white, cold,* and *round,* the powers to produce those *ideas* in us as they are in the snowball I call *qualities*; and as they are sensations or perceptions in our understandings, I call them *ideas*; which *ideas*, if I speak of sometimes as in the things themselves, I would be understood to mean those qualities in the objects which produce them in us.

9. Qualities thus considered in bodies are:

First, such as are utterly inseparable from the body, in what state soever it be; such as in all the alterations and changes it suffers, all the force can be used upon it, it constantly keeps; and such as sense constantly finds in every particle of matter which has bulk enough to be perceived; and the mind finds inseparable from every particle of matter, though less than to make itself singly be perceived by our senses. V.g., take a grain of wheat, divide it into two parts, each part has still *solidity, extension, figure,* and *mobility*; divide it again, and it retains still the same qualities; and so divide it on, till the parts become insensible: they must retain still each of them all those qualities. For division (which is all that a mill or pestle or any other body does upon another in reducing it to insensible parts) can never take away either solidity, extension, figure, or mobility from any body, but only makes two or more distinct separate masses of matter, of that which was but one before; all which distinct masses, reckoned as so many distinct bodies, after division make a certain number. These I call *original* or *primary qualities* of body; which I think we may observe to produce simple *ideas* in us, viz. solidity, extension, figure, motion or rest, and number.

10. Secondly, such *qualities* which in truth are nothing in the objects themselves but powers to produce various sensations in us by their *primary qualities*, i.e. by the bulk, figure, texture, and motion of their insensible parts, as colours, sounds, tastes, etc. These I call *secondary qualities*. To these might be added a third sort, which are allowed to be barely powers, though they are as much real qualities in the subject as those which I, to comply with the common way of speaking, call *qualities*, but for distinction, *secondary qualities*. For the power in fire to produce a new colour, or consistency in wax or clay, by its primary qualities, is as much a quality in fire as the power it has to produce in me a new *idea* or sensation of warmth or burning, which I felt not before, by the same primary qualities, viz. the bulk, texture, and motion of its insensible parts.

11. The next thing to be considered is how *bodies* produce *ideas* in us; and that is manifestly *by impulse*, the only way which we can conceive bodies operate in.

12. If then external objects be not united to our minds when they produce *ideas* in it and yet we perceive *these original qualities* in such of them as singly fall under our senses, it is evident that some motion must be thence continued by our nerves or animal spirits, by some parts of our bodies, to the brain or the seat of sensation, there to *produce in our minds the particular* ideas *we have of them*. And since the extension, figure, number, and motion of bodies of an observable bigness may be perceived at a distance *by* the sight, it is evident some singly imperceptible bodies must come from them to the eyes, and thereby convey to the brain some *motion*, which produces these *ideas* which we have of them in us.

13. After the same manner that the *ideas* of these original qualities are produced in us, we may conceive that the *ideas of secondary qualities* are also *produced*, viz. *by the operation of insensible particles on our senses*. For it being manifest that there are bodies and good store of bodies, each whereof are so small that we cannot by any of our senses discover either their bulk, figure, or motion, as is evident in the particles of the air and water and others extremely smaller than those, perhaps as much smaller than the particles of air or water as the particles of air or water are smaller than peas or hail-stones: let us suppose at present that the different motions and figures, bulk and number, of such particles, affecting the several organs of our senses, produce in us those different sensations which we have from the colours and smells of bodies: v.g. that a violet, by the impulse of such insensible particles of matter, of peculiar figures and bulks, and in different degrees and modifications of their motions, causes the *ideas* of the blue colour and sweet scent of that flower to be produced in our minds. It being no more impossible to conceive that God should annex such *ideas* to such motions, with which they have no similitude, than that he should annex the *idea* of pain to the motion of a piece of steel dividing our flesh, with which that *idea* hath no resemblance.

14. What I have said concerning *colours* and *smells* may be understood also of *tastes* and *sounds, and other the like sensible qualities*; which, whatever reality we by mistake attribute to them, are in truth nothing in the objects themselves but powers to produce various sensations in us, and depend *on those primary qualities*, viz. bulk, figure, texture, and motion of parts, as I have said.

15.   From whence I think it easy to draw this observation: that the *ideas of primary qualities* of bodies *are resemblances* of them, and their patterns do really exist in the bodies themselves; but the *ideas produced* in us *by* these *secondary qualities have no resemblance* of them at all. There is nothing like our *ideas* existing in the bodies themselves. They are, in the bodies we denominate from them, only a power to produce those sensations in us; and what is sweet, blue, or warm in *idea* is but the certain bulk, figure, and motion of the insensible parts in the bodies themselves, which we call so.

16.   *Flame* is denominated *hot* and *light*; *snow, white* and *cold*; and *manna, white* and *sweet*, from the *ideas* they produce in us. Which qualities are commonly thought to be the same in those bodies that those *ideas* are in us, the one the perfect resemblance of the other, as they are in a mirror, and it would by most men be judged very extravagant if one should say otherwise. And yet he that will consider that *the same fire* that at one distance *produces* in us the sensation of *warmth* does, at a nearer approach, produce in us the far different sensation of *pain*, ought to bethink himself what reason he has to say that his *idea* of *warmth*, which was produced in him by the fire, is actually *in the fire*; and his *idea* of *pain*, which the same fire produced in him the same way, is *not* in the *fire*. Why are whiteness and coldness in snow, and pain not, when it produces the one and the other *idea* in us; and can do neither, but by the bulk, figure, number, and motion of its solid parts?

17.   The particular *bulk, number, figure, and motion of the parts of fire or snow are really in them*, whether anyone's senses perceive them or no; and therefore they may be called *real qualities*, because they really exist in those bodies. But *light, heat, whiteness*, or *coldness are no more really in them than sickness or pain is in* manna. Take away the sensation of them; let not the eyes see light or colours, nor the ears hear sounds; let the palate not taste, nor the nose smell; and all colours, tastes, odours, and sounds, as they are such particular *ideas*, vanish and cease, and are reduced to their causes, i.e. bulk, figure, and motion of parts.

18.   A piece of *manna* of a sensible bulk is able to produce in us the *idea* of a round or square figure; and by being removed from one place to another, the *idea* of motion. This *idea* of motion represents it as it really is in the *manna* moving; a circle or square are the same, whether in *idea* or existence, in the mind or in the *manna*; and this, both *motion and figure, are really in the manna*, whether we take notice of them or no: this everybody is ready to agree to. Besides, *manna*, by the bulk, figure, texture,

and motion of its parts, has a power to produce the sensations of sickness, and sometimes of acute pains or gripings in us. That these *ideas* of *sickness and pain are not in the* manna, but effects of its operations on us, and are nowhere when we feel them not: this also everyone readily agrees to. And yet men are hardly to be brought to think that *sweetness and whiteness are not really in manna,* which are but the effects of the operations of *manna,* by the motion, size, and figure of its particles, on the eyes and palate, as the pain and sickness caused by *manna* are confessedly nothing but the effects of its operations on the stomach and guts, by the size, motion, and figure of its insensible parts (for by nothing else can a body operate, as has been proved): as if it could not operate on the eyes and palate and thereby produce in the mind particular distinct *ideas* which in itself it has not, as well as we allow it can operate on the guts and stomach and thereby produce distinct *ideas* which in itself it has not. These *ideas* being all effects of the operations of *manna* on several parts of our bodies by the size, figure, number, and motion of its parts, why those produced by the eyes and palate should rather be thought to be really in the *manna* than those produced by the stomach and guts; or why the pain and sickness, *ideas* that are the effects of *manna,* should be thought to be nowhere, when they are not felt: and yet the sweetness and whiteness, effects of the same *manna* on other parts of the body by ways equally as unknown, should be thought to exist in the *manna,* when they are not seen nor tasted, would need some reason to explain.

19. Let us consider the red and white colours in *porphyry.* Hinder light but from striking on it, and its colours vanish: it no longer produces any such *ideas* in us; upon the return of light it produces these appearances on us again. Can anyone think any real alterations are made in the *porphyry* by the presence or absence of light; and that those *ideas* of whiteness and redness are really in *porphyry* in the light, when it is plain *it has no colour in the dark*? It has, indeed, such a configuration of particles, both night and day, as are apt, by the rays of light rebounding from some parts of that hard stone, to produce in us the *idea* of redness, and from others the *idea* of whiteness; but whiteness or redness are not in it at any time, but such a texture that hath the power to produce such a sensation in us.

20. Pound an almond, and the clear white *colour* will be altered into a dirty one, and the sweet *taste* into an oily one. What real alteration can the beating of the pestle make in any body, but an alteration of the *texture* of it?

21. *Ideas* being thus distinguished and understood, we may be

able to give an account how the same water, at the same time, may produce the *idea* of cold by one hand and of heat by the other, whereas it is impossible that the same water, if those *ideas* were really in it, should at the same time be both hot and cold.   For if we imagine *warmth* as it is *in our hands* to be *nothing but a certain sort and degree of motion in the minute particles of our nerves, or animal spirits,* we may understand how it is possible that the same water may at the same time produce the sensation of heat in one hand and cold in the other; which yet figure never does, that never producing the *idea* of a square by one hand which has produced the *idea* of a globe by another. But if the sensation of heat and cold be nothing but the increase or diminution of the motion of the minute parts of our bodies, caused by the corpuscles of any other body, it is easy to be understood that, if that motion be greater in one hand than in the other, if a body be applied to the two hands, which has in its minute particles a greater motion than in those of one of the hands, and a less than in those of the other, it will increase the motion of the one hand and lessen it in the other, and so cause the different sensations of heat and cold that depend thereon.

22.   I have in what just goes before been engaged in physical inquiries a little further than perhaps I intended.   But, it being necessary to make the nature of sensation a little understood; and to make the *difference between the qualities in bodies, and the* ideas *produced by them in the mind,* to be distinctly conceived, without which it were impossible to discourse intelligibly of them: I hope I shall be pardoned this little excursion into natural philosophy, it being necessary in our present inquiry to distinguish the *primary* and *real qualities* of bodies, which are always in them (viz. solidity, extension, figure, number, and motion or rest; and are sometimes perceived by us, viz. when the bodies they are in are big enough singly to be discerned), from those *secondary* and *imputed qualities,* which are but the powers of several combinations of those primary ones, when they operate without being distinctly discerned; whereby we also may come to know what *ideas* are, and what are not, resemblances of something really existing in the bodies we denominate from them.

23.   The *qualities,* then, that are in *bodies,* rightly considered, are of *three sorts*:

First, The *bulk, figure, number, situation,* and *motion or rest* of their solid parts.   Those are in them, whether we perceive them or no; and when they are of that size that we can discover them, we have by these an *idea* of the thing as it is in itself, as is plain in artificial things. These I call *primary qualities*.

Secondly, The *power* that is in any body, by reason of *its* insensible *primary qualities*, to operate after a peculiar manner on any of our senses, and thereby *produce in us* the *different ideas* of several colours, sounds, smells, tastes, etc. These are usually called sensible qualities.

Thirdly, The *power* that is in any body, *by* reason of the particular constitution of *its primary qualities*, *to* make such a *change* in the *bulk, figure, texture, and motion of another body*, as to make it operate on our senses differently from what it did before. Thus the sun has a power to make wax white, and fire to make lead fluid. These *are* usually called powers.

The first of these, as has been said, I think may be properly called *real, original*, or *primary qualities*, because they are in the things themselves, whether they are perceived or no; and upon their different modifications it is that the secondary qualities depend.

The other two are only powers to act differently upon other things, which powers result from the different modifications of those primary qualities.

24.   But though *these two latter sorts of qualities are powers barely*, and nothing but powers relating to several other bodies and resulting from the different modifications of the original qualities, yet they are generally otherwise thought of. For *the second sort*, viz. the powers to produce several *ideas* in us by our senses, *are looked upon as real qualities in the things* thus affecting us; but *the third sort are called and esteemed barely powers*, v.g. the *idea* of heat or light which we receive by our eyes or touch from the sun are commonly thought *real qualities* existing in the sun and something more than mere powers in it. But when we consider the sun in reference to wax, which it melts or blanches, we look upon the whiteness and softness produced in the wax not as qualities in the sun but effects produced by *powers* in it: whereas, if rightly considered, these qualities of light and warmth, which are perceptions in me when I am warmed or enlightened by the sun, are no otherwise in the sun than the changes, made in the wax when it is blanched or melted, are in the sun. They are all of them equally powers in the sun, depending on its primary qualities; whereby it is able in the one case so to alter the bulk, figure, texture, or motion of some of the insensible parts of my eyes or hands as thereby to produce in me the *idea* of light or heat; and in the other, it is able so to alter the bulk, figure, texture, or motion of the insensible parts of the wax, as to make them fit to produce in me the distinct

ideas of white and fluid.

25. The reason *why the one are ordinarily taken for real qualities and the other only for bare powers* seems to be because the *ideas* we have of distinct colours, sounds, etc., containing nothing at all in them of bulk, figure, or motion, we are not apt to think them the effects of these primary qualities which appear not to our senses to operate in their production, and with which they have not any apparent congruity or conceivable connexion. Hence it is that we are so forward to imagine that those *ideas* are the resemblances of something really existing in the objects themselves, since sensation discovers nothing of bulk, figure, or motion of parts in their production, nor can reason show how bodies by their bulk, figure, and motion should produce in the mind the *ideas* of blue or yellow, etc. But in the other case, in the operations of bodies changing the qualities one of another, we plainly discover that the quality produced hath commonly no resemblance with anything in the thing producing it; wherefore we look on it as a bare effect of power. For, though receiving the *idea* of heat or light from the sun, we are apt to think it is a perception and resemblance of such a quality in the sun: yet when we see wax or a fair face receive change of colour from the sun, we cannot imagine that to be the reception or resemblance of anything in the sun, because we find not those different colours in the sun itself. For, our senses being able to observe a likeness or unlikeness of sensible qualities in two different external objects, we forwardly enough conclude the production of any sensible quality in any subject to be an effect of bare power, and not the communication of any quality which was really in the efficient, when we find no such sensible quality in the thing that produced it. But our senses not being able to discover any unlikeness between the *idea* produced in us and the quality of the object producing it, we are apt to imagine that our *ideas* are resemblances of something in the objects, and not the effects of certain powers placed in the modification of their primary qualities, with which primary qualities the *ideas* produced in us have no resemblance.

26. To conclude, beside those before-mentioned *primary qualities* in bodies, viz. bulk, figure, extension, number, and motion of their solid parts: all the rest, whereby we take notice of bodies and distinguish them one from another, are nothing else but several powers in them, depending on those primary qualities; whereby they are fitted, either by immediately operating on our bodies to produce several different *ideas* in us, or else, by operating on other bodies, so to change their primary

qualities as to render them capable of producing *ideas* in us different from what before they did. The former of these, I think, may be called *secondary qualities immediately perceivable,* the latter *secondary qualities, mediately perceivable.*

CHAPTER IX

OF PERCEPTION

1. PERCEPTION, as it is the first faculty of the mind exercised about our *ideas,* so it is the first and simplest *idea* we have from reflection, and is by some called thinking in general. Though thinking, in the propriety of the *English* tongue, signifies that sort of operation in the mind about its *ideas,* wherein the mind is active, where it, with some degree of voluntary attention, considers anything. For in bare naked *perception,* the mind is, for the most part, only passive; and what it perceives, it cannot avoid perceiving.

2. *What perception is,* everyone will know better by reflecting on what he does himself, when he sees, hears, feels, etc., or thinks, than by any discourse of mine. Whoever reflects on what passes in his own mind cannot miss it. And if he does not reflect, all the words in the world cannot make him have any notion of it.

3. This is certain: that whatever alterations are made in the body, if they reach not the mind; whatever impressions are made on the outward parts, if they are not taken notice of within, there is no perception. Fire may burn our bodies with no other effect than it does a billet, unless the motion be continued to the brain, and there the sense of heat, or *idea* of pain, be produced in the mind; wherein consists *actual perception.*

4. How often may a man observe in himself that, whilst his mind is intently employed in the contemplation of some objects, and curiously surveying some *ideas* that are there, it takes no notice of impressions of sounding bodies made upon the organ of hearing, with the same alteration that used to be for the producing the idea of sound. A sufficient impulse there may be on the organ, but it not reaching the observation of the mind, there follows no perception; and though the motion that used to produce the *idea* of sound be made in the ear, yet no sound is heard. Want of sensation, in this case, is not through any defect in the organ, or that the man's ears are less affected than at other times when he does hear: but that which used to produce the *idea,*

though conveyed in by the usual organ, not being taken notice of in the understanding, and so imprinting no *idea* on the mind, there follows no sensation. *So that wherever there is sense* or *perception, there some* idea *is actually produced, and present in the understanding.*

5. Therefore I doubt not but *children,* by the exercise of their senses about objects that affect them *in the womb, receive some few* ideas, before they are born, as the unavoidable effects either of the bodies that environ them or else of those wants or diseases they suffer; amongst which (if one may conjecture concerning things not very capable of examination) I think the *ideas* of hunger and warmth are two: which probably are some of the first that children have and which they scarce ever part with again.

6. But though it be reasonable to imagine that *children* receive some *ideas* before they come into the world, yet these simple *ideas* are *far from* those *innate principles* which some contend for and we above have rejected. These here mentioned, being the effects of sensation, are only from some affections of the body which happen to them there, and so depend on something exterior to the mind, no otherwise differing in their manner of production from other *ideas* derived from sense but only in the precedency of time; whereas those innate principles are supposed to be quite of another nature, not coming into the mind by any accidental alterations in or operations on the body, but, as it were, original characters impressed upon it in the very first moment of its being and constitution.

7. As there are some *ideas* which we may reasonably suppose may be introduced into the minds of children in the womb, subservient to the necessities of their life and being there, so after they are born *those* ideas are the *earliest imprinted which happen to be the sensible qualities which first occur* to them; amongst which light is not the least considerable nor of the weakest efficacy. And how covetous the mind is to be furnished with all such *ideas* as have no pain accompanying them may be a little guessed by what is observable in children new-born, who always turn their eyes to that part from whence the light comes, lay them how you please. But the *ideas* that are most familiar at first, being various according to the divers circumstances of children's first entertainment in the world, the order wherein the several *ideas* come at first into the mind is very various and uncertain also; neither is it much material to know it.

8. We are further to consider concerning perception that the *ideas we receive by sensation are often* in grown people *altered by*

the judgment, without our taking notice of it. When we set before our eyes a round globe of any uniform colour, v.g. gold, alabaster, or jet, it is certain that the *idea* thereby imprinted in our mind is of a flat circle, variously shadowed, with several degrees of light and brightness coming to our eyes. But we having, by use, been accustomed to perceive what kind of appearance convex bodies are wont to make in us, what alterations are made in the reflections of light by the difference of the sensible figures of bodies: the judgment presently, by an habitual custom, alters the appearances into their causes. So that from that which truly is variety of shadow or colour, collecting the figure, it makes it pass for a mark of figure and frames to itself the perception of a convex figure and an uniform colour, when the *idea* we receive from thence is only a plane variously coloured, as is evident in painting. To which purpose I shall here insert a problem of that very ingenious and studious promoter of real knowledge, the learned and worthy Mr. *Molyneux*, which he was pleased to send me in a letter some months since; and it is this: *Suppose a man born blind, and now adult, and taught by his touch to distinguish between a cube and a sphere of the same metal, and nighly of the same bigness, so as to tell, when he felt one and the other, which is the cube, which the sphere. Suppose then the cube and sphere placed on a table, and the blind man to be made to see:* quaere, *whether by his sight, before he touched them, he could now distinguish and tell which is the globe, which the cube?* To which the acute and judicious proposer answers: *Not. For, though he has obtained the experience of how a globe, how a cube affects his touch, yet he has not yet obtained the experience that what affects his touch so or so must affect his sight so or so; or that a protuberant angle in the cube, that pressed his hand unequally, shall appear to his eye as it does in the cube.* I agree with this thinking gentleman, whom I am proud to call my friend, in his answer to this problem; and am of opinion that the blind man, at first sight, would not be able with certainty to say which was the globe, which the cube, whilst he only saw them, though he could unerringly name them by his touch, and certainly distinguish them by the difference of their figures felt. This I have set down and leave with my reader as an occasion for him to consider how much he may be beholding to experience, improvement, and acquired notions, where he thinks he has not the least use of or help from them; and the rather, because this observing *gentleman* further adds that, *having upon the occasion of my book proposed this to divers very ingenious men, he hardly ever met with one that at first gave the answer to it which he thinks true, till by hearing his reasons they were convinced.*

9.   But this is not, I think, usual in any of our *ideas*, but those received by *sight*. Because sight, the most comprehensive of all our senses, conveying to our minds the *ideas* of light and colours, which are peculiar only to that sense; and also the far different *ideas* of space, figure, and motion, the several varieties whereof change the appearances of its proper object, viz. light and colours: we bring ourselves by use to judge of the one by the other. This, in many cases by a settled habit, in things whereof we have frequent experience, is performed so constantly and so quick, that we take that for the perception of our sensation which is an *idea* formed by our judgment; so that one, viz. that of sensation, serves only to excite the other, and is scarce taken notice of itself; as a man who reads or hears with attention and understanding, takes little notice of the characters or sounds, but of the *ideas* that are excited in him by them.

10.   Nor need we wonder that this is done with so little notice, if we consider how very *quick* the *actions of the mind* are performed; for, as itself is thought to take up no space, to have no extension, so its actions seem to require no time, but many of them seem to be crowded into an instant. I speak this in comparison to the actions of the body. Anyone may easily observe this in his own thoughts, who will take the pains to reflect on them. How, as it were in an instant, do our minds, with one glance, see all the parts of a demonstration, which may very well be called a long one, if we consider the time it will require to put it into words, and step by step show it another? *Secondly*, we shall not be so much surprised that this is done in us with so little notice, if we consider how the facility which we get of doing things by a custom of doing makes them often pass in us without our notice. *Habits*, especially such as are begun very early, come at last to *produce actions in us which often escape our observation.* How frequently do we, in a day, cover our eyes with our eye-lids, without perceiving that we are at all in the dark? Men that by custom have got the use of a by-word do almost in every sentence pronounce sounds which though taken notice of by others they themselves neither hear nor observe. And therefore it is not so strange that our mind should often change the *idea* of its sensation into that of its judgment, and make one serve only to excite the other, without our taking notice of it.

15.   *Perception* then being the *first step and degree towards knowledge and the inlet of all the materials of it*: the fewer senses any man, as well as any other creature, hath; and the fewer and

duller the impressions are that are made by them; and the duller the faculties are that are employed about them: the more remote are they from that knowledge which is to be found in some men. But this, being in great variety of degrees (as may be perceived amongst men), cannot certainly be discovered in the several species of animals, much less in their particular individuals. It suffices me only to have remarked here that perception is the first operation of all our intellectual faculties, and the inlet of all knowledge into our minds. And I am apt, too, to imagine that it is perception in the lowest degree of it which puts the boundaries between animals and the inferior ranks of creatures. But this I mention only as my conjecture by the by, it being indifferent to the matter in hand which way the learned shall determine of it.

Chapter X

OF RETENTION

1. THE next faculty of the mind, whereby it makes a further progress towards knowledge, is that which I call *retention*, or the keeping of those simple *ideas* which from sensation or reflection it hath received. This is done two ways. First, by keeping the *idea* which is brought into it, for some time actually in view, which is called *contemplation*.

2. The other way of retention is the power to revive again in our minds those *ideas* which, after imprinting, have disappeared, or have been as it were laid aside out of sight; and thus we do, when we conceive heat or light, yellow or sweet, the object being removed. This is *memory*, which is as it were the storehouse of our *ideas*. For, the narrow mind of man not being capable of having many *ideas* under view and consideration at once, it was necessary to have a repository, to lay up those *ideas* which, at another time, it might have use of. But, our *ideas* being nothing but actual perceptions in the mind, which cease to be anything when there is no perception of them, this *laying up* of our *ideas* in the repository of the memory signifies no more but this: that the mind has a power in many cases to revive perceptions which it has once had, with this additional perception annexed to them, that it has had them before. And in this sense it is that our *ideas* are said to be in our memories, when indeed they are actually nowhere; but only there is an ability in the mind when it will to revive them again, and as it were

paint them anew on itself, though some with more, some with less difficulty, some more lively, and others more obscurely. And thus it is by the assistance of this faculty that we are said to have all those *ideas* in our understandings which, though we do not actually contemplate, yet we can bring in sight and make appear again and be the objects of our thoughts, without the help of those sensible qualities which first imprinted them there.

3.   *Attention* and *repetition help* much to the fixing any *ideas* in *the memory*; but those which naturally at first make the deepest and most lasting impression are those which are accompanied with *pleasure* or *pain*. The great business of the senses being to make us take notice of what hurts or advantages the body, it is wisely ordered by nature (as has been shown) that pain should accompany the reception of several *ideas*; which, supplying the place of consideration and reasoning in children, and acting quicker than consideration in grown men, makes both the young and old avoid painful objects with that haste which is necessary for their preservation, and in both settles in the memory a caution for the future.

4.   Concerning the several *degrees of* lasting, wherewith *ideas* are imprinted on the *memory*, we may observe that some of them have been produced in the understanding by an object affecting the senses once only and no more than once; others that have more than once offered themselves to the senses have yet been little taken notice of: the mind either heedless, as in children, or otherwise employed, as in men, intent only on one thing, not setting the stamp deep into itself. And in some, where they are set on with care and repeated impressions, either through the temper of the body or some other default, the memory is very weak. In all these cases, *ideas* in the mind quickly fade and often vanish quite out of the understanding, leaving no more footsteps or remaining characters of themselves than shadows do flying over fields of corn; and the mind is as void of them as if they never had been there.

5.   Thus many of those *ideas* which were produced in the minds of children in the beginning of their sensation (some of which, perhaps, as of some pleasures and pains, were before they were born and others in their infancy) if in the future course of their lives they are not repeated again, are quite lost without the least glimpse remaining of them. This may be observed in those who by some mischance have lost their sight when they were very young, in whom the *ideas* of colours, having been but slightly taken notice of and ceasing to be repeated, do quite wear out; so that some years after there is no more notion nor memory of

colours left in their minds than in those of people born blind. The memory in some men, it is true, is very tenacious, even to a miracle; but yet there seems to be a constant decay of all our *ideas*, even of those which are struck deepest and in minds the most retentive: so that, if they be not sometimes renewed by repeated exercise of the senses or reflection on those kind of objects which at first occasioned them, the print wears out and at last there remains nothing to be seen. Thus the *ideas* as well as children of our youth often die before us; and our minds represent to us those tombs to which we are approaching: where, though the brass and marble remain, yet the inscriptions are effaced by time and the imagery moulders away. *The pictures drawn in our minds are laid in fading colours*, and if not sometimes refreshed, vanish and disappear. How much the constitution of our bodies and the make of our animal spirits are concerned in this, and whether the temper of the brain make this difference that in some it retains the characters drawn on it like marble, in others like freestone, and in others little better than sand, I shall not here inquire, though it may seem probable that the constitution of the body does sometimes influence the memory, since we oftentimes find a disease quite strip the mind of all its *ideas*, and the flames of a fever, in a few days, calcine all those images to dust and confusion which seemed to be as lasting as if graved in marble.

Chapter XI

OF DISCERNING, AND OTHER OPERATIONS OF THE MIND

1. ANOTHER faculty we may take notice of in our minds is that of *discerning* and distinguishing between the several *ideas* it has. It is not enough to have a confused perception of something in general; unless the mind had a distinct perception of different objects and their qualities, it would be capable of very little knowledge, though the bodies that affect us were as busy about us as they are now, and the mind were continually employed in thinking. On this faculty of distinguishing one thing from another depends the *evidence and certainty* of several, even very general, propositions, which have passed for innate truths: because men, overlooking the true cause why those propositions find universal assent, impute it wholly to native uniform impressions; whereas it in truth *depends upon this clear discerning faculty* of the mind whereby it perceives two *ideas* to be the

same, or different. But of this more hereafter.

2. How much the imperfection of accurately discriminating *ideas* one from another lies either in the dullness or faults of the organs of sense, or want of acuteness, exercise, or attention in the understanding, or hastiness and precipitancy natural to some tempers, I will not here examine; it suffices to take notice that this is one of the operations that the mind may reflect on and observe in itself. It is of that consequence to its other knowledge that, so far as this faculty is in itself dull or not rightly made use of, for the distinguishing one thing from another, so far our notions are confused, and our reason and judgment disturbed or misled. If in having our *ideas* in the memory ready at hand consists quickness of parts: in this, of having them unconfused and being able nicely to distinguish one thing from another, where there is but the least difference, consists, in a great measure, the exactness of judgment and clearness of reason which is to be observed in one man above another. And hence perhaps may be given some reason of that common observation, that men who have a great deal of wit, and prompt memories, have not always the clearest judgment or deepest reason. For *wit* lying most in the assemblage of *ideas*, and putting those together with quickness and variety, wherein can be found any resemblance or congruity, thereby to make up pleasant pictures and agreeable visions in the fancy: *judgment*, on the contrary, lies quite on the other side, in separating carefully, one from another, *ideas* wherein can be found the least difference, thereby to avoid being misled by similitude, and by affinity to take one thing for another. This is a way of proceeding quite contrary to metaphor and allusion, wherein for the most part lies that entertainment and pleasantry of wit, which strikes so lively on the fancy, and therefore is so acceptable to all people: because its beauty appears at first sight, and there is required no labour of thought to examine what truth or reason there is in it. The mind, without looking any further, rests satisfied with the agreeableness of the picture and the gaiety of the fancy; and it is a kind of affront to go about to examine it by the severe rules of truth and good reason; whereby it appears that it consists in something that is not perfectly conformable to them.

3. To the well distinguishing our *ideas*, it chiefly contributes that they be *clear and determinate*; and when they are so, *it will not breed any confusion* or mistake about them, though the senses should (as sometimes they do) convey them from the same object differently on different occasions, and so seem to err. For, though a man in a fever should from sugar have a

bitter taste, which at another time would produce a sweet one, yet the *idea* of bitter in that man's mind would be as clear and distinct from the *idea* of sweet as if he had tasted only gall. Nor does it make any more confusion between the two *ideas* of sweet and bitter that the same sort of body produces at one time, one and at another time another *idea* by the taste, than it makes a confusion in two *ideas* of white and sweet or white and round that the same piece of sugar produces them both in the mind at the same time. And the *ideas* of orange colour and azure that are produced in the mind by the same parcel of the infusion of *lignum nephriticum* are no less distinct *ideas* than those of the same colours, taken from two very different bodies.

4.   The COMPARING them one with another, in respect of extent, degrees, time, place, or any other circumstances, is another operation of the mind about its *ideas*, and is that upon which depends all that large tribe of *ideas* comprehended under *relation*; which, of how vast an extent it is, I shall have occasion to consider hereafter.

5.   How far brutes partake in this faculty is not easy to determine. I imagine they have it not in any great degree: for though they probably have several *ideas* distinct enough, yet it seems to me to be the prerogative of human understanding, when it has sufficiently distinguished any *ideas*, so as to perceive them to be perfectly different and so consequently two, to cast about and consider in what circumstances they are capable to be compared. And therefore, I think, *beasts compare* not their *ideas* further than some sensible circumstances annexed to the objects themselves. The other power of comparing, which may be observed in men, belonging to general *ideas*, and useful only to abstract reasonings, we may probably conjecture beasts have not.

6.   The next operation we may observe in the mind about its *ideas* is COMPOSITION, whereby it puts together several of those simple ones it has received from sensation and reflection, and combines them into complex ones. Under this of composition may be reckoned also that of ENLARGING, wherein, though the composition does not so much appear as in more complex ones, yet it is nevertheless a putting several *ideas* together, though of the same kind. Thus, by adding several units together, we make the *idea* of a dozen; and putting together the repeated *ideas* of several perches, we frame that of furlong.

7.   In this also, I suppose, *brutes* come far short of men. For, though they take in and retain together several combinations of simple *ideas*, as possibly the shape, smell, and voice of his

master make up the complex *idea* a dog has of him, or rather are so many distinct marks whereby he knows him: yet I *do not* think they do of themselves ever compound them and *make complex* ideas. And perhaps even where we think they have complex *ideas*, it is only one simple one that directs them in the knowledge of several things, which possibly they distinguish less by their sight than we imagine. For I have been credibly informed that a bitch will nurse, play with, and be fond of young foxes, as much as and in place of her puppies, if you can but get them once to suck her so long that her milk may go through them. And those animals, which have a numerous brood of young ones at once, appear not to have any knowledge of their number; for though they are mightily concerned for any of their young that are taken from them whilst they are in sight or hearing, yet if one or two of them be stolen from them in their absence or without noise, they appear not to miss them or to have any sense that their number is lessened.

8. When children have, by repeated sensations, got *ideas* fixed in their memories, they begin by degrees to learn the use of signs. And when they have got the skill to apply the organs of speech to the framing of articulate sounds, they begin to make *use of words* to signify their *ideas* to others. These verbal signs they sometimes borrow from others and sometimes make themselves, as one may observe among the new and unusual names children often give to things in their first use of language.

9. The use of words then being to stand as outward marks of our internal *ideas*, and those *ideas* being taken from particular things, if every particular *idea* that we take in should have a dictinct name, names must be endless. To prevent this, the mind makes the particular *ideas* received from particular objects to become general; which is done by considering them as they are in the mind such appearances, separate from all other existences and the circumstances of real existence, as time, place, or any other concomitant *ideas*. This is called ABSTRACTION, whereby *ideas* taken from particular beings become general representatives of all of the same kind; and their names, general names, applicable to whatever exists conformable to such abstract *ideas*. Such precise, naked appearances in the mind, without considering how, whence, or with what others they came there, the understanding lays up (with names commonly annexed to them) as the standards to rank real existences into sorts, as they agree with these patterns, and to *denominate* them accordingly. Thus the same colour being observed to-day in chalk or snow, which the mind yesterday received from milk,

it considers that appearance alone, makes it a representative of all of that kind; and having given it the name *whiteness*, it by that sound signifies the same quality wheresoever to be imagined or met with; and thus universals, whether *ideas* or terms, are made.

10. If it may be doubted whether *beasts* compound and enlarge their *ideas* that way to any degree: this, I think, I may be positive in, that the power of *abstracting* is not at all in them; and that the having of general *ideas* is that which puts a perfect distinction betwixt man and brutes, and is an excellency which the faculties of brutes do by no means attain to. For it is evident we observe no footsteps in them of making use of general signs for universal *ideas*; from which we have reason to imagine that they have not the faculty of abstracting, or making general *ideas*, since they have no use of words or any other general signs.

14. These I think are the first faculties and operations of the mind which it makes use of in understanding; and though they are exercised about all its *ideas* in general, yet the instances I have hitherto given have been chiefly in simple *ideas*. And I have subjoined the explication of these faculties of the mind to that of simple *ideas* before I come to what I have to say concerning complex ones, for these following reasons:

First, Because several of these faculties being exercised at first principally about simple *ideas*, we might, by following nature in its ordinary method, trace and discover them in their rise, progress, and gradual improvements.

Secondly, Because, observing the faculties of the mind, how they operate about simple *ideas*, which are usually, in most men's minds, much more clear, precise, and distinct than complex ones, we may the better examine and learn how the mind abstracts, denominates, compares, and exercises its other operations about those which are complex, wherein we are much more liable to mistake.

Thirdly, Because these very operations of the mind about *ideas* received from *sensation* are themselves, when reflected on, another set of *ideas*, derived from that other source of our knowledge, which I call *reflection*, and therefore fit to be considered in this place after the simple *ideas* of *sensation*. Of compounding, comparing, abstracting, etc., I have but just spoken, having occasion to treat of them more at large in other places.

15. And thus I have given a short and, I think, true *history of the first beginnings of human knowledge*: whence the mind has its first objects, and by what steps it makes its progress to the laying in and storing up those *ideas* out of which is to be framed all the

knowledge it is capable of; wherein I must appeal to experience and observation whether I am in the right, the best way to come to truth being to examine things as really they are, and not to conclude they are as we fancy of ourselves or have been taught by others to imagine.

16. To deal truly, *this is the only way* that I can discover *whereby* the *ideas* of things *are brought into the understanding*. If other men have either innate *ideas* or infused principles, they have reason to enjoy them; and if they are sure of it, it is impossible for others to deny them the privilege that they have above their neighbours. I can speak but of what I find in myself and is agreeable to those notions, which, if we will examine the whole course of men in their several ages, countries, and educations, seem to depend on those foundations which I have laid and to correspond with this method, in all the parts and degrees thereof.

17. I pretend not to teach, but to inquire; and therefore cannot but confess here again that external and internal sensation are the only passages that I can find of knowledge to the understanding. These alone, as far as I can discover, are the windows by which light is let into this *dark room*. For, methinks, the *understanding* is not much unlike a closet wholly shut from light, with only some little opening left, to let in external visible resemblances, or *ideas* of things without; would the pictures coming into such a dark room but stay there, and lie so orderly as to be found upon occasion, it would very much resemble the understanding of a man in reference to all objects of sight and the *ideas* of them.

These are my guesses concerning the means whereby the understanding comes to have and retain simple *ideas* and the modes of them, with some other operations about them. I proceed now to examine some of these simple *ideas* and their modes a little more particularly.

CHAPTER XII

OF COMPLEX IDEAS

1. WE have hitherto considered those *ideas* in the reception whereof the mind is only passive, which are those simple ones received from *sensation* and *reflection* before mentioned, whereof

the mind cannot make one to itself, nor have any *idea* which does not wholly consist of them. But as the mind is wholly passive in the reception of all its simple *ideas*, so it exerts several acts of its own whereby out of its simple *ideas*, as the materials and foundations of the rest, the others are framed. The acts of the mind, wherein it exerts its power over its simple *ideas*, are chiefly these three: (1) Combining several simple *ideas* into one compound one; and thus all complex *ideas* are made. (2) The second is bringing two *ideas*, whether simple or complex, together, and setting them by one another, so as to take a view of them at once, without uniting them into one; by which way it gets all its *ideas* of relations. (3) The third is separating them from all other *ideas* that accompany them in their real existence: this is called *abstraction*; and thus all its general *ideas* are made. This shows man's power, and its way of operation, to be much the same in the material and intellectual world. For the materials in both being such as he has no power over either to make or destroy, all that man can do is either to unite them together, or to set them by one another, or wholly separate them. I shall here begin with the first of these in the consideration of complex *ideas*, and come to the other two in their due places. As simple *ideas* are observed to exist in several combinations united together, so the mind has a power to consider several of them united together as one *idea*, and that not only as they are united in external objects, but as itself has joined them. *Ideas* thus made up of several simple ones put together, I call *complex*, such as are *beauty, gratitude, a man, an army, the universe*; which, though complicated of various simple *ideas*, or *complex ideas* made up of simple ones, yet are, when the mind pleases, considered each by itself as one entire thing, and signified by one name.

2. In this faculty of repeating and joining together its *ideas*, the mind has great power in varying and multiplying the objects of its thoughts, infinitely beyond what *sensation* or *reflection* furnished it with, but all this still confined to those simple *ideas* which it received from those two sources, and which are the ultimate materials of all its compositions. For simple *ideas* are all from things themselves, and of these *the mind can* have no more, nor other than what are suggested to it. It can have no other *ideas* of sensible qualities than what come from without by the senses; nor any *ideas* of other kind of operations of a thinking substance, than what it finds in itself. But when it has once got these simple *ideas* it is not confined barely to observation and what offers itself from without: it can, by its own power, put

together those *ideas* it has and *make new complex ones*, which it never received so united.

3.   *Complex ideas*, however compounded and decompounded, though their number be infinite and the variety endless wherewith they fill and entertain the thoughts of men, yet I think they may be all reduced under these three heads:

> 1. *Modes.*
> 2. *Substances.*
> 3. *Relations.*

4.   First, *Modes* I call such complex *ideas* which, however compounded, contain not in them the supposition of subsisting by themselves, but are considered as dependences on, or affections of substances; such are the *ideas* signified by the words *triangle, gratitude, murder*, etc. And if in this I use the word *mode* in somewhat a different sense from its ordinary signification, I beg pardon: it being unavoidable in discourses differing from the ordinary received notions either to make new words or to use old words in somewhat a new signification, the latter whereof in our present case is perhaps the more tolerable of the two.

5.   Of these *modes*, there are two sorts which deserve distinct consideration: First, there are some which are only variations, or different combinations of the same simple *idea*, without the mixture of any other, as a dozen, or score; which are nothing but the *ideas* of so many distinct units added together; and these I call *simple modes* as being contained within the bounds of one simple *idea*. Secondly, there are others compounded of simple *ideas* of several kinds, put together to make one complex one: v.g. *beauty*, consisting of a certain composition of colour and figure, causing delight in the beholder; *theft*, which being the concealed change of the possession of anything, without the consent of the proprietor, contains, as is visible, a combination of several *ideas* of several kinds: and these I call *mixed modes*.

6.   Secondly, the *ideas* of *substances* are such combinations of simple *ideas* as are taken to represent distinct particular things subsisting by themselves, in which the supposed or confused *idea* of substance, such as it is, is always the first and chief. Thus if to substance be joined the simple *idea* of a certain dull whitish colour, with certain degrees of weight, hardness, ductility, and fusibility, we have the *idea* of *lead*; and a combination of the *ideas* of a certain sort of figure, with the powers of motion, thought, and reasoning, joined to substance, make the ordinary *idea* of *a man*. Now of substances also, there are two sorts of

ideas: one of single substances, as they exist separately, as of *a man* or *a sheep;* the other of several of those put together, as an *army* of men, or *flock* of sheep; which *collective* ideas *of* several *substances* thus put together are as much each of them one single *idea* as that of a man or an unit.

7. Thirdly, the last sort of complex *ideas* is that we call *relation,* which consists in the consideration and comparing one *idea* with another.

Of these several kinds we shall treat in their order.

8. If we will trace the progress of our minds, and with attention observe how it repeats, adds together, and unites its simple *ideas* received from sensation or reflection, it will lead us further than at first perhaps we should have imagined. And I believe we shall find, if we warily observe the originals of our notions, that even *the most abstruse ideas,* how remote soever they may seem from sense, or from any operation of our own minds, are yet only such as the understanding frames to itself, by repeating and joining together *ideas* that it had either from objects of sense, or from its own operations about them: so that those even large *and abstract* ideas *are derived from sensation or reflection,* being no other than what the mind, by the ordinary use of its own faculties, employed about *ideas* received from objects of sense or from the operations it observes in itself about them, may and does attain unto. This I shall endeavour to show in the *ideas* we have of *space, time,* and *infinity,* and some few other that seem the most remote from those originals.

Chapter XIII

OF SIMPLE MODES; AND FIRST, OF THE SIMPLE MODES OF SPACE

1. Though in the foregoing part I have often mentioned simple *ideas,* which are truly the materials of all our knowledge, yet having treated of them there rather in the way that they come into the mind than as distinguished from others more compounded, it will not be perhaps amiss to take a view of some of them again under this consideration, and examine those different *modifications of the same* idea, which the mind either finds in things existing, or is able to make within itself without the help of any extrinsical object, or any foreign suggestion.

Those *modifications of any one simple* idea (which, as has been said, I call *simple modes*) are as perfectly different and distinct *ideas* in the mind as those of the greatest distance or contrariety. For the *idea* of *two* is as distinct from that of *one*, as *blueness* from *heat*, or either of them from any number: and yet it is made up only of that simple *idea* of an unit repeated; and repetitions of this kind joined together make those distinct *simple modes*, of a *dozen*, a *gross*, a *million*.

2. I shall begin with the *simple idea* of *space*. I have shown above, ch. iv, that we get the *idea* of space, both by our sight and touch; which, I think, is so evident that it would be as needless to go to prove that men perceive, by their sight, a distance between bodies of different colours, or between the parts of the same body, as that they see colours themselves; nor is it less obvious that they can do so in the dark by feeling and touch.

3. This space, considered barely in length between any two beings, without considering anything else between them, is called *distance*; if considered in length, breadth, and thickness, I think it may be called *capacity*. The term extension is usually applied to it in what manner soever considered.

4. Each different distance is a different modification of space; and *each* idea *of any different distance, or space, is a simple mode of this* idea. Men, for the use and by the custom of measuring, settle in their minds the *ideas* of certain stated lengths, such as are an *inch, foot, yard, fathom, mile, diameter of the earth,* etc., which are so many distinct *ideas* made up only of space. When any such stated lengths or measures of space are made familiar to men's thoughts, they can in their minds repeat them as often as they will without mixing or joining to them the *idea* of body or anything else; and frame to themselves the *ideas* of long, square, or cubic, *feet, yards,* or *fathoms,* here amongst the bodies of the universe, or else beyond the utmost bounds of all bodies; and by adding these still one to another, enlarge their *idea* of space as much as they please. This power of repeating or doubling any *idea* we have of any distance and adding it to the former as often as we will without being ever able to come to any stop or stint, let us enlarge it as much as we will, is that which gives us the *idea* of *immensity*.

5. There is another modification of this *idea* which is nothing but the relation which the parts of the termination of extension or circumscribed space have amongst themselves. This the touch discovers in sensible bodies whose extremities come within our reach, and the eye takes both from bodies and colours whose boundaries are within its view; where observing how the extremities terminate either in straight lines, which meet at discernible angles, or in crooked lines, wherein no angles can be

perceived: by considering these as they relate to one another in all parts of the extremities of any body or space, it has that *idea* we call *figure*, which affords to the mind infinite variety. For, besides the vast number of different figures that do really exist in the coherent masses of matter, the stock that the mind has in its power, by varying the *idea* of space and thereby making still new compositions by repeating its own *ideas* and joining them as it pleases, is perfectly inexhaustible. And so it can multiply figures *in infinitum*.

6. For the mind having a power to repeat the *idea* of any length directly stretched out, and join it to another in the same direction, which is to double the length of that straight line or else join it to another with what inclination it thinks fit and so make what sort of angle it pleases: and being able also to shorten any line it imagines by taking from it one-half or one-fourth or what part it pleases, without being able to come to an end of any such divisions, it can make an angle of any bigness. So also the lines that are its sides, of what length it pleases, which joining again to other lines of different lengths and at different angles till it has wholly enclosed any space, it is evident that it can multiply *figures* both in their shape and capacity *in infinitum*; all which are but so many different *simple modes of space*.

The same that it can do with straight lines, it can do also with crooked, or crooked and straight together; and the same it can do in lines, it can also in superficies, by which we may be led into further thoughts of the endless variety of *figures* that the mind has a power to make and thereby to multiply the *simple modes* of space.

7. Another *idea* coming under this head and belonging to this tribe is that we call *place*. As in simple space, we consider the relation of distance between any two bodies or points; so in our *idea* of *place*, we consider the relation of distance betwixt anything, and any two or more points, which are considered as keeping the same distance one with another, and so considered as at rest. For when we find anything at the same distance now which it was yesterday, from any two or more points which have not since changed their distance one with another, and with which we then compared it, we say it hath kept the same *place*; but if it hath sensibly altered its distance with either of those points, we say it hath changed its place, though, vulgarly speaking, in the common notion of *place*, we do not always exactly observe the distance from precise points, but from larger portions of sensible objects, to which we consider the thing placed to bear relation, and its distance from which we have some

reason to observe.

8. Thus, a company of chess-men standing on the same squares of the chess-board where we left them, we say they are all in the *same place*, or unmoved, though perhaps the chess-board hath been in the meantime carried out of one room into another; because we compared them only to the parts of the chess-board, which keep the same distance one with another. The chess-board, we also say, is in the *same place* it was, if it remain in the same part of the cabin, though perhaps the ship which it is in sails all the while. And the ship is said to be in the *same place*, supposing it kept the same distance with the parts of the neighbouring land, though perhaps the earth hath turned round; and so both chess-men, and board, and ship, have every one *changed place*, in respect of remoter bodies, which have kept the same distance one with another. But yet the distance from certain parts of the board being that which determines the place of the chess-men; and the distance from the fixed parts of the cabin (with which we made the comparison) being that which determined the place of the chess-board; and the fixed parts of the earth that by which we determined the place of the ship : these things may be said properly to be in the *same place* in those respects; though their distance from some other things, which in this matter we did not consider, being varied, they have undoubtedly *changed place* in that respect; and we ourselves shall think so, when we have occasion to compare them with those other.

9. But this modification of distance we call *place*, being made by men for their common use, that by it they might be able to design the particular position of things where they had occasion for such designation: men consider and determine of this *place* by reference to those adjacent things which best served to their present purpose, without considering other things which to another purpose would better *determine the place* of the same thing. Thus in the chess-board, the use of the *designation of* the *place* of each chess-man being determined only within that chequered piece of wood, it would cross that purpose to measure it by anything else; but when these very chess-men are put up in a bag, if anyone should ask where the black king is, it would be proper to *determine the place* by the parts of the room it was in and not by the chess-board: there being another use of *designing the place* it is now in than when in play it was on the chess-board, and so must be determined by other bodies. So if anyone should ask in what place are the verses which report the story of *Nisus* and *Eurialus*, it would be very improper to

determine this place by saying they were in such a part of the earth, or in *Bodley's* library; but the right designation of the place would be by the parts of *Virgil's* works; and the proper answer would be that these verses were about the middle of the ninth book of his *Aeneids*, and that they have been always constantly in the same place ever since *Virgil* was printed; which is true, though the book itself hath moved a thousand times, the use of the *idea* of place here being to know only in what part of the book that story is, that so, upon occasion, we may know where to find it and have recourse to it for our use.

10. That our *idea* of place is nothing else but such a relative position of anything as I have before mentioned, I think is plain and will be easily admitted, when we consider that we can have no *idea* of the place of the universe, though we can of all the parts of it; because beyond that, we have not the *idea* of any fixed, distinct, particular beings, in reference to which we can imagine it to have any relation of distance, but all beyond it is one uniform space or expansion, wherein the mind finds no variety, no marks. For to say that the world is somewhere means no more than that it does exist; this, though a phrase borrowed from place, signifying only its existence, not location; and when one can find out and frame in his mind clearly and distinctly the place of the universe, he will be able to tell us whether it moves or stands still in the undistinguishable *inane* of infinite space: though it be true that the word place has sometimes a more confused sense and stands for that space which any body takes up; and so the universe is in a place. The *idea* therefore of *place* we have by the same means that we get the *idea* of space (whereof this is but a particular limited consideration), viz. by our sight and touch, by either of which we receive into our minds the *ideas* of extension or distance.

11. There are some that would persuade us that *body and extension are the same thing*, who either change the signification of words, which I would not suspect them of, they having so severely condemned the philosophy of others because it hath been too much placed in the uncertain meaning or deceitful obscurity of doubtful or insignificant terms. If therefore they mean by *body and extension the same* that other people do, viz. by *body*, something that is solid and extended, whose parts are separable and movable different ways; and by *extension*, only the space that lies between the extremities of those solid coherent parts, and which is possessed by them, they confound very different *ideas* one with another. For I appeal to every man's own thoughts whether the *idea* of space be not as distinct from that of

solidity as it is from the *idea* of scarlet colour? It is true, solidity cannot exist without extension, neither can scarlet colour exist without extension; but this hinders not but that they are distinct *ideas*. Many *ideas* require others as necessary to their existence or conception which yet are very distinct *ideas*. Motion can neither be nor be conceived without space, and yet motion is not space nor space motion; space can exist without it and they are very distinct *ideas*; and so, I think, are those of space and solidity. Solidity is so inseparable an *idea* from body that upon that depends its filling of space, its contact, impulse, and communication of motion upon impulse. And if it be a reason to prove that spirit is different from body because thinking includes not the *idea* of extension in it, the same reason will be as valid, I suppose, to prove that *space is not body*, because it includes not the *idea* of solidity in it: *space* and *solidity* being *as distinct ideas* as thinking and extension, and as wholly separable in the mind one from another. *Body* then and *extension*, it is evident, are two distinct *ideas*. For,

12.   *First, Extension* includes no solidity, nor resistance to the motion of *body*, as body does.

13.   *Secondly,* The parts of pure space are inseparable one from the other; so that the continuity cannot be separated, neither really nor mentally. For I demand of anyone to remove any part of it from another, with which it is continued, even so much as in thought. To divide and separate actually is, as I think, by removing the parts one from another, to make two superficies, where before there was a continuity; and to divide mentally is to make in the mind two superficies, where before there was a continuity, and consider them as removed one from the other; which can only be done in things considered by the mind as capable of being separated and, by separation, of acquiring new distinct superficies, which they then have not, but are capable of. But neither of these ways of separation, whether real or mental, is, as I think, compatible to pure *space*.

It is true, a man may consider so much of such a *space* as is answerable or commensurate to a foot, without considering the rest; which is indeed a partial consideration, but not so much a mental separation or division, since a man can no more mentally divide without considering two superficies separate one from the other, than he can actually divide without making two superficies disjoined one from the other; but a partial consideration is not separating. A man may consider light in the sun without its heat, or mobility in body without its extension, without thinking of their separation. One is only a partial consideration, terminating in one alone; and the other is a consideration of both as existing separately.

14. *Thirdly*, The parts of pure *space* are immovable, which follows from their inseparability, *motion* being nothing but change of distance between any two things; but this cannot be between parts that are inseparable, which, therefore, must needs be at perpetual rest one amongst another.

Thus the determined *idea* of simple *space* distinguishes it plainly and sufficiently from *body*, since its parts are inseparable, immovable, and without resistance to the motion of body.

15. If anyone ask me *what* this *space* I speak of *is*, I will tell him when he tells me what his *extension* is. For to say, as is usually done, that extension is to have *partes extra partes* is to say only that *extension* is *extension*. For what am I the better informed in the nature of *extension* when I am told that *extension is to have parts that are extended, exterior to parts that are extended*, i.e. *extension* consists of extended parts? As if one asking what a fibre was, I should answer him that it was a thing made up of several fibres. Would he hereby be enabled to understand what a fibre was better than he did before? Or rather, would he not have reason to think that my design was to make sport with him, rather than seriously to instruct him?

16. Those who contend that *space and body are the same* bring this *dilemma*: either this *space* is something or nothing; if nothing be between two bodies, they must necessarily touch; if it be allowed to be something, they ask: Whether it be body or spirit? To which I answer by another question: Who told them that there was, or could be, nothing but solid beings which could not think, and thinking beings that were not extended? Which is all they mean by the terms *body* and *spirit*.

17. If it be demanded (as usually it is) whether this *space*, void of *body*, be *substance* or *accident*, I shall readily answer I know not, nor shall be ashamed to own my ignorance, till they that ask show me a clear distinct *idea* of *substance*.

18. I endeavour as much as I can to deliver myself from those fallacies which we are apt to put upon ourselves, by taking words for things. It helps not our ignorance to feign a knowledge where we have none by making a noise with sounds, without clear and distinct significations. Names made at pleasure neither alter the nature of things, nor make us understand them, but as they are signs of and stand for determined *ideas*. And I desire those who lay so much stress on the sound of these two syllables, *substance*, to consider whether applying it as they do to the

infinite incomprehensible GOD, to finite spirit, and to body, it be in the same sense; and whether it stands for the same *idea*, when each of those three so different beings are called *substances*? If so, whether it will not thence follow that God, spirits, and body, agreeing in the same common nature of *substance*, differ not any otherwise than in a bare different modification of that *substance*: as a tree and a pebble, being in the same sense body and agreeing in the common nature of body, differ only in a bare modification of that common matter; which will be a very harsh doctrine. If they say that they apply it to God, finite spirits, and matter in three different significations, and that it stands for one *idea* when GOD is said to be a *substance*, for another when the soul is called *substance*, and for a third when a body is called so: if the name *substance* stands for three several distinct *ideas*, they would do well to make known those distinct *ideas*, or at least to give three distinct names to them, to prevent in so important a notion the confusion and errors that will naturally follow from the promiscuous use of so doubtful a term; which is so far from being suspected to have three distinct, that in ordinary use it has scarce one clear distinct signification. And if they can thus make three distinct *ideas* of *substance*, what hinders why another may not make a fourth?

19.   They who first ran into the notion of *accidents*, as a sort of real beings that needed something to inhere in, were forced to find out the word *substance* to support them. Had the poor *Indian* philosopher (who imagined that the earth also wanted something to bear it up) but thought of this word *substance*, he needed not to have been at the trouble to find an elephant to support it, and a tortoise to support his elephant: the word *substance* would have done it effectually. And he that inquired might have taken it for as good an answer from an *Indian* philosopher that *substance*, without knowing what it is, is that which supports the earth, as we take it for a sufficient answer and good doctrine from our *European* philosophers that *substance*, without knowing what it is, is that which supports *accidents*. So that of *substance*, we have no *idea* of what it is, but only a confused, obscure one of what it does.

20.   Whatever a learned man may do here, an intelligent *American*, who inquired into the nature of things, would scarce take it for a satisfactory account if, desiring to learn our architecture, he should be told that a pillar was a thing supported by a *basis* and a *basis* something that supported a pillar. Would he not think himself mocked instead of taught with such an

account as this? And a stranger to them would be very liberally instructed in the nature of books and the things they contained if he should be told that all learned books consisted of paper and letters, and that letters were things inhering in paper and paper a thing that held forth letters: a notable way of having clear *ideas* of letters and paper! But were the *Latin* words *inhaerentia* and *substantia* put into the plain *English* ones that answer them, and were called *sticking on* and *under-propping*, they would better discover to us the very great clearness there is in the doctrine of *substance* and *accidents*, and show of what use they are in deciding of questions in philosophy.

21. But to return to our *idea* of *space*. If *body* be not supposed infinite (which I think no one will affirm), I would ask whether, if GOD placed a man at the extremity of corporeal beings, he could not stretch his hand beyond his body? If he could, then he would put his arm where there was before *space* without *body*; and if there he spread his fingers, there would still be *space* between them without *body*. If he could not stretch out his hand, it must be because of some external hindrance (for we suppose him alive, with such a power of moving the parts of his body that he hath now, which is not in itself impossible if GOD so pleased to have it; or at least it is not impossible for God so to move him); and then I ask whether that which hinders his hand from moving outwards be substance or accident, something or nothing? And when they have resolved that, they will be able to resolve themselves what that is which is, or may be between two bodies at a distance, that is not body, has no solidity. In the meantime, the argument is at least as good that where nothing hinders (as beyond the utmost bounds of all bodies), a *body* put into motion may move on, as where there is nothing between, there two bodies must necessarily touch; for pure *space* between is sufficient to take away the necessity of mutual contact, but bare *space* in the way is not sufficient to stop motion. The truth is, these men must either own that they think body infinite, though they are loath to speak it out, or else affirm that *space* is not *body*. For I would fain meet with that thinking man that can in his thoughts set any bounds to space, more than he can to duration, or by thinking hope to arrive at the end of either. And therefore, if his *idea* of eternity be infinite, so is his *idea* of immensity: they are both finite or infinite alike.

22. Further, those who assert the impossibility of *space* existing without *matter*, must not only make body infinite, but must also deny a power in God to annihilate any part of matter. No one,

I suppose, will deny that God can put an end to all motion that is in matter, and fix all the bodies of the universe in a perfect quiet and rest and continue them as long as he pleases. Whoever then will allow that God can, during such a general rest, annihilate either this book or the body of him that reads it, must necessarily admit the possibility of a *vacuum*; for it is evident that the space that was filled by the parts of the annihilated body will still remain and be a space without body. For the circumambient bodies being in perfect rest are a wall of adamant and in that state make it a perfect impossibility for any other body to get into that space. And indeed the necessary motion of one particle of matter into the place from whence another particle of matter is removed is but a consequence from the supposition of plenitude; which will therefore need some better proof than a supposed matter of fact, which experiment can never make out: our own clear and distinct *ideas* plainly satisfying us that there is no necessary connexion between *space* and *solidity*, since we can conceive the one without the other. And those who dispute for or against a *vacuum* do thereby confess they have distinct *ideas* of *vacuum* and *plenum*, i.e. that they have an *idea* of extension void of solidity, though they deny its existence; or else they dispute about nothing at all. For they who so much alter the signification of words as to call *extension*, *body*, and consequently make the whole essence of body to be nothing but pure extension without solidity, must talk absurdly whenever they speak of *vacuum*, since it is impossible for extension to be without extension. For *vacuum*, whether we affirm or deny its existence, signifies space without body, whose very existence no one can deny to be possible who will not make matter infinite and take from God a power to annihilate any particle of it.

23.   But not to go so far as beyond the utmost bounds of body in the universe, nor appeal to God's omnipotency to find a *vacuum*, the *motion* of bodies that are in our view and neighbourhood seem to me plainly to evince it. For I desire anyone so to divide a solid body, of any dimension he pleases, as to make it possible for the solid parts to move up and down freely every way within the bounds of that superficies, if there be not left in it a void space as big as the least part into which he has divided the said solid body. And if, where the least particle of the body divided is as big as a mustard-seed, a void space equal to the bulk of a mustard-seed be requisite to make room for the free motion of the parts of the divided body within the bounds of its superficies, where the particles of matter are

100,000,000 less than a mustard-seed, there must also be a space void of solid matter as big as 100,000,000th part of a mustard-seed; for if it hold in one it will hold in the other, and so on *in infinitum*. And let this void space be as little as it will, it destroys the hypothesis of *plenitude*. For if there can be a space void of body equal to the smallest separate particle of matter now existing in nature, it is still space without body and makes as great a difference between space and body as if it were μέγα χάσμα, a distance as wide as any in nature. And therefore, if we suppose not the void space necessary to motion equal to the least parcel of the divided solid matter, but to one-tenth or one-thousandth of it, the same consequence will always follow of space without matter.

24. But the question being here, whether the *idea of space* or *extension* be *the same with the idea of body*, it is not necessary to prove the real existence of a *vacuum*, but the *idea* of it; which it is plain men have when they inquire and dispute whether there be a *vacuum* or no. For if they had not the *idea* of space without body, they could not make a question about its existence; and if their *idea* of body did not include in it something more than the bare *idea* of space, they could have no doubt about the plenitude of the world; and it would be as absurd to demand whether there were space without body, as whether there were space without space, or body without body, since these were but different names of the same *idea*.

Chapter XIV

OF DURATION AND ITS SIMPLE MODES

1. There is another sort of distance, or length, the *idea* whereof we get not from the permanent parts of space, but from the fleeting and perpetually perishing parts of succession. This we call *duration*: the simple modes whereof are any different lengths of it whereof we have distinct *ideas*, as *hours, days, years,* etc., *time* and *eternity*.

2. The answer of a great man, to one who asked what time was, *Si non rogas intelligo* (which amounts to this: The more I set myself to think of it, the less I understand it), might perhaps persuade one that *time*, which reveals all other things, is itself not to be discovered. *Duration, time,* and *eternity* are, not without reason, thought to have something very abstruse in their nature. But however remote these may seem from our

comprehension, yet if we trace them right to their originals, I doubt not but one of those sources of all our knowledge, viz. *sensation* and *reflection*, will be able to furnish us with these *ideas*, as clear and distinct as many others which are thought much less obscure; and we shall find that the *idea* of eternity itself is derived from the same common original with the rest of our *ideas*.

3.   To understand *time* and *eternity* aright, we ought with attention to consider what *idea* it is we have of *duration*, and how we came by it.   It is evident, to anyone who will but observe what passes in his own mind, that there is a train of *ideas* which constantly succeed one another in his understanding, as long as he is awake.   *Reflection* on these appearances of several *ideas* one after another in our minds is that which furnishes us with the *idea* of *succession*; and the distance between any parts of that succession, or between the appearance of any two *ideas* in our minds, is that we call *duration*.   For whilst we are thinking or whilst we receive successively several *ideas* in our minds, we know that we do exist; and so we call the existence or the continuation of the existence of ourselves, or anything else commensurate to the succession of any *ideas* in our minds, the *duration* of ourselves or any such other thing co-existing with our thinking.

4.   That we have our notion of *succession* and *duration* from this original, viz. from reflection on the train of *ideas* which we find to appear one after another in our own minds, seems plain to me in that we have no perception of *duration* but by considering the train of *ideas* that take their turns in our understandings. When that succession of *ideas* ceases, our perception of duration ceases with it; which everyone clearly experiments in himself, whilst he sleeps soundly, whether an hour or a day, a month or a year; of which duration of things, while he sleeps or thinks not, he has no perception at all, but it is quite lost to him; and the moment wherein he leaves off to think, till the moment he begins to think again, seems to him to have no distance.   And so I doubt not but it would be to a waking man, if it were possible for him to keep only one *idea* in his mind, without variation and the succession of others; and we see that one who fixes his thoughts very intently on one thing so as to take but little notice of the succession of *ideas* that pass in his mind whilst he is taken up with that earnest contemplation, lets slip out of his account a good part of that duration and thinks that time shorter than it is.   But if sleep commonly unites the distant parts of duration, it is because during that time we have no succession of *ideas* in

our minds. For if a man during his sleep dreams, and variety of *ideas* make themselves perceptible in his mind one after another, he hath then, during such a dreaming, a sense of *duration* and of the length of it. By which it is to me very clear that men derive their *ideas* of duration from their *reflection on the train of the* ideas they observe to succeed one another in their own understandings, without which observation they can have no notion of *duration*, whatever may happen in the world.

5. Indeed a man having, from reflecting on the succession and number of his own thoughts, got the notion or *idea* of *duration*, he can apply that notion to things which exist while he does not think: as he that has got the *idea* of extension from bodies by his sight or touch can apply it to distances, where no body is seen or felt. And therefore, though a man has no perception of the length of duration which passed whilst he slept or thought not: yet, having observed the revolution of days and nights and found the length of their duration to be in appearance regular and constant, he can, upon the supposition that that revolution has proceeded after the same manner whilst he was asleep or thought not, as it used to do at other times, he can, I say, imagine and make allowance for the length of *duration* whilst he slept. But if *Adam* and *Eve* (when they were alone in the world) instead of their ordinary night's sleep, had passed the whole twenty-four hours in one continued sleep, the duration of that twenty-four hours had been irrecoverably lost to them, and been forever left out of their account of time.

6. Thus *by reflecting on the appearing of various* ideas *one after another in our understandings, we get the notion of succession*; which if anyone should think we did rather get from our observation of motion by our senses, he will perhaps be of my mind when he considers that even motion produces in his mind an *idea* of succession no otherwise than as it produces there a continued train of distinguishable *ideas*. For a man looking upon a body really moving perceives yet no motion at all unless that motion produces a constant train *of successive* ideas: v.g. a man becalmed at sea, out of sight of land, in a fair day, may look on the sun, or sea, or ship a whole hour together and perceive no motion at all in either, though it be certain that two, and perhaps all of them, have moved during that time a great way; but as soon as he perceives either of them to have changed distance with some other body, as soon as this motion produces any new *idea* in him, then he perceives that there has been motion. But wherever a man is with all things at rest about him, without perceiving any motion at all, if during this hour of quiet he has

been thinking, he will perceive the various *ideas* of his own thoughts in his own mind appearing one after another, and thereby observe and find succession where he could observe no motion.

7.   And this, I think, is the reason *why motions very slow*, though they are constant, *are not perceived* by us: because in their remove from one sensible part towards another, their change of distance is so slow that it causes no new *ideas* in us, but a good while one after another.   And so not causing a constant train of new *ideas* to follow one another immediately in our minds, we have no perception of motion; which consisting in a constant succession, we cannot perceive that succession without a constant succession of varying *ideas* arising from it.

8.   On the contrary, *things that move* so swift as not to affect the senses distinctly with several distinguishable distances of their motion, and so cause not any train of *ideas* in the mind, *are not* also *perceived* to move.   For anything that moves round about in a circle, in less time than our *ideas* are wont to succeed one another in our minds, is not perceived to move, but seems to be a perfect entire circle of that matter or colour, and not a part of a circle in motion.

9.   Hence I leave it to others to judge whether it be not probable that our *ideas* do, whilst we are awake, succeed one another in our minds at certain distances, not much unlike the images in the inside of a lantern, turned round by the heat of a candle.   This appearance of theirs in train, though perhaps it may be sometimes faster and sometimes slower, yet, I guess, varies not very much in a waking man: there seem to be *certain bounds to the quickness and slowness of the succession of* those *ideas* one to another in our minds beyond which they can neither delay nor hasten.

10.   The reason I have for this odd conjecture is from observing that, in the impressions made upon any of our senses, we can but to a certain degree perceive any succession; which if exceeding quick, the sense of succession is lost, even in cases where it is evident that there is a real succession.   Let a cannon-bullet pass through a room, and in its way take with it any limb or fleshy parts of a man, it is as clear as any demonstration can be that it must strike successively the two sides of the room; it is also evident that it must touch one part of the flesh first, and another after, and so in succession; and yet, I believe, nobody who ever felt the pain of such a shot, or heard the blow against the two distant walls, could perceive any succession either in the pain or sound of so swift a stroke.   Such a part of duration as this,

wherein we perceive no succession, is that which we may call an *instant,* and is *that which takes up the time of only one idea* in our minds, without the succession of another, wherein therefore we perceive no succession at all.

11. This also happens *where the motion is* so *slow* as not to supply a constant train of fresh *ideas* to the senses, as fast as the mind is capable of receiving new ones into it; and so other *ideas* of our own thoughts having room to come into our minds between those offered to our senses by the moving body, *there the sense of motion is lost*; and the body, though it really moves, yet not changing perceivable distance with some other bodies as fast as the *ideas* of our own minds do naturally follow one another in train, the thing seems to stand still; as is evident in the hands of clocks, and shadows of sun-dials, and other constant but slow motions where, though after certain intervals we perceive by the change of distance that it hath moved, yet the motion itself we perceive not.

12. So that to me it seems that *the constant and regular succession of ideas* in a waking man *is*, as it were, *the measure* and standard *of all other successions*: whereof, if anyone either exceeds the pace of our *ideas*, as where two sounds or pains, etc., take up in their succession the duration of but one *idea*, or else where any motion or succession is so slow as that it keeps not pace with the *ideas* in our minds or the quickness in which they take their turns, as when any one or more *ideas* in their ordinary course come into our mind between those which are offered to the sight by the different perceptible distances of a body in motion, or between sounds or smells following one another, there also the sense of a constant continued succession is lost, and we perceive it not but with certain gaps of rest between.

CHAPTER XVI

OF NUMBER

1. AMONGST all the *ideas* we have, as there is none suggested to the mind by more ways, so there is none more simple, than that *of unity*, or one: it has no shadow of variety or composition in it; every object our senses are employed about, every *idea* in our understandings, every thought of our minds, brings this *idea* along with it. And therefore it is the most intimate to our thoughts, as well as it is, in its agreement to all other things, the most universal *idea* we have. For number applies itself to men,

angels, actions, thoughts: everything that either doth exist, or can be imagined.

2.   By repeating this *idea* in our minds, and adding the repetitions together, we come by the *complex* ideas *of the modes of it.* Thus, by adding one to one, we have the complex *idea* of a couple; by putting twelve units together, we have the complex *idea* of a dozen; and of a score, or a million, or any other number.

3.   *The simple modes* of *number are of all other the most distinct*: every the least variation, which is an unit, making each combination as clearly different from that which approacheth nearest to it, as the most remote; two being as distinct from one, as two hundred; and the *idea* of two as distinct from the *idea* of three, as the magnitude of the whole earth is from that of a mite. This is not so in other simple modes, in which it is not so easy, nor perhaps possible, for us to distinguish betwixt two approaching *ideas*, which yet are really different. For who will undertake to find a difference between the white of this paper and that of the next degree to it; or can form distinct *ideas* of every the least excess in extension?

4.   The clearness and *distinctness of each mode of number* from all others, even those that approach nearest, makes me apt to think that demonstrations in numbers, if they are not more evident and exact than in extension, yet they are more general in their use, and more determinate in their application. Because the *ideas* of numbers are more precise and distinguishable than in extension, where every equality and excess are not so easy to be observed or measured; because our thoughts cannot in space arrive at any determined smallness beyond which it cannot go, as an unit; and therefore the quantity or proportion of any the least excess cannot be discovered; which is clear otherwise in number where, as has been said, 91 is as distinguishable from 90 as from 9000, though 91 be the next immediate excess to 90. But it is not so in extension, where whatsoever is more than just a foot or an inch is not distinguishable from the standard of a foot or an inch; and in lines which appear of an equal length, one may be longer than the other by innumerable parts; nor can anyone assign an angle which shall be the next biggest to a right one.

5.   By the repeating, as has been said, of the *idea* of an unit, and joining it to another unit, we make thereof one collective *idea*, marked by the name *two*. And whosoever can do this and proceed on, still adding one more to the last collective *idea* which he had of any number and gave a name to it, may count or have *ideas* for several collections of units, distinguished one from another, as far as he hath a series of names for following num-

bers, and a memory to retain that series, with their several names: all *numeration* being but still the adding of one unit more and giving to the whole together, as comprehended in one *idea*, a new or distinct name or sign, whereby to know it from those before and after and distinguish it from every smaller or greater multitude of unities. So that he that can add one to one, and so to two, and so go on with his tale, taking still with him the distinct names belonging to every progression, and so again, by subtracting an unit from each collection, retreat and lessen them, is capable of all the *ideas* of numbers, within the compass of his language, or for which he hath names, though not perhaps, of more. For the several simple modes of numbers being in our minds but so many combinations of units, which have no variety nor are capable of any other difference but more or less, names or marks for each distinct combination seem more necessary than in any other sort of *ideas*. For without such names or marks, we can hardly well make use of numbers in reckoning, especially where the combination is made up of any great multitude of units; which put together, without a name or mark to distinguish that precise collection, will hardly be kept from being a heap in confusion.

Chapter XVII

OF INFINITY

1. HE that would know what kind of *idea* it is to which we give the name of *infinity* cannot do it better than by considering to what infinity is by the mind more immediately attributed, and then how the mind comes to frame it.

Finite and *infinite* seem to me to be looked upon by the mind as the *modes of quantity*, and to be attributed primarily in their first designation only to those things which have parts, and are capable of increase or diminution by the addition or subtraction of any the least part; and such are the *ideas* of space, duration, and number, which we have considered in the foregoing chapters. It is true that we cannot but be assured that the great GOD, of whom and from whom are all things, is incomprehensibly infinite; but yet, when we apply to that first and supreme Being our idea of infinite, in our weak and narrow thoughts, we do it primarily in respect of his duration and ubiquity, and, I think, more figuratively to his power, wisdom, and goodness, and other attributes, which are properly inexhaustible and incomprehensible, etc. For, when we call them infinite, we have no other *idea* of this infinity but what carries with it some reflection on and intimation of that number or extent of the acts or objects of God's power, wisdom, and goodness which can never be supposed so great or so many which these attributes will not always surmount and exceed—let us multiply them in our thoughts as far as we can—with all the infinity of endless number. I do not pretend to say how these attributes are in GOD, who is infinitely beyond the reach of our narrow capacities; they do, without doubt, contain in them all possible perfection: but this, I say, is our way of conceiving them and these our *ideas* of their infinity.

2.   Finite then, and infinite being by the mind looked on as modifications of expansion and duration, the next thing to be considered is: *how the mind comes by* them. As for the *idea of finite*, there is no great difficulty. The obvious portions of extension that affect our senses carry with them into the mind the *idea* of finite; and the ordinary periods of succession, whereby we measure time and duration, as hours, days, and years, are bounded lengths. The difficulty is how we come by those boundless *ideas* of *eternity* and *immensity*, since the objects which we converse with come so much short of any approach or proportion to that largeness.

3.   Everyone that has any *idea* of any stated lengths of space, as a foot, finds that he can repeat that *idea*; and joining it to the former, make the *idea* of two feet; and by the addition of a third, three feet; and so on, without ever coming to an end of his additions, whether of the same *idea* of a foot, or, if he pleases, of doubling it, or any other *idea* he has of any length, as a mile, or diameter of the earth, or of the *orbis magnus*: for whichsoever of these he takes, and how often soever he doubles or any otherwise multiplies it, he finds that, after he has continued his doubling in his thoughts and enlarged his *idea* as much as he pleases, he has no more reason to stop, nor is one jot nearer the end of such addition than he was at first setting out: the power of enlarging his *idea* of space by further additions remaining still the same, he hence takes *the idea of infinite space*.

4.   This, I think, is the way whereby the mind gets the *idea of infinite space*. It is a quite different consideration to examine whether the mind has the *idea* of such a *boundless space actually existing*, since our *ideas* are not always proofs of the existence of things; but yet, since this comes here in our way, I suppose I may say that we are apt to think that space in itself is actually

boundless, to which imagination the *idea* of space or expansion of itself naturally leads us. For, it being considered by us either as the extension of body, or as existing by itself, without any solid matter taking it up (for of such a void space we have not only the *idea*, but I have proved, as I think, from the motion of body, its necessary existence), it is impossible the mind should be ever able to find or suppose any end of it, or be stopped anywhere in its progress in this space, how far soever it extends its thoughts. Any bounds made with body, even adamantine walls, are so far from putting a stop to the mind in its further progress in space and extension that it rather facilitates and enlarges it. For so far as that body reaches, so far no one can doubt of extension; and when we are come to the utmost extremity of body, what is there that can there put a stop and satisfy the mind that it is at the end of space, when it perceives it is not; nay, when it is satisfied that body itself can move into it? For if it be necessary for the motion of body that there should be an empty space, though never so little, here amongst bodies; and it be possible for body to move in or through that empty space; nay, it is impossible for any particle of matter to move but into an empty space: the same possibility of a body's moving into a void space, beyond the utmost bounds of body as well as into a void space interspersed amongst bodies, will always remain clear and evident, the *idea* of empty pure space, whether within or beyond the confines of all bodies, being exactly the same, differing not in nature though in bulk, and there being nothing to hinder body from moving into it. So that wherever the mind places itself by any thought, either amongst or remote from all bodies, it can, in this uniform *idea* of space, nowhere find any bounds, any end, and so must necessarily conclude it, by the very nature and *idea* of each part of it, to be actually infinite.

5. As, by the power we find in ourselves of repeating, as often as we will, any *idea* of space, we get the *idea* of immensity: so, by being able to repeat the *idea* of any length of duration we have in our minds, with all the endless addition of number, we come by the *idea* of *eternity*. For we find in ourselves we can no more come to an end of such repeated *ideas* than we can come to the end of number; which everyone perceives he cannot. But here again it is another question, quite different from our having an *idea* of eternity, to know whether there were *any real being*, whose duration has been *eternal*. And as to this, I say, he that considers something now existing, must necessarily come to something eternal. But having spoken of this in another place, I shall say here no more of it, but proceed on to some other

considerations of our *idea* of infinity.

6.   If it be so, that our *idea* of infinity be got from the power
we observe in ourselves of repeating, without end, our own
ideas, it may be demanded: *Why we do not attribute infinity to
other* ideas, *as well as those of space and duration*, since they may
be as easily, and as often, repeated in our minds as the other;
and yet nobody ever thinks of infinite sweetness, or infinite
whiteness, though he can repeat the *idea* of sweet or white as
frequently as those of a yard or a day.   To which I answer: All
the *ideas* that are considered as having parts, and are capable of
increase by the addition of any equal or less parts, afford us, by
their repetition, the *idea* of infinity; because, with this endless
repetition, there is continued an enlargement of which there can
be no end. But in other *ideas* it is not so. For to the largest *idea*
of extension or duration that I at present have, the addition of
any the least part makes an increase; but to the perfectest *idea* I
have of the whitest whiteness, if I add another of a less or equal
whiteness (and of a whiter than I have, I cannot add the *idea*),
it makes no increase, and enlarges not my *idea* at all; and therefore the different *ideas* of whiteness, etc., are called degrees.
For those *ideas* that consist of parts are capable of being augmented by every addition of the least part; but if you take the
idea of white, which one parcel of snow yielded yesterday to
your sight, and another *idea* of white from another parcel of
snow you see today, and put them together in your mind, they
embody, as it were, and run into one, and the *idea* of whiteness
is not at all increased; and if we add a less degree of whiteness to
a greater, we are so far from increasing, that we diminish it.
Those *ideas* that consist not of parts, cannot be augmented to
what proportion men please, or be stretched beyond what they
have received by their senses; but space, duration, and number,
being capable of increase by repetition, leave in the mind an
idea of an endless room for more; nor can we conceive anywhere
a stop to a further addition or progression; and so those *ideas*
alone lead our minds towards the thought of infinity.

CHAPTER XVIII

OF OTHER SIMPLE MODES

1.   THOUGH I have in the foregoing chapters shown how, from
simple *ideas* taken in by sensation, the mind comes to extend

itself even to infinity (which, however it may of all others seem most remote from any sensible perception, yet at last hath nothing in it but what is made out of simple *ideas*: received into the mind by the senses, and afterwards there put together, by the faculty the mind has to repeat its own *ideas*) though, I say, these might be instances enough of simple modes of the simple *ideas* of sensation, and suffice to show how the mind comes by them, yet I shall, for method's sake, though briefly, give an account of some few more, and then proceed to more complex *ideas*.

2. To *slide, roll, tumble, walk, creep, run, dance, leap, skip,* and abundance of others that might be named, are words which are no sooner heard but everyone who understands *English* has presently in his mind distinct *ideas*, which are all but the different modifications of motion. *Modes of motion* answer those of extension; *swift* and *slow* are two different *ideas* of motion, the measures whereof are made of the distances of time and space put together; so they are complex *ideas*, comprehending time and space with motion.

3. The like variety have we in sounds. Every articulate word is a different *modification of sound*; by which we see that from the sense of hearing by such modifications the mind may be furnished with distinct *ideas* to almost an infinite number. Sounds also, besides the distinct cries of birds and beasts, are modified by diversity of notes of different length put together, which make that complex *idea* called a *tune*, which a musician may have in his mind when he hears or makes no sound at all, by reflecting on the *ideas* of those sounds so put together silently in his own fancy.

4. Those of colours are also very various: some we take notice of as the different degrees or, as they are termed, *shades of the same colour*. But since we very seldom make assemblages of colours, either for use or delight, but figure is taken in also, and has its part in it, as in painting, weaving, needleworks, etc., those which are taken notice of do most commonly belong to mixed modes, as being made up of *ideas* of divers kinds, viz. figure and colour, such as *beauty, rainbow,* etc.

5. All *compounded tastes and smells* are also modes, made up of these simple *ideas* of those senses. But they, being such as generally we have no names for, are less taken notice of and cannot be set down in writing, and therefore must be left without enumeration to the thoughts and experience of my reader.

6. In general it may be observed that those *simple modes which are considered but as different degrees of the same simple* idea, though they are in themselves many of them very distinct *ideas*,

yet *have ordinarily no distinct names*, nor are much taken notice of, as distinct *ideas*, where the difference is but very small between them. Whether men have neglected these modes and given no names to them, as wanting measures nicely to distinguish them, or because, when they were so distinguished, that knowledge would not be of general or necessary use, I leave it to the thoughts of others: it is sufficient to my purpose to show that all our simple *ideas* come to our minds only by sensation and reflection, and that when the mind has them, it can variously repeat and compound them, and so make new complex *ideas*. But, though white, red, or sweet, etc., have not been modified or made into complex *ideas* by several combinations, so as to be named and thereby ranked into species, yet some others of the simple *ideas*, viz. those of unity, duration, motion, etc., above instanced in, as also power and thinking, have been thus modified to a great variety of complex *ideas*, with names belonging to them.

7. *The reason whereof*, I suppose, has been this: that the great concernment of men being with men one amongst another, the knowledge of men, and their actions, and the signifying of them to one another was most necessary; and therefore they made *ideas* of actions very nicely modified, and gave those complex *ideas* names, that they might the more easily record and discourse of those things they were daily conversant in, without long ambages and circumlocutions, and that the things they were continually to give and receive information about might be the easier and quicker understood. That this is so and that men, in framing different complex *ideas* and giving them names, have been much governed by the end of speech in general (which is a very short and expedite way of conveying their thoughts one to another) is evident in the names which in several arts have been found out and applied to several complex *ideas* of modified actions belonging to their several trades for dispatch sake, in their direction or discourses about them. Which *ideas* are not generally framed in the minds of men not conversant about these operations. And thence the words that stand for them, by the greatest part of men of the same language, are not understood. V.g., *colshire, drilling, filtration, cohobation* are words standing for certain complex *ideas* which, being seldom in the minds of any but those few whose particular employments do at every turn suggest them to their thoughts, those names of them are not generally understood but by smiths and chemists; who, having framed the complex *ideas* which these words stand for, and having given names to them or received them from others

upon hearing of these names in communication, readily conceive those *ideas* in their minds, as by *cohobation*: all the simple *ideas* of distilling and the pouring the liquor, distilled from anything back upon the remaining matter and distilling it again. Thus we see that there are great varieties of simple *ideas*, as of tastes and smells, which have no names; and of modes many more; which either not having been generally enough observed, or else not being of any great use to be taken notice of in the affairs and converse of men, they have not had names given to them, and so pass not for species. This we shall have occasion hereafter to consider more at large, when we come to speak of words.

Chapter XIX

OF THE MODES OF THINKING

1. WHEN the mind turns its view inwards upon itself, and contemplates its own actions, *thinking* is the first that occurs. In it the mind observes a great variety of modifications, and from thence receives distinct *ideas*. Thus the perception which actually accompanies and is annexed to any impression on the body made by an external object, being distinct from all other modifications of *thinking*, furnishes the mind with a distinct *idea*, which we call *sensation*; which is, as it were, the actual entrance of any *idea* into the understanding by the senses. The same *idea*, when it again recurs without the operation of the like object on the external sensory, is *remembrance*; if it be sought after by the mind, and with pain and endeavour found, and brought again in view, it is *recollection*; if it be held there long under attentive consideration, it is *contemplation*; when *ideas* float in our mind, without any reflection or regard of the understanding, it is that which the *French* call *rêverie* (our language has scarce a name for it); when the *ideas* that offer themselves (for as I have observed in another place, whilst we are awake there will always be a train of *ideas* succeeding one another in our minds) are taken notice of and, as it were, registered in the memory, it is *attention*; when the mind with great earnestness and of choice fixes its view on any *idea*, considers it on all sides and will not be called off by the ordinary solicitation of other *ideas*, it is that we call *intention* or *study*; sleep, without dreaming, is rest from all these. And *dreaming* itself is the having of *ideas* (whilst the outward senses are stopped, so that they re-

ceive not outward objects with their usual quickness) in the mind not suggested by any external objects or known occasion, nor under any choice or conduct of the understanding at all; and whether that which we call *ecstasy* be not dreaming with the eyes open, I leave to be examined.

2.   These are some few instances of those various *modes of thinking* which the mind may observe in itself and so have as distinct *ideas* of as it hath of *white* and *red*, a *square* or a *circle*. I do not pretend to enumerate them all, nor to treat at large of this set of *ideas* which are got from *reflection*; that would be to make a volume. It suffices to my present purpose to have shown here, by some few examples, of what sort these *ideas* are and how the mind comes by them, especially since I shall have occasion hereafter to treat more at large of *reasoning, judging, volition*, and *knowledge*, which are some of the most considerable operations of the mind and *modes of thinking*.

3.   But perhaps it may not be an unpardonable digression nor wholly impertinent to our present design, if we reflect here upon *the different state of the mind in thinking*, which those instances of attention, *rêverie*, and dreaming, etc., before mentioned, naturally enough suggest. That there are *ideas*, some or other, always present in the mind of a waking man, everyone's experience convinces him, though the mind employs itself about them with several degrees of attention. Sometimes the mind fixes itself with so much earnestness on the contemplation of some objects that it turns their *ideas* on all sides, remarks their relations and circumstances, and views every part so nicely and with such intention that it shuts out all other thoughts and takes no notice of the ordinary impressions made then on the senses, which at another season would produce very sensible perceptions; at other times, it barely observes the train of ideas that succeed in the understanding, without directing and pursuing any of them; and at other times it lets them pass almost quite unregarded, as faint shadows that make no impression.

4.   This difference of *intention* and *remission* of the mind in thinking, with a great variety of degrees between earnest study and very near minding nothing at all, everyone, I think, has experimented in himself. Trace it a little further, and you find the mind in sleep retired as it were from the senses, and out of the reach of those motions made on the organs of sense, which at other times produce very vivid and sensible *ideas*. I need not, for this, instance in those who sleep out whole stormy nights without hearing the thunder or seeing the lightning or feeling the shaking of the house, which are sensible enough to those who

are waking. But in this retirement of the mind from the senses it often retains a yet more loose and incoherent manner of *thinking* which we call *dreaming*; and last of all, sound sleep closes the scene quite and puts an end to all appearances. This, I think, almost everyone has experience of in himself and his own observation without difficulty leads him thus far. That which I would further conclude from hence is that, since the mind can sensibly put on, at several times, several degrees of *thinking* and be sometimes even in a waking man so remiss as to have thoughts dim and obscure to that degree that they are very little removed from none at all; and at last in the dark retirements of sound sleep, loses the sight perfectly of all *ideas* whatsoever: since, I say, this is evidently so in matter of fact and constant experience, I ask whether it be not probable that *thinking is the action and not the essence of the soul*? since the operations of agents will easily admit of intention and remission; but the essences of things are not conceived capable of any such variation. But this by the by.

Chapter XX

OF MODES OF PLEASURE AND PAIN

1. AMONGST the simple *ideas* which we receive both from *sensation* and *reflection*, *pain* and *pleasure* are two very considerable ones. For as in the body there is sensation barely in itself, or accompanied with *pain* or *pleasure*, so the thought or perception of the mind is simply so, or else accompanied also with *pleasure* or *pain*, delight or trouble, call it how you please. These, like other simple *ideas*, cannot be described, nor their names defined; the way of knowing them is, as of the simple *ideas* of the senses, only by experience. For, to define them by the presence of good or evil is no otherwise to make them known to us than by making us reflect on what we feel in ourselves, upon the several and various operations of good and evil upon our minds, as they are differently applied to or considered by us.

2. Things then are good or evil only in reference to pleasure or pain. That we call *good* which *is apt to cause or increase pleasure, or diminish pain in us, or else to procure or preserve us the possession of any other good or absence of any evil*. And, on the contrary, we name that *evil* which *is apt to produce or increase any pain, or*

diminish any pleasure in us, or else to procure us any evil, or deprive us of any good. By pleasure and pain, I must be understood to mean of body or mind, as they are commonly distinguished, though in truth they be only different constitutions of the mind, sometimes occasioned by disorder in the body, sometimes by thoughts of the mind.

3. *Pleasure* and *pain* and that which causes them, good and evil, are the hinges on which our *passions* turn. And if we reflect on ourselves and observe how these, under various considerations, operate in us, what modifications or tempers of mind, what internal sensations (if I may so call them) they produce in us, we may thence form to ourselves the *ideas* of our *passions*.

4. Thus anyone reflecting upon the thought he has of the delight which any present or absent thing is apt to produce in him has the *idea* we call *love*. For when a man declares in autumn when he is eating them, or in spring when there are none, that he *loves* grapes, it is no more but that the taste of grapes delights him; let an alteration of health or constitution destroy the delight of their taste, and he then can be said to *love* grapes no longer.

5. On the contrary, the thought of the pain which anything present or absent is apt to produce in us is what we call *hatred*. Were it my business here to inquire any further than into the bare *ideas* of our passions as they depend on different modifications of pleasure and pain, I should remark that our *love* and *hatred* of inanimate insensible beings is commonly founded on that pleasure and pain which we receive from their use and application any way to our senses, though with their destruction. But *hatred* or *love*, to beings capable of happiness or misery, is often the uneasiness or delight which we find in ourselves arising from a consideration of their very being or happiness. Thus the being and welfare of a man's children or friends producing constant delight in him, he is said constantly to *love* them. But it suffices to note that our *ideas* of *love* and *hatred* are but the dispositions of the mind in respect of pleasure and pain in general, however caused in us.

6. The uneasiness a man finds in himself upon the absence of anything whose present enjoyment carries the *idea* of delight with it is that we call *desire*; which is greater or less, as that uneasiness is more or less vehement. Where, by the by, it may perhaps be of some use to remark that the chief, if not only, spur to human industry and action is uneasiness. For whatever good is proposed, if its absence carries no displeasure nor pain

with it, if a man be easy and content without it, there is no desire of it nor endeavour after it; there is no more but a bare *velleity*, the term used to signify the lowest degree of desire and that which is next to none at all, when there is so little uneasiness in the absence of anything that it carries a man no further than some faint wishes for it, without any more effectual or vigorous use of the means to attain it. *Desire* also is stopped or abated by the opinion of the impossibility or unattainableness of the good proposed, as far as the uneasiness is cured or allayed by that consideration. This might carry our thoughts further, were it seasonable in this place.

Chapter XXI

OF POWER

1. The mind—being every day informed by the senses of the alteration of those simple *ideas* it observes in things without; and taking notice how one comes to an end, and ceases to be, and another begins to exist which was not before; reflecting also on what passes within itself, and observing a constant change of its *ideas*, sometimes by the impression of outward objects on the senses, and sometimes by the determination of its own choice; and concluding from what it has so constantly observed to have been, that the like changes will for the future be made in the same things, by like agents, and by the like ways—considers in one thing the possibility of having any of its simple *ideas* changed, and in another the possibility of making that change; and so comes by that *idea* which we call *power*. Thus we say fire has a *power* to melt gold, i.e. to destroy the consistency of its insensible parts, and consequently its hardness, and make it fluid; and gold has a *power* to be melted; that the sun has a *power* to blanch wax, and wax a *power* to be blanched by the sun, whereby the yellowness is destroyed, and whiteness made to exist in its room. In which, and the like cases, the *power* we consider is in reference to the change of perceivable *ideas*. For we cannot observe any alteration to be made in, or operation upon anything, but by the observable change of its sensible *ideas*, nor conceive any alteration to be made but by conceiving a change of some of its *ideas*.

2. *Power* thus considered is two-fold, viz. as able to make, or able to receive, any change; the one may be called *active*, and

the other *passive power*. Whether matter be not wholly destitute of *active power*, as its author GOD is truly above all *passive power*, and whether the intermediate state of created spirits be not that alone which is capable of both *active* and *passive* power, may be worth consideration. I shall not now enter into that inquiry, my present business being not to search into the original of power but how we come by the *idea* of it. But since *active powers* make so great a part of our complex *ideas* of natural substances (as we shall see hereafter) and I mention them as such according to common apprehension, yet they being not, perhaps, so truly *active powers* as our hasty thoughts are apt to represent them, I judge it not amiss, by this intimation, to direct our minds to the consideration of GOD and spirits for the clearest *idea* of *active power*.

3. I confess *power includes in it some kind of relation* (a relation to action or change), as indeed which of our *ideas*, of what kind soever, when attentively considered, does not? For our *ideas* of extension, duration, and number, do they not all contain in them a secret relation of the parts? Figure and motion have something relative in them much more visibly; and sensible qualities, as colours and smells, etc., what are they but the *powers* of different bodies in relation to our perception, etc.? And, if considered in the things themselves, do they not depend on the bulk, figure, texture, and motion of the parts? All which include some kind of relation in them. Our *idea* therefore of *power*, I think, may well have a place amongst other simple *ideas* and be considered as one of them, being one of those that make a principal ingredient in our complex *ideas* of substances, as we shall hereafter have occasion to observe.

4. We are abundantly furnished with the *idea* of *passive power* by almost all sorts of sensible things. In most of them we cannot avoid observing their sensible qualities, nay, their very substances, to be in a continual flux; and therefore with reason we look on them as liable still to the same change. Nor have we of *active power* (which is the more proper signification of the word *power*) fewer instances. Since whatever change is observed, the mind must collect a power somewhere able to make that change, as well as a possibility in the thing itself to receive it. But yet, if we will consider it attentively, bodies, by our senses, do not afford us so clear and distinct an *idea* of *active power*, as we have from reflection on the operations of our minds. For all *power* relating to action, and there being but two sorts of action whereof we have any *idea*, viz. thinking and motion, let us consider whence we have the clearest *ideas* of the *powers* which

produce these actions. (1) Of thinking, body affords us no *idea* at all; it is only from reflection that we have that. (2) Neither have we from body any *idea* of the beginning of motion. A body at rest affords us no *idea* of any *active power* to move; and when it is set in motion itself, that motion is rather a passion than an action in it. For, when the ball obeys the stroke of a billiard-stick, it is not any action of the ball, but bare passion; also when by impulse it sets another ball in motion that lay in its way, it only communicates the motion it had received from another, and loses in itself so much as the other received: which gives us but a very obscure *idea* of an *active power* of moving in body, whilst we observe it only to transfer, but not produce, any motion. For it is but a very obscure *idea* of *power* which reaches not the production of the action but the continuation of the passion. For so is motion in a body impelled by another, the continuation of the alteration made in it from rest to motion being little more an action than the continuation of the alteration of its figure by the same blow is an action. The *idea* of the beginning of motion we have only from reflection on what passes in ourselves, where we find by experience that barely by willing it, barely by a thought of the mind, we can move the parts of our bodies which were before at rest. So that it seems to me we have from the observation of the operation of bodies by our senses but a very imperfect obscure *idea* of *active power*, since they afford us not any *idea* in themselves of the *power* to begin any action, either motion or thought. But if, from the impulse bodies are observed to make one upon another, anyone thinks he has a clear *idea* of *power*, it serves as well to my purpose, *sensation* being one of those ways whereby the mind comes by its *ideas*; only I thought it worthwhile to consider here by the way whether the mind doth not receive its *idea* of *active power* clearer from reflection on its own operations than it doth from any external sensation.

5. This, at least, I think evident: that we find in ourselves a *power* to begin or forbear, continue or end several actions of our minds and motions of our bodies, barely by a thought or preference of the mind ordering or, as it were commanding, the doing or not doing such or such a particular action. This *power* which the mind has thus to order the consideration of any *idea*, or the forbearing to consider it, or to prefer the motion of any part of the body to its rest, and *vice versa*, in any particular instance, is that which we call the *will*. The actual exercise of that power, by directing any particular action, or its forbearance, is that which we call *volition* or *willing*. The forbearance of that

action, consequent to such order or command of the mind, is called *voluntary*. And whatsoever action is performed without such a thought of the mind is called *involuntary*. The power of perception is that which we call the *understanding*. Perception, which we make the act of the understanding, is of three sorts: (1) The perception of *ideas* in our minds. (2) The perception of the signification of signs. (3) The perception of the connexion or repugnancy, agreement or disagreement, that there is between any of our *ideas*. All these are attributed to the *understanding* or perceptive power, though it be the two latter only that use allows us to say we understand.

6.   These powers of the mind, viz. of *perceiving* and of *preferring*, are usually called by another name; and the ordinary way of speaking is that the *understanding* and *will* are two *faculties* of the mind: a word proper enough, if it be used, as all words should be, so as not to breed any confusion in men's thoughts, by being supposed (as I suspect it has been) to stand for some real beings in the soul that performed those actions of understanding and volition. For when we say the *will* is the commanding and superior faculty of the soul; that it is or is not free; that it determines the inferior faculties; that it follows the dictates of the *understanding*, etc.; though these and the like expressions, by those that carefully attend to their own *ideas* and conduct their thoughts more by the evidence of things than the sound of words, may be understood in a clear and distinct sense: yet I suspect, I say, that this way of speaking of *faculties* has misled many into a confused notion of so many distinct agents in us, which had their several provinces and authorities and did command, obey, and perform several actions, as so many distinct beings; which has been no small occasion of wrangling, obscurity, and uncertainty in questions relating to them.

7.   Everyone, I think, finds in himself a *power* to begin or forbear, continue or put an end to several actions in himself. From the consideration of the extent of this power of the mind over the actions of the man, which everyone finds in himself, arise the *ideas* of *liberty* and *necessity*.

8.   All the actions that we have any *idea* of, reducing themselves, as has been said, to these two, viz. thinking and motion: so far as a man has a power to think or not to think, to move or not to move, according to the preference or direction of his own mind, so far is a man *free*. Wherever any performance or forbearance are not equally in a man's power, wherever doing or not doing will not equally follow upon the preference of his mind directing

it, there he is not *free*, though perhaps the action may be voluntary. So that the *idea* of *liberty* is the *idea* of a power in any agent to do or forbear any particular action, according to the determination or thought of the mind, whereby either of them is preferred to the other; where either of them is not in the power of the agent to be produced by him according to his *volition*, there he is not at *liberty*: that agent is under *necessity*. So that *liberty* cannot be where there is no thought, no volition, no will; but there may be thought, there may be will, there may be volition, where there is no *liberty*. A little consideration of an obvious instance or two may make this clear.

9. A tennis ball, whether in motion by the stroke of a racket, or lying still at rest, is not by anyone taken to be a *free agent*. If we inquire into the reason, we shall find it is because we conceive not a tennis ball to think, and consequently not to have any volition, or preference of motion to rest, or *vice versa*; and therefore has not *liberty*, is not a free agent; but all its both motion and rest come under our *idea* of *necessary*, and are so called. Likewise, a man falling into the water (a bridge breaking under him) has not herein liberty, is not a free agent. For though he has volition, though he prefers his not falling to falling, yet the forbearance of that motion not being in his power, the stop or cessation of that motion follows not upon his volition; and therefore therein he is not *free*. So a man striking himself or his friend by a convulsive motion of his arm, which it is not in his power by volition or the direction of his mind to stop or forbear, nobody thinks he has in this *liberty*; everyone pities him as acting by necessity and constraint.

10. Again, suppose a man be carried whilst fast asleep into a room where is a person he longs to see and speak with, and be there locked fast in, beyond his power to get out; he awakes and is glad to find himself in so desirable company, which he stays willingly in, i.e. prefers his stay to going away. I ask, is not this stay voluntary? I think nobody will doubt it; and yet being locked fast in, it is evident he is not at liberty not to stay, he has not freedom to be gone. So that *liberty is not an* idea *belonging to volition*, or preferring, but to the person having the power of doing or forbearing to do, according as the mind shall choose or direct. Our *idea* of liberty reaches as far as that power and no further. For wherever restraint comes to check that power, or compulsion takes away that indifference of ability on either side to act or to forbear acting, there *liberty*, and our notion of it, presently ceases.

11. We have instances enough and often more than enough in

our own bodies. A man's heart beats and the blood circulates, which it is not in his power by any thought or volition to stop; and therefore in respect of these motions, where rest depends not on his choice nor would follow the determination of his mind if it should prefer it, he is not a *free agent*. Convulsive motions agitate his legs so that, though he *wills* it never so much, he cannot by any power of his mind stop their motion (as in that odd disease called *chorea Sancti Viti*), but he is perpetually dancing; he is not at liberty in this action but under as much necessity of moving as a stone that falls or a tennis ball struck with a racket. On the other side, a palsy or the stocks hinder his legs from obeying the determination of his mind if it would thereby transfer his body to another place. In all these there is want of *freedom*, though the sitting still even of a paralytic, whilst he prefers it to a removal, is truly voluntary. *Voluntary* then *is not opposed to necessary, but to involuntary*. For a man may prefer what he can do to what he cannot do; the state he is in, to its absence or change, though necessity has made it in itself unalterable.

12. As it is in the motions of the body, so it is in the thoughts of our minds: where anyone is such that we have power to take it up, or lay it by, according to the preference of the mind, there we are *at liberty*. A waking man, being under the necessity of having some *ideas* constantly in his mind, is not at *liberty* to think or not to think, no more than he is at *liberty* whether his body shall touch any other or no; but whether he will remove his contemplation from one *idea* to another is many times in his choice, and then he is, in respect of his *ideas*, as much at *liberty* as he is in respect of bodies he rests on; he can at pleasure remove himself from one to another. But yet some *ideas* to the mind, like some motions to the body, are such as in certain circumstances it cannot avoid, nor obtain their absence by the utmost effort it can use. A man on the rack is not at *liberty* to lay by the *idea* of pain, and divert himself with other contemplations; and sometimes a boisterous passion hurries our thoughts, as a hurricane does our bodies, without leaving us the liberty of thinking on other things, which we would rather choose. But as soon as the mind regains the power to stop or continue, begin or forbear any of these motions of the body without, or thoughts within, according as it thinks fit to prefer either to the other, we then consider the man as a *free agent* again.

13. Wherever thought is wholly wanting or the power to act or forbear according to the direction of thought, there *necessity* takes place. This, in an agent capable of volition when the

beginning or continuation of any action is contrary to that preference of his mind, is called *compulsion*; when the hindering or stopping any action is contrary to his volition, it is called *restraint*. Agents that have no thought, no volition at all, are in everything *necessary* agents.

14. If this be so (as I imagine it is), I leave it to be considered whether it may not help to put an end to that long agitated and, I think, unreasonable because unintelligible, question, viz. *whether man's will be free or no*. For if I mistake not, it follows from what I have said that the question itself is altogether improper; and it is as insignificant to ask whether man's *will* be free, as to ask whether his sleep be swift, or his virtue square: *liberty* being as little applicable to the *will*, as swiftness of motion is to sleep, or squareness to virtue. Everyone would laugh at the absurdity of such a question as either of these, because it is obvious that the modifications of motion belong not to sleep, nor the difference of figure to virtue; and when anyone well considers it, I think he will as plainly perceive that *liberty*, which is but a power, belongs only to agents and cannot be an attribute or modification of the *will*, which is also but a power.

15. Such is the difficulty of explaining and giving clear notions of internal actions by sounds that I must here warn my reader that *ordering, directing, choosing, preferring*, etc., which I have made use of, will not distinctly enough express *volition*, unless he will reflect on what he himself does when he *wills*. For example, *preferring*, which seems perhaps best to express the act of *volition*, does it not precisely. For though a man would prefer flying to walking, yet who can say he ever *wills* it? *Volition*, it is plain, is an act of the mind knowingly exerting that dominion it takes itself to have over any part of the man, by employing it in, or withholding it from, any particular action. And what is the *will* but the faculty to do this? And is that faculty anything more in effect than a power, the power of the mind to determine its thought to the producing, continuing, or stopping any action as far as it depends on us? For can it be denied that whatever agent has a power to think on its own actions, and to prefer their doing or omission either to other, has that faculty called *will*? *Will*, then, is nothing but such a power. *Liberty*, on the other side, is the power a man has to do or forbear doing any particular action according as its doing or forbearance has the actual preference in the mind; which is the same thing as to say according as he himself *wills* it.

16. It is plain then that the *will* is nothing but one power or ability, and *freedom* another power or ability, so that to ask

whether the *will has freedom* is to ask whether one power has another power, one ability another ability: a question at first sight too grossly absurd to make a dispute, or need an answer. For who is it that sees not that *powers* belong only to *agents* and *are attributes only of substances, and not of powers* themselves? So that this way of putting the question (viz. whether the *will be free*) is in effect to ask whether the *will* be a substance, an agent, or at least to suppose it, since freedom can properly be attributed to nothing else. If freedom can with any propriety of speech be applied to power, it may be attributed to the power that is in a man to produce or forbear producing motion in parts of his body by choice or preference; which is that which denominates him free and is freedom itself. But if anyone should ask whether freedom were free, he would be suspected not to understand well what he said; and he would be thought to deserve *Midas's* ears, who, knowing that rich was a denomination from the possession of riches, should demand whether riches themselves were rich.

17. However, the *name faculty*, which men have given to this power called the *will*, and whereby they have been led into a way of talking of the *will* as acting, may, by an appropriation that disguises its true sense, serve a little to palliate the absurdity; yet the *will*, in truth, signifies nothing but a power or ability to prefer or choose; and when the *will*, under the name of a *faculty*, is considered, as it is, barely as an ability to do something, the absurdity in saying it is free or not free will easily discover itself. For if it be reasonable to suppose and talk of *faculties* as distinct beings that can act (as we do, when we say the *will* orders, and the *will* is free), it is fit that we should make a speaking *faculty*, and a walking *faculty*, and a dancing *faculty*, by which those actions are produced, which are but several modes of motion, as well as we make the *will* and *understanding* to be *faculties* by which the actions of choosing and perceiving are produced, which are but several modes of thinking. And we may as properly say that it is the singing *faculty* sings, and the dancing *faculty* dances, as that the *will* chooses, or that the understanding conceives; or, as is usual, that the *will* directs the understanding, or the understanding obeys or obeys not the *will*: it being altogether as proper and intelligible to say that the power of speaking directs the power of singing, or the power of singing obeys or disobeys the power of speaking.

18. This way of talking, nevertheless, has prevailed and, as I guess, produced great confusion. For these being all different powers in the mind or in the man to do several actions, he

exerts them as he thinks fit. But the power to do one action is not operated on by the power of doing another action. For the power of thinking operates not on the power of choosing, nor the power of choosing on the power of thinking, no more than the power of dancing operates on the power of singing, or the power of singing on the power of dancing, as anyone who reflects on it will easily perceive. And yet this is it which we say when we thus speak, that *the will operates on the understanding, or the understanding on the will.*

19. I grant that this or that actual thought may be the occasion of volition, or exercising the power a man has to choose, or the actual choice of the mind, the cause of actual thinking on this or that thing, as the actual singing of such a tune may be the occasion of dancing such a dance, and the actual dancing of such a dance the occasion of singing such a tune. But in all these it is not one *power* that operates on another, but it is the mind that operates and exerts these powers; it is the man that does the action, it is the agent that has power, or is able to do. For *powers* are relations, not agents; and *that which has the power or not the power to operate is that alone which is or is not free,* and not the power itself. For freedom, or not freedom, can belong to nothing but what has or has not a power to act.

20. The attributing to *faculties* that which belonged not to them has given occasion to this way of talking; but the introducing into discourses concerning the mind, with the name of *faculties*, a notion of their operating has, I suppose, as little advanced our knowledge in that part of ourselves as the great use and mention of the like invention of *faculties* in the operations of the body has helped us in the knowledge of physic. Not that I deny there are *faculties*, both in the body and mind: they both of them have their *powers* of operating, else neither the one nor the other could operate. For nothing can operate that is not able to operate; and that is not able to operate that has no *power* to operate. Nor do I deny that those words and the like are to have their place in the common use of languages that have made them current. It looks like too much affectation wholly to lay them by; and philosophy itself, though it likes not a gaudy dress, yet when it appears in public must have so much complacency as to be clothed in the ordinary fashion and language of the country, so far as it can consist with truth and perspicuity. But the fault has been that faculties have been spoken of and represented as so many distinct agents. For it being asked, what it was that digested the meat in our stomachs, it was a ready and very satisfactory answer to say that it was the *digestive faculty*.

What was it that made anything come out of the body? The *expulsive faculty*. What moved? The *motive faculty*. And so in the mind, the *intellectual faculty*, or the understanding, understood; and the *elective faculty*, or the will, willed or commanded; which is, in short, to say that the ability to digest digested, and the ability to move moved, and the ability to understand understood. For *faculty*, *ability*, and *power*, I think, are but different names of the same things; which ways of speaking, when put into more intelligible words, will, I think, amount to thus much: that digestion is performed by something that is able to digest, motion by something able to move, and understanding by something able to understand. And, in truth, it would be very strange if it should be otherwise, as strange as it would be for a man to be free without being able to be free.

21.   To return, then, to the inquiry about liberty, I think *the question is not proper, whether the will be free, but whether a man be free*. Thus, I think,

(1) That so far as anyone can, by the direction or choice of his mind, preferring the existence of any action to the non-existence of that action, and *vice versa*, make it to exist or not exist, so far he is *free*. For if I can, by a thought directing the motion of my finger, make it move when it was at rest, or *vice versa*, it is evident that in respect of that I am free; and if I can, by a like thought of my mind, preferring one to the other, produce either words or silence, I am at liberty to speak or hold my peace; and *as far as this power reaches, of acting or not acting, by the determination of his own thought preferring either, so far is a man free*. For how can we think anyone freer than to have the power to do what he will? And so far as anyone can, by preferring any action to its not being, or rest to any action, produce that action or rest, so far can he do what he will. For such a preferring of action to its absence is the willing of it; and we can scarce tell how to imagine any *being* freer than to be able to do what he *wills*. So that in respect of actions within the reach of such a power in him, a man seems as free as it is possible for freedom to make him.

22.   But the inquisitive mind of man, willing to shift off from himself as far as he can all thoughts of guilt, though it be by putting himself into a worse state than that of fatal necessity, is not content with this: freedom, unless it reaches further than this will not serve the turn; and it passes for a good plea that a man is not free at all, if he be not as free to will as he is to act what he wills. Concerning a man's liberty, there yet, therefore, is raised this further question, *whether a man be free to will,*

which I think is what is meant when it is disputed whether the *will* be free. And as to that I imagine:

23. (2) That *willing*, or *volition*, being an action, and freedom consisting in a power of acting or not acting, *a man in respect of willing or the act of volition, when any action in his power is once proposed to his thoughts, as presently to be done, cannot be free*. The reason whereof is very manifest: for, it being un-avoidable that the action depending on his *will* should exist or not exist, and its existence or not-existence following perfectly the determination and preference of his will, he cannot avoid willing the existence or not-existence of that action; it is absolutely necessary that he *will* the one or the other, i.e., *prefer* the one to the other, since one of them must necessarily follow; and that which does follow, follows by the choice and determination of his mind, that is, by his *willing it*: for if he did not *will* it, it would not be. So that in respect of the act of *willing*, a man in such case is not free: liberty consisting in a power to act or not to act, which in regard of volition a man, upon such a proposal, has not. For it is unavoidably necessary to prefer the doing or forbearance of an action in a man's power, which is once so proposed to his thoughts: a man must necesarily *will* the one or the other of them, upon which preference or volition the action or its forbearance certainly follows and is truly voluntary; but the act of volition, or preferring one of the two, being that which he cannot avoid, a man, in respect of that act of *willing*, is under a necessity, and so cannot be free, unless necessity and freedom can consist together and a man can be free and bound at once.

24. This then is evident, that in all proposals of present action *a man is not at liberty to will or not to will because he cannot forbear willing*: liberty consisting in a power to act or to forbear acting, and in that only. For a man that sits still is said yet to be at liberty, because he can walk if he *wills* it. But if a man sitting still has not a power to remove himself, he is not at liberty; so likewise a man falling down a precipice, though in motion, is not at liberty, because he cannot stop that motion if he would. This being so, it is plain that a man that is walking, to whom it is proposed to give off walking, is not at liberty whether he *will* determine himself to walk or give off walking, or no: he must necessarily prefer one or the other of them: walking or not walking; and so it is in regard of all other actions in our power so proposed, which are the far greater number. For considering the vast number of voluntary actions that succeed one another every moment that we are awake, in the course of our lives, there

are but few of them that are thought on or proposed to the *will*, until the time they are to be done. And in all such actions, as I have shown, the mind, in respect of *willing*, has not a power to act or not to act, wherein consists liberty; the mind in that case has not a power to forbear *willing*: it cannot avoid some determination concerning them, let the consideration be as short, the thought as quick, as it will: it either leaves the man in the state he was before thinking or changes it, continues the action or puts an end to it. Whereby it is manifest that it orders and directs one, in preference to or with neglect of the other, and thereby either the continuation or change becomes unavoidably voluntary.

25. Since then it is plain that in most cases a man is not at liberty whether he will *will* or no, the next thing demanded is *whether a man be at liberty to will which of the two he pleases, motion or rest*. This question carries the absurdity of it so manifestly in itself that one might thereby sufficiently be convinced that liberty concerns not the will. For to ask whether a man be at liberty to will either motion or rest, speaking or silence, which he pleases, is to ask whether a man can *will* what he *wills*, or be pleased with what he is pleased with. A question which, I think, needs no answer; and they who can make a question of it must suppose one will to determine the acts of another, and another to determine that and so on *in infinitum*.

26. To avoid these and the like absurdities, nothing can be of greater use than to establish in our minds determined *ideas* of the things under consideration. If the *ideas* of liberty and volition were well fixed in our understandings and carried along with us in our minds, as they ought, through all the questions that are raised about them, I suppose a great part of the difficulties that perplex men's thoughts and entangle their understandings would be much easier resolved; and we should perceive where the confused signification of terms, or where the nature of the thing caused the obscurity.

27. *First* then, it is carefully to be remembered that *freedom consists in the dependence of the existence or not-existence of any action upon our volition of it, and not in the dependence of any action or its contrary on our preference*. A man standing on a cliff is at liberty to leap twenty yards downwards into the sea, not because he has a power to do the contrary action, which is to leap twenty yards upwards, for that he cannot do; but he is therefore free because he has a power to leap or not to leap. But if a greater force than his either holds him fast or tumbles him down, he is no longer free in that case: because the doing

or forbearance of that particular action is no longer in his power. He that is a close prisoner in a room twenty-foot-square, being at the north side of his chamber, is at liberty to walk twenty feet southward, because he can walk or not walk it; but is not, at the same time, at liberty to do the contrary, i.e. to walk twenty feet northward.

In this, then, consists freedom, viz. in our being able to act or not to act according as we shall choose or *will*.

28. *Secondly*, we must remember that *volition* or *willing* is an act of the mind directing its thought to the production of any action, and thereby exerting its power to produce it. To avoid multiplying of words, I would crave leave here, under the word *action*, to comprehend the forbearance too of any action proposed: *sitting still*, or *holding one's peace*, when *walking* or *speaking* are proposed, though mere forbearances, requiring as much the determination of the *will* and being often as weighty in their consequences as the contrary actions, may, on that consideration, well enough pass for actions too. But this I say that I may not be mistaken if for brevity's sake I speak thus.

29. *Thirdly*, the *will* being nothing but a power in the mind to direct the operative faculties of a man to motion or rest, as far as they depend on such direction: to the question, What is it determines the will? the true and proper answer is, the mind. For that which determines the general power of directing, to this or that particular direction, is nothing but the agent itself exercising the power it has that particular way. If this answer satisfies not, it is plain the meaning of the question, *What determines the will?* is this: What moves the mind, in every particular instance, to determine its general power of directing to this or that particular motion or rest? And to this I answer: The motive for continuing in the same state or action is only the present satisfaction in it; the motive to change is always some *uneasiness*: nothing setting us upon the change of state, or upon any new action, but some *uneasiness*. This is the great motive that works on the mind to put it upon action, which for shortness's sake we will call *determining of the will*, which I shall more at large explain.

30. But in the way to it, it will be necessary to premise that, though I have above endeavoured to express the act of *volition*, by *choosing*, *preferring*, and the like terms, that signify *desire* as well as *volition*, for want of other words to mark that act of the mind whose proper name is *willing* or *volition*, yet it being a very simple act, whosoever desires to understand what it is will better find it by reflecting on his own mind and observing what it does

when it *wills*, than by any variety of articulate sounds whatsoever. This caution of being careful not to be misled by expressions that do not enough keep up the difference between the *will* and several acts of the mind that are quite distinct from it I think the more necessary, because I find the will often confounded with several of the affections, especially *desire*, and one put for the other, and that by men who would not willingly be thought not to have had very distinct notions of things and not to have writ very clearly about them. This I imagine has been no small occasion of obscurity and mistake in this matter and therefore is, as much as may be, to be avoided. For he that shall turn his thoughts inwards upon what passes in his mind when he *wills* shall see that the *will* or power of *volition* is conversant about nothing but that particular determination of the mind whereby, barely by a thought, the mind endeavours to give rise, continuation, or stop to any action which it takes to be in its power. This, well considered, plainly shows that the *will* is perfectly distinguished from *desire*; which, in the very same action, may have a quite contrary tendency from that which our *will* sets us upon. A man, whom I cannot deny, may oblige me to use persuasions to another, which, at the same time I am speaking, I may wish may not prevail on him. In this case, it is plain the *will* and *desire* run counter. I will the action that tends one way, whilst my desire tends another, and that the direct contrary. A man who, by a violent fit of the gout in his limbs, finds a doziness in his head or a want of appetite in his stomach removed, desires to be eased too of the pain of his feet or hands (for wherever there is pain there is a desire to be rid of it) though yet, whilst he apprehends that the removal of the pain may translate the noxious humour to a more vital part, his *will* is never determined to any one action that may serve to remove this pain. Whence it is evident that *desiring* and *willing* are two distinct acts of the mind, and consequently that the *will*, which is but the power of *volition*, is much more distinct from *desire*.

31.   To return, then, to the inquiry, *What is it that determines the will in regard to our actions?* And that, upon second thoughts, I am apt to imagine is not, as is generally supposed, the greater good in view, but some (and for the most part the most pressing) *uneasiness* a man is at present under. This is that which successively determines the *will* and sets us upon those actions we perform. This *uneasiness* we may call, as it is, *desire*; which is an *uneasiness* of the mind for want of some absent good. All pain of the body, of what sort soever, and disquiet of the mind, is *uneasiness*; and with this is always joined

desire, equal to the pain or *uneasiness* felt, and is scarce distinguishable from it. For *desire* being nothing but an *uneasiness* in the want of an absent good, in reference to any pain felt, ease is that absent good; and till that ease be attained, we may call it *desire*, nobody feeling pain that he wishes not to be eased of, with a desire equal to that pain, and inseparable from it. Besides this desire of ease from pain, there is another of absent positive good; and here also the desire and *uneasiness* are equal. As much as we desire any absent good, so much are we in pain for it. But here all absent good does not, according to the greatness it has, or is acknowledged to have, cause pain equal to that greatness, as all pain causes desire equal to itself: because the absence of good is not always a pain, as the presence of pain is. And therefore absent good may be looked on and considered without *desire*. But so much as there is anywhere of *desire*, so much there is of *uneasiness*.

32.   That *desire* is a state of *uneasiness* everyone who reflects on himself will quickly find. Who is there that has not felt in *desire* what the wise man says of hope (which is not much different from it), that it being *deferred makes the heart sick*, and that still proportionable to the greatness of the *desire* which sometimes raises the *uneasiness* to that pitch that it makes people cry out, *give me children*, give me the thing desired, *or I die*? Life itself, and all its enjoyments, is a burden cannot be borne under the lasting and unremoved pressure of such an *uneasiness*.

33.   Good and evil, present and absent, it is true, work upon the mind; but that which immediately determines the *will*, from time to time, to every voluntary action, is the *uneasiness* of *desire*, fixed on some absent good: either negative, as indolence to one in pain; or positive, as enjoyment of pleasure. That it is this *uneasiness* that determines the *will* to the successive voluntary actions, whereof the greatest part of our lives is made up, and by which we are conducted through different courses to different ends, I shall endeavour to show, both from experience and the reason of the thing.

34.   When a man is perfectly content with the state he is in, which is when he is perfectly without any *uneasiness*, what industry, what action, what *will* is there left but to continue in it? Of this every man's observation will satisfy him. And thus we see our all-wise Maker, suitable to our constitution and frame, and knowing what it is that determines the *will*, has put into man the *uneasiness* of hunger and thirst, and other natural desires, that return at their seasons, to move and determine their

wills for the preservation of themselves, and the continuation of their species. For I think we may conclude that, if the bare contemplation of these good ends to which we are carried by these several *uneasinesses* had been sufficient to determine the *will* and set us on work, we should have had none of these natural pains, and perhaps in this world little or no pain at all. *It is better to marry than to burn*, says St. *Paul*, where we may see what it is that chiefly drives men into the enjoyments of a conjugal life. A little burning felt pushes us more powerfully than greater pleasures in prospect draw or allure.

42. *Happiness*, then, in its full extent, is the utmost pleasure we are capable of, and *misery* the utmost pain; and the lowest degree of what can be called *happiness* is so much ease from all pain, and so much present pleasure, as without which anyone cannot be content. Now, because pleasure and pain are produced in us by the operation of certain objects either on our minds or our bodies and in different degrees, therefore, what has an aptness to produce pleasure in us is that we call *good*, and what is apt to produce pain in us we call *evil*, for no other reason but for its aptness to produce pleasure and pain in us, wherein consists our *happiness* and *misery*. Further, though what is apt to produce any degree of pleasure be in itself *good*, and what is apt to produce any degree of pain be *evil*, yet it often happens that we do not call it so when it comes in competition with a greater of its sort, because, when they come in competition, the degrees also of pleasure and pain have justly a preference. So that if we will rightly estimate what we call *good* and *evil*, we shall find it lies much in comparison: for the cause of every less degree of pain, as well as every greater degree of pleasure, has the nature of *good*, and *vice versa*.

51. As therefore the highest perfection of intellectual nature lies in a careful and constant pursuit of true and solid happiness, so the care of ourselves, that we mistake not imaginary for real happiness, is the necessary foundation of our *liberty*. The stronger ties we have to an unalterable pursuit of happiness in general, which is our greatest good and which, as such, our desires always follow, the more are we free from any necessary determination of our *will* to any particular action, and from a necessary compliance with our desire, set upon any particular, and then appearing preferable good, till we have duly examined whether it has a tendency to, or be inconsonant with, our real happiness; and therefore, till we are as much informed upon this inquiry as the weight of the matter and the nature of the case demands, we are, by the necessity of preferring and pursu-

ing true happiness as our greatest good, obliged to suspend the satisfaction of our desire in particular cases.

52. This is the hinge on which turns the *liberty* of intellectual beings, in their constant endeavours after and a steady prosecution of true felicity, that they can *suspend* this prosecution in particular cases, till they have looked before them and informed themselves whether that particular thing which is then proposed or desired lies in the way to their main end, and make a real part of that which is their greatest good; for the inclination and tendency of their nature to happiness is an obligation and motive to them to take care not to mistake or miss it, and so necessarily puts them upon caution, deliberation, and wariness in the direction of their particular actions, which are the means to obtain it. Whatever necessity determines to the pursuit of real bliss, the same necessity, with the same force, establishes *suspense*, *deliberation*, and scrutiny of each successive desire, whether the satisfaction of it does not interfere with our true happiness and mislead us from it. This, as seems to me, is the great privilege of finite intellectual beings; and I desire it may be well considered whether the great inlet and exercise of all the *liberty* men have, are capable of, or can be useful to them, and that whereon depends the turn of their actions, does not lie in this: that they can *suspend* their desires and stop them from determining their *wills* to any action, till they have duly and fairly *examined* the good and evil of it, as far forth as the weight of the thing requires. This we are able to do; and when we have done it, we have done our duty, and all that is in our power, and indeed all that needs. For, since the *will* supposes knowledge to guide its choice, all that we can do is to hold our *wills* undetermined, till we have *examined* the good and evil of what we desire. What follows after that follows in a chain of consequences, linked one to another, all depending on the last determination of the judgment, which, whether it shall be upon a hasty and precipitate view, or upon a due and mature *examination*, is in our power: experience showing us that in most cases we are able to suspend the present satisfaction of any desire.

53. But if any extreme disturbance (as sometimes it happens) possesses our whole mind, as when the pain of the rack, an impetuous *uneasiness*, as of love, anger, or any other violent passion, running away with us, allows us not the liberty of thought, and we are not masters enough of our own minds to consider thoroughly and examine fairly, God, who knows our frailty, pities our weakness, and requires of us no more than we are able to do, and sees what was and what was not in our power,

will judge as a kind and merciful father. But the forbearance of a too hasty compliance with our desires, the moderation and restraint of our passions, so that our understandings may be *free* to examine, and reason unbiased give its judgment, being that whereon a right direction of our conduct to true happiness depends: it is in this we should employ our chief care and endeavours. In this we should take pains to suit the relish of our minds to the true intrinsic good or ill that is in things, and not permit an allowed or supposed possible great and weighty good to slip out of our thoughts, without leaving any relish, any desire of itself there, till, by a due consideration of its true worth, we have formed appetites in our minds suitable to it and made ourselves uneasy in the want of it, or in the fear of losing it. And how much this is in everyone's power, by making resolutions to himself such as he may keep, is easy for everyone to try. Nor let anyone say he cannot govern his passions, nor hinder them from breaking out, and carrying him into action; for what he can do before a prince or a great man, he can do alone or in the presence of God, if he will.

56.   These things duly weighed, will give us, as I think, a clear view into the state of human liberty. Liberty, it is plain, consists in a power to do, or not to do; to do, or forbear doing, as we *will*. This cannot be denied. But this seeming to comprehend only the actions of a man consecutive to volition, it is further inquired whether he be at liberty to *will* or no. And to this it has been answered that, in most cases, a man is not at liberty to forbear the act of volition: he must exert an act of his *will*, whereby the action proposed is made to exist or not to exist. But yet there is a case wherein a man is at liberty in respect of *willing*, and that is the choosing of a remote good as an end to be pursued. Here a man may suspend the act of his choice from being determined for or against the thing proposed, till he has examined whether it be really of a nature, in itself and consequences, to make him happy or no. For when he has once chosen it, and thereby it is become a part of his happiness, it raises desire, and that proportionably gives him uneasiness which determines his *will* and sets him at work in pursuit of his choice on all occasions that offer. And here we may see how it comes to pass that a man may justly incur punishment, though it be certain that in all the particular actions that he *wills*, he does and necessarily does will that which he then judges to be good. For though his *will* be always determined by that which is judged good by his understanding, yet it excuses him not: because, by a too hasty choice of his own making, he has

imposed on himself wrong measures of good and evil, which, however false and fallacious, have the same influence on all his future conduct as if they were true and right. He has vitiated his own palate and must be answerable to himself for the sickness and death that follows from it. The eternal law and nature of things must not be altered to comply with his ill-ordered choice. If the neglect or abuse of the liberty he had to examine what would really and truly make for his happiness misleads him, the miscarriages that follow on it must be imputed to his own election. He had a power to suspend his determination; it was given him that he might examine and take care of his own happiness and look that he were not deceived. And he could never judge that it was better to be deceived than not, in a matter of so great and near concernment.

What has been said may also discover to us the reason why men in this world prefer different things and pursue happiness by contrary courses. But yet, since men are always constant and in earnest in matters of happiness and misery, the question still remains, *how men come often to prefer the worse to the better*, and to choose that, which, by their own confession, has made them miserable.

69. The last inquiry, therefore, concerning this matter is whether it be in a man's power to change the pleasantness and unpleasantness that accompanies any sort of action; and, to that, it is plain in many cases he can. Men may and should correct their palates and give a relish to what either has, or they suppose has, none. The relish of the mind is as various as that of the body, and like that too may be altered; and it is a mistake to think that men cannot change the displeasingness or indifference that is in actions into pleasure and desire, if they will do but what is in their power. A due consideration will do it in some cases; and practice, application, and custom in most. Bread or tobacco may be neglected where they are shown to be useful to health, because of an indifference or disrelish to them; reason and consideration at first recommends and begins their trial, and use finds or custom makes them pleasant. That this is so in virtue, too, is very certain. Actions are pleasing or displeasing, either in themselves, or considered as a means to a greater and more desirable end. The eating of a well-seasoned dish, suited to a man's palate, may move the mind by the delight itself that accompanies the eating, without reference to any other end; to which the consideration of the pleasure there is in health and strength (to which that meat is subservient) may add a new gusto, able to make us swallow an ill-relished potion. In

the latter of these, any action is rendered more or less pleasing only by the contemplation of the end and the being more or less persuaded of its tendency to it or necessary connexion with it; but the pleasure of the action itself is best acquired or increased by use and practice. Trials often reconcile us to that which at a distance we looked on with aversion, and by repetitions wear us into a liking of what possibly, in the first essay, displeased us. Habits have powerful charms and put so strong attractions of easiness and pleasure into what we accustom ourselves to, that we cannot forbear to do, or at least be easy in the omission of, actions which habitual practice has suited and thereby recommends to us. Though this be very visible and everyone's experience shows him he can do, yet it is a part, in the conduct of men towards their happiness, neglected to a degree that it will be possibly entertained as a paradox, if it be said that men can make things or actions more or less pleasing to themselves, and thereby remedy that to which one may justly impute a great deal of their wandering. Fashion and the common opinion having settled wrong notions, and education and custom ill habits, the just values of things are misplaced and the palates of men corrupted. Pains should be taken to rectify these; and contrary habits change our pleasures and give a relish to that which is necessary or conducive to our happiness. This everyone must confess he can do; and when happiness is lost and misery overtakes him, he will confess he did amiss in neglecting it and condemn himself for it; and I ask everyone whether he has not often done so?

70.   I shall not now enlarge any further on the *wrong judgments* and neglect of what is in their power, whereby men mislead themselves. This would make a volume and is not my business. But whatever false notions or shameful neglect of what is in their power may put men out of their way to happiness and distract them, as we see, into so different courses of life, this yet is certain: that morality, established upon its true foundations, cannot but determine the choice in anyone that will but consider; and he that will not be so far a rational creature as to reflect seriously upon infinite happiness and misery must needs condemn himself as not making that use of his understanding he should. The rewards and punishments of another life, which the Almighty has established as the enforcements of his law, are of weight enough to determine the choice against whatever pleasure or pain this life can show, when the eternal state is considered but in its bare possibility, which nobody can make any doubt of. He that will allow exquisite and endless happiness

to be but the possible consequence of a good life here, and the contrary state, the possible reward of a bad one, must own himself to judge very much amiss if he does not conclude that a virtuous life, with the certain expectation of everlasting bliss which may come, is to be preferred to a vicious one with the fear of that dreadful state of misery which, it is very possible, may overtake the guilty, or at best the terrible uncertain hope of annihilation. This is evidently so, though the virtuous life here had nothing but pain, and the vicious, continual pleasure: which yet is, for the most part, quite otherwise, and wicked men have not much the odds to brag of, even in their present possession; nay, all things rightly considered have, I think, even the worst part here. But when infinite happiness is put in one scale against infinite misery in the other; if the worst that comes to the pious man, if he mistakes, be the best that the wicked can attain to; if he be in the right, who can without madness run the venture? Who in his wits would choose to come within a possibility of infinite misery, which if he miss, there is yet nothing to be got by that hazard? Whereas on the other side, the sober man ventures nothing against infinite happiness to be got, if his expectation comes to pass. If the good man be in the right, he is eternally happy; if he mistakes, he is not miserable, he feels nothing. On the other side, if the wicked be in the right, he is not happy; if he mistakes, he is infinitely miserable. Must it not be a most manifest wrong judgment that does not presently see to which side, in this case, the preference is to be given? I have forborne to mention anything of the certainty or probability of a future state, designing here to show the *wrong judgment* that anyone must allow he makes upon his own principles, laid how he pleases, who prefers the short pleasures of a vicious life upon any consideration, whilst he knows and cannot but be certain that a future life is at least possible.

Chapter XXII

OF MIXED MODES

1. HAVING treated of *simple modes* in the foregoing chapters and given several instances of some of the most considerable of them, to show what they are and how we come by them, we are now in the next place to consider those we call *mixed modes*; such are the complex *ideas* we mark by the names *obligation, drunkenness,* a *lie,* etc.; which consisting of several combinations of simple

ideas of different kinds, I have called *mixed modes*, to distinguish them from the more simple modes, which consist only of simple *ideas* of the same kind. These mixed modes, being also such combinations of simple *ideas* as are not looked upon to be characteristical marks of any real beings that have a steady existence, but scattered and independent *ideas* put together by the mind, are thereby distinguished from the complex *ideas* of substances.

2. That the mind, in respect of its simple *ideas*, is wholly passive and receives them all from the existence and operations of things, such as sensation or reflection offers them, without being able to make any one *idea*, experience shows us. But if we attentively consider these *ideas* I call *mixed modes* we are now speaking of, we shall find their original quite different. *The mind* often *exercises an active power in making these* several *combinations*; for, it being once furnished with simple *ideas*, it can put them together in several compositions and so make variety of complex *ideas* without examining whether they exist so together in nature. And hence I think it is that these *ideas* are called *notions*: as if they had their original, and constant existence more in the thoughts of men than in the reality of things; and to form such *ideas*, it sufficed that the mind put the parts of them together, and that they were consistent in the understanding, without considering whether they had any real being, though I do not deny but several of them might be taken from observation and the existence of several simple *ideas* so combined, as they are put together in the understanding. For the man who first framed the *idea* of *hypocrisy* might have either taken it at first from the observation of one who made show of good qualities which he had not, or else have framed that *idea* in his mind without having any such pattern to fashion it by. For it is evident that, in the beginning of languages and societies of men, several of those complex *ideas*, which were consequent to the constitutions established amongst them, must needs have been in the minds of men before they existed anywhere else, and that many names that stood for such complex *ideas* were in use, and so those *ideas* framed, before the combinations they stood for ever existed.

3. Indeed, now that languages are made and abound with words standing for such combinations, *an usual way of getting these complex* ideas *is by the explication of those terms that stand for them*. For, consisting of a company of simple *ideas* combined, they may, by words standing for those simple *ideas*, be represented to the mind of one who understands those words,

though that complex combination of simple *ideas* were never offered to his mind by the real existence of things. Thus a man may come to have the *idea* of *sacrilege* or *murder*, by enumerating to him the simple *ideas* which these words stand for, without ever seeing either of them committed.

4. Every *mixed mode* consisting of many distinct simple *ideas*, it seems reasonable to inquire *whence it has its unity*, and how such a precise multitude comes to make but one *idea*, since that combination does not always exist together in nature. To which I answer it is plain it has its unity from an act of the mind combining those several simple *ideas* together, and considering them as one complex one, consisting of those parts; and the mark of this union, or that which is looked on generally to complete it, is one name given to that combination. For it is by their names that men commonly regulate their account of their distinct species of mixed modes, seldom allowing or considering any number of simple *ideas* to make one complex one, but such collections as there be names for. Thus, though the killing of an old man be as fit in nature to be united into one complex *idea* as the killing a man's father, yet there being no name standing precisely for the one as there is the name of *parricide* to mark the other, it is not taken for a particular complex *idea* nor a distinct species of actions from that of killing a young man, or any other man.

5. If we should inquire a little further to see *what* it is that *occasions men to make several combinations of simple* ideas into distinct and, as it were, settled *modes*, and neglect others, which in the nature of things themselves have as much an aptness to be combined and make distinct *ideas*, we shall find the reason of it to be the end of language; which being to mark or communicate men's thoughts to one another with all the dispatch that may be, they usually make such collections of *ideas* into complex modes and affix names to them, as they have frequent use of in their way of living and conversation, leaving others, which they have but seldom an occasion to mention, loose and without names that tie them together: they rather choosing to enumerate (when they have need) such *ideas* as make them up by the particular names that stand for them, than to trouble their memories by multiplying of complex *ideas* with names to them, which they shall seldom or never have any occasion to make use of.

6. This shows us *how it comes to pass that there are in every language many particular words which cannot be rendered by any one single word of another*. For the several fashions,

customs, and manners of one nation making several combinations of *ideas* familiar and necessary in one, which another people have had never any occasion to make, or perhaps so much as take notice of, names come of course to be annexed to them, to avoid long periphrases in things of daily conversation, and so they become so many distinct complex *ideas* in their minds. Thus ὀστρακισμός amongst the *Greeks* and *proscriptio* amongst the *Romans* were words which other languages had no names that exactly answered, because they stood for complex *ideas* which were not in the minds of the men of other nations. Where there was no such custom, there was no notion of any such actions, no use of such combinations of *ideas* as were united and, as it were, tied together by those terms: and therefore in other countries there were no names for them.

7.   Hence also we may see the reason *why languages constantly change*, take up new and lay by old terms. Because change of customs and opinions bringing with it new combinations of *ideas*, which it is necessary frequently to think on and talk about, new names, to avoid long descriptions, are annexed to them; and so they become new species of complex modes. What a number of different *ideas* are by this means wrapped up in one short sound and how much of our time and breath is thereby saved, anyone will see who will but take the pains to enumerate all the *ideas* that either *reprieve* or *appeal* stand for, and instead of either of those names, use a periphrasis to make anyone understand their meaning.

8.   Though I shall have occasion to consider this more at large, when I come to treat of words and their use, yet I could not avoid to take thus much notice here of the names of *mixed modes* which, being fleeting and transient combinations of simple *ideas*, which have but a short existence anywhere but in the minds of men, and there too have no longer any existence than whilst they are thought on, *have not so much anywhere the appearance of a constant and lasting existence as in their names*; which are therefore, in these sort of *ideas*, very apt to be taken for the *ideas* themselves. For if we should inquire where the *idea* of a *triumph* or *apotheosis* exists, it is evident they could neither of them exist altogether anywhere in the things themselves, being actions that required time to their performance, and so could never all exist together; and as to the minds of men, where the *ideas* of these actions are supposed to be lodged, they have there too a very uncertain existence, and therefore we are apt to annex them to the names that excite them in us.

9.   There are therefore *three ways whereby we get the complex*

ideas *of mixed modes*: (1) By experience and *observation* of things themselves: thus, by seeing two men wrestle or fence, we get the *idea* of wrestling or fencing. (2) By *invention*, or voluntary putting together of several simple *ideas* in our own minds: so he that first invented printing or etching, had an *idea* of it in his mind before it ever existed. (3) Which is the most usual way, by *explaining the names* of actions we never saw, or motions we cannot see; and by enumerating, and thereby, as it were, setting before our imaginations all those *ideas* which go to the making them up, and are the constituent parts of them. For, having by *sensation* and *reflection* stored our minds with simple *ideas*, and by use got the names that stand for them, we can by those names represent to another any complex *idea* we would have him conceive, so that it has in it no simple *ideas* but what he knows and has with us the same name for. For all our complex *ideas* are ultimately resolvable into simple *ideas*, of which they are compounded and originally made up, though perhaps their immediate ingredients, as I may so say, are also complex *ideas*. Thus the *mixed mode* which the word *lie* stands for is made of these simple *ideas*: (1) articulate sounds; (2) certain *ideas* in the mind of the speaker; (3) those words the signs of those *ideas*; (4) those signs put together by affirmation or negation, otherwise than the *ideas* they stand for, are in the mind of the speaker. I think I need not go any further in the analysis of that complex *idea* we call a *lie*, what I have said is enough to show that it is made up of simple *ideas*; and it could not be but an offensive tediousness to my reader to trouble him with a more minute enumeration of every particular simple *idea* that goes to this complex one; which, from what has been said, he cannot but be able to make out to himself. The same may be done in all our complex *ideas* whatsoever, which, however compounded and decompounded, may at last be resolved into simple *ideas*, which are all the materials of knowledge or thought we have or can have. Nor shall we have reason to fear that the mind is hereby stinted to too scanty a number of *ideas*, if we consider what an inexhaustible stock of simple modes number and figure alone afford us. How far then *mixed modes*, which admit of the various combinations of different simple *ideas* and their infinite modes, are from being few and scanty we may easily imagine. So that before we have done we shall see that nobody need be afraid he shall not have scope and compass enough for his thoughts to range in, though they be, as I pretend, confined only to simple *ideas* received from sensation or reflection and their several combinations.

10.   It is worth our observing *which of all our simple* ideas *have been most modified and had most mixed modes made out of them with names given to them*; and those have been these three: thinking and motion (which are the two *ideas* which comprehend in them all action) and power, from whence these actions are conceived to flow.   These simple *ideas*, I say, of thinking, motion, and power have been those which have been most modified, and out of whose modifications have been made most complex modes with names to them.   For action being the great business of mankind, and the whole matter about which all laws are conversant, it is no wonder that the several modes of thinking and motion should be taken notice of, the *ideas* of them observed and laid up in the memory and have names assigned to them, without which laws could be but ill-made, or vice and disorder repressed.   Nor could any communication be well had amongst men without such complex *ideas* with names to them; and therefore men have settled names, and supposed settled *ideas* in their minds, of modes of actions distinguished by their causes, means, objects, ends, instruments, time, place, and other circumstances; and also of their powers fitted for those actions, v.g., boldness is the power to speak or do what we intend, before others, without fear or disorder; and the *Greeks* call the confidence of speaking by a peculiar name, παρρησία, which power or ability in man of doing anything, when it has been acquired by frequent doing the same thing, is that *idea* we name *habit*; when it is forward and ready upon every occasion to break into action, we *call* it *disposition.* Thus *testiness* is a disposition or aptness to be angry.

To conclude, let us examine any *modes of action,* v.g. *consideration* and *assent,* which are actions of the mind; *running* and *speaking,* which are actions of the body; *revenge* and *murder,* which are actions of both together; and we shall find them but so many *collections of simple ideas,* which together make up the complex ones signified by those names.

11.   *Power* being the source from whence all action proceeds, the substances wherein these powers are, when they exert this power into act, are called *causes*; and the substances which thereupon are produced, or the simple *ideas* which are introduced into any subject by the exerting of that power, are called *effects.* The *efficacy* whereby the new substance or *idea* is produced is called, in the subject exerting that power, *action*; but in the subject wherein any simple idea is changed or produced, it is called *passion*: which efficacy however various, and the effects almost infinite, yet we can, I think, conceive it, in intellectual agents,

to be nothing else but modes of thinking and willing; in corporeal agents, nothing else but modifications of motion. I say, I think we cannot conceive it to be any other but these two. For whatever sort of action, besides these, produces any effects, I confess myself to have no notion or *idea* of; and so it is quite remote from my thoughts, apprehensions, and knowledge, and as much in the dark to me as five other senses, or as the *ideas* of colours to a blind man; and therefore *many words which seem to express some action* signify nothing of the action or *modus operandi* at all, *but* barely *the effect*, with some circumstances of the subject wrought on, or cause operating: v.g. creation, annihilation, contain in them no *idea* of the action or manner whereby they are produced, but barely of the cause and the thing done. And when a countryman says the cold freezes water, though the word freezing seems to import some *action*, yet truly it signifies nothing but the effect, viz. that water that was before fluid is become hard and consistent, without containing any *idea* of the action whereby it is done.

12. I think I shall not need to remark here that, though power and action make the greatest part of mixed modes, marked by names and familiar in the minds and mouths of men, yet other simple *ideas* and their several combinations are *not* excluded; much less, I think, will it be *necessary* for me *to enumerate all the mixed modes* which have been settled, with names to them. That would be to make a dictionary of the greatest part of the words made use of in divinity, ethics, law, and politics, and several other sciences. All that is requisite to my present design is to show what sort of *ideas* those are which I call *mixed modes*, how the mind comes by them, and that they are compositions made up of simple *ideas* got from sensation and reflection; which, I suppose, I have done.

Chapter XXIII

OF OUR COMPLEX IDEAS OF SUBSTANCES

1. The mind being, as I have declared, furnished with a great number of the simple *ideas* conveyed in by the *senses*, as they are found in exterior things, or by *reflection* on its own operations, takes notice also that a certain number of these simple *ideas* go constantly together; which, being presumed to belong to one

thing, and words being suited to common apprehensions and made use of for quick dispatch, are called, so united in one subject, by one name; which, by inadvertency, we are apt afterward to talk of and consider as one simple *idea*, which indeed is a complication of many *ideas* together: because, as I have said, not imagining how these simple *ideas* can subsist by themselves, we accustom ourselves to suppose some *substratum* wherein they do subsist, and from which they do result; which therefore we call *substance*.

2.   So that if anyone will examine himself concerning his *notion of pure substance in general*, he will find he has no other *idea* of it at all, but only a supposition of he knows not what support of such qualities which are capable of producing simple *ideas* in us; which qualities are commonly called accidents.   If anyone should be asked what is the subject wherein colour or weight inheres, he would have nothing to say but, the solid extended parts; and if he were demanded what is it that that solidity and extension adhere in, he would not be in a much better case than the *Indian* before-mentioned who, saying that the world was supported by a great elephant, was asked what the elephant rested on, to which his answer was, a great tortoise; but being again pressed to know what gave support to the broad-backed tortoise, replied, something, he knew not what.   And thus here, as in all other cases where we use words without having clear and distinct *ideas*, we talk like children who, being questioned what such a thing is which they know not, readily give this satisfactory answer, that it is *something*; which in truth signifies no more, when so used, either by children or men, but that they know not what, and that the thing they pretend to know and talk of is what they have no distinct *idea* of at all, and so are perfectly ignorant of it and in the dark.   The *idea* then we have, to which we give the general name substance, being nothing but the supposed, but unknown, support of those qualities we find existing, which we imagine cannot subsist *sine re substante*, without something to support them, we call that support *substantia*; which, according to the true import of the word, is, in plain *English, standing under* or *upholding*.

3.   An obscure and relative *idea* of substance in general being thus made, we come to have the *ideas of particular sorts of substances* by collecting such combinations of simple *ideas* as are, by experience and observation of men's senses, taken notice of to exist together, and are therefore supposed to flow from the particular internal constitution or unknown essence of that substance.   Thus we come to have the *ideas* of a man, horse, gold,

water, etc.; of which substances, whether anyone has any other clear *idea*, further than of certain simple *ideas* co-existing together, I appeal to everyone's own experience. It is the ordinary qualities observable in iron, or a diamond, put together that make the true complex *idea* of those substances, which a smith or a jeweller commonly knows better than a philosopher; who, whatever substantial forms he may talk of, has no other *idea* of those substances than what is framed by a collection of those simple *ideas* which are to be found in them: only we must take notice that our complex *ideas* of substances, besides all these simple *ideas* they are made up of, have always the confused *idea* of *something* to which they belong, and in which they subsist; and therefore when we speak of any sort of substance, we say it is a *thing* having such or such qualities: as body is a *thing* that is extended, figured, and capable of motion; a spirit, a *thing* capable of thinking; and so hardness, friability, and power to draw iron, we say, are qualities to be found in a loadstone. These and the like fashions of speaking intimate that the substance is supposed always *something* besides the extension, figure, solidity, motion, thinking or other observable *ideas*, though we know not what it is.

4. Hence, when we talk or think of any particular sort of corporeal substances, as *horse, stone*, etc., though the *idea* we have of either of them be but the complication or collection of those several simple *ideas* of sensible qualities, which we use to find united in the thing called *horse* or *stone*: yet, because we cannot conceive how they should subsist alone, nor one in another, we suppose them existing in and supported by some common subject; *which support we denote by the name substance*, though it be certain we have no clear or distinct *idea* of that *thing* we suppose a support.

5. The same thing happens concerning the operations of the mind, viz. thinking, reasoning, fearing, etc., which we concluding not to subsist of themselves, nor apprehending how they can belong to body or be produced by it, we are apt to think these the actions of some other *substance*, which we call *spirit*; whereby yet it is evident that, having no other *idea* or notion of matter but *something* wherein those many sensible qualities which affect our senses do subsist, by supposing a substance wherein *thinking, knowing, doubting*, and a power of moving, etc., do subsist, *we have as clear a notion of the substance of spirit as we have of body*: the one being supposed to be (without knowing what it is) the *substratum* to those simple *ideas* we have from without; and the other supposed (with a like ignorance of what it is) to be the

substratum to those operations which we experiment in ourselves within. It is plain then that the *idea* of corporeal *substance* in matter is as remote from our conceptions and apprehensions as that of spiritual *substance*, or *spirit;* and therefore, from our not having any notion of the *substance* of spirit, we can no more conclude its non-existence than we can, for the same reason, deny the existence of body: it being as rational to affirm there is no body, because we have no clear and distinct *idea* of the *substance* of matter, as to say there is no spirit, because we have no clear and distinct *idea* of the *substance* of a spirit.

6.   Whatever therefore be the secret and abstract nature of *substance* in general, all *the* ideas *we have of particular distinct sorts of substances* are nothing but several combinations of simple *ideas*, co-existing in such, though unknown, cause of their union as makes the whole subsist of itself. It is by such combinations of simple *ideas* and nothing else that we represent particular sorts of *substances* to ourselves; such are the *ideas* we have of their several species in our minds; and such only do we, by their specific names, signify to others, v.g. *man, horse, sun, water, iron;* upon hearing which words, everyone who understands the language frames in his mind a combination of those several simple *ideas* which he has usually observed or fancied to exist together under that denomination, all which he supposes to rest in and be, as it were, adherent to that unknown common subject which inheres not in anything else. Though in the meantime it be manifest, and everyone upon inquiry into his own thoughts will find, that he has no other *idea* of any *substance*, v.g., let it be *gold, horse, iron, man, vitriol, bread*, but what he has barely of those sensible qualities which he supposes to inhere, with a supposition of such a *substratum* as gives, as it were, a support to those qualities or simple *ideas* which he has observed to exist united together. Thus, the *idea* of the *sun*, what is it but an aggregate of those several simple *ideas*, bright, hot, roundish, having a constant regular motion, at a certain distance from us, and perhaps some other: as he who thinks and discourses of the *sun* has been more or less accurate in observing those sensible qualities, *ideas*, or properties, which are in that thing which he calls the *sun*.

7.   For he has the perfectest *idea* of any of the particular sorts of *substances*, who has gathered and put together most of those simple *ideas* which do exist in it; among which are to be reckoned its active powers and passive capacities, which, though not simple *ideas*, yet in this respect, for brevity's sake, may conveniently enough be reckoned amongst them. Thus, the power of drawing

iron is one of the *ideas* of the complex one of that substance we call a *loadstone*; and a power to be so drawn is a part of the complex one we call *iron*: which powers pass for inherent qualities in those subjects. Because every *substance*, being as apt, by the powers we observe in it, to change some sensible qualities in other subjects as it is to produce in us those simple *ideas* which we receive immediately from it, does, by those new sensible qualities introduced into other subjects, discover to us those powers which do thereby mediately affect our senses, as regularly as its sensible qualities do it immediately: v.g. we immediately by our senses perceive in *fire* its heat and colour, which are, if rightly considered, nothing but powers in it to produce those *ideas* in us; we also by our senses perceive the colour and brittleness of *charcoal*, whereby we come by the knowledge of another power in fire, which it has to change the colour and consistency of wood. By the former, fire immediately, by the latter, it mediately discovers to us these several powers; which therefore we look upon to be a part of the qualities of fire, and so make them a part of the complex *idea* of it. For all those powers that we take cognizance of terminating only in the alteration of some sensible qualities in those subjects on which they operate, and so making them exhibit to us new sensible *ideas*, therefore it is that I have reckoned these powers amongst the simple *ideas* which make the complex ones of the sorts of *substances*, though these powers considered in themselves are truly complex *ideas*. And in this looser sense, I crave leave to be understood when I name any of these *potentialities amongst the simple ideas*, which we recollect in our minds when we think *of particular substances*. For the powers that are severally in them are necessary to be considered, if we will have true distinct notions of the several sorts of substances.

8. Nor are we to wonder that *powers make a great part of our complex* ideas *of substances*, since their secondary qualities are those which in most of them serve principally to distinguish substances one from another, and commonly make a considerable part of the complex *idea* of the several sorts of them. For, our senses failing us in the discovery of the bulk, texture, and figure of the minute parts of bodies, on which their real constitutions and differences depend, we are fain to make use of their secondary qualities as the characteristical notes and marks whereby to frame *ideas* of them in our minds and distinguish them one from another: all which secondary qualities, as has been shown, are nothing but bare powers. For the colour and taste of *opium* are, as well as its soporific or anodyne virtues, mere powers,

depending on its primary qualities, whereby it is fitted to produce different operations on different parts of our bodies.

9.   *The* ideas *that make our complex ones of corporeal substances* are of these three sorts.   *First*, the *ideas* of the primary qualities of things, which are discovered by our senses, and are in them even when we perceive them not; such are the bulk, figure, number, situation, and motion of the parts of bodies, which are really in them, whether we take notice of them or no. *Secondly*, the sensible secondary qualities, which, depending on these, are nothing but the powers those substances have to produce several *ideas* in us by our senses; which *ideas* are not in the things themselves otherwise than as anything is in its cause. *Thirdly*, the aptness we consider in any substance to give or receive such alterations of primary qualities, as that the substance so altered should produce in us different *ideas* from what it did before: these are called active and passive powers; all which powers, as far as we have any notice or notion of them, terminate only in sensible simple *ideas*.   For whatever alteration a *loadstone* has the power to make in the minute particles of iron, we should have no notion of any power it had at all to operate on iron, did not its sensible motion discover it; and I doubt not but there are a thousand changes that bodies we daily handle have a power to cause in one another, which we never suspect, because they never appear in sensible effects.

10.   *Powers* therefore justly *make a great part of our complex* ideas *of substances*.   He that will examine his complex *idea* of gold will find several of its *ideas* that make it up to be only powers, as the power of being melted, but of not spending itself in the fire, of being dissolved in *aqua regia*, are *ideas* as necessary to make up our complex *idea* of gold as its colour and weight; which, if duly considered, are also nothing but different powers. For, to speak truly, yellowness is not actually in gold, but is a power in gold to produce that *idea* in us by our eyes, when placed in a due light; and the heat, which we cannot leave out of our *idea* of the sun, is no more really in the sun, than the white colour it introduces into wax.   These are both equally powers in the sun, operating, by the motion and figure of its insensible parts, so on a man as to make him have the *idea* of heat; and so on wax, as to make it capable to produce in a man the *idea* of white.

11.   Had we senses acute enough to discern the minute particles of bodies and the real constitution on which their sensible qualities depend, I doubt not but they would produce quite different *ideas* in us; and that which is now the yellow colour of

gold would then disappear, and instead of it we should see an admirable texture of parts, of a certain size and figure. This microscopes plainly discover to us; for what to our naked eyes produces a certain colour is, by thus augmenting the acuteness of our senses, discovered to be quite a different thing; and the thus altering, as it were, the proportion of the bulk of the minute parts of a coloured object to our usual sight produces different *ideas* from what it did before. Thus sand, or pounded glass, which is opaque and white to the naked eye, is pellucid in a microscope; and a hair seen this way loses its former colour and is in a great measure pellucid, with a mixture of some bright sparkling colours, such as appear from the refraction of diamonds and other pellucid bodies. Blood to the naked eye appears all red, but by a good microscope, wherein its lesser parts appear, shows only some few globules of red, swimming in a pellucid liquor; and how these red globules would appear, if glasses could be found that yet could magnify them a thousand or ten thousand times more, is uncertain.

12. The infinite wise Contriver of us and all things about us hath fitted our senses, faculties, and organs to the conveniences of life, and the business we have to do here. We are able, by our senses, to know and distinguish things, and to examine them so far as to apply them to our uses, and several ways to accommodate the exigencies of this life. We have insight enough into their admirable contrivances and wonderful effects to admire and magnify the wisdom, power, and goodness of their Author. Such a knowledge as this, which is suited to our present condition, we want not faculties to attain. But it appears not that God intended we should have a perfect, clear, and adequate knowledge of them: that perhaps is not in the comprehension of any finite being. We are furnished with faculties (dull and weak as they are) to discover enough in the creatures to lead us to the knowledge of the Creator and the knowledge of our duty, and we are fitted well enough with abilities to provide for the conveniences of living: these are our business in this world. But were our senses altered and made much quicker and acuter, the appearance and outward scheme of things would have quite another face to us and, I am apt to think, would be inconsistent with our being, or at least well-being in this part of the universe which we inhabit. He that considers how little our constitution is able to bear a remove into parts of this air, not much higher than that we commonly breathe in, will have reason to be satisfied that in this globe of earth allotted for our mansion, the all-wise Architect has suited our organs, and the

bodies that are to affect them, one to another. If our sense of hearing were but a thousand times quicker than it is, how would a perpetual noise distract us. And we should in the quietest retirement be less able to sleep or meditate than in the middle of a sea-fight. Nay, if that most instructive of our senses, seeing, were in any man 1000 or 100,000 times more acute than it is now by the best microscope, things, several millions of times less than the smallest object of his sight now would then be visible to his naked eyes, and so he would come nearer the discovery of the texture and motion of the minute parts of corporeal things, and in many of them probably get *ideas* of their internal constitutions; but then he would be in a quite different world from other people: nothing would appear the same to him and others, the visible *ideas* of everything would be different. So that I doubt whether he and the rest of men could discourse concerning the objects of sight, or have any communication about colours, their appearances being so wholly different. And perhaps such a quickness and tenderness of sight could not endure bright sunshine or so much as open daylight, nor take in but a very small part of any object at once, and that too only at a very near distance. And if by the help of such microscopical eyes (if I may so call them), a man could penetrate further than ordinary into the secret composition and radical texture of bodies, he would not make any great advantage by the change, if such an acute sight would not serve to conduct him to the market and exchange, if he could not see things he was to avoid at a convenient distance, nor distinguish things he had to do with, by those sensible qualities others do. He that was sharp-sighted enough to see the configuration of the minute particles of the spring of a clock, and observe upon what peculiar structure and impulse its elastic motion depends, would no doubt discover something very admirable; but if eyes so framed could not view at once the hand and the characters of the hour-plate, and thereby at a distance see what o'clock it was, their owner could not be much benefited by that acuteness, which, whilst it discovered the secret contrivance of the parts of the machine, made him lose its use.

13. And here give me leave to propose an extravagant conjecture of mine, viz. that, since we have some reason (if there be any credit to be given to the report of things that our philosophy cannot account for) to imagine that spirits can assume to themselves bodies of different bulk, figure, and conformation of parts, whether one great advantage some of them have over us may not lie in this: that they can so frame and shape to themselves

organs of sensation or perception as to suit them to their present design and the circumstances of the object they would consider. For how much would that man exceed all others in knowledge who had but the faculty so to alter the structure of his eyes, that one sense, as to make it capable of all the several degrees of vision which the assistance of glasses (casually at first lighted on) has taught us to conceive? What wonders would he discover who could so fit his eye to all sorts of objects as to see, when he pleased, the figure and motion of the minute particles in the blood and other juices of animals as distinctly as he does, at other times, the shape and motion of the animals themselves. But to us, in our present state, unalterable organs so contrived as to discover the figure and motion of the minute parts of bodies whereon depend those sensible qualities we now observe in them would, perhaps, be of no advantage. God has, no doubt, made us so as is best for us in our present condition. He hath fitted us for the neighbourhood of the bodies that surround us and we have to do with; and though we cannot, by the faculties we have, attain to a perfect knowledge of things, yet they will serve us well enough for those ends above-mentioned, which are our great concernment. I beg my reader's pardon for laying before him so wild a fancy concerning the ways of perception in beings above us; but how extravagant soever it be, I doubt whether we can imagine anything about the knowledge of angels but after this manner, some way or other, in proportion to what we find and observe in ourselves. And though we cannot but allow that the infinite power and wisdom of God may frame creatures with a thousand other faculties and ways of perceiving things without them than what we have, yet our thoughts can go no further than our own, so impossible it is for us to enlarge our very guesses beyond the *ideas* received from our own sensation and reflection. The supposition, at least, that angels do sometimes assume bodies need not startle us, since some of the most ancient and most learned fathers of the Church seemed to believe that they had bodies; and this is certain, that their state and way of existence is unknown to us.

14. But to return to the matter in hand, the *ideas* we have of substances and the ways we come by them: I say *our specific* ideas *of substances* are nothing else but *a collection of a certain number of simple* ideas, *considered as united in one thing*. These *ideas* of substances, though they are commonly called simple apprehensions, and the names of them simple terms, yet in effect are complex and compounded. Thus the *idea* which an *Englishman* signifies by the name *swan* is white colour, long neck, red

beak, black legs, and whole feet, and all these of a certain size, with a power of swimming in the water, and making a certain kind of noise, and perhaps, to a man who has long observed this kind of birds, some other properties: which all terminate in sensible simple *ideas*, all united in one common subject.

15.   Besides the complex *ideas* we have of material sensible substances, of which I have last spoken, by the simple *ideas* we have taken from those operations of our own minds which we experiment daily in ourselves, as thinking, understanding, willing, knowing and power of beginning motion, etc., coexisting in some substance, we are able to frame *the complex* idea *of an immaterial spirit*. And thus, by putting together the *ideas* of thinking, perceiving, liberty, and power of moving themselves and other things, we have as clear a perception and notion of immaterial substances as we have of material.   For putting together the *ideas* of thinking and willing, or the power of moving or quieting corporeal motion, joined to substance, of which we have no distinct *idea*, we have the *idea* of an immaterial spirit; and by putting together the *ideas* of coherent solid parts, and a power of being moved, joined with substance, of which likewise we have no positive *idea*, we have the *idea* of matter. The one is as clear and distinct an *idea* as the other: the *idea* of thinking, and moving a body, being as clear and distinct *ideas* as the *ideas* of extension, solidity, and being moved.   For our *idea* of substance is equally obscure, or none at all, in both: it is but a supposed I know not what, to support those *ideas* we call accidents.   It is for want of reflection that we are apt to think that our senses show us nothing but material things.   Every act of sensation, when duly considered, gives us an equal view of both parts of nature, the corporeal and spiritual.   For whilst I know, by seeing or hearing, etc., that there is some corporeal being without me, the object of that sensation, I do more certainly know that there is some spiritual being within me that sees and hears.   This, I must be convinced, cannot be the action of bare insensible matter; nor ever could be, without an immaterial thinking being.

16.   By the complex *idea* of extended, figured, coloured, and all other sensible qualities, which is all that we know of it, we are as far from the *idea* of the substance of body, as if we knew nothing at all; *nor* after all the acquaintance and familiarity which we imagine we *have* with matter, and the many qualities *men* assure themselves they perceive and know in bodies, will it perhaps upon examination be found that they have any *more or clearer primary* ideas *belonging to body than they have belonging to*

immaterial spirit.

17. *The primary* ideas *we have peculiar to body,* as contradistinguished to spirit, *are the cohesion of solid,* and consequently separable, *parts, and a power of communicating motion by impulse.* These, I think, are the original *ideas* proper and peculiar to body; for figure is but the consequence of finite extension.

18. *The* ideas *we have* belonging and *peculiar to spirit are thinking and will,* or a power of putting body into motion by thought, and, which is consequent to it, liberty. For, as body cannot but communicate its motion by impulse to another body, which it meets with at rest, so the mind can put bodies into motion, or forbear to do so, as it pleases. The *ideas* of existence, duration, and mobility are common to them both.

19. There is no reason why it should be thought strange that I make *mobility belong to spirit*; for, having no other *idea* of motion but change of distance with other beings that are considered as at rest, and finding that spirits as well as bodies cannot operate but where they are, and that spirits do operate at several times in several places, I cannot but attribute change of place to all finite spirits; (for of the infinite spirit I speak not here). For my soul, being a real being as well as my body, is certainly as capable of changing distance with any other body or being, as body itself, and so is capable of motion. And if a mathematician can consider a certain distance, or a change of that distance between two points, one may certainly conceive a distance and a change of distance between two spirits, and so conceive their motion, their approach or removal, one from another.

20. Everyone finds in himself that his soul can think, will, and operate on his body in the place where that is, but cannot operate on a body, or in a place, an hundred miles distant from it. Nobody can imagine that his soul can think or move a body at *Oxford* whilst he is at *London,* and cannot but know that, being united to his body, it constantly changes place all the whole journey between *Oxford* and *London,* as the coach or horse does that carries him, and I think may be said to be truly all that while in motion; or, if that will not be allowed to afford us a clear *idea* enough of its motion, its being separated from the body in death I think will; for to consider it as going out of the body, or leaving it and yet to have no *idea* of its motion, seems to me impossible.

21. If it be said by anyone that it cannot change place because it hath none, for spirits are not in *loco* but *ubi,* I suppose that way of talking will not now be of much weight to many in an

age that is not much disposed to admire or suffer themselves to be deceived by such unintelligible ways of speaking. But if anyone thinks there is any sense in that distinction, and that it is applicable to our present purpose, I desire him to put it into intelligible *English*, and then from thence draw a reason to show that immaterial spirits are not capable of motion. Indeed motion cannot be attributed to GOD, not because he is an immaterial, but because he is an infinite spirit.

22. Let us *compare* then our complex *idea* of an immaterial spirit with our complex *idea* of body and see whether there be any more obscurity in one than in the other, and in which most. Our *idea* of body, as I think, is an extended solid substance, capable of communicating motion by impulse; and our *idea* of our soul, as an immaterial spirit, is of a substance that thinks, and has a power of exciting motion in body, by will or thought. These, I think, are *our complex* ideas *of soul and body, as contradistinguished*; and now let us examine which has most obscurity in it and difficulty to be apprehended. I know that people whose thoughts are immersed in matter and have so subjected their minds to their senses that they seldom reflect on anything beyond them, are apt to say they cannot comprehend a thinking thing, which perhaps is true; but I affirm, when they consider it well, they can no more comprehend an extended thing.

23. If anyone say he knows not what it is thinks in him, he means he knows not what the substance is of that thinking thing; no more, say I, knows he what the substance is of that solid thing. Further, if he says he knows not how he thinks, I answer: neither knows he how he is extended, how the solid parts of body are united or cohere together to make extension. For though the pressure of the particles of air may account for the *cohesion of several parts of matter* that are grosser than the particles of air, and have pores less than the corpuscles of air, yet the weight or pressure of the air will not explain, nor can be a cause of, the coherence of the particles of air themselves. And if the pressure of the aether, or any subtiler matter than the air, may unite and hold fast together the parts of a particle of air, as well as other bodies, yet it cannot make bonds for itself and hold together the parts that make up every the least corpuscle of that *materia subtilis*. So that that hypothesis, how ingeniously soever explained, by showing that the parts of sensible bodies are held together by the pressure of other external insensible bodies, reaches not the parts of the aether itself; and by how much the more evident it proves that the parts of other bodies are held together by the external pressure of the aether, and can have no

other conceivable cause of their cohesion and union, by so much the more it leaves us in the dark concerning the cohesion of the parts of the corpuscles of the aether itself; which we can neither conceive without parts, they being bodies and divisible, nor yet how their parts cohere, they wanting that cause of cohesion which is given of the cohesion of the parts of all other bodies.

24. But in truth, *the pressure of any ambient fluid*, how great soever, *can be no* intelligible *cause of the cohesion of the solid parts of matter*. For though such a pressure may hinder the avulsion of two polished superficies one from another in a line perpendicular to them, as in the experiment of two polished marbles, yet it can never in the least hinder the separation by a motion in a line parallel to those surfaces. Because the ambient fluid, having a full liberty to succeed in each point of space deserted by a lateral motion, resists such a motion of bodies so joined, no more than it would resist the motion of that body, were it on all sides environed by that fluid and touched no other body; and therefore, if there were no other cause of cohesion, all parts of bodies must be easily separable by such a lateral sliding motion. For if the pressure of the aether be the adequate cause of cohesion, wherever that cause operates not, there can be no cohesion. And since it cannot operate against such a lateral separation (as has been shown), therefore in every imaginary plane intersecting any mass of matter, there could be no more cohesion than of two polished surfaces, which will always, notwithstanding any imaginable pressure of a fluid, easily slide one from another. So that, perhaps, how clear an *idea* soever we think we have of the extension of body, which is nothing but the cohesion of solid parts, he that shall well consider it in his mind may have reason to conclude that it is *as easy* for him *to have a clear* idea *how the soul thinks as how body is extended*. For, since body is no further nor otherwise extended than by the union and cohesion of its solid parts, we shall very ill comprehend the *extension* of body, without understanding wherein consists the union and cohesion of its parts; which seems to me as incomprehensible as the manner of thinking, and how it is performed.

25. I allow it is usual for most people to wonder how anyone should find a difficulty in what they think they every day observe. Do we not see, will they be ready to say, the parts of bodies stick firmly together? Is there anything more common? And what doubt can there be made of it? And the like I say concerning *thinking* and *voluntary motion*: do we not every moment experiment it in ourselves, and therefore can it be doubted? The matter of fact is clear, I confess; but when we

would a little nearer look into it and consider how it is done, there I think we are at a loss, both in the one and the other, and can as little understand how the parts of body cohere as how we ourselves perceive or move. I would have anyone intelligibly explain to me how the parts of gold or brass (that but now in fusion were as loose from one another as the particles of water or the sands of an hour-glass) come in a few moments to be so united and adhere so strongly one to another that the utmost force of men's arms cannot separate them; a considering man will, I suppose, be here at a loss to satisfy his own or another man's understanding.

26.   The little bodies that compose that fluid we call *water* are so extremely small that I have never heard of anyone who by a microscope (and yet I have heard of some that have magnified to 10,000; nay, to much above 100,000 times) pretended to perceive their distinct bulk, figure, or motion; and the particles of *water* are also so perfectly loose one from another that the least force sensibly separates them. Nay, if we consider their perpetual motion, we must allow them to have no cohesion one with another; and yet let but a sharp cold come and they unite, they consolidate, these little atoms cohere and are not, without great force, separable. He that could find the bonds that tie these heaps of loose little bodies together so firmly, he that could make known the cement that makes them stick so fast one to another, would discover a great and yet unknown secret; and yet when that was done, would he be far enough from making the extension of body (which is the cohesion of its solid parts) intelligible, till he could show wherein consisted the union or consolidation of the parts of those bonds or of that cement or of the least particle of matter that exists? Whereby it appears that this primary and supposed obvious quality of body will be found, when examined, to be as incomprehensible as anything belonging to our minds, and *a solid extended substance as hard to be conceived as a thinking immaterial one*, whatever difficulties some would raise against it.

27.   For to extend our thoughts a little further, that pressure which is brought to explain the cohesion of bodies is as unintelligible as the cohesion itself. For if matter be considered, as no doubt it is, finite, let anyone send his contemplation to the extremities of the universe and there see what conceivable hoops, what bond he can imagine to hold this mass of matter in so close a pressure together, from whence steel has its firmness, and the parts of a diamond their hardness and indissolubility. If matter be finite, it must have its extremes, and there must be something

to hinder it from scattering asunder. If, to avoid this difficulty, anyone will throw himself into the supposition and abyss of infinite matter, let him consider what light he thereby brings to the *cohesion* of body, and whether he be ever the nearer making it intelligible, by resolving it into a supposition the most absurd and most incomprehensible of all other: so far is our extension of body (which is nothing but the cohesion of solid parts) from being clearer or more distinct, when we would inquire into the nature, cause, or manner of it, than the *idea* of thinking.

28. Another *idea* we have of body is the power of *communication of motion by impulse*; and of our souls, the power of *exciting of motion by thought*. These *ideas*, the one of body, the other of our minds, every day's experience clearly furnishes us with; but if here again we inquire how this is done, we *are equally in the dark*. For in the communication of motion by impulse, wherein as much motion is lost to one body as is got to the other, which is the ordinariest case, we can have no other conception but of the passing of motion out of one body into another; which, I think, is as obscure and inconceivable as how our minds move or stop our bodies by thought, which we every moment find they do. The increase of motion by impulse, which is observed or believed sometimes to happen, is yet harder to be understood. We have by daily experience clear evidence of motion produced both by impulse and by thought, but the manner how hardly comes within our comprehension: we are equally at a loss in both. So that however we consider motion and its communication either from body or spirit, *the* idea *which belongs to spirit is at least as clear as that that belongs to body*. And if we consider the active power of moving or, as I may call it, *motivity*, it is much clearer in spirit than body, since two bodies, placed by one another at rest, will never afford us the *idea* of a power in the one to move the other, but by a borrowed motion; whereas the mind every day affords us *ideas* of an active power of moving of bodies; and therefore it is worth our consideration whether active power be not the proper attribute of spirits, and passive power of matter. Hence may be conjectured that created spirits are not totally separate from matter, because they are both active and passive. Pure spirit, viz. God, is only active; pure matter is only passive; those beings that are both active and passive we may judge to partake of both. But, be that as it will, I think, we have as many and as clear *ideas* belonging to spirit as we have belonging to body, the substance of each being equally unknown to us, and the *idea* of thinking in spirit as clear as of extension in body; and the communication of motion by

thought which we attribute to spirit is as evident as that by impulse, which we ascribe to body. Constant experience makes us sensible of both of these, though our narrow understandings can comprehend neither. For when the mind would look beyond those original *ideas* we have from sensation or reflection and penetrate into their causes and manner of production, we find still it discovers nothing but its own short-sightedness.

29. To conclude. Sensation convinces us that there are solid, extended substances, and reflection, that there are thinking ones; experience assures us of the existence of such beings, and that the one hath a power to move body by impulse, the other by thought: this we cannot doubt of. Experience, I say, every moment furnishes us with the clear *ideas* both of the one and the other. But beyond these *ideas*, as received from their proper sources, our faculties will not reach. If we would inquire further into their nature, causes, and manner, we perceive not the nature of extension clearer than we do of thinking. If we would explain them any further, one is as easy as the other; and there is no more difficulty to conceive how a substance we know not should, by thought, set body into motion, than how a substance we know not should, by impulse, set body into motion. So that we are no more able to discover wherein the *ideas* belonging to body consist than those belonging to spirit. From whence it seems probable to me that the simple *ideas* we receive from sensation and reflection are the boundaries of our thoughts; beyond which the mind, whatever efforts it would make, is not able to advance one jot; nor can it make any discoveries, when it would pry into the nature and hidden causes of those *ideas*.

30. So that, in short, *the idea* we have *of spirit, compared with the* idea we have *of body*, stands thus: the substance of spirit is unknown to us, and so is the substance of body equally unknown to us. Two primary qualities or properties of body, viz. solid coherent parts and impulse, we have distinct clear *ideas* of; so likewise we know and have distinct clear *ideas* of two primary qualities or properties of spirit, viz. thinking, and a power of action, i.e. a power of beginning or stopping several thoughts or motions. We have also the *ideas* of several qualities inherent in bodies, and have the clear distinct *ideas* of them; which qualities are but the various modifications of the extension of cohering solid parts, and their motion. We have likewise the *ideas* of the several modes of thinking, viz. believing, doubting, intending, fearing, hoping, all which are but the several modes of thinking. We have also the *ideas* of willing, and moving the body consequent to it, and with the body itself too; for, as has

been shown, spirit is capable of motion.

31.   Lastly, if this notion of immaterial spirit may have, per-haps, some difficulties in it not easily to be explained, we have therefore no more reason to deny or doubt the existence of such spirits than we have to deny or doubt the existence of body, because the notion of body is cumbered with some difficulties very hard, and perhaps impossible, to be explained or under-stood by us.   For I would fain have instanced anything in our notion of spirit more perplexed or nearer a contradiction than the very notion of body includes in it, the divisibility *in infinitum* of any finite extension involving us, whether we grant or deny it, in consequences impossible to be explicated or made in our apprehensions consistent: consequences that carry greater difficulty and more apparent absurdity than any-thing can follow from the notion of an immaterial knowing substance.

32.   Which we are not at all to wonder at, since we, having but some few superficial *ideas* of things, discovered to us only by the senses from without or by the mind reflecting on what it experi-ments in itself within, have no knowledge beyond that, much less of the internal constitution and true nature of things, being destitute of faculties to attain it.   And therefore experimenting and discovering in ourselves knowledge and the power of voluntary motion, as certainly as we experiment or discover in things without us the cohesion and separation of solid parts, which is the extension and motion of bodies, *we have as much reason to be satisfied with our notion of immaterial spirit as with our notion of body, and the existence of the one as well as the other*.   For it being no more a contradiction that thinking should exist separate and independent from solidity than it is a con-tradiction that solidity should exist separate and independent from thinking, they being both but simple *ideas* independent one from another; and having as clear and distinct *ideas* in us of thinking as of solidity, I know not why we may not as well allow a thinking thing without solidity, i.e. *immaterial*, to exist, as a solid thing without thinking, i.e. *matter*, to exist, especially since it is no harder to conceive how thinking should exist without matter than how matter should think. For whensoever we would proceed beyond these simple *ideas* we have from sensation and reflection and dive further into the nature of things, we fall presently into darkness and obscurity, perplexedness and difficulties, and can discover nothing further but our own blindness and ignorance.   But which ever of these complex *ideas* be clearest, that of body or immaterial spirit, this is

evident, that the simple *ideas* that make them up are no other than what we have received from sensation or reflection; and so is it of all our other *ideas* of substances, even of God himself.

33.   For if we examine the *idea* we have of the incomprehensible supreme Being, we shall find that we come by it the same way, and that the complex *ideas* we have both of God and separate spirits are made up of the simple *ideas* we receive from *reflection*: v.g., having, from what we experiment in ourselves, got the *ideas* of existence and duration, of knowledge and power, of pleasure and happiness, and of several other qualities and powers which it is better to have than to be without; when we would frame an *idea* the most suitable we can to the supreme Being, we enlarge every one of these with our *idea* of infinity, and so, putting them together, make our complex *idea of God*. For that the mind has such a power of enlarging some of its *ideas*, received from sensation and reflection, has been already shown.

34.   If I find that I know some few things and some of them or all perhaps imperfectly, I can frame an *idea* of knowing twice as many; which I can double again as often as I can add to number and thus enlarge my *idea* of knowledge by extending its comprehension to all things existing or possible. The same also I can do of knowing them more perfectly: i.e., all their qualities, powers, causes, consequences and relations, etc., till all be perfectly known that is in them or can any way relate to them, and thus frame the *idea* of infinite or boundless knowledge. The same may also be done of power till we come to that we call infinite, and also of the duration of existence without beginning or end, and so frame the *idea* of an eternal being. The degrees or extent wherein we ascribe existence, power, wisdom and all other perfection (which we can have any *ideas* of) to that sovereign being which we call God being all boundless and infinite, we frame the best *idea* of him our minds are capable of; all which is done, I say, by enlarging those simple *ideas* we have taken from the operations of our own minds by reflection or by our senses from exterior things to that vastness to which infinity can extend them.

35.   For it is infinity which, joined to our *ideas* of existence, power, knowledge, etc., makes that complex *idea* whereby we represent to ourselves, the best we can, the supreme Being. For, though in his own essence (which certainly we do not know, not knowing the real essence of a pebble, or a fly, or of our own selves) God be simple and uncompounded, yet I think I may say we have no other *idea* of him but a complex one of existence, knowledge, power, happiness, etc., infinite and

eternal; which are all distinct *ideas,* and some of them, being relative, are again compounded of others; all which, being as has been shown originally got from *sensation* and *reflection,* go to make up the *idea* or notion we have of God.

36. This further is to be observed, that there is no *idea* we attribute to God, bating infinity, which is not also a part of our complex *idea* of other spirits. Because, being capable of no other simple *ideas,* belonging to anything but body, but those which by reflection we receive from the operation of our own minds, we can attribute to spirits no other but what we receive from thence; and all the difference we can put between them in our contemplation of spirits is only in the several extents and degrees of their knowledge, power, duration, happiness, etc. For that in our *ideas,* as well *of spirits* as of other things, we are *restrained to those we receive from sensation and reflection* is evident from hence: that in our *ideas* of spirits, how much soever advanced in perfection beyond those of bodies, even to that of infinite, we cannot yet have any *idea* of the manner wherein they discover their thoughts one to another, though we must necessarily conclude that separate spirits, which are beings that have perfecter knowledge and greater happiness than we, must needs have also a perfecter way of communicating their thoughts than we have who are fain to make use of corporeal signs and particular sounds; which are therefore of most general use as being the best and quickest we are capable of. But of immediate communication, having no experiment in ourselves and consequently no notion of it at all, we have no *idea* how spirits which use not words can, with quickness, or much less, how spirits that have no bodies can be masters of their own thoughts and communicate or conceal them at pleasure, though we cannot but necessarily suppose they have such a power.

37. And thus we have seen *what kind of* ideas *we have of substances of all kinds,* wherein they consist, and how we come by them. From whence, I think, it is very evident:

First, That all our *ideas* of the several sorts of substances are nothing but collections of simple *ideas,* with a supposition of something to which they belong, and in which they subsist, though of this supposed something we have no clear distinct *idea* at all.

Secondly, That all the simple *ideas* that, thus united in one common *substratum,* make up our complex *ideas* of several sorts of the substances are no other but such as we have received from *sensation* or *reflection.* So that even in those which we think we are most intimately acquainted with, and come nearest the comprehension of our most enlarged conceptions, we cannot reach beyond those simple *ideas*. And even in those which seem most remote from all we have to do with and do infinitely surpass anything we can perceive in ourselves by *reflection* or discover by *sensation* in other things, we can attain to nothing but those simple *ideas* which we originally received from *sensation* or *reflection*, as is evident in the complex *ideas* we have of angels and particularly of God himself.

Thirdly, That most of the simple *ideas* that make up our complex *ideas* of substances, when truly considered, are only powers, however we are apt to take them for positive qualities: v.g. the greatest part of the *ideas* that make our complex *idea* of *gold* are yellowness, great weight, ductility, fusibility, and solubility in *aqua regia*, etc., all united together in an unknown *substratum*; all which *ideas* are nothing else but so many relations to other substances, and are not really in the gold, considered barely in itself, though they depend on those real and primary qualities of its internal constitution, whereby it has a fitness differently to operate and be operated on by several other substances.

Chapter XXV

OF RELATION

1. BESIDES the *ideas*, whether simple or complex, that the mind has of things as they are in themselves, there are others it gets from their comparison one with another. The understanding, in the consideration of anything, is not confined to that precise object: it can carry any *idea*, as it were, beyond itself or, at least, look beyond it to see how it stands in conformity to any other. When the mind so considers one thing that it does, as it were, bring it to and set it by another and carry its view from one to the other, this is, as the words import, *relation* and *respect*; and the denominations given to positive things, intimating that respect, and serving as marks to lead the thoughts beyond the subject itself denominated to something distinct from it, are what we call *relatives*; and the things so brought together, *related*. Thus, when the mind considers *Caius* as such a positive being, it takes nothing into that *idea* but what really exists in *Caius*: v.g. when I consider him as a man, I have nothing in my mind but the complex *idea* of the species, man. So likewise, when I say *Caius* is a white man, I have nothing but the bare consideration of man who hath that white colour. But when I give *Caius* the name *husband*, I intimate some other person; and when I give him the name *whiter*, I intimate some other thing; in both cases my thought is led to something beyond *Caius*, and there are two things brought into consideration. And since any *idea*, whether simple or complex, may be the occasion why the mind thus brings two things together and, as it were, takes a view of them at once, though still considered as distinct, therefore any of our *ideas* may be the foundation of relation. As in the above-mentioned instance, the contract and ceremony of marriage with *Sempronia* is the occasion of the denomination or relation of husband, and the colour white the occasion why he is said whiter than freestone.

2. These and the like *relations expressed by relative terms that have others answering them with a reciprocal intimation,* as father and son, bigger and less, cause and effect, *are very obvious* to everyone, and everybody at first sight perceives the relation. For father and son, husband and wife, and such other correlative terms seem so nearly to belong one to another and, through custom, do so readily chime and answer one another in people's memories, that upon the naming of either of them the thoughts are presently carried beyond the things so named; and nobody overlooks or doubts of a relation where it is so plainly intimated. But where languages have failed to give correlative names, there the relation is not always so easily taken notice of. *Concubine* is, no doubt, a relative name as well as wife; but in languages where this and the like words have not a correlative term, there people are not so apt to take them to be so, as wanting that evident mark of relation which is between correlatives, which seem to explain one another and not to be able to exist but together. Hence it is that many of those names, which duly considered do include evident relations, have been called external denominations. But all names that are more than empty sounds must signify some *idea* which is either in the thing to which the name is applied, and then it is positive and is looked on as united to and existing in the thing to which the denomination is given, or else it arises from the respect the mind finds in it to something distinct from it, with which it considers it, and then it includes a relation.

3. Another sort of *relative terms* there is, which are not looked on to be either relative or so much as external denominations; *which* yet, under the form and appearance of signifying something absolute in the subject, do conceal a tacit, though less observable, relation. Such are the *seemingly positive* terms of

old, great, imperfect, etc., whereof I shall have occasion to speak more at large in the following chapters.

4. This further may be observed, that the *ideas* of relation may be the same in men who have far different *ideas* of the things that are related, or that are thus compared: v.g. those who have far different *ideas* of a *man* may yet agree in the notion of a *father,* which is a notion superinduced to the substance, or man, and refers only to an act of that thing called man whereby he contributed to the generation of one of his own kind, let man be what it will.

5. The *nature* therefore *of relation* consists in the referring or comparing two things one to another, from which comparison one or both comes to be denominated. And if either of those things be removed or cease to be, the relation ceases, and the denomination consequent to it, though the other receive in itself no alteration at all: v.g. *Caius,* whom I consider today as a father, ceases to be so tomorrow only by the death of his son, without any alteration made in himself. Nay, barely by the mind's changing the object to which it compares anything, the same thing is capable of having contrary denominations at the same time: v.g. *Caius,* compared to several persons, may truly be said to be older and younger, stronger and weaker, etc.

6. Whatsoever doth or can exist or be considered as one thing is positive; and so not only simple *ideas* and substances, but modes also, are positive beings, though the parts of which they consist are very often relative one to another; but the whole together considered as one thing, and producing in us the complex *idea* of one thing, which *idea* is in our minds as one picture, though an aggregate of divers parts and under one name, it is a positive or absolute thing, or *idea.* Thus a triangle, though the parts thereof compared one to another be *relative,* yet the *idea* of the whole is a positive absolute *idea.* The same may be said of a family, a tune, etc.; for there can be no relation but betwixt two things considered as two things. There must always be in relation two *ideas* or things, either in themselves really separate, or considered as distinct, and then a ground or occasion for their comparison.

7. Concerning relation in general, these things may be considered:

First, That there is *no one thing,* whether simple *idea,* substance, mode, or relation, or name of either of them, *which is not capable of almost an infinite number of* considerations in reference to other things; and therefore this makes no small part of men's thoughts and words. V.g., one single man may at once be concerned in and sustain all these following *relations*, and many more, viz. father, brother, son, grandfather, grandson, father-in-law, son-in-law, husband, friend, enemy, subject, general, judge, patron, client, professor, *European*, *Englishman*, islander, servant, master, possessor, captain, superior, inferior, bigger, less, older, younger, contemporary, like, unlike, etc., to an almost infinite number: he being capable of as many relations as there can be occasions of comparing him to other things, in any manner of agreement, disagreement, or respect whatsoever For, as I said, *relation* is a way of comparing or considering two things together and giving one or both of them some appellation from that comparison, and sometimes giving even the relation itself a name.

8. *Secondly*, This further may be considered concerning *relation*: that, though it be not contained in the real existence of things, but something extraneous and superinduced, yet the *ideas* which relative words stand for are often clearer and more distinct than of those substances to which they do belong. The notion we have of a father or brother is a great deal clearer and more distinct than that we have of a man; or, if you will, *paternity* is a thing whereof it is easier to have a clear *idea* than of *humanity*. And I can much easier conceive what a friend is than what God, because the knowledge of one action or one simple *idea* is oftentimes sufficient to give me the notion of a relation; but to the knowing of any substantial being, an accurate collection of sundry *ideas* is necessary. A man, if he compares two things together, can hardly be supposed not to know what it is wherein he compares them, so that, when he compares any things together, he cannot but have a very clear *idea* of that relation. The *ideas*, then, of *relations are capable* at least *of being more perfect and distinct in our minds than those of substances*. Because it is commonly hard to know all the simple *ideas* which are really in any substance, but for the most part easy enough to know the simple *ideas* that make up any relation I think on, or have a name for: v.g. comparing two men in reference to one common parent, it is very easy to frame the *ideas* of brothers, without having yet the perfect *idea* of a man. For significant relative words, as well as others, standing only for *ideas*, and those being all either simple or made up of simple ones, it suffices, for the knowing the precise *idea* the relative term stands for, to have a clear conception of that which is the foundation of the relation; which may be done without having a perfect and clear *idea* of the thing it is attributed to. Thus having the notion that one laid the egg out of which the other was hatched,

I have a clear *idea* of the relation of *dam* and *chick*, between the two cassowaries in St. *James'* Park, though perhaps I have but a very obscure and imperfect *idea* of those birds themselves.

9.   *Thirdly*, Though there be a great number of considerations wherein things may be compared one with another, and so a multitude of *relations*, yet they *all terminate in* and are concerned about those *simple ideas*, either of sensation or reflection; which I think to be the whole materials of all our knowledge. To clear this, I shall show it in the most considerable relations that we have any notion of, and in some that seem to be the most remote from *sense* or *reflection*; which yet will appear to have their *ideas* from thence and leave it past doubt that the notions we have of them are but certain simple *ideas*, and so originally derived from sense or reflection.

10.   *Fourthly*, That *relation* being the considering of one thing with another which is extrinsical to it, it is evident that all words that necessarily lead the mind to any other *ideas* than are supposed really to exist in that thing to which the word is applied are *relative words*: v.g. a *man, black, merry, thoughtful, thirsty, angry, extended*; these and the like are all absolute, because they neither signify nor intimate anything but what does or is supposed really to exist in the man thus denominated; but *father, brother, king, husband, blacker, merrier*, etc., are words which, together with the thing they denominate, imply also something else separate and exterior to the existence of that thing.

11.   Having laid down these premises concerning *relation* in general, I shall now proceed to show in some instances how all the *ideas* we have of *relation* are made up, as the others are, only of simple *ideas*, and that they all, how refined or remote from sense soever they seem, terminate at last in simple *ideas*. I shall begin with the most comprehensive relation wherein all things that do or can exist are concerned, and that is the relation of *cause* and *effect*. The *idea* whereof, how derived from the two fountains of all our knowledge, *sensation* and *reflection*, I shall in the next place consider.

Chapter XXVI

OF CAUSE AND EFFECT, AND OTHER RELATIONS

1.   IN the notice that our senses take of the constant vicissitude of things, we cannot but observe that several particular, both

qualities and substances, begin to exist, and that they receive this their existence from the due application and operation of some other being. From this observation we get our *ideas* of *cause* and *effect*. That which produces any simple or complex *idea* we denote by the general name, *cause*, and that which is produced, *effect*. Thus, finding that, in that substance which we call wax, fluidity, which is a simple *idea* that was not in it before, is constantly produced by the application of a certain degree of heat, we call the simple *idea* of heat, in relation to fluidity in wax, the cause of it, and fluidity the effect. So also, finding that the substance, wood, which is a certain collection of simple *ideas* so called, by the application of fire is turned into another substance, called ashes, i.e. another complex *idea*, consisting of a collection of simple *ideas*, quite different from that complex *idea* which we call wood, we consider fire, in relation to ashes, as cause, and the ashes, as effect. So that whatever is considered by us to conduce or operate to the producing any particular simple *idea*, or collection of simple *ideas* whether substance or mode, which did not before exist, hath thereby in our minds the relation of a cause, and so is denominated by us.

2. Having thus, from what our senses are able to discover in the operations of bodies on one another, got the notion of *cause* and *effect*, viz. that a *cause* is that which makes any other thing, either simple *idea*, substance, or mode, begin to be, and an *effect* is that which had its beginning from some other thing: the mind finds no great difficulty to distinguish the several originals of things into two sorts:

First, When the thing is wholly made new, so that no part thereof did ever exist before, as when a new particle of matter doth begin to exist *in rerum natura*, which had before no being; and this we call *creation*.

Secondly, When a thing is made up of particles which did all of them before exist, but that very thing, so constituted of preexisting particles which, considered all together, make up such a collection of simple *ideas*, had not any *existence* before, as this man, this egg, rose, or cherry, etc. And this, when referred to a substance, produced in the ordinary course of nature by an internal principle, but set on work by and received from some external agent or cause, and working by insensible ways which we perceive not, we call *generation*. When the cause is extrinsical, and the effect produced by a sensible separation or *juxtaposition* of discernible parts, we call it *making*; and such are all artificial things. When any simple *idea* is produced which was not in that subject before, we call it *alteration*. Thus a man is generated, a picture made; and either of them altered, when any new sensible quality or simple *idea* is produced in either of them, which was not there before; and the things thus made to exist, which were not there before, are *effects*; and those things which operated to the existence, *causes*. In which and all other cases, we may observe that the notion of *cause* and *effect* has its rise from *ideas* received by sensation or reflection, and that this relation, how comprehensive soever, terminates at last in them. For to have the *idea* of *cause* and *effect*, it suffices to consider any simple *idea* or substance as beginning to exist by the operation of some other, without knowing the manner of that operation.

CHAPTER XXVII

OF IDENTITY AND DIVERSITY

1. ANOTHER occasion the mind often takes of comparing is the very being of things, when, considering anything as existing at any determined time and place, we compare it with itself existing at another time, and thereon form the *ideas* of *identity* and *diversity*. When we see anything to be in any place in any instant of time, we are sure (be it what it will) that it is that very thing, and not another which at that same time exists in another place, how like and undistinguishable soever it may be in all other respects; and in this consists *identity*, when the *ideas* it is attributed to vary not at all from what they were that moment wherein we consider their former existence, and to which we compare the present. For we never finding nor conceiving it possible that two things of the same kind should exist in the same place at the same time, we rightly conclude that whatever exists anywhere at any time, excludes all of the same kind, and is there itself alone. When therefore we demand whether anything be the same or no, it refers always to something that existed such a time in such a place, which it was certain, at that instant, was the same with itself, and no other; from whence it follows that one thing cannot have two beginnings of existence, nor two things one beginning: it being impossible for two things of the same kind to be or exist in the same instant in the very same place, or one and the same thing in different places. That, therefore, that had one beginning is the same thing; and that which had a different beginning in time and place from that is not the same, but diverse. That which has made the difficulty about this

relation has been the little care and attention used in having precise notions of the things to which it is attributed.

2. We have the *ideas* but of three sorts of substances: (1) God. (2) Finite intelligences. (3) *Bodies*. First, God is without beginning, eternal, unalterable, and everywhere, and therefore concerning his identity there can be no doubt. Secondly, Finite spirits having had each its determinate time and place of beginning to exist, the relation to that time and place will always determine to each of them its identity, as long as it exists.

Thirdly, The same will hold of every particle of matter to which, no addition or subtraction of matter being made, it is the same. For, though these three sorts of substances, as we term them, do not exclude one another out of the same place, yet we cannot conceive but that they must necessarily each of them exclude any of the same kind out of the same place; or else the notions and names of identity and diversity would be in vain, and there could be no such distinction of substances, or anything else one from another. For example: could two bodies be in the same place at the same time, then those two parcels of matter must be one and the same, take them great or little; nay, all bodies must be one and the same. For by the same reason that two particles of matter may be in one place, all bodies may be in one place: which, when it can be supposed, takes away the distinction of identity and diversity of one and more, and renders it ridiculous. But it being a contradiction that two or more should be one, identity and diversity are relations and ways of comparing well-founded and of use to the understanding. All other things being but modes or relations ultimately terminated in substances, the identity and diversity of each particular existence of them too will be by the same way determined; only as to things whose existence is in succession, such as are the actions of finite beings, v.g. *motion* and *thought*, both which consist in a continued train of succession, concerning their diversity there can be no question: because each perishing the moment it begins, they cannot exist in different times or in different places, as permanent beings can at different times exist in distant places; and therefore no motion or thought, considered as at different times, can be the same, each part thereof having a different beginning of existence.

3. From what has been said, it is easy to discover what is so much inquired after, the *principium individuationis*; and that, it is plain, is existence itself, which determines a being of any sort to a particular time and place, incommunicable to two beings of the same kind. This, though it seems easier to conceive in

simple substances or modes, yet, when reflected on, is not more difficult in compounded ones, if care be taken to what it is applied: v.g. let us suppose an atom, i.e. a continued body under one immutable superficies, existing in a determined time and place; it is evident, that, considered in any instant of its existence, it is in that instant the same with itself. For, being at that instant what it is, and nothing else, it is the same, and so must continue as long as its existence is continued; for so long it will be the same, and no other. In like manner, if two or more atoms be joined together into the same mass, every one of those atoms will be the same, by the foregoing rule; and whilst they exist united together, the mass, consisting of the same atoms, must be the same mass, or the same body, let the parts be never so differently jumbled; but if one of these atoms be taken away, or one new one added, it is no longer the same mass or the same body. In the state of living creatures, their identity depends not on a mass of the same particles but on something else. For them the variation of great parcels of matter alters not the identity: an oak growing from a plant to a great tree, and then lopped, is still the same oak; and a colt grown up to a horse, sometimes fat, sometimes lean, is all the while the same horse, though in both these cases there may be a manifest change of the parts, so that truly they are not either of them the same masses of matter, though they be truly one of them the same oak, and the other the same horse. The reason whereof is that, in these two cases of a mass of matter and a living body, *identity* is not applied to the same thing.

4. We must therefore consider wherein an oak differs from a mass of matter; and that seems to me to be in this: that the one is only the cohesion of particles of matter any how united; the other such a disposition of them as constitutes the parts of an oak, and such an organization of those parts as is fit to receive and distribute nourishment, so as to continue and frame the wood, bark, and leaves, etc., of an oak, in which consists the vegetable life. That being then one plant which has such an organization of parts in one coherent body, partaking of one common life, it continues to be the same plant as long as it partakes of the same life, though that life be communicated to new particles of matter vitally united to the living plant, in a like continued organization, conformable to that sort of plants. For this organization, being at any one instant in any one collection of *matter*, is in that particular concrete distinguished from all other and is that individual life; which existing constantly from that moment both forwards and backwards, in the

same continuity of insensibly succeeding parts united to the living body of the plant, it has that identity which makes the same plant and all the parts of it parts of the same plant during all the time that they exist united in that continued organization, which is fit to convey that common life to all the parts so united.

5.   The case is not so much different in *brutes* but that anyone may hence see what makes an animal and continues it the same. Something we have like this in machines and may serve to illustrate it. For example, what is a watch? It is plain it is nothing but a fit organization or construction of parts to a certain end, which, when a sufficient force is added to it, it is capable to attain. If we would suppose this machine one continued body, all whose organized parts were repaired, increased, or diminished by a constant addition or separation of insensible parts, with one common life, we should have something very much like the body of an animal, with this difference: that in an animal the fitness of the organization and the motion wherein life consists begin together, the motion coming from within; but in machines, the force, coming sensibly from without, is often away when the organ is in order and well-fitted to receive it.

6.   This also shows wherein the identity of the same *man* consists: viz. in nothing but a participation of the same continued life, by constantly fleeting particles of matter, in succession vitally united to the same organized body. He that shall place the *identity* of man in anything else but, like that of other animals, in one fitly organized body, taken in any one instant and from thence continued under one organization of life in several successively fleeting particles of matter united to it, will find it hard to make an *embryo*, one of years, mad, and sober, the same man, by any supposition that will not make it possible for *Seth, Ismael, Socrates, Pilate, St. Austin,* and *Caesar Borgia* to be the same man. For if the *identity* of soul alone makes the same man, and there be nothing in the nature of matter why the same individual spirit may not be united to different bodies, it will be possible that those men living in distant ages, and of different tempers, may have been the same man: which way of speaking must be, from a very strange use of the word *man,* applied to an *idea* out of which body and shape are excluded. And that way of speaking would agree yet worse with the notions of those philosophers who allow of transmigration and are of opinion that the souls of men may, for their miscarriages, be detruded into the bodies of beasts, as fit habitations, with organs suited to the satisfaction of their brutal inclinations. But yet I think, nobody, could he be sure that the soul of *Heliogabalus*

were in one of his hogs, would yet say that hog were a *man* or *Heliogabalus*.

7.   It is not therefore unity of substance that comprehends all sorts of *identity* or will determine it in every case; but to conceive and judge of it aright, we must consider what *idea* the word it is applied to stands for: it being one thing to be the same *substance*, another the same *man*, and a third the same *person*, if *person*, *man*, and *substance* are three names standing for three different *ideas*; for such as is the *idea* belonging to that name, such must be the *identity*; which, if it had been a little more carefully attended to, would possibly have prevented a great deal of that confusion which often occurs about this matter, with no small seeming difficulties, especially concerning *personal identity*, which therefore we shall in the next place a little consider.

8.   An animal is a living organized body; and consequently the same animal, as we have observed, is the same continued life communicated to different particles of matter as they happen successively to be united to that organized living body.   And whatever is talked of other definitions, ingenuous observation puts it past doubt that the *idea* in our minds of which the sound *man* in our mouths is the sign, is nothing else but of an animal of such a certain form: since I think I may be confident that whoever should see a creature of his own shape and make, though it had no more reason all its life than a *cat* or a *parrot*, would call him still a *man*; or whoever should hear a *cat* or a *parrot* discourse, reason, and philosophize would call or think it nothing but a *cat* or a *parrot* and say the one was a dull irrational *man*, and the other a very intelligent rational *parrot*.   A relation we have in an author of great note sufficient to countenance the supposition of a rational *parrot*.   His words[1] are:

'I had a mind to know from Prince *Maurice's* own mouth the account of a common but much credited story, that I had heard so often from many others, of an old *parrot* he had in *Brazil* during his government there, that spoke and asked and answered common questions like a reasonable creature, so that those of his train there generally concluded it to be witchery or possession; and one of his chaplains, who lived long afterwards in *Holland*, would never from that time endure a *parrot* but said they all had a devil in them.   I had heard many particulars of this story and assevered by people hard to be discredited, which made me ask Prince *Maurice* what there was of it.   He

[1] Temple, Sir Wm. *Memoirs of what past in ,Christendom, begun* 1672 *to* . . . 1679. 1692. pp. 57-60.

said, with his usual plainness and dryness in talk, there was something true but a great deal false of what had been reported. I desired to know of him what there was of the first? He told me short and coldly that he had heard of such an old *parrot* when he came to *Brazil*; and though he believed nothing of it and it was a good way off, yet he had so much curiosity as to send for it; that it was a very great and a very old one; and when it came first into the room where the Prince was, with a great many *Dutchmen* about him, it said presently: *What a company of white men are here?* They asked it what he thought that man was, pointing at the Prince. It answered, *some general or other.* When they brought it close to him, he asked it: *D'où venez-vous?* It answered: *De Marinnan.* The Prince: *À qui êtes-vous?* The parrot: *À un Portugais.* Prince: *Que fais-tu là?* Parrot: *Je garde les poules.* The Prince laughed and said: *Vous gardez les poules?* The parrot answered: *Oui, moi, & je sais bien faire,* and made the chuck four or five times that people use to make to chickens when they call them. I set down the words of this worthy dialogue in *French*, just as Prince *Maurice* said them to me. I asked him in what language the *parrot* spoke and he said in *Brazilian.* I asked whether he understood *Brazilian*; he said no, but he had taken care to have two interpreters by him, the one a *Dutchman* that spoke *Brazilian*, and the other a *Brazilian* that spoke *Dutch*; that he asked them separately and privately, and both of them agreed in telling him just the same thing that the *parrot* said. I could not but tell this odd story because it is so much out of the way, and from the first hand, and what may pass for a good one; for I dare say this Prince at least believed himself in all he told me, having ever passed for a very honest and pious man. I leave it to naturalists to reason, and to other men to believe as they please upon it; however, it is not perhaps amiss to relieve or enliven a busy scene sometimes with such digressions, whether to the purpose or no.'

I have taken care that the reader should have the story at large in the author's own words, because he seems to me not to have thought it incredible; for it cannot be imagined that so able a man as he, who had sufficiency enough to warrant all the testimonies he gives of himself, should take so much pains, in a place where it had nothing to do, to pin so close not only on a man whom he mentions as his friend, but on a prince, in whom he acknowledges very great honesty and piety, a story which, if he himself thought incredible, he could not but also think ridiculous. The Prince, it is plain, who vouches this story, and our author who relates it from him, both of them call this talker a *parrot*; and I ask anyone else who thinks such a story fit to be told, whether, if this *parrot* and all of its kind had always talked, as we have a prince's word for it, as this one did, whether, I say, they would not have passed for a race of *rational animals*; but yet whether for all that they would have been allowed to be men and not *parrots*? For I presume it is not the *idea* of a thinking or rational being alone that makes the *idea* of a *man* in most people's sense, but of a body so and so shaped, joined to it; and if that be the *idea* of a *man*, the same successive body not shifted all at once must, as well as the same immaterial spirit, go to the making of the same *man*.

9.   This being premised, to find wherein *personal identity* consists, we must consider what *person* stands for; which, I think, is a thinking intelligent being that has reason and reflection and can consider itself as itself, the same thinking thing in different times and places; which it does only by that consciousness which is inseparable from thinking and, as it seems to me, essential to it: it being impossible for anyone to perceive without perceiving that he does perceive. When we see, hear, smell, taste, feel, meditate, or will anything, we know that we do so. Thus it is always as to our present sensations and perceptions, and by this everyone is to himself that which he calls *self*: it not being considered in this case whether the same *self* be continued in the same or divers substances. For since consciousness always accompanies thinking, and it is that that makes everyone to be what he calls *self*, and thereby distinguishes himself from all other thinking things: in this alone consists *personal identity*, i.e. the sameness of a rational being. And as far as this consciousness can be extended backwards to any past action or thought, so far reaches the identity of that *person*: it is the same *self* now it was then, and it is by the same *self* with this present one that now reflects on it, that that action was done.

10.   But it is further inquired whether it be the same identical substance? This, few would think they had reason to doubt of, if these perceptions, with their consciousness, always remained present in the mind whereby the same thinking thing would be always consciously present and, as would be thought, evidently the same to itself. But that which seems to make the difficulty is this: that this consciousness being interrupted always by forgetfulness, there being no moment of our lives wherein we have the whole train of all our past actions before our eyes in one view, but even the best memories losing the sight of one part whilst they are viewing another; and we sometimes, and that the greatest part of our lives, not reflecting on our past selves, being

intent on our present thoughts, and in sound sleep having no thoughts at all, or at least none with that consciousness which remarks our waking thoughts; I say, in all these cases, our consciousness being interrupted, and we losing the sight of our past *selves*, doubts are raised whether we are the same thinking thing, i.e. the same substance, or no. Which, however reasonable or unreasonable, concerns not *personal identity* at all: the question being what makes the same *person*, and not whether it be the same identical substance, which always thinks in the same person; which, in this case, matters not at all: different substances, by the same consciousness (where they do partake in it) being united into one person, as well as different bodies by the same life are united into one animal, whose *identity* is preserved in that change of substances by the unity of one continued life. For, it being the same consciousness that makes a man be himself to himself, *personal identity* depends on that only, whether it be annexed only to one individual substance, or can be continued in a succession of several substances. For as far as any intelligent being can repeat the *idea* of any past action with the same consciousness it had of it at first, and with the same consciousness it has of any present action, so far it is the same *personal self*. For it is by the consciousness it has of its present thoughts and actions that it is *self* to *itself* now, and so will be the same *self* as far as the same consciousness can extend to actions past or to come, and would be by distance of time or change of substance no more two *persons* than a man be two men by wearing other clothes today than he did yesterday, with a long or short sleep between: the same consciousness uniting those distant actions into the same *person*, whatever substances contributed to their production.

11. That this is so, we have some kind of evidence in our very bodies, all whose particles, whilst vitally united to this same thinking conscious self so that we feel when they are touched and are affected by and conscious of good or harm that happens to them, are a part of our *selves*, i.e. of our thinking conscious *self*. Thus, the limbs of his body are to everyone a part of *himself*; he sympathizes and is concerned for them. Cut off a hand, and thereby separate it from that consciousness he had of its heat, cold, and other affections, and it is then no longer a part of that which is *himself*, any more than the remotest part of matter. Thus, we see the *substance* whereof *personal self* consisted at one time may be varied at another, without the change of personal *identity*: there being no question about the same person, though the limbs, which but now were a part of it, be

cut off.

12.   But the question is whether, if the same substance, which thinks, be changed, it can be the same person, or, remaining the same, it can be different persons.

And to this I answer, first, this can be no question at all to those who place thought in a purely material animal constitution, void of an immaterial substance. For, whether their supposition be true or no, it is plain they conceive personal identity preserved in something else than identity of substance, as animal identity is preserved in identity of life and not of substance. And therefore those who place thinking in an immaterial substance only, before they can come to deal with these men, must show why personal identity cannot be preserved in the change of immaterial substances, or variety of particular immaterial substances, as well as animal identity is preserved in the change of material substances, or variety of particular bodies: unless they will say, it is one immaterial spirit that makes the same life in brutes, as it is one immaterial spirit that makes the same person in men; which the *Cartesians* at least will not admit, for fear of making brutes thinking things too.

13.   But next, as to the first part of the question, whether, if the same thinking substance (supposing immaterial substances only to think) be changed, it can be the same person, I answer: That cannot be resolved but by those who know what kind of substances they are that do think, and whether the consciousness of past actions can be transferred from one thinking substance to another. I grant, were the same consciousness the same individual action, it could not; but, it being but a present representation of a past action, why it may not be possible that that may be represented to the mind to have been which really never was, will remain to be shown. And therefore how far the consciousness of past actions is annexed to any individual agent, so that another cannot possibly have it, will be hard for us to determine, till we know what kind of action it is that cannot be done without a reflex act of perception accompanying it, and how performed by thinking substances, who cannot think without being conscious of it. But that which we call the *same consciousness* not being the same individual act, why one intellectual substance may not have represented to it, as done by itself, what it never did, and was perhaps done by some other agent: why, I say, such a representation may not possibly be without reality of matter of fact, as well as several representations in dreams are, which yet whilst dreaming we take for true, will be difficult to conclude from the nature of things. And that it never is so will

by us, till we have clearer views of the nature of thinking substances, be best resolved into the goodness of God, who, as far as the happiness or misery of any of his sensible creatures is concerned in it, will not, by a fatal error of theirs, transfer from one to another that consciousness which draws reward or punishment with it. How far this may be an argument against those who would place thinking in a system of fleeting animal spirits, I leave to be considered. But yet, to return to the question before us, it must be allowed that, if the same consciousness (which, as has been shown, is quite a different thing from the same numerical figure or motion in body) can be transferred from one thinking substance to another, it will be possible that two thinking substances may make but one person. For the same consciousness being preserved, whether in the same or different substances, the personal identity is preserved.

14. As to the second part of the question, whether, the same immaterial substance remaining, there may be two distinct persons, which question seems to me to be built on this: whether the same immaterial being, being conscious of the actions of its past duration, may be wholly stripped of all the consciousness of its past existence and lose it beyond the power of ever retrieving again and so, as it were beginning a new account from a new period, have a consciousness that cannot reach beyond this new state. All those who hold pre-existence are evidently of this mind, since they allow the soul to have no remaining consciousness of what it did in that pre-existent state, either wholly separate from body, or informing any other body; and if they should not, it is plain experience would be against them. So that, personal identity reaching no further than consciousness reaches, a pre-existent spirit, not having continued so many ages in a state of silence, must needs make different persons. Suppose a *Christian Platonist* or *Pythagorean* should, upon God's having ended all his works of creation the seventh day, think his soul hath existed ever since, and should imagine it has revolved in several human bodies, as I once met with one who was persuaded his had been the soul of *Socrates* (how reasonably I will not dispute; this I know, that in the post he filled, which was no inconsiderable one, he passed for a very rational man, and the press has shown that he wanted not parts or learning); would anyone say that he, being not conscious of any of *Socrates*'s actions or thoughts, could be the same person with *Socrates*? Let anyone reflect upon himself and conclude that he has in himself an immaterial spirit, which is that which thinks in him and in the constant change of his body keeps him

the same and is that which he calls himself; let him also suppose it to be the same soul that was in *Nestor* or *Thersites* at the siege of *Troy* (for souls being, as far as we know anything of them, in their nature indifferent to any parcel of matter, the supposition has no apparent absurdity in it), which it may have been, as well as it is now the soul of any other man; but he now having no consciouness of any of the actions either of *Nestor* or *Thersites*, does or can he conceive himself the same person with either of them? Can he be concerned in either of their actions, attribute them to himself, or think them his own, more than the actions of any other men that ever existed? So that, this consciousness not reaching to any of the actions of either of those men, he is no more one *self* with either of them than if the soul or immaterial spirit that now informs him had been created and began to exist, when it began to inform his present body, though it were never so true that the same spirit that informed *Nestor's* or *Thersites's* body were numerically the same that now informs his. For this would no more make him the same person with *Nestor* than if some of the particles of matter that were once a part of *Nestor* were now a part of this man: the same immaterial substance, without the same consciousness, no more making the same person by being united to any body than the same particle of matter, without consciousness, united to any body, makes the same person. But let him once find himself conscious of any of the actions of *Nestor*, he then finds himself the same person with *Nestor*.

15. And thus we may be able, without any difficulty, to conceive the same person at the resurrection, though in a body not exactly in make or parts the same which he had here, the same consciousness going along with the soul that inhabits it. But yet the soul alone, in the change of bodies, would scarce, to anyone but to him that makes the soul the *man*, be enough to make the same *man*. For should the soul of a prince, carrying with it the consciousness of the prince's past life, enter and inform the body of a cobbler as soon as deserted by his own soul, everyone sees he would be the same person with the prince, accountable only for the prince's actions; but who would say it was the same man? The body too goes to the making the man and would, I guess, to everybody, determine the man in this case, wherein the soul, with all its princely thoughts about it, would not make another man: but he would be the same cobbler to everyone besides himself. I know that in the ordinary way of speaking, the same person and the same man stand for one and the same thing. And indeed, everyone will always have a liberty to speak as he pleases and to apply what articulate sounds to what *ideas* he

thinks fit, and change them as often as he pleases. But yet when we will inquire what makes the same *spirit, man,* or *person,* we must fix the *ideas* of *spirit, man,* or *person* in our minds; and having resolved with ourselves what we mean by them, it will not be hard to determine in either of them or the like when it is the *same* and when not.

16. But though the same immaterial substance or soul does not alone, wherever it be, and in whatsoever state, make the same man: yet, it is plain, consciousness, as far as ever it can be extended, should it be to ages past, unites existences and actions very remote in time into the same person, as well as it does the existence and actions of the immediately preceding moment, so that whatever has the consciousness of present and past actions is the same person to whom they both belong. Had I the same consciousness that I saw the ark and *Noah's* flood as that I saw an overflowing of the *Thames* last winter, or as that I write now, I could no more doubt that I that write this now, that saw the *Thames* overflowed last winter, and that viewed the flood at the general deluge, was the same *self,* place that *self* in what substance you please, than I that write this am the same *myself* now whilst I write (whether I consist of all the same substance, material or immaterial, or no) that I was yesterday. For as to this point of being the same *self,* it matters not whether this present *self* be made up of the same or other substances, I being as much concerned and as justly accountable for any action that was done a thousand years since, appropriated to me now by this self-consciousness, as I am for what I did the last moment.

17. *Self* is that conscious thinking thing (whatever substance made up of, whether spiritual or material, simple or compounded, it matters not) which is sensible or conscious of pleasure and pain, capable of happiness or misery, and so is concerned for *itself,* as far as that consciousness extends. Thus everyone finds that, whilst comprehended under that consciousness, the little finger is as much a part of *itself* as what is most so. Upon separation of this little finger, should this consciousness go along with the little finger and leave the rest of the body, it is evident the little finger would be the *person,* the *same person*; and self then would have nothing to do with the rest of the body. As in this case it is the consciousness that goes along with the substance, when one part is separate from another, which makes the same *person* and constitutes this inseparable *self*: so it is in reference to substance remote in time. That with which the *consciousness* of this present thinking thing can join itself makes the same *person* and is one *self* with it, and with nothing else,

and so attributes to *itself* and owns all the actions of that thing as its own, as far as that consciousness reaches, and no further; as everyone who reflects will perceive.

18.   In this *personal identity* is founded all the right and justice of reward and punishment: happiness and misery being that for which everyone is concerned for *himself*, not mattering what becomes of any substance not joined to or affected with that consciousness. For, as it is evident in the instance I gave but now, if the consciousness went along with the little finger when it was cut off, that would be the same *self* which was concerned for the whole body yesterday, as making part of *itself*, whose actions then it cannot but admit as its own now. Though, if the same body should still live and immediately from the separation of the little finger have its own peculiar consciousness, whereof the little finger knew nothing, it would not at all be concerned for it as a part of *itself*, or could own any of its actions, or have any of them imputed to him.

19.   This may show us wherein *personal identity* consists: not in the identity of substance but, as I have said, in the identity of *consciousness*, wherein, if *Socrates* and the present mayor of *Queenborough* agree, they are the same person; if the same *Socrates* waking and sleeping do not partake of the same *consciousness*, *Socrates* waking and sleeping is not the same person. And to punish *Socrates* waking for what sleeping *Socrates* thought, and waking *Socrates* was never conscious of, would be no more of right than to punish one twin for what his brother-twin did, whereof he knew nothing, because their outsides were so like that they could not be distinguished; for such twins have been seen.

20.   But yet possibly it will still be objected, suppose I wholly lose the memory of some parts of my life beyond a possibility of retrieving them, so that perhaps I shall never be conscious of them again: yet am I not the same person that did those actions, had those thoughts that I once was conscious of, though I have now forgot them? To which I answer that we must here take notice what the word *I* is applied to, which, in this case, is the man only. And the same man being presumed to be the same person, *I* is easily here supposed to stand also for the same person. But if it be possible for the same man to have distinct incommunicable consciousness at different times, it is past doubt the same man would at different times make different persons; which, we see, is the sense of mankind in the solemnest declaration of their opinions, human laws not punishing the *mad man* for the *sober man's* actions, nor the *sober man* for what the

mad man did, thereby making them two persons: which is some-what explained by our way of speaking in *English* when we say such an one *is not himself*, or is *beside himself*; in which phrases it is insinuated, as if those who now, or at least first used them, thought that *self* was changed, the *self*-same person was no longer in that man.

21. But yet it is hard to conceive that *Socrates*, the same individual man, should be two persons. To help us a little in this, we must consider what is meant by *Socrates* or the same individual *man*.

First, it must be either the same individual, immaterial, thinking substance; in short, the same numerical soul, and nothing else.

Secondly, or the same animal, without any regard to an immaterial soul.

Thirdly, or the same immaterial spirit united to the same animal.

Now, take which of these suppositions you please, it is im-possible to make personal identity to consist in anything but consciousness, or reach any further than that does.

For, by the first of them, it must be allowed possible that a man born of different women, and in distant times, may be the same man. A way of speaking which, whoever admits, must allow it possible for the same man to be two distinct persons, as any two that have lived in different ages without the knowledge of one another's thoughts.

By the second and third, *Socrates*, in this life and after it, cannot be the same man any way but by the same conscious-ness; and so, making *human identity* to consist in the same thing wherein we place *personal identity*, there will be no difficulty to allow the same man to be the same person. But then they who place *human identity* in consciousness only, and not in some-thing else, must consider how they will make the infant *Socrates* the same man with *Socrates* after the resurrection. But whatso-ever to some men makes a *man*, and consequently the same individual man, wherein perhaps few are agreed, personal identity can by us be placed in nothing but consciousness (which is that alone which makes what we call *self*), without involving us in great absurdities.

22. But is not a man drunk and sober the same person, why else is he punished for the fact he commits when drunk, though he be never afterwards conscious of it? Just as much the same person as a man that walks and does other things in his sleep is the same person and is answerable for any mischief he shall do

in it. Human laws punish both, with a justice suitable to their way of knowledge; because, in these cases, they cannot distinguish certainly what is real, what counterfeit; and so the ignorance in drunkenness or sleep is not admitted as a plea. For, though punishment be annexed to personality, and personality to consciousness, and the drunkard perhaps be not conscious of what he did, yet human judicatures justly punish him, because the fact is proved against him, but want of consciousness cannot be proved for him. But in the Great Day, wherein the secrets of all hearts shall be laid open, it may be reasonable to think no one shall be made to answer for what he knows nothing of, but shall receive his doom, his conscience accusing or excusing him. 23. Nothing but consciousness can unite remote existences into the same person: the identity of substance will not do it; for whatever substance there is however framed, without consciousness there is no person; and a carcass may be a person, as well as any sort of substance be so, without consciousness.

Could we suppose two distinct incommunicable consciousnesses acting the same body, the one constantly by day, the other by night; and, on the other side, the same consciousness, acting by intervals, two distinct bodies: I ask, in the first case whether the *day-* and the *night-man* would not be two as distinct persons as *Socrates* and *Plato*? And whether, in the second case, there would not be one person in two distinct bodies, as much as one man is the same in two distinct clothings? Nor is it at all material to say that this same and this distinct *consciousness*, in the cases above mentioned, is owing to the same and distinct immaterial substances, bringing it with them to those bodies; which, whether true or no, alters not the case, since it is evident the *personal identity* would equally be determined by the consciousness, whether that consciousness were annexed to some individual immaterial substance or no. For, granting that the thinking substance in man must be necessarily supposed immaterial, it is evident that immaterial thinking thing may sometimes part with its past consciousness and be restored to it again, as appears in the forgetfulness men often have of their past actions; and the mind many times recovers the memory of a past consciousness, which it had lost for twenty years together. Make these intervals of memory and forgetfulness to take their turns regularly by day and night, and you have two persons with the same immaterial spirit, as much as in the former instance two persons with the same body. So that *self* is not determined by identity or diversity of substance, which it cannot be sure of, but only by identity of consciousness.

26. *Person*, as I take it, is the name for this *self*. Wherever a man finds what he calls *himself*, there, I think, another may say is the *same person*. It is a forensic term, appropriating actions and their merit, and so belongs only to intelligent agents, capable of a law, and happiness and misery. This personality extends *itself* beyond present existence to what is past, only by consciousness; whereby it becomes concerned and accountable, owns and imputes to *itself* past actions, just upon the same ground and for the same reason that it does the present. All which is founded in a concern for happiness, the unavoidable concomitant of consciousness: that which is conscious of pleasure and pain desiring that that self that is conscious should be happy. And therefore whatever past actions it cannot reconcile or appropriate to that present *self* by consciousness, it can be no more concerned in than if they had never been done; and to receive pleasure or pain, i.e. reward or punishment, on the account of any such action, is all one as to be made happy or miserable in its first being, without any demerit at all. For supposing a man punished now for what he had done in another life, whereof he could be made to have no consciousness at all, what difference is there between that punishment and being created miserable? And therefore conformable to this, the Apostle tells us, that at the Great Day, when everyone shall *receive according to his doings, the secrets of all hearts shall be laid open*. The sentence shall be justified by the consciousness all persons shall have that they *themselves*, in what bodies soever they appear, or what substances soever that consciousness adheres to, are the *same* that committed those actions and deserve that punishment for them.

CHAPTER XXVIII

OF OTHER RELATIONS

1. BESIDES the before-mentioned occasions of time, place, and causality of comparing or referring things one to another, there are, as I have said, infinite others, some whereof I shall mention.

First, The first I shall name is some one simple *idea* which, being capable of parts or degrees, affords an occasion of comparing the subjects wherein it is to one another, in respect of that simple *idea*, v.g. *whiter, sweeter, bigger, equal, more*, etc. These relations, depending on the equality and excess of the same simple *idea* in several subjects may be called, if one will, *proportional*; and that these are only conversant about those simple *ideas* received from sensation or reflection is so evident that nothing need be said to evince it.

2.   *Secondly*, Another occasion of comparing things together, or considering one thing so as to include in that consideration some other thing, is the circumstances of their origin or beginning; which, being not afterwards to be altered, make the relations depending thereon as lasting as the subjects to which they belong, v.g. *father* and *son, brothers, cousin-germans*, etc., which have their relations by one community of blood, wherein they partake in several degrees; *countrymen*, i.e. those who were born in the same country or tract of ground; and these I call *natural relations*, wherein we may observe that mankind have fitted their notions and words to the use of common life and not to the truth and extent of things. For it is certain that in reality the relation is the same betwixt the begetter and the begotten in the several races of other animals as well as men; but yet it is seldom said this bull is the grandfather of such a calf, or that two pigeons are cousin-germans. It is very convenient that by distinct names these relations should be observed and marked out in mankind, there being occasion, both in laws and other communications one with another, to mention and take notice of men under these relations; from whence also arise the obligations of several duties amongst men; whereas in brutes, men having very little or no cause to mind these relations, they have not thought fit to give them distinct and peculiar names. This, by the way, may give us some light into the different state and growth of languages; which, being suited only to the convenience of communication, are proportioned to the notions men have, and the commerce of thoughts familiar amongst them, and not to the reality or extent of things, nor to the various respects might be found among them, nor the different abstract considerations might be framed about them. Where they had no philosophical notions, there they had no terms to express them; and it is no wonder men should have framed no names for those things they found no occasion to discourse of. From whence it is easy to imagine why, as in some countries, they may not have so much as the name for a horse, and in others, where they are more careful of the pedigrees of their horses than of their own, that there they may have not only names for particular horses but also of their several relations of kindred one to another.

3.   *Thirdly*, Sometimes the foundation of considering things, with reference to one another, is some act whereby anyone comes by a moral right, power, or obligation to do something.

Thus, a *general* is one that hath power to command an army; and an army under a general is a collection of armed men obliged to obey one man. A *citizen*, or a *burgher*, is one who has a right to certain privileges in this or that place. All this sort depending upon men's wills or agreement in society, I call *instituted* or *voluntary*, and may be distinguished from the natural in that they are most, if not all of them, some way or other alterable and separable from the persons to whom they have sometimes belonged, though neither of the substances so related be destroyed. Now, though these are all reciprocal, as well as the rest, and contain in them a reference of two things one to the other, yet, because one of the two things often wants a relative name importing that reference, men usually take no notice of it and the relation is commonly overlooked: v.g. a *patron* and *client* are easily allowed to be relations, but a *constable* or *dictator* are not so readily at first hearing considered as such, because there is no peculiar name for those who are under the command of a dictator or constable, expressing a relation to either of them, though it be certain that either of them hath a certain power over some others, and so is so far related to them as well as a patron is to his client of general to his army.

4. *Fourthly,* There is another sort of relation which is the conformity or disagreement men's voluntary actions have to a rule to which they are referred, and by which they are judged of; which, I think, may be called *moral relation*, as being that which denominates our moral actions, and deserves well to be examined, there being no part of knowledge wherein we should be more careful to get determined *ideas* and avoid, as much as may be, obscurity and confusion. Human actions, when with their various ends, objects, manners, and circumstances they are framed into distinct complex *ideas*, are, as has been shown, so many *mixed modes*, a great part whereof have names annexed to them. Thus, supposing gratitude to be a readiness to acknowledge and return kindness received, polygamy to be the having more wives than one at once: when we frame these notions thus in our minds, we have there so many determined *ideas* of mixed modes. But this is not all that concerns our actions; it is not enough to have determined *ideas* of them and to know what names belong to such and such combinations of *ideas*. We have a further and greater concernment, and that is to know whether such actions so made up are morally good or bad.

5. Good and evil, as hath been shown (Bk. II, chap. xx, § 2, and chap. xxi, § 42), are nothing but pleasure or pain, or that which occasions or procures pleasure or pain to us. *Morally good*

and evil, then, is only the conformity or disagreement of our voluntary actions to some law, whereby good or evil is drawn on us from the will and power of the law-maker; which good and evil, pleasure or pain, attending our observance or breach of the law by the decree of the law-maker, is that we call *reward* and *punishment*.

6. Of these *moral rules* or laws to which men generally refer, and by which they judge of the rectitude or pravity of their actions, there seem to me to be *three sorts* with their three different enforcements or rewards and punishments. For since it would be utterly in vain to suppose a rule set to the free actions of man without annexing to it some enforcement of good and evil to determine his will, we must, wherever we suppose a law, suppose also some reward or punishment annexed to that law. It would be in vain for one intelligent being to set a rule to the actions of another if he had it not in his power to reward the compliance with and punish deviation from his rule by some good and evil that is not the natural product and consequence of the action itself. For that, being a natural convenience or inconvenience, would operate of itself without a law. This, if I mistake not, is the true nature of all *law*, properly so called.

7. The laws that men generally refer their actions to, to judge of their rectitude or obliquity, seem to me to be these three: (1) The *divine* law. (2) The *civil* law. (3) The law of *opinion* or *reputation*, if I may so call it. By the relation they bear to the first of these, men judge whether their actions are sins or duties; by the second, whether they be criminal or innocent; and by the third, whether they be virtues or vices.

8. *First*, The *divine* law, whereby I mean that law which God has set to the actions of men, whether promulgated to them by the light of nature or the voice of revelation. That God has given a rule whereby men should govern themselves, I think there is nobody so brutish as to deny. He has a right to do it, we are his creatures; he has goodness and wisdom to direct our actions to that which is best; and he has power to enforce it by rewards and punishments of infinite weight and duration in another life; for nobody can take us out of his hands. This is the only true touchstone of *moral rectitude*; and by comparing them to this law, it is that men judge of the most considerable *moral good* or *evil* of their actions: that is, whether, as *duties or sins*, they are like to procure them happiness or misery from the hands of the ALMIGHTY.

9. *Secondly*, The *civil* law, the rule set by the commonwealth to the actions of those who belong to it, is another rule to which

men refer their actions, to judge whether they be *criminal* or no. This law nobody overlooks, the rewards and punishments that enforce it being ready at hand and suitable to the power that makes it; which is the force of the commonwealth, engaged to protect the lives, liberties, and possessions of those who live according to its laws, and has power to take away life, liberty, or goods from him who disobeys; which is the punishment of offences committed against this law.

10. *Thirdly,* The *law of opinion or reputation.* Virtue and vice are names pretended and supposed everywhere to stand for actions in their own nature right and wrong; and as far as they really are so applied, they so far are coincident with the *divine law* above mentioned. But yet, whatever is pretended, this is visible: that these names, *virtue* and *vice,* in the particular instances of their application, through the several nations and societies of men in the world, are constantly attributed only to such actions as in each country and society are in reputation or discredit. Nor is it to be thought strange that men everywhere should give the name of *virtue* to those actions which amongst them are judged praiseworthy, and call that *vice* which they account blamable: since otherwise they would condemn themselves, if they should think anything *right* to which they allowed not commendation, anything *wrong* which they let pass without blame. Thus the measure of what is everywhere called and esteemed *virtue* and *vice* is this approbation or dislike, praise or blame, which by a secret and tacit consent establishes itself in the several societies, tribes, and clubs of men in the world, whereby several actions come to find credit or disgrace amongst them according to the judgment, maxims, or fashions of that place. For though men, uniting into politic societies, have resigned up to the public the disposing of all their force, so that they cannot employ it against any fellow-citizen any further than the law of the country directs, yet they retain still the power of thinking well or ill, approving or disapproving of the actions of those whom they live amongst and converse with; and by this approbation and dislike they establish amongst themselves what they will call *virtue* and *vice.*

11. That this is the common *measure of virtue and vice* will appear to anyone who considers that, though that passes for *vice* in one country which is counted a *virtue,* or at least not *vice,* in another, yet everywhere *virtue* and praise, *vice* and blame, go together. *Virtue* is everywhere that which is thought praiseworthy; and nothing else but that which has the allowance of

public esteem is called *virtue*.[1] *Virtue* and praise are so united

[1] Our author, in his Preface to the 2nd Edition, taking notice how apt men have been to mistake him, added what here follows: Of this the ingenious author of the *Discourse concerning the Nature of Man* has given me a late instance, to mention no other. For the civility of his expressions and the candour that belongs to his order forbid me to think that he would have closed his Preface with an insinuation, as if in what I had said, Book II, Chapter xxviii, concerning the third rule which men refer their actions to, I went about to make *virtue vice*, and *vice virtue*, unless he had mistaken my meaning; which he could not have done if he had but given himself the trouble to consider what the argument was I was then upon, and what was the chief design of that chapter, plainly enough set down in the fourth section and those following. For I was there not laying down moral rules, but showing the original and nature of moral *ideas*, and enumerating the rules men make use of in moral relations, whether those rules were true or false; and pursuant thereunto, I tell what has everywhere that denomination, which in the language of that place answers to *virtue* and *vice* in ours, which *alters not the nature of things*, though men generally do judge of and denominate their actions according to the esteem and fashion of the place or sect they are of.

If he had been at the pains to reflect on what I had said, B. I, c. iii, section 18, and in this present chapter, sections 13, 14, 15, and 20, he would have known what I think of the eternal and unalterable nature of right and wrong and what I call *virtue* and *vice*; and if he had observed that, in the place he quotes, I only report as matter of fact what others call *virtue* and *vice*, he would not have found it liable to any great exception. For I think I am not much out in saying that one of the rules made use of in the world for a ground or measure of a moral relation is that esteem and reputation which several sorts of actions find variously in the several societies of men, according to which they are there called *virtues* or *vices*; and whatever authority the learned Mr. *Lowde* places in his *old English dictionary*, I dare say it nowhere tells him (if I should appeal to it) that the same action is not in credit called and counted a *virtue* in one place which, being in disrepute, passes for and under the name of *vice* in another. The taking notice that men bestow the names of *virtue* and *vice* according to this rule of reputation is all I have done, or can be laid to my charge to have done, towards the making *vice virtue* and *virtue vice*. But the good man does well, and as becomes his calling, to be watchful in such points and to take the alarm, even at expressions which, standing alone by themselves, might sound ill and be suspected.

It is to this zeal, allowable in his function, that I forgive his citing as he does these words of mine in section 11 of this chapter (*The exhortations of inspired teachers have not feared to appeal to common repute, whatsoever things lovely, whatsoever things are of good report, if there be any virtue, if there be any praise*, etc., *Phil.* iv, 8) without taking notice of those immediately preceding, which introduce them and run thus: *Whereby in the corruption of manners, the true boundaries of the law of nature, which ought to be the rule of virtue and vice, were pretty well preserved. So that even the exhortations of inspired teachers*, etc. By which words and the rest of that section, it is plain that I brought that passage of St. *Paul* not to prove that the general measure of what men call *virtue* and *vice* throughout the world was the reputation and fashion of each particular society within itself, but to show that, though it were so, yet, for reasons I there give, men, in that way of denominating their actions, did not for the most part much vary from the law of nature, which is that standing and unalterable rule by which they ought to judge of the moral rectitude and pravity of their actions and accordingly denominate them *virtues* or *vices*. Had Mr. *Lowde* considered this, he would have found it little to his purpose to have quoted that passage in a sense I used it not and would, I imagine, have spared the explication he subjoins to it as not very necessary. But I hope this Second Edition will give him satisfaction in the point, and that this matter is now so expressed as to show him there was no cause of scruple.

Though I am forced to differ from him in those apprehensions he has expressed in the latter end of his Preface concerning what I had said about *virtue* and *vice*, yet we are better agreed than he thinks in what he says in his third chapter, p. 78, concerning *natural inscription* and *innate notions*. I shall not deny him the privilege he claims, p. 52, to state the question as he pleases, especially when he states it so as to leave nothing in it contrary to what I have said: for, according to him, *innate notions being conditional things, depending upon the concurrence of several other circumstances in*

that they are called often by the same name. *Sunt sua praemia laudi*, says *Virgil*; and so *Cicero, nihil habet natura praestantius, quam honestatem, quam laudem, quam dignitatem, quam decus,* which he tells you are all names for the same thing, *Tuscul. Quaest.*, lib. ii, 20. This is the language of the heathen philosophers who well understood wherein their notions of *virtue* and *vice* consisted. And though, perhaps, by the different temper, education, fashion, maxims, or interest of different sorts of men, it fell out that what was thought praiseworthy in one place escaped not censure in another, and so in different societies, *virtues* and *vices* were changed: yet as to the main, they for the most part kept the same everywhere. For since nothing can be more natural than to encourage with esteem and reputation that wherein everyone finds his advantage, and to blame and discountenance the contrary, it is no wonder that esteem and discredit, virtue and vice, should in a great measure everywhere correspond with the unchangeable rule of right and wrong, which the law of God hath established: there being nothing that so directly and visibly secures and advances the general good of mankind in this world as obedience to the laws he has set them, and nothing that breeds such mischiefs and confusion as the neglect of them. And therefore men, without renouncing all sense and reason and their own interest, which they are so constantly true to, could not generally mistake in placing their

---

order to the soul's exerting them, all that he says for *innate, imprinted, impressed notions* (for of *innate ideas* he says nothing at all) amounts at last only to this: that there are certain propositions which, though the soul from the beginning or when a man is born does not know, yet by *assistance from the outward senses and the help of some previous cultivation* it may afterwards come certainly to know the truth of; which is no more than what I have affirmed in my First Book. For I suppose by the *soul's* exerting them he means its beginning to know them, or else the *soul's exerting of notions* will be to me a very unintelligible expression; and I think at best is a very unfit one in this case, it misleading men's thoughts by an insinuation, as if these notions were in the mind before the *soul exerts them*, i.e. before they are known; whereas truly, before they are known, there is nothing of them in the mind but a capacity to know them, when the *concurrence of those circumstances*, which this ingenious author thinks necessary, *in order to the soul's exerting them*, brings them into our knowledge.

Page 52, I find him express it thus: *These natural notions are not so imprinted upon the soul as that they naturally and necessarily exert themselves (even in children and idiots) without any assistance from the outward senses or without the help of some previous cultivation.* Here he says: *they exert themselves*, as, p. 78, that the *soul exerts them.* When he has explained to himself or others what he means by the *soul's exerting innate notions* or *their exerting themselves*, and what that *previous cultivation* and *circumstances*, *in order* to their being *exerted*, are, he will, I suppose, find there is so little of controversy between him and me in the point, bating that he calls that *exerting of notions* which I in a more vulgar style call *knowing*, that I have reason to think he brought in my name upon this occasion only out of the pleasure he has to speak civilly of me, which I must gratefully acknowledge he has done everywhere he mentions me, not without conferring on me, as some others have done, a title I have no right to.

commendation and blame on that side that really deserved it not. Nay, even those men whose practice was otherwise failed not to give their approbation right, few being depraved to that degree as not to condemn at least in others the faults they themselves were guilty of: whereby even in the corruption of manners, the true boundaries of the law of nature, which ought to be the rule of virtue and vice, were pretty well preserved. So that even the exhortations of inspired teachers have not feared to appeal to common repute. *Whatsoever is lovely, whatsoever is of good report, if there be any virtue, if there be any praise,* etc. (Phil. iv, 8.)

15. To conceive rightly of *moral actions*, we must take notice of them under this two-fold consideration. *First,* as they are in themselves, each made up of such a collection of simple *ideas.* Thus *drunkenness* or *lying* signify such or such a collection of simple *ideas*, which I call mixed modes; and in this sense they are as much *positive absolute ideas,* as the drinking of a horse, or speaking of a parrot. *Secondly,* our actions are considered as good, bad, *or* indifferent; and in this respect they are *relative,* it being their conformity to, or disagreement with, some rule that makes them to be regular or irregular, good or bad; and so, as far as they are compared with a rule, and thereupon denominated, they come under relation. Thus the challenging and fighting with a man, as it is a certain positive mode or particular sort of action, by particular *ideas* distinguished from all others, is called *duelling*: which, when considered in relation to the law of God, will deserve the name of sin; to the law of fashion, in some countries, valour and virtue; and to the municipal laws of some governments, a capital crime. In this case, when the positive mode has one name, and another name as it stands in relation to the law, the distinction may as easily be observed as it is in substances, where one name, v.g. *man,* is used to signify the thing, another, v.g. *father,* to signify the relation.

16. But because very frequently the positive *idea* of the action and its moral relation are comprehended together under one name, and the same word made use of to express both the mode or action and its moral rectitude or obliquity, therefore the relation itself is less taken notice of; and there is often no *distinction* made *between the positive idea* of the action *and the reference it has to a rule.* By which confusion of these two distinct considerations under one term, those who yield too easily to the impressions of sounds and are forward to take names for things are often misled in their judgment of actions.

Thus the taking from another what is his, without his knowledge or allowance, is properly called *stealing*; but that name being commonly understood to signify also the moral pravity of the action and to denote its contrariety to the law, men are apt to condemn whatever they hear called stealing as an ill action, disagreeing with the rule of right. And yet the private taking away his sword from a madman to prevent his doing mischief, though it be properly denominated *stealing*, as the name of such a *mixed mode*: yet when compared to the law of God and considered in its relation to that supreme rule, it is no sin or transgression, though the name *stealing* ordinarily carries such an intimation with it.

Chapter XXIX

OF CLEAR AND OBSCURE, DISTINCT AND CONFUSED IDEAS

1. HAVING shown the original of our *ideas* and taken a view of their several sorts; considered the difference between the simple and the complex, and observed how the complex ones are divided into those of modes, substances, and relations: all which, I think, is necessary to be done by anyone who would acquaint himself thoroughly with the progress of the mind in its apprehension and knowledge of things: it will, perhaps, be thought I have dwelt long enough upon the examination of *ideas*. I must, nevertheless, crave leave to offer some few other considerations concerning them. The first is that some are *clear* and others *obscure*, some *distinct* and others *confused*.

2. The perception of the mind being most aptly explained by words relating to the sight, we shall best understand what is meant by *clear* and *obscure* in our *ideas* by reflecting on what we call *clear* and *obscure* in the objects of sight. Light being that which discovers to us visible objects, we give the name of *obscure* to that which is not placed in a light sufficient to discover minutely to us the figure and colours which are observable in it, and which, in a better light, would be discernible. In like manner, our *simple ideas* are *clear*, when they are such as the objects themselves from whence they were taken did or might, in a well-ordered sensation or perception, present them. Whilst the memory retains them thus and can produce them to the mind whenever it has occasion to consider them, they are *clear ideas*. So far as they either want anything of that original exact-

ness, or have lost any of their first freshness and are, as it were, faded or tarnished by time, so far are they *obscure*. *Complex ideas*, as they are made up of simple ones, so they are *clear*, when the *ideas* that go to their composition are clear; and the number and order of those simple *ideas* that are the ingredients of any complex one is determinate and certain.

3. The *cause* of *obscurity*, in simple *ideas*, seems to be either dull organs, or very slight and transient impressions made by the objects, or else a weakness in the memory, not able to retain them as received. For to return again to visible objects, to help us to apprehend this matter: if the organs or faculties of perception, like wax over-hardened with cold, will not receive the impression of the seal from the usual impulse wont to imprint it; or, like wax of a temper too soft, will not hold it well, when well imprinted; or else supposing the wax of a temper fit, but the seal not applied with a sufficient force to make a clear impression: in any of these cases, the print left by the seal will be *obscure*. This, I suppose, needs no application to make it plainer.

4. As a *clear idea* is that whereof the mind has such a full and evident perception as it does receive from an outward object operating duly on a well-disposed organ, so a *distinct idea* is that wherein the mind perceives a difference from all other; and a *confused idea* is such an one as is not sufficiently distinguishable from another, from which it ought to be different.

5. If no *idea* be *confused* but such as is not sufficiently distinguishable from another, from which it should be different, it will be hard, may anyone say, to find anywhere a *confused idea*. For let any *idea* be as it will, it can be no other but such as the mind perceives it to be; and that very perception sufficiently distinguishes it from all other *ideas* which cannot be other, i.e. different, without being perceived to be so. No *idea* therefore can be indistinguishable from another from which it ought to be different, unless you would have it different from itself: for from all other it is evidently different.

6. To remove this difficulty, and to help us to conceive aright what it is that makes the *confusion ideas* are at any time chargeable with, we must consider that things ranked under distinct names are supposed different enough to be distinguished, that so each sort, by its peculiar name, may be marked and discoursed of apart upon any occasion. And there is nothing more evident than that the greatest part of different names are supposed to stand for different things. Now every *idea* a man has being visibly what it is and distinct from all other *ideas* but

itself, that which makes it *confused* is, when it is such, that it may as well be called by another name as that which it is expressed by: the difference which keeps the things (to be ranked under those two different names) distinct, and makes some of them belong rather to the one and some of them to the other of those names, being left out, and so the distinction which was intended to be kept up by those different names is quite lost.

CHAPTER XXX

OF REAL AND FANTASTICAL IDEAS

1. BESIDES what we have already mentioned concerning *ideas*, other considerations belong to them in reference to things from whence they are taken, or which they may be supposed to represent; and thus, I think, they may come under a threefold distinction, and are:

First, either real or fantastical;

Secondly, adequate or inadequate;

Thirdly, true or false.

First, By *real ideas*, I mean such as have a foundation in nature, such as have a conformity with the real being and existence of things, or with their archetypes. *Fantastical or chimerical* I call such as have no foundation in nature, nor have any conformity with that reality of being to which they are tacitly referred, as to their archetypes. If we examine the several sorts of *ideas* before-mentioned, we shall find that:

2. *First*, Our *simple* ideas *are all real*, all agree to the reality of things, not that they are all of them the images or representations of what does exist; the contrary whereof, in all but the primary qualities of bodies, hath been already shown. But, though whiteness and coldness are no more in snow than pain is, yet those *ideas* of whiteness and coldness, pain, etc., being in us the effects of powers in things without us, ordained by our Maker to produce in us such sensations, they are real *ideas* in us whereby we distinguish the qualities that are really in things themselves. For these several appearances being designed to be the marks whereby we are to know and distinguish things which we have to do with, our *ideas* do as well serve us to that purpose and are as real distinguishing characters, whether they be only constant effects or else exact resemblances of something in the things themselves: the reality lying in that steady correspondence they have with the distinct constitutions of real beings. But whether

they answer to those constitutions, as to causes or patterns, it matters not: it suffices that they are constantly produced by them. And thus our simple *ideas* are all real and true, because they answer and agree to those powers of things which produce them in our minds, that being all that is requisite to make them real and not fictions at pleasure. For in simple *ideas* (as has been shown) the mind is wholly confined to the operation of things upon it, and can make to itself no simple *idea* more than what it has received.

3. Though the mind be wholly passive in respect of its simple *ideas*, yet, I think, we may say it is not so in respect of its complex *ideas*; for those being combinations of simple *ideas* put together and united under one general name, it is plain that the mind of man uses some kind of liberty in forming those complex *ideas*: how else comes it to pass that one man's *idea* of gold or justice is different from another's but because he has put in or left out of his, some simple *idea* which the other has not? The question then is which of these are real and which barely imaginary combinations? What collections agree to the reality of things and what not? And to this I say that:

4. *Secondly, Mixed modes and relations* having no other *reality* but what they have in the minds of men, there is nothing more required to this kind of *ideas* to make them *real*, but that they be so framed that there be a possibility of existing conformable to them. These *ideas*, being themselves archetypes, cannot differ from their archetypes and so *cannot be chimerical*, unless anyone will jumble together in them inconsistent *ideas*. Indeed, as any of them have the names of a known language assigned to them, by which he that has them in his mind would signify them to others, so bare possibility of existing is not enough: they must have a conformity to the ordinary signification of the name that is given them, that they may not be thought fantastical, as if a man would give the name of justice to that *idea* which common use calls liberality. But this fantasticalness relates more to propriety of speech than reality of *ideas*; for a man to be undisturbed in danger, sedately to consider what is fittest to be done, and to execute it steadily is a mixed mode or a complex *idea* of an action which may exist. But to be undisturbed in danger, without using one's reason or industry, is what is also possible to be, and so is as real an *idea* as the other. Though the first of these, having the name *courage* given to it, may in respect of that name be a right or wrong *idea*; but the other, whilst it has not a common received name of any known language assigned to it, is not capable of any deformity, being made with no

reference to anything but itself.

5.   *Thirdly,* Our *complex* ideas *of substances,* being made all of them in reference to things existing without us, and intended to be representations of substances as they really are, are no further *real* than as they are such combinations of simple *ideas* as are really united and co-exist in things without us. On the contrary, those are *fantastical* which are made up of such collections of simple *ideas* as were really never united, never were found together in any substance: v.g. a rational creature, consisting of a horse's head, joined to a body of human shape, or such as the *centaurs* are described; or a body yellow, very malleable, fusible, and fixed, but lighter than common water; or an uniform, unorganized body, consisting, as to sense, all of similar parts, with perception and voluntary motion joined to it. Whether such substances as these can possibly exist or no, it is probable we do not know; but, be that as it will, these *ideas* of substances being made conformable to no pattern existing that we know, and consisting of such collections of *ideas* as no substance ever showed us united together, they ought to pass with us for barely imaginary; but much more are those complex *ideas* so, which contain in them any inconsistency or contradiction of their parts.

CHAPTER XXXI

OF ADEQUATE AND INADEQUATE IDEAS

1.   OF our real *ideas,* some are adequate, and some are inadequate. Those I call *adequate* which perfectly represent those archetypes which the mind supposes them taken from, which it intends them to stand for, and to which it refers them. *Inadequate ideas* are such which are but a partial or incomplete representation of those archetypes to which they are referred. Upon which account it is plain,

2.   *First,* That *all our simple* ideas *are adequate.* Because, being nothing but the effects of certain powers in things, fitted and ordained by GOD to produce such sensations in us, they cannot but be correspondent and adequate to those powers; and we are sure they agree to the reality of things. For, if sugar produce in us the *ideas* which we call whiteness and sweetness, we are sure there is a power in sugar to produce those *ideas* in our minds, or else they could not have been produced by it. And so

each sensation answering the power that operates on any of
our senses, the *idea* so produced is a real *idea* (and not a fiction
of the mind, which has no power to produce any simple *idea*)
and cannot but be adequate, since it ought only to answer that
power; and so all simple *ideas* are adequate. It is true, the
things producing in us these simple *ideas* are but few of them
denominated by us as if they were only the causes of them, but
as if those *ideas* were real beings in them. For though fire be
called painful to the touch, whereby is signified the power of
producing in us the *idea* of pain, yet it is denominated also light
and hot, as if light and heat were really something in the fire,
more than a power to excite these *ideas* in us, and therefore are
called *qualities* in or of the fire. But these being nothing, in
truth, but powers to excite such *ideas* in us, I must in that sense
be understood when I speak of secondary *qualities* as being in
things, or of their *ideas* as being in the objects that excite them
in us. Such ways of speaking, though accommodated to the
vulgar notions without which one cannot be well understood,
yet truly signify nothing but those powers which are in things to
excite certain sensations or *ideas* in us: since, were there no fit
organs to receive the impressions fire makes on the sight and
touch, nor a mind joined to those organs to receive the *ideas* of
light and heat by those impressions from the fire or the sun,
there would yet be no more light or heat in the world than there
would be pain if there were no sensible creature to feel it,
though the sun should continue just as it is now, and Mount
Aetna flame higher than ever it did. Solidity and extension and
the termination of it, figure, with motion and rest, whereof we
have the *ideas*, would be really in the world as they are whether
there were any sensible being to perceive them or no, and therefore those we have reason to look on as the real modifications of
matter, and such as are the exciting causes of all our various
sensations from bodies. But this being an inquiry not belonging
to this place, I shall enter no further into it, but proceed to
show what complex *ideas* are *adequate* and what not.
3.   *Secondly*, Our *complex* ideas *of modes*, being voluntary collections of simple *ideas*, which the mind puts together without
reference to any real archetypes or standing patterns existing
anywhere, *are* and cannot but be *adequate ideas*. Because they,
not being intended for copies of things really existing, but for
archetypes made by the mind to rank and denominate things by,
cannot want anything: they having each of them that combination of *ideas* and thereby that perfection which the mind intended
they should, so that the mind acquiesces in them and can find

nothing wanting. Thus, by having the *idea* of a figure with three sides meeting at three angles, I have a complete *idea* wherein I require nothing else to make it perfect. That the mind is satisfied with the perfection of this its *idea* is plain, in that it does not conceive that any understanding hath, or can have, a more complete or perfect *idea* of that thing it signifies by the word *triangle*, supposing it to exist, than itself has in that complex *idea* of three sides and three angles, in which is contained all that is or can be essential to it or necessary to complete it, wherever or however it exists. But in our *ideas* of *substances* it is otherwise. For there, desiring to copy things as they really do exist, and to represent to ourselves that constitution on which all their properties depend, we perceive our *ideas* attain not that perfection we intend: we find they still want something we should be glad were in them, and so are all *inadequate*. But *mixed modes* and *relations*, being archetypes without patterns, and so having nothing to represent but themselves, cannot but be adequate, everything being so to itself. He that at first put together the *idea* of danger perceived, absence of disorder from fear, sedate consideration of what was justly to be done, and executing that without disturbance or being deterred by the danger of it, had certainly in his mind that complex *idea* made up of that combination; and intending it to be nothing else but what it is, nor to have in it any other simple *ideas* but what it hath, it could not also but be an *adequate idea*; and laying this up in his memory, with the name *courage* annexed to it to signify it to others, and denominate from thence any action he should observe to agree with it, had thereby a standard to measure and denominate actions by, as they agreed to it. This *idea*, thus made and laid up for a pattern, must necessarily be *adequate*, being referred to nothing else but itself, nor made by any other original but the good-liking and will of him that first made this combination.

4.   Indeed another, coming after and in conversation learning from him the word *courage*, may make an *idea*, to which he gives that name *courage*, different from what the first author applied it to and has in his mind when he uses it. And in this case, if he designs that his *idea* in thinking should be conformable to the other's *idea*, as the name he uses in speaking is conformable in sound to his from whom he learned it, his *idea* may be very wrong and *inadequate*. Because in this case, making the other man's *idea* the pattern of his *idea* in thinking, as the other man's word or sound is the pattern of his in speaking, his *idea* is so far defective and *inadequate* as it is distant from the archetype

and pattern he refers it to and intends to express and signify by
the name he uses for it, which name he would have to be a sign
of the other man's *idea* (to which, in its proper use, it is primarily annexed) and of his own, as agreeing to it: to which, if
his own does not exactly correspond, it is faulty and inadequate.
5.   Therefore these *complex* ideas *of modes*, when they are
referred by the mind and intended to correspond to the *ideas*
in the mind of some other intelligent being, expressed by the
names we apply to them, they *may be* very deficient, wrong, and
inadequate, because they agree not to that which the mind
designs to be their archetype and pattern: in which respect only
any *idea* of *modes* can be wrong, imperfect, or *inadequate*. And
on this account our *ideas* of *mixed modes* are the most liable to
be faulty of any other; but this refers more to proper speaking
than knowing right.
6.   *Thirdly*, What *ideas we have of substances*, I have above
shown. Now, those *ideas* have in the mind a double reference:
(1) Sometimes they are referred to a supposed real essence of
each species of things. (2) Sometimes they are only designed to
be pictures and representations in the mind of things that do
exist, by *ideas* of those qualities that are discoverable in them.
In both which ways these copies of those originals and archetypes *are* imperfect and *inadequate*.
    First, It is usual for men to make the names of substances
stand for things as supposed to have certain real essences, whereby they are of this or that species; and names standing for
nothing but the *ideas* that are in men's minds, they must consequently refer their *ideas* to such real essences, as to their
archetypes. That men (especially such as have been bred up in
the learning taught in this part of the world) do suppose certain
specific essences of substances, which each individual in its
several kinds is made conformable to and partakes of, is so far
from needing proof that it will be thought strange if anyone
should do otherwise. And thus they ordinarily apply the specific
names they rank particular substances under to things as distinguished by such specific real essences. Who is there almost,
who would not take it amiss if it should be doubted whether he
called himself man with any other meaning than as having the
real essence of a man? And yet if you demand what those real
essences are, it is plain men are ignorant and know them not.
From whence it follows that the *ideas* they have in their minds,
being referred to real essences, as to archetypes which are
unknown, must be so far from being *adequate* that they cannot
be supposed to be any representation of them at all. The com-

plex *ideas* we have of substances are, as it has been shown, certain collections of simple *ideas* that have been observed or supposed constantly to exist together. But such a complex *idea* cannot be the real essence of any substance; for then the properties we discover in that body would depend on that complex *idea* and be deducible from it, and their necessary connexion with it be known: as all properties of a triangle depend on and, as far as they are discoverable, are deducible from the complex *idea* of three lines including a space. But it is plain that in our complex *ideas* of substances are not contained such *ideas*, on which all the other qualities that are to be found in them do depend. The common *idea* men have of *iron* is a body of a certain colour, weight, and hardness; and a property that they look on as belonging to it is malleableness. But yet this property has no necessary connexion with that complex *idea*, or any part of it; and there is no more reason to think that malleableness depends on that colour, weight, and hardness than that that colour or that weight depends on its malleableness. And yet, though we know nothing of these real essences, there is nothing more ordinary than that men should attribute the sorts of things to such essences. The particular parcel of matter which makes the ring I have on my finger is forwardly by most men supposed to have a real essence whereby it is *gold*, and from whence those qualities flow which I find in it, viz. its peculiar colour, weight, hardness, fusibility, fixedness, and change of colour upon a slight touch of mercury, etc. This essence, from which all these properties flow, when I inquire into it and search after it, I plainly perceive I cannot discover: the furthest I can go is only to presume that, it being nothing but body, its real essence or internal constitution, on which these qualities depend, can be nothing but the figure, size, and connexion of its solid parts; of neither of which I having any distinct perception at all, I can have no *idea* of its essence, which is the cause that it has that particular shining yellowness, a greater weight than anything I know of the same bulk, and a fitness to have its colour changed by the touch of quicksilver. If anyone will say that the real essence and internal constitution on which these properties depend is not the figure, size, and arrangement or connexion of its solid parts, but something else called its particular *form*, I am further from having any *idea* of its real essence than I was before; for I have an *idea* of figure, size, and situation of solid parts in general, though I have none of the particular figure, size, or putting together of parts whereby the qualities above-mentioned are produced; which qualities I find in that particular

parcel of matter that is on my finger, and not in another parcel
of matter with which I cut the pen I write with. But when I
am told that something besides the figure, size, and posture of
the solid parts of that body is its essence, something called
substantial form, of that I confess I have no *idea* at all, but only
of the sound *form*; which is far enough from an *idea* of its real
essence or constitution. The like ignorance as I have of the real
essence of this particular substance, I have also of the real
essence of all other natural ones: of which essences, I confess, I
have no distinct *ideas* at all; and I am apt to suppose others,
when they examine their own knowledge, will find in themselves, in this one point, the same sort of ignorance.

7. Now then, when men apply to this particular parcel of
matter on my finger a general name already in use and denominate it *gold*, do they not ordinarily or are they not understood to
give it that name as belonging to a particular species of bodies,
having a real internal essence, by having of which essence this
particular substance comes to be of that species and to be called
by that name? If it be so, as it is plain it is, the name by which
things are marked as having that essence must be referred
primarily to that essence; and consequently the *idea* to which
that name is given must be referred also to that essence and be
intended to represent it. Which essence, since they who so use
the names know not, their ideas *of substances* must be *all inadequate* in that respect, as not containing in them that real
essence which the mind intends they should.

8. *Secondly*, Those who, neglecting that useless supposition of
unknown real essences, whereby they are distinguished, endeavour to copy the substances that exist in the world by putting
together the *ideas* of those sensible qualities which are found
co-existing in them, though they come much nearer a likeness of
them than those who imagine they know not what real specific
essences, yet they arrive not at perfectly adequate *ideas* of those
substances they would thus copy into their minds; nor do those
copies exactly and fully contain all that is to be found in their
archetypes. Because those qualities and powers of substances,
whereof we make their complex *ideas*, are so many and various
that no man's complex *idea* contains them all. That our abstract
ideas of substances do not contain in them all the simple *ideas*
that are united in the things themselves is evident in that men
do rarely put into their complex *idea* of any substance all the
simple *ideas* they do know to exist in it. Because, endeavouring
to make the signification of their specific names as clear and as
little cumbersome as they can, they make their specific *ideas* of

the sorts of substances, for the most part, of a few of those simple *ideas* which are to be found in them; but these having no original precedency or right to be put in and make the specific *idea* more than others that are left out, it is plain that, both these ways, *our* ideas *of substances* are deficient and *inadequate*. The simple *ideas* whereof we make our complex ones of substances are all of them (bating only the figure and bulk of some sorts) powers; which being relations to other substances, we can never be sure that we know all the powers that are in any one body till we have tried what changes it is fitted to give to or receive from other substances in their several ways of application; which being impossible to be tried upon any one body, much less upon all, it is impossible we should have adequate *ideas* of any substance made up of a collection of all its properties.

9. Whosoever first lighted on a parcel of that sort of substance we denote by the word *gold* could not rationally take the bulk and figure he observed in that lump to depend on its real essence or internal constitution. Therefore those never went into his *idea* of that species of body; but its peculiar colour, perhaps, and weight were the first he abstracted from it to make the complex *idea* of that species. Which both are but powers, the one to affect our eyes after such a manner and to produce in us that *idea* we call yellow, and the other to force upwards any other body of equal bulk, they being put into a pair of equal scales one against another. Another, perhaps, added to these the *ideas* of fusibility and fixedness, two other passive powers, in relation to the operation of fire upon it; another, its ductility and solubility in *aqua regia*, two other powers relating to the operation of other bodies in changing its outward figure or separation of it into insensible parts. These, or part of these, put together, usually make the complex *idea* in men's minds of that sort of body we call *gold*.

10. But no one who hath considered the properties of bodies in general, or this sort in particular, can doubt that this, called *gold*, has infinite other properties not contained in that complex *idea*. Some, who have examined this species more accurately, could, I believe, enumerate ten times as many properties in *gold*, all of them as inseparable from its internal constitution as its colour or weight; and it is probable, if anyone knew all the properties that are by divers men known of this metal, there would an hundred times as many *ideas* go to the complex *idea* of *gold* as any one man yet has in his, and yet, perhaps, that not be the thousandth part of what is to be discovered in it: the changes that that one body is apt to receive and make in other bodies,

upon a due application, exceeding far not only what we know
but what we are apt to imagine. Which will not appear so much
a paradox to anyone who will but consider how far men are yet
from knowing all the properties of that one, no very compound
figure, a *triangle*, though it be no small number that are already
by mathematicians discovered of it.

11.   So that *all our complex* ideas *of substances are* imperfect
and *inadequate*.   Which would be so also in mathematical
figures, if we were to have our complex *ideas* of them only by
collecting their properties in reference to other figures.   How
uncertain and imperfect would our *ideas* be of an *ellipsis*, if we
had no other *idea* of it but some few of its properties? Whereas,
having in our plain *idea* the whole essence of that figure, we
from thence discover those properties, and demonstratively see
how they flow and are inseparable from it.

12.   Thus the mind has three sorts of abstract *ideas* or nominal
essences:

First, Simple ideas, which *are* ἔκτυπα or *copies*, but yet certainly *adequate*.   Because, being intended to express nothing
but the power in things to produce in the mind such a sensation,
that sensation, when it is produced, cannot but be the effect of
that power.   So the paper I write on having the power in the
light (I speak according to the common notion of light) to
produce in me the sensation which I call white, it cannot but
be the effect of such a power in something without the mind,
since the mind has not the power to produce any such *idea* in
itself; and being meant for nothing else but the effect of such a
power, that simple *idea* is real and *adequate*; the sensation of
white in my mind, being the effect of that power which is in the
paper to produce it, is perfectly *adequate* to that power, or else
that power would produce a different *idea*.

13.   *Secondly*, The *complex* ideas *of substances are ectypes*,
copies too, but not perfect ones, not *adequate*; which is very
evident to the mind, in that it plainly perceives that, whatever
collection of simple *ideas* it makes of any substance that exists,
it cannot be sure that it exactly answers all that are in that substance; since, not having tried all the operations of all other
substances upon it and found all the alterations it would
receive from or cause in other substances, it cannot have an
exact *adequate* collection of all its active and passive capacities;
and so *not* have an *adequate* complex *idea* of the powers of any
substance existing and its relations, which is that sort of complex *idea* of substances we have.   And, after all, if we could
have and actually had in our complex *idea* an exact collection of

all the secondary qualities or powers of any substance, we should not yet thereby have an *idea* of the essence of that thing. For, since the powers or qualities that are observable by us are not the real essence of that substance but depend on it and flow from it, any collection whatsoever of these qualities cannot be the real essence of that thing. Whereby it is plain that our *ideas* of substances are not *adequate*, are not what the mind intends them to be. Besides, a man has no *idea* of substance in general, nor knows what substance is in itself.

14. *Thirdly, Complex* ideas *of modes and relations are* originals and *archetypes*, are not copies, nor made after the pattern of any real existence to which the mind intends them to be conformable and exactly to answer. These being such collections of simple *ideas* that the mind itself puts together, and such collections that each of them contains in it precisely all that the mind intends it should, they are archetypes and essences of modes that may exist, and so are designed only for and belong only to such modes as, when they do exist, have an exact conformity with those complex *ideas*. The *ideas*, therefore, of modes and relations cannot but be *adequate*.

Chapter XXXII

OF TRUE AND FALSE IDEAS

1. **Though** truth and falsehood belong, in propriety of speech, only to propositions, yet *ideas* are oftentimes termed *true or false* (as what words are there that are not used with great latitude and with some deviation from their strict and proper significations?): though I think that, when *ideas* themselves are termed true or false, there is still some secret or tacit proposition which is the foundation of that denomination, as we shall see if we examine the particular occasions wherein they come to be called true or false. In all which we shall find some kind of affirmation or negation, which is the reason of that denomination. For our *ideas*, being nothing but bare appearances or perceptions in our minds, cannot properly and simply in themselves be said to be *true* or *false*, no more than a single name of anything can be said to be *true* or *false*.

2. Indeed both *ideas* and words *may* be said to be *true, in a metaphysical sense* of the word truth, as all other things that any

way exist are said to be true, i.e. really to be such as they exist: though in things called *true* even in that sense, there is perhaps a secret reference to our *ideas*, looked upon as the standards of that truth; which amounts to a mental proposition, though it be usually not taken notice of.

3.   But it is not in that metaphysical sense of truth which we inquire here, when we examine whether our *ideas* are capable of being *true* or *false*, but in the more ordinary acceptation of those words; and so I say that the *ideas* in our minds, being only so many perceptions or appearances there, none of them are *false*: the *idea* of a centaur having no more falsehood in it when it appears in our minds than the name centaur has falsehood in it when it is pronounced by our mouths or written on paper. For truth or falsehood lying always in some affirmation or negation, mental or verbal, our *ideas* are *not capable*, any of them, *of being false*, till the mind passes some judgment on them, that is, affirms or denies something of them.

4.   Whenever the mind refers any of its *ideas* to anything extraneous to them, they are then *capable to be called true or false*. Because the mind, in such a reference, makes a tacit supposition of their conformity to that thing; which supposition as it happens to be *true* or *false*, so the *ideas* themselves come to be denominated. The most usual cases wherein this happens are these following:

5.   *First*, When the mind supposes any *idea* it has *conformable to* that in *other men's* minds, called by the same common name: v.g. when the mind intends or judges its *ideas* of *justice, temperance, religion* to be the same with what other men give those names to.

   Secondly, When the mind supposes any *idea* it has in itself to be *conformable to some real existence*. Thus the two *ideas* of a man and a centaur, supposed to be the *ideas* of real substances, are the one *true* and the other *false*: the one having a conformity to what has really existed, the other not.

   Thirdly, When the mind *refers* any of its *ideas to* that *real* constitution and *essence* of anything whereon all its properties depend; and thus the greatest part, if not all our *ideas* of substances are *false*.

6.   These suppositions the mind is very apt tacitly to make concerning its own *ideas*. But yet, if we will examine it, we shall find it is chiefly, if not only, concerning its abstract complex *ideas*. For the natural tendency of the mind being towards knowledge, and finding that, if it should proceed by and dwell upon only particular things, its progress would be very slow and its

work endless: therefore to shorten its way to knowledge and make each perception the more comprehensive, the first thing it does as the foundation of the easier enlarging its knowledge, either by contemplation of the things themselves that it would know or conference with others about them, is to bind them into bundles and rank them so into sorts, that what knowledge it gets of any of them it may thereby with assurance extend to all of that sort, and so advance by larger steps in that which is its great business, knowledge. This, as I have elsewhere shown, is the reason why we collect things under comprehensive *ideas*, with names annexed to them, into *genera* and *species*, i.e. into kinds and sorts.

7. If therefore we will warily attend to the motions of the mind and observe what course it usually takes in its way to knowledge, we shall, I think, find that, the mind having got any *idea* which it thinks it may have use of either in contemplation or discourse, the first thing it does is to abstract it, and then get a name to it, and so lay it up in its storehouse, the memory, as containing the essence of a sort of things of which that name is always to be the mark. Hence it is that we may often observe that, when anyone sees a new thing of a kind that he knows not, he presently asks what it is, meaning by that inquiry nothing but the name, as if the name carried with it the knowledge of the species or the essence of it, whereof it is indeed used as the mark and is generally supposed annexed to it.

8. But, this abstract *idea* being something in the mind between the thing that exists and the name that is given to it, it is in our *ideas* that both the rightness of our knowledge and the propriety or intelligibleness of our speaking consists. And hence it is that men are so forward to suppose that the abstract *ideas* they have in their minds are such as agree to the things existing without them to which they are referred, and are the same also to which the names they give them do by the use and propriety of that language belong. For without this *double conformity of* their *ideas*, they find they should both think amiss of things in themselves, and talk of them unintelligibly to others.

9. *First*, then, I say that, *when the truth of our* ideas *is judged of by the conformity they have to the* ideas *which other men have and commonly signify by the same name, they may be any of them false*. But yet *simple* ideas are *least* of all *liable to be so mistaken*, because a man, by his senses and every day's observation, may easily satisfy himself what the simple *ideas* are which their several names that are in common use stand for: they being but few in number and such as, if he doubts or mistakes in, he

may easily rectify by the objects they are to be found in. There-fore it is seldom that anyone mistakes in his names of simple *ideas*, or applies the name *red* to the *idea* of green, or the name sweet to the *idea* bitter; much less are men apt to confound the names of *ideas* belonging to different senses and call a colour by the name of a taste, etc., whereby it is evident that the simple *ideas* they call by any name are commonly the same that others have and mean when they use the same names.

10. *Complex* ideas *are much more liable to be false in this respect; and the complex* ideas *of mixed modes, much more than those of substances*; because in substances (especially those which the common and unborrowed names of any language are applied to) some remarkable sensible qualities, serving ordi-narily to distinguish one sort from another, easily preserve those who take any care in the use of their words from applying them to sorts of substances to which they do not at all belong. But in mixed modes we are much more uncertain: it being not so easy to determine of several actions whether they are to be called *justice* or *cruelty*, *liberality* or *prodigality*. And so in referring our *ideas* to those of other men, called by the same names, ours may be *false*; and the *idea* in our minds which we express by the word *justice* may perhaps be that which ought to have another name.

11. But whether or no our *ideas* of mixed modes are more liable than any sort to be different from those of other men which are marked by the same names, this at least is certain: that *this sort of falsehood is much more familiarly attributed to* our *ideas* of *mixed modes than to any other*. When a man is thought to have a false *idea* of *justice*, or *gratitude*, or *glory*, it is for no other reason but that his agrees not with the *ideas* which each of those names are the signs of in other men.

12. *The reason whereof* seems to me to be this: that the abstract *ideas* of mixed modes being men's voluntary combina-tions of such a precise collection of simple *ideas*, and so the essence of each species being made by men alone, whereof we have no other sensible standard existing anywhere but the name itself, or the definition of that name: we have nothing else to refer these our *ideas* of mixed modes to, as a standard to which we would conform them, but the *ideas* of those who are thought to use those names in their most proper significations; and so, as our *ideas* conform or differ from them, they pass for true or false. And thus much concerning the *truth* and *falsehood* of our *ideas* in reference to their names.

13. *Secondly,* As to the *truth and falsehood of our* ideas *in*

reference to the *real existence* of things: when that is made the standard of their truth, none of them can be termed false, but only our complex *ideas* of substances.

14.   *First*, Our simple *ideas* being barely such perceptions as God has fitted us to receive and given power to external objects to produce in us by established laws and ways, suitable to his wisdom and goodness, though incomprehensible to us, their truth consists in nothing else but in such appearances as are produced in us and must be suitable to those powers he has placed in external objects, or else they could not be produced in us; and thus answering those powers, they are what they should be, *true ideas*. Nor do they become liable to any imputation of *falsehood*, if the mind (as in most men I believe it does) judges these *ideas* to be in the things themselves. For God in his wisdom having set them as marks of distinction in things whereby we may be able to discern one thing from another and so choose any of them for our uses, as we have occasion, it alters not the nature of our simple *idea* whether we think that the *idea* of blue be in the violet itself or in our mind only; and only the power of producing it, by the texture of its parts reflecting the particles of light after a certain manner, to be in the violet itself. For that texture in the object, by a regular and constant operation, producing the same *idea* of blue in us, it serves us to distinguish, by our eyes, that from any other thing: whether that distinguishing mark, as it is really in the *violet*, be only a peculiar texture of parts or else that very colour, the *idea* whereof (which is in us) is the exact resemblance. And it is equally from that appearance to be denominated *blue*, whether it be that real colour or only a peculiar texture in it that causes in us that *idea*: since the name *blue* notes properly nothing but that mark of distinction that is in a *violet*, discernible only by our eyes, whatever it consists in, that being beyond our capacities distinctly to know and, perhaps, would be of less use to us if we had faculties to discern.

15.   Neither would it carry any imputation of *falsehood* to our simple *ideas if*, by the different structure of our organs, it were so ordered that *the same object should produce in several men's minds different* ideas at the same time: v.g. if the *idea* that a *violet* produced in one man's mind by his eyes were the same that a *marigold* produced in another man's, and *vice versa*. For, since this could never be known, because one man's mind could not pass into another man's body to perceive what appearances were produced by those organs, neither the *ideas* hereby, nor the names, would be at all confounded, or any *falsehood* be in either.

For all things that had the texture of a *violet* producing constantly the *idea* which he called *blue*, and those which had the texture of a *marigold* producing constantly the *idea* which he as constantly called *yellow*, whatever those appearances were in his mind, he would be able as regularly to distinguish things for his use by those appearances, and understand and signify those distinctions marked by the names *blue* and *yellow*, as if the appearances or *ideas* in his mind, received from those two flowers, were exactly the same with the *ideas* in other men's minds. I am nevertheless very apt to think that the sensible *ideas* produced by any object in different men's minds are most commonly very near and undiscernibly alike. For which opinion, I think, there might be many reasons offered; but, that being besides my present business, I shall not trouble my reader with them, but only mind him that the contrary supposition, if it could be proved, is of little use either for the improvement of our knowledge or conveniency of life, and so we need not trouble ourselves to examine it.

16. From what has been said concerning our simple *ideas*, I think it evident that our *simple* ideas can *none of them* be *false in respect of things* existing without us. For the truth of these appearances or perceptions in our minds consisting, as has been said, only in their being answerable to the powers in external objects to produce by our senses such appearances in us, and each of them being in the mind such as it is suitable to the power that produced it, and which alone it represents, it cannot upon that account, or as referred to such a pattern, be *false*. *Blue* or *yellow*, *bitter* or *sweet*, can never be false *ideas*: these perceptions in the mind are just such as they are there, answering the powers appointed by God to produce them, and so are truly what they are and are intended to be. Indeed the names may be misapplied, but that in this respect makes no falsehood in the *ideas*, as if a man ignorant in the *English* tongue should call *purple scarlet*.

17. *Secondly, Neither can* our *complex* ideas *of modes, in reference to the essence of anything really existing, be false*; because whatever complex *idea* I have of any mode, it hath no reference to any pattern existing and made by nature; it is not supposed to contain in it any other *ideas* than what it hath, nor to represent anything but such a complication of *ideas* as it does. Thus, when I have the *idea* of such an action of a man who forbears to afford himself such meat, drink, and clothing, and other conveniencies of life as his riches and estate will be sufficient to supply and his station requires, I have no *false idea* but such an

one as represents an action either as I find or imagine it, and so is capable of neither *truth* nor *falsehood*. But when I give the name *frugality* or *virtue* to this action, then it may be called a *false idea*, if thereby it be supposed to agree with that *idea* to which, in propriety of speech, the name of *frugality* doth belong, or to be conformable to that law which is the standard of virtue and vice.

18.   *Thirdly,* Our complex *ideas of substances, being all referred to patterns in things themselves, may be false.* That they are all *false,* when looked upon as the representations of the unknown essences of things, is so evident that there needs nothing to be said of it. I shall therefore pass over that chimerical supposition and consider them as collections of simple *ideas* in the mind, taken from combinations of simple *ideas* existing together constantly in things, of which patterns they are the supposed copies; and in this reference of them to the existence of things, they *are false* ideas: (1) *when* they put together simple *ideas,* which in the real existence of things have no union; as when, to the shape and size that exist together in a horse is joined in the same complex *idea* the power of barking like a dog: which three *ideas,* however put together into one in the mind, were never united in nature; and this therefore may be called a *false idea* of an horse. (2) *Ideas* of substances are in this respect also *false,* when, from any collection of simple *ideas* that do always exist together, there is separated, by a direct negation, any other simple *idea* which is constantly joined with them. Thus, if to extension, solidity, fusibility, the peculiar weightiness, and yellow colour of gold, anyone join in his thoughts the negation of a greater degree of fixedness than is in lead or copper, he may be said to have a false complex *idea,* as well as when he joins to those other simple ones the *idea* of perfect absolute fixedness. For either way, the complex *idea* of gold, being made up of such simple ones as have no union in nature, may be termed false. But if he leave out of this his complex *idea* that of fixedness quite, without either actually joining to or separating of it from the rest in his mind, it is, I think, to be looked on as an inadequate and imperfect *idea* rather than a *false* one, since, though it contains not all the simple *ideas* that are united in nature, yet it puts none together but what do really exist together.

19.   Though in compliance with the ordinary way of speaking, I have shown in what sense and upon what ground our *ideas* may be sometimes called *true* or *false,* yet if we will look a little nearer into the matter in all cases, where any *idea* is called *true*

or *false*, it is from some judgment that the mind makes or is supposed to make that is *true* or *false*. For *truth or falsehood* being *never without some affirmation or negation*, express or tacit, it is not to be found but where signs are joined or separated, according to the agreement or disagreement of the things they stand for. The signs we chiefly use are either *ideas* or words, wherewith we make either mental or verbal propositions. *Truth* lies in so joining or separating these representatives as the things they stand for do in themselves agree or disagree; and *falsehood* in the contrary, as shall be more fully shown hereafter.

Chapter XXXIII

OF THE ASSOCIATION OF IDEAS

1.   There is scarce anyone that does not observe something that seems odd to him, and is in itself really extravagant, in the opinions, reasonings, and actions of other men. The least flaw of this kind, if at all different from his own, everyone is quicksighted enough to espy in another, and will by the authority of reason forwardly condemn, though he be guilty of much greater unreasonableness in his own tenets and conduct, which he never perceives and will very hardly, if at all, be convinced of.

2.   This proceeds not wholly from self-love, though that has often a great hand in it. Men of fair minds, and not given up to the overweening of self-flattery, are frequently guilty of it; and in many cases one with amazement hears the arguings and is astonished at the obstinacy of a worthy man who yields not to the evidence of reason, though laid before him as clear as daylight.

3.   This sort of unreasonableness is usually imputed to education and prejudice, and for the most part truly enough, though that reaches not the bottom of the disease nor shows distinctly enough whence it rises or wherein it lies. Education is often rightly assigned for the cause, and prejudice is a good general name for the thing itself; but yet, I think, he ought to look a little further, who would trace this sort of madness to the root it springs from and so explain it, as to show whence this flaw has its original in very sober and rational minds, and wherein it consists.

4.   I shall be pardoned for calling it by so harsh a name as *madness*, when it is considered that opposition to reason deserves that name and is really madness; and there is scarce a man so

free from it but that, if he should always on all occasions argue or do as in some cases he constantly does, would not be thought fitter for *Bedlam* than civil conversation. I do not here mean when he is under the power of an unruly passion, but in the steady calm course of his life. That which will yet more apologize for this harsh name and ungrateful imputation on the greatest part of mankind is that, inquiring a little by the by into the nature of madness (bk. II, chap. xi, § 13), I found it to spring from the very same root and to depend on the very same cause we are here speaking of. This consideration of the thing itself, at a time when I thought not the least on the subject which I am now treating of, suggested it to me. And if this be a weakness to which all men are so liable, if this be a taint which so universally infects mankind, the greater care should be taken to lay it open under its due name, thereby to excite the greater care in its prevention and cure.

5. Some of our *ideas* have a natural correspondence and connexion one with another; it is the office and excellency of our reason to trace these, and hold them together in that union and correspondence which is founded in their peculiar beings. Besides this, there is another connexion of *ideas* wholly owing to chance or custom: *ideas*, that in themselves are not at all of kin, come to be so united in some men's minds that it is very hard to separate them, they always keep in company, and the one no sooner at any time comes into the understanding but its associate appears with it; and if they are more than two which are thus united, the whole gang, always inseparable, show themselves together.

6. This strong combination of *ideas*, not allied by nature, the mind makes in itself either voluntarily or by chance; and hence it comes in different men to be very different, according to their different inclinations, educations, interests, etc. Custom settles habits of thinking in the understanding, as well as of determining in the will, and of motions in the body: all which seem to be but trains of motion in the animal spirits, which, once set a-going, continue in the same steps they have been used to; which, by often treading, are worn into a smooth path, and the motion in it becomes easy and, as it were, natural. As far as we can comprehend thinking, thus *ideas* seem to be produced in our minds; or, if they are not, this may serve to explain their following one another in an habitual train, when once they are put into that track, as well as it does to explain such motions of the body. A musician used to any tune will find that, let it but once begin in his head, the *ideas* of the several notes of it will

follow one another orderly in his understanding, without any
care or attention, as regularly as his fingers move orderly over
the keys of the organ to play out the tune he has begun, though
his unattentive thoughts be elsewhere a-wandering. Whether
the natural cause of these *ideas*, as well as of that regular dancing
of his fingers, be the motion of his animal spirits, I will not
determine, how probable soever, by this instance, it appears to
be so; but this may help us a little to conceive of intellectual
habits and of the tying together of *ideas*.

7. That there are such associations of them made by custom
in the minds of most men, I think nobody will question who has
well considered himself or others; and to this, perhaps, might
be justly attributed most of the sympathies and antipathies
observable in men, which work as strongly and produce as
regular effects as if they were natural; and are therefore called
so, though they at first had no other original but the accidental
connexion of two *ideas*, which either the strength of the first
impression or future indulgence so united that they always
afterwards kept company together in that man's mind, as if they
were but one *idea*. I say most of the antipathies, I do not say
all: for some of them are truly natural, depend upon our original
constitution, and are born with us; but a great part of those
which are counted natural would have been known to be from
unheeded, though perhaps early, impressions or wanton fancies
at first, which would have been acknowledged the original of
them, if they had been warily observed. A grown person sur-
feiting with honey no sooner hears the name of it, but his fancy
immediately carries sickness and qualms to his stomach, and he
cannot bear the very *idea* of it; other *ideas* of dislike and sickness and vomiting presently accompany it, and he is disturbed,
but he knows from whence to date this weakness and can tell
how he got this indisposition: had this happened to him by an
overdose of honey when a child, all the same effects would have
followed, but the cause would have been mistaken, and the
antipathy counted natural.

8. I mention this not out of any great necessity there is in this
present argument to distinguish nicely between natural and
acquired antipathies, but I take notice of it for another purpose,
viz. that those who have children or the charge of their education would think it worth their while diligently to watch and
carefully to prevent the undue connexion of *ideas* in the minds
of young people. This is the time most susceptible of lasting
impressions; and though those relating to the health of the body
are by discreet people minded and fenced against, yet I am apt

to dou t that those which relate more peculiarly to the mind, and termin te in the understanding or passions, have been much less heeded than the thing deserves: nay, those relating purely to the understanding have, as I suspect, been by most men wholly overlooked.

9. This wrong connexion in our minds of *ideas*, in themselves loose and independent one of another, has such an influence and is of so great force to set us awry in our actions as well moral as natural, passions, reasonings, and notions themselves, that perhaps there is not any one thing that deserves more to be looked after.

10. The *ideas* of *goblins* and *sprites* have really no more to do with darkness than light: yet let but a foolish maid inculcate these often on the mind of a child and raise them there together, possibly he shall never be able to separate them again so long as he lives, but darkness shall ever afterwards bring with it those frightful *ideas*, and they shall be so joined that he can no more bear the one than the other.

11. A man receives a sensible injury from another, thinks on the man and that action over and over, and by ruminating on them strongly, or much, in his mind, so cements those two *ideas* together that he makes them almost one; never thinks on the man, but the pain and displeasure he suffered comes into his mind with it, so that he scarce distinguishes them, but has as much an aversion for the one as the other. Thus hatreds are often begotten from slight and almost innocent occasions, and quarrels propagated and continued in the world.

12. A man has suffered pain or sickness in any place, he saw his friend die in such a room: though these have in nature nothing to do one with another, yet when the *idea* of the place occurs to his mind, it brings (the impression being once made) that of the pain and displeasure with it, he confounds them in his mind, and can as little bear the one as the other.

13. When this combination is settled and whilst it lasts, it is not in the power of reason to help us and relieve us from the effects of it. *Ideas* in our minds, when they are there, will operate according to their natures and circumstances; and here we see the cause why time cures certain affections, which reason, though in the right and allowed to be so, has not power over nor is able against them to prevail with those who are apt to hearken to it in other cases. The death of a child, that was the daily delight of his mother's eyes and joy of her soul, rends from her heart the whole comfort of her life and gives her all the torment imaginable; use the consolations of reason in this case,

and you were as good preach ease to one on the rack and hope to allay, by rational discourses, the pain of his joints tearing asunder. Till time has by disuse separated the sense of that enjoyment and its loss from the *idea* of the child returning to her memory, all representations, though never so reasonable, are in vain; and therefore some in whom the union between these *ideas* is never dissolved spend their lives in mourning and carry an incurable sorrow to their graves.

14.   A friend of mine knew one perfectly cured of madness by a very harsh and offensive operation. The gentleman, who was thus recovered, with great sense of gratitude and acknowledgement owned the cure all his life after as the greatest obligation he could have received; but whatever gratitude and reason suggested to him, he could never bear the sight of the operator: that image brought back with it the *idea* of that agony which he suffered from his hands, which was too mighty and intolerable for him to endure.

15.   Many children, imputing the pain they endured at school to their books they were corrected for, so join those *ideas* together that a book becomes their aversion; and they are never reconciled to the study and use of them all their lives after; and thus reading becomes a torment to them, which otherwise possibly they might have made the great pleasure of their lives. There are rooms convenient enough that some men cannot study in; and fashions of vessels which, though never so clean and commodious, they cannot drink out of, and that by reason of some accidental *ideas* which are annexed to them and make them offensive; and who is there that hath not observed some man to flag at the appearance or in the company of some certain person, not otherwise superior to him, but because having once on some occasion got the ascendant, the *idea* of authority and distance goes along with that of the person, and he that has been thus subjected is not able to separate them.

16.   Instances of this kind are so plentiful everywhere that, if I add one more, it is only for the pleasant oddness of it. It is of a young gentleman, who having learnt to dance, and that to great perfection, there happened to stand an old trunk in the room where he learnt. The *idea* of this remarkable piece of household stuff had so mixed itself with the turns and steps of all his dances that, though in that chamber he could dance excellently well, yet it was only whilst that trunk was there; nor could he perform well in any other place, unless that or some such other trunk had its due position in the room. If this story shall be suspected to be dressed up with some comical circum-

stances, a little beyond precise nature, I answer for myself that I had it some years since from a very sober and worthy man, upon his own knowledge, as I report it; and I dare say there are very few inquisitive persons who read this, who have not met with accounts, if not examples, of this nature that may parallel, or at least justify this.

17.   Intellectual habits and defects, this way contracted, are not less frequent and powerful, though less observed. Let the *ideas* of being and matter be strongly joined, either by education or much thought: whilst these are still combined in the mind, what notions, what reasonings will there be about separate spirits? Let custom from the very childhood have joined figure and shape to the *idea* of God, and what absurdities will that mind be liable to about the Deity?

Let the *idea* of infallibility be inseparably joined to any person, and these two constantly together possess the mind; and then one body in two places at once shall unexamined be swallowed for a certain truth, by an implicit faith, whenever that imagined infallible person dictates and demands assent without inquiry.

18.   Some such wrong and unnatural combinations of *ideas* will be found to establish the irreconcilable opposition between different sects of philosophy and religion; for we cannot imagine everyone of their followers to impose wilfully on himself and knowingly refuse truth offered by plain reason.   Interest, though it does a great deal in the case, yet cannot be thought to work whole societies of men to so universal a perverseness as that every one of them to a man should knowingly maintain falsehood: some at least must be allowed to do what all pretend to, i.e. to pursue truth sincerely; and therefore there must be something that blinds their understandings and makes them not see the falsehood of what they embrace for real truth.   That which thus captivates their reasons and leads men of sincerity blindfold from common sense will, when examined, be found to be what we are speaking of: some independent *ideas* of no alliance to one another are, by education, custom, and the constant din of their party, so coupled in their minds that they always appear there together, and they can no more separate them in their thoughts than if they were but one *idea*, and they operate as if they were so.   This gives sense to *jargon*, demonstration to absurdities, and consistency to nonsense, and is the foundation of the greatest, I had almost said of all, the errors in the world; or if it does not reach so far, it is at least the most dangerous one, since, so far as it obtains, it hinders men from

seeing and examining. When two things, in themselves disjoined, appear to the sight constantly united, if the eye sees
these things riveted which are loose, where will you begin to
rectify the mistakes that follow in two *ideas* that they have been
accustomed so to join in their minds as to substitute one for the
other and, as I am apt to think, often without perceiving it
themselves? This, whilst they are under the deceit of it, makes
them incapable of conviction, and they applaud themselves as
zealous champions for truth, when indeed they are contending
for error; and the confusion of two different *ideas*, which a
customary connexion of them in their minds hath to them made
in effect but one, fills their heads with false views and their
reasonings with false consequences.

19.   Having thus given an account of the original, sorts, and
extent of our *ideas*, with several other considerations about these
(I know not whether I may say) instruments, or materials of
our knowledge, the method I at first proposed to myself would
now require that I should immediately proceed to show what
use the understanding makes of them, and what knowledge we
have by them. This was that which, in the first general view I
had of this subject, was all that I thought I should have to do;
but, upon a nearer approach, I find that there is so close a connexion between *ideas* and words, and our abstract *ideas* and
general words have so constant a relation one to another, that it
is impossible to speak clearly and distinctly of our knowledge,
which all consists in propositions, without considering first the
nature, use, and signification of language; which, therefore,
must be the business of the next book.

BOOK III

OF WORDS

CHAPTER I

OF WORDS OR LANGUAGE IN GENERAL

1. GOD, having designed man for a sociable creature, made him not only with an inclination and under a necessity to have fellowship with those of his own kind, but furnished him also with language, which was to be the great instrument and common tie of society. *Man*, therefore, had by nature his organs so fashioned as to be *fit to frame articulate sounds*, which we call words. But this was not enough to produce language; for parrots and several other birds will be taught to make articulate sounds distinct enough, which yet by no means are capable of language.

2. Besides articulate sounds, therefore, it was further necessary that he should be *able to use these sounds as signs of internal conceptions*, and to make them stand as marks for the *ideas* within his own mind, whereby they might be made known to others, and the thoughts of men's minds be conveyed from one to another.

3. But neither was this sufficient to make words so useful as they ought to be. It is not enough for the perfection of language that sounds can be made signs of *ideas*, unless those *signs* can be so made use of as *to comprehend several particular things*: for the multiplication of words would have perplexed their use, had every particular thing need of a distinct name to be signified by. To remedy this inconvenience, language had yet a further improvement in the use of general terms, whereby one word was made to mark a multitude of particular existences, which advantageous use of sounds was obtained only by the difference of the *ideas* they were made signs of: those names becoming general which are made to stand for general *ideas*, and those remaining particular where the *ideas* they are used for are particular.

4. Besides these names which stand for *ideas*, there be other words which men make use of, not to signify any *idea*, but the want or absence of some *ideas*, simple or complex, or all *ideas*

together: such as are *nihil* in Latin, and in English, *ignorance* and *barrenness*. All which negative or privative words cannot be said properly to belong to or signify no *ideas*, for then they would be perfectly insignificant sounds; but they relate to positive *ideas*, and signify their absence.

5.   It may also lead us a little towards the original of all our notions and knowledge, if we remark how great a dependence our *words* have on common sensible *ideas*, and how those which are made use of to stand for actions and notions quite removed from sense *have their rise from thence, and from obvious sensible* ideas *are transferred to more abstruse significations*, and made to stand for *ideas* that come not under the cognizance of our senses: v.g. to *imagine, apprehend, comprehend, adhere, conceive, instil, disgust, disturbance, tranquillity*, etc., are all words taken from the operations of sensible things, and applied to certain modes of thinking. *Spirit*, in its primary signification, is breath; *angel*, a messenger; and I doubt not but, if we could trace them to their sources, we should find in all languages the names, which stand for things that fall not under our senses, to have had their first rise from sensible *ideas*. By which we may give some kind of guess what kind of notions they were and whence derived, which filled their minds who were the first beginners of languages, and how nature, even in the naming of things, unawares suggested to men the originals and principles of all their knowledge: whilst, to give names that might make known to others any operations they felt in themselves, or any other *ideas* that came not under their senses, they were fain to borrow words from ordinary known *ideas* of sensation, by that means to make others the more easily to conceive those operations they experimented in themselves, which made no outward sensible appearances; and then, when they had got known and agreed names to signify those internal operations of their own minds, they were sufficiently furnished to make known by words all their other *ideas*, since they could consist of nothing but either of outward sensible perceptions, or of the inward operations of their minds about them: we having, as has been proved, no *ideas* at all, but what originally come either from sensible objects without, or what we feel within ourselves, from the inward workings of our own spirits, of which we are conscious to ourselves within.

6.   But to understand better the use and force of language, as subservient to instruction and knowledge, it will be convenient to consider:

First, To what it is that names, in the use of language, are immediately applied.

Secondly, Since all (except proper) names are general, and so stand not particularly for this or that single thing, but for sorts and ranks of things, it will be necessary to consider in the next place what the sorts and kinds or, if you rather like the Latin names, *what the species and genera of things* are, wherein they consist, and how they come to be made. These being (as they ought) well looked into, we shall the better come to find the right use of words, the natural advantages and defects of language, and the remedies that ought to be used, to avoid the inconveniences of obscurity or uncertainty in the signification of words, without which it is impossible to discourse with any clearness or order concerning knowledge, which, being conversant about propositions, and those most commonly universal ones, has greater connexion with words than perhaps is suspected.

These considerations, therefore, shall be the matter of the following chapters.

CHAPTER II

OF THE SIGNIFICATION OF WORDS

1. MAN, though he have great variety of thoughts, and such from which others as well as himself might receive profit and delight, yet they are all within his own breast, invisible and hidden from others, nor can of themselves be made to appear. The comfort and advantage of society not being to be had without communication of thoughts, it was necessary that man should find out some external sensible signs whereby those invisible *ideas,* which his thoughts are made up of, might be made known to others. For this purpose nothing was so fit, either for plenty or quickness, as those articulate sounds which with so much ease and variety he found himself able to make. Thus we may conceive how *words,* which were by nature so well adapted to that purpose, come to be made use of by men as *the signs of* their *ideas*: not by any natural connexion that there is between particular articulate sounds and certain *ideas,* for then there would be but one language amongst all men; but by a voluntary imposition whereby such a word is made arbitrarily the mark of such an *idea.* The use, then, of words is to be sensible marks of *ideas,* and the *ideas* they stand for are their proper and im-

mediate signification.

2.   The use men have of these marks being either to record their own thoughts for the assistance of their own memory or, as it were, to bring out their *ideas* and lay them before the view of others: *words, in their primary or immediate signification, stand for nothing but the* ideas *in the mind of him that uses them,* how imperfectly soever or carelessly those *ideas* are collected from the things which they are supposed to represent. When a man speaks to another, it is that he may be understood; and the end of speech is that those sounds, as marks, may make known his *ideas* to the hearer. That then which words are the marks of are the *ideas* of the speaker; nor can anyone apply them as marks, immediately, to anything else but the *ideas* that he himself hath, for this would be to make them signs of his own conceptions and yet apply them to other *ideas*, which would be to make them signs and not signs of his *ideas* at the same time, and so in effect to have no signification at all. Words being voluntary signs, they cannot be voluntary signs imposed by him on things he knows not. That would be to make them signs of nothing, sounds without signification. A man cannot make his words the signs either of qualities in things or of conceptions in the mind of another, whereof he has none in his own. Till he has some *ideas* of his own, he cannot suppose them to correspond with the conceptions of another man; nor can he use any signs for them: for thus they would be the signs of he knows not what, which is in truth to be the signs of nothing. But when he represents to himself other men's *ideas* by some of his own, if he consent to give them the same names that other men do, it is still to his own *ideas*: to *ideas* that he has, and not to *ideas* that he has not.

3.   This is so necessary in the use of language that in this respect the knowing and the ignorant, the learned and unlearned, use the *words* they speak (with any meaning) all alike. They, *in every man's mouth, stand for the* ideas *he has*, and which he would express by them. A child having taken notice of nothing in the metal he hears called gold but the bright shining yellow colour, he applies the word gold only to his own *idea* of that colour and nothing else, and therefore calls the same colour in a peacock's tail gold. Another that hath better observed adds to shining yellow great weight, and then the sound gold, when he uses it, stands for a complex *idea* of a shining yellow and very weighty substance. Another adds to those qualities fusibility, and then the word gold to him signifies a body, bright, yellow, fusible, and very heavy. Another adds malleability. Each of

these uses equally the word gold, when they have occasion to express the *idea* which they have applied it to; but it is evident that each can apply it only to his own *idea*, nor can he make it stand as a sign of such a complex *idea* as he has not.

4. But though words, as they are used by men, can properly and immediately signify nothing but the *ideas* that are in the mind of the speaker, yet they in their thoughts give them a secret reference to two other things.

First, they suppose their words to be marks of the ideas *in the minds also of other men, with whom they communicate*: for else they should talk in vain and could not be understood, if the sounds they applied to one *idea* were such as by the hearer were applied to another, which is to speak two languages. But in this, men stand not usually to examine whether the *idea* they and those they discourse with have in their minds be the same, but think it enough that they use the word as they imagine in the common acceptation of that language, in which they suppose that the *idea* they make it a sign of is precisely the same to which the understanding men of that country apply that name.

5. *Secondly,* because *men* would not be thought to talk *barely* of their own imaginations, but of things as really they are, therefore they *often suppose their words to stand also for the reality of things.* But this relating more particularly to substances and their names, as perhaps the former does to simple *ideas* and modes, we shall speak of these two different ways of applying words more at large, when we come to treat of the names of mixed môdes and substances in particular: though give me leave here to say that it is a perverting the use of words, and brings unavoidable obscurity and confusion into their signification, whenever we make them stand for anything but those *ideas* we have in our own minds.

6. Concerning words also it is further to be considered: *First,* That they being immediately the signs of men's *ideas* and, by that means, the instruments whereby men communicate their conceptions and express to one another those thoughts and imaginations they have within their own breasts, *there comes by constant use* to be such *a connexion between certain sounds and the* ideas *they stand for* that the names heard almost as readily excite certain *ideas* as if the objects themselves, which are apt to produce them, did actually affect the senses. Which is manifestly so in all obvious sensible qualities, and in all substances that frequently and familiarly occur to us.

7. *Secondly,* That though the proper and immediate signification of words are *ideas* in the mind of the speaker, yet,

because by familiar use from our cradles we come to learn certain articulate sounds very perfectly and have them readily on our tongues and always at hand in our memories, but yet are not always careful to examine or settle their significations perfectly, it *often* happens that *men*, even when they would apply themselves to an attentive consideration, do *set their thoughts more on words than things*. Nay, because words are many of them learned before the *ideas* are known for which they stand: therefore some, not only children but men, speak several words no otherwise than parrots do, only because they have learned them and have been accustomed to those sounds. But so far as words are of use and signification, so far is there a constant connexion between the sound and the *idea*, and a designation that the one stand for the other: without which application of them, they are nothing but so much insignificant noise.

8. *Words*, by long and familiar use, as has been said, come to excite in men certain *ideas*, so constantly and readily that they are apt to suppose a natural connexion between them. But that they *signify* only men's peculiar *ideas*, and that *by a perfectly arbitrary imposition*, is evident in that they often fail to excite in others (even that use the same language) the same *ideas* we take them to be the signs of; and every man has so inviolable a liberty to make words stand for what *ideas* he pleases that no one hath the power to make others have the same *ideas* in their minds that he has, when they use the same words that he does. And therefore the great *Augustus* himself, in the possession of that power which ruled the world, acknowledged he could not make a new Latin word, which was as much as to say that he could not arbitrarily appoint what *idea* any sound should be a sign of, in the mouths and common language of his subjects. It is true, common use, by a tacit consent, appropriates certain sounds to certain *ideas* in all languages, which so far limits the signification of that sound that, unless a man applies it to the same *idea*, he does not speak properly. And let me add that, unless a man's words excite the same *ideas* in the hearer which he makes them stand for in speaking, he does not speak intelligibly. But whatever be the consequence of any man's using of words differently, either from their general meaning or the particular sense of the person to whom he addresses them, this is certain: their signification, in his use of them, is limited to his *ideas*, and they can be signs of nothing else.

1. ALL things that exist being particulars, it may perhaps be thought reasonable that words, which ought to be conformed to things, should be so too, I mean in their signification, but yet we find the quite contrary. The far *greatest part of words* that make all languages *are general terms*: which has not been the effect of neglect or chance, but of reason and necessity.

2. *First, It is impossible that every particular thing should have a distinct peculiar name.* For, the signification and use of words depending on that connexion which the mind makes between its *ideas* and the sounds it uses as signs of them, it is necessary, in the application of names to things, that the mind should have distinct *ideas* of the things, and retain also the particular name that belongs to every one, with its peculiar appropriation to that *idea*. But it is beyond the power of human capacity to frame and retain distinct *ideas* of all the particular things we meet with: every bird and beast men saw, every tree and plant that affected the senses could not find a place in the most capacious understanding. If it be looked on as an instance of a prodigious memory that some generals have been able to call every soldier in their army by his proper name, we may easily find a reason why men have never attempted to give names to each sheep in their flock or crow that flies over their heads, much less to call every leaf of plants or grain of sand that came in their way by a peculiar name.

3. *Secondly,* If it were possible, *it would yet be useless,* because it would not serve to the chief end of language. Men would in vain heap up names of particular things, that would not serve them to communicate their thoughts. Men learn names and use them in talk with others only that they may be understood: which is then only done when, by use or consent, the sound I make by the organs of speech excites, in another man's mind who hears it, the *idea* I apply it to in mine when I speak it. This cannot be done by names applied to particular things, whereof I alone having the *ideas* in my mind, the names of them could not be significant or intelligible to another who was not acquainted with all those very particular things which had fallen under my notice.

4. *Thirdly,* But yet granting this also feasible (which I think

is not), yet *a distinct name for every particular thing would not be of any great use for the improvement of knowledge,* which, though founded in particular things, enlarges itself by general views, to which things reduced into sorts, under general names, are properly subservient. These, with the names belonging to them, come within some compass and do not multiply every moment, beyond what either the mind can contain or use requires. And therefore, in these, men have for the most part stopped, but yet not so as to hinder themselves from distinguishing particular things by appropriated names, where convenience demands it. And therefore in their own species, which they have most to do with and wherein they have often occasion to mention particular persons, they make use of proper names, and there distinct individuals have distinct denominations.

5.   Besides persons, countries also, cities, rivers, mountains, and other the like distinctions of place have usually found peculiar names, and that for the same reason: they being such as men have often an occasion to mark particularly and, as it were, set before others in their discourses with them. And I doubt not but, if we had reason to mention particular horses as often as we have to mention particular men, we should have *proper names* for the one as familiar as for the other, and *Bucephalus* would be a word as much in use as *Alexander*. And therefore we see that, amongst jockeys, horses have their proper names to be known and distinguished by as commonly as their servants: because amongst them there is often occasion to mention this or that particular horse, when he is out of sight.

6.   The next thing to be considered is *how general words come to be made.* For since all things that exist are only particulars, how come we by general terms, or where find we those general natures they are supposed to stand for? Words become general by being made the signs of general *ideas*; and *ideas* become general by separating from them the circumstances of time and place and any other *ideas* that may determine them to this or that particular existence. By this way of abstraction they are made capable of representing more individuals than one: each of which, having in it a conformity to that abstract *idea,* is (as we call it) of that sort.

7.   But to deduce this a little more distinctly, it will not perhaps be amiss to trace our notions and names from their beginning and observe by what degrees we proceed and by what steps we enlarge our *ideas* from our first infancy. There is nothing more evident than that the *ideas* of the persons children converse

with (to instance in them alone) are, like the persons themselves, only particular. The *ideas* of the nurse and the mother are well framed in their minds and, like pictures of them there, represent only those individuals. The names they first gave to them are confined to these individuals, and the names of *nurse* and *mamma* the child uses determine themselves to those persons. Afterwards, when time and a larger acquaintance have made them observe that there are a great many other things in the world that, in some common agreements of shape and several other qualities, resemble their father and mother and those persons they have been used to, they frame an *idea* which they find those many particulars do partake in, and to that they give, with others, the name *man*, for example. And *thus they come to have a general name*, and a general *idea*. Wherein they make nothing new, but only leave out of the complex *idea* they had of *Peter* and *James*, *Mary* and *Jane* that which is peculiar to each, and retain only what is common to them all.

8. By the same way that they come by the general name and *idea* of *man*, they easily *advance to more general names* and notions. For, observing that several things that differ from their *idea of man* and cannot therefore be comprehended under that name have yet certain qualities wherein they agree with *man*, by retaining only those qualities and uniting them into one *idea*, they have again another and a more general *idea*, to which, having given a name, they make a term of a more comprehensive extension: which new *idea* is made, not by any new addition, but only as before, by leaving out the shape and some other properties signified by the name *man*, and retaining only a body, with life, sense, and spontaneous motion, comprehended under the name *animal*.

9. That this is the *way whereby men first formed general* ideas, *and general names to them*, I think is so evident that there needs no other proof of it but the considering of a man's self, or others, and the ordinary proceedings of their minds in knowledge; and he that thinks general natures or notions are anything else but such abstract and partial *ideas* of more complex ones, taken at first from particular existences, will I fear be at a loss where to find them. For let anyone reflect and then tell me wherein does his *idea* of *man* differ from that of *Peter* and *Paul*, or his *idea* of *horse* from that of *Bucephalus*, but in the leaving out something that is peculiar to each individual, and retaining so much of those particular complex *ideas* of several particular existences as they are found to agree in. Of the complex *ideas* signified by the names *man* and *horse*, leaving out but those

particulars wherein they differ, and retaining only those wherein they agree, and of those making a new distinct complex *idea*, and giving the name *animal* to it, one has a more general term that comprehends with man several other creatures. Leave out of the *idea* of *animal* sense and spontaneous motion, and the remaining complex *idea*, made up of the remaining simple ones of body, life, and nourishment, becomes a more general one, under the more comprehensive term, *vivens*. And not to dwell longer upon this particular, so evident in itself, by the same way the mind proceeds to *body*, *substance*, and at last to *being*, *thing*, and such universal terms which stand for any of our *ideas* whatsoever. To conclude: this whole *mystery* of *genera* and *species*, which make such a noise in the schools and are with justice so little regarded out of them, is nothing else but abstract *ideas*, more or less comprehensive, with names annexed to them. In all which, this is constant and unvariable: that every more general term stands for such an *idea* as is but a part of any of those contained under it.

10.   This may show us the reason *why, in the defining of words*, which is nothing but declaring their signification, *we make use of the genus*, or next general word that comprehends it. Which is not out of necessity, but only to save the labour of enumerating the several simple *ideas* which the next general word or *genus* stands for, or, perhaps, sometimes the shame of not being able to do it. But though defining by *genus* and *differentia* (I crave leave to use these terms of art, though originally Latin, since they most properly suit those notions they are applied to) I say, though defining by the *genus* be the shortest way, yet I think it may be doubted whether it be the best. This I am sure, it is not the only, and so not absolutely necessary. For, definition being nothing but making another understand by words what *idea* the term defined stands for, a definition is best made by enumerating those simple *ideas* that are combined in the signification of the term defined; and if, instead of such an enumeration, men have accustomed themselves to use the next general term, it has not been out of necessity or for greater clearness, but for quickness and dispatch sake. For I think that, to one who desired to know what *idea* the word *man* stood for, if it should be said that *man* was a solid extended substance, having life, sense, spontaneous motion, and the faculty of reasoning, I doubt not but the meaning of the term *man* would be as well understood, and the *idea* it stands for be at least as clearly made known, as when it is defined to be a *rational animal*; which, by the several definitions of *animal*, *vivens*, and *corpus*, resolves itself into

those enumerated *ideas*. I have, in explaining the term *man*, followed here the ordinary definition of the schools, which, though perhaps not the most exact, yet serves well enough to my present purpose. And one may, in this instance, see what gave occasion to the rule that a definition must consist of *genus* and *differentia*; and it suffices to show us the little necessity there is of such a rule, or advantage in the strict observing of it. For definitions, as has been said, being only the explaining of one word by several others so that the meaning or *idea* it stands for may be certainly known, languages are not always so made according to the rules of logic that every term can have its signification exactly and clearly expressed by two others. Experience sufficiently satisfies us to the contrary, or else those who have made this rule have done ill, that they have given us so few definitions conformable to it. But of definitions, more in the next chapter.

11.   To return to general words: it is plain, by what has been said, that *general* and *universal* belong not to the real existence of things, but *are the inventions* and *creatures of the understanding*, made by it for its own use, *and concern only signs*, whether words or *ideas*. Words are general, as has been said, when used for signs of general *ideas*, and so are applicable indifferently to many particular things; and *ideas* are general when they are set up as the representatives of many particular things: but universality belongs not to things themselves, which are all of them particular in their existence, even those words and *ideas* which in their signification are general. When therefore we quit particulars, the generals that rest are only creatures of our own making: their general nature being nothing but the capacity they are put into, by the understanding, of signifying or representing many particulars. For the signification they have is nothing but a relation that, by the mind of man, is added to them.

12.   The next thing therefore to be considered is *what kind of signification it is that general words have*. For, as it is evident that they do not signify barely one particular thing, for then they would not be general terms but proper names, so on the other side it is as evident they do not signify a plurality, for man and men would then signify the same, and the distinction of numbers (as grammarians call them) would be superfluous and useless. That then which general words signify is a sort of things, and each of them does that by being a sign of an abstract *idea* in the mind; to which *idea*, as things existing are found to agree, so they come to be ranked under that name or, which is all one, be of that sort. Whereby it is evident that the *essences of* the *sorts or* (if the Latin word pleases better) *species* of things are

nothing else but these abstract *ideas*. For, the having the essence of any species being that which makes any thing to be of that species, and the conformity to the *idea* to which the name is annexed being that which gives a right to that name, the having the essence and the having that conformity must needs be the same thing, since to be of any species and to have a right to the name of that species is all one. As for example, to be a *man* or of the species *man* and to have right to the name *man* is the same thing. Again, to be a *man* or of the same species *man* and have the essence of a *man* is the same thing. Now, since nothing can be a *man* or have a right to the name *man* but what has a conformity to the abstract *idea* the name *man* stand for, nor anything be a man or have a right to the species *man* but what has the essence of that species, it follows that the abstract *idea* for which the name stands and the essence of the species is one and the same. From whence it is easy to observe that the essences of the sorts of things and, consequently, the sorting of things is the workmanship of the understanding that abstracts and makes those general *ideas*.

13. I would not here be thought to forget, much less to deny, that nature, in the production of things, makes several of them alike: there is nothing more obvious, especially in the races of animals, and all things propagated by seed. But yet I think we may say the *sorting* of them under names *is the workmanship of the understanding, taking occasion, from the similitude* it observes amongst them, to make abstract general *ideas*, and set them up in the mind, with names annexed to them, as patterns or forms (for in that sense the word form has a very proper signification), to which, as particular things existing are found to agree, so they come to be of that species, have that denomination, or are put into that *classis*. For when we say: this is a *man*, that a *horse*; this *justice*, that *cruelty*; this a *watch*, that a *jack*, what do we else but rank things under different specific names as agreeing to those abstract *ideas* of which we have made those names the signs? And what are the essences of those species, set out and marked by names, but those abstract ideas in the mind, which are, as it were, the bonds between particular things that exist and the names they are to be ranked under? And when general names have any connexion with particular beings, these abstract *ideas* are the *medium* that unites them: so that the essences of species, as distinguished and denominated by us, neither are nor can be anything but those precise abstract *ideas* we have in our minds. And therefore the supposed real essences of substances, if different from our abstract *ideas*, cannot be the

essences of the species we rank things into. For two species may be one, as rationally as two different essences be the essence of one species; and I demand, What are the alterations which may or may not be made in a *horse* or *lead*, without making either of them to be of another species? In determining the species of things by our abstract *ideas*, this is easy to resolve; but if any-one will regulate himself herein by supposed real essences, he will, I suppose, be at a loss, and he will never be able to know when any thing precisely ceases to be of the species of a *horse* or *lead*.
14. Nor will anyone wonder that I say these *essences* or abstract *ideas* (which are the measures of name and the boundaries of species) are *the workmanship of the understanding*, who con-siders that at least the complex ones are often, in several men, different collections of simple *ideas*, and therefore that is *covet-ousness* to one man which is not so to another. Nay, even in substances, where their abstract *ideas* seem to be taken from the things themselves, they are not constantly the same; no, not in that species which is most familiar to us and with which we have the most intimate acquaintance, it having been more than once doubted whether the *foetus* born of a woman were a *man*, even so far as that it hath been debated whether it were or were not to be nourished and baptized: which it could not be if the abstract *idea* or essence to which the name man belonged were of nature's making, and were not the uncertain and various collection of simple *ideas* which the understanding puts together, and then abstracting it, affixed a name to it. So that in truth *every distinct abstract* idea *is a distinct essence*, and the names that stand for such distinct *ideas* are the names of things essentially different. Thus a circle is as essentially different from an oval as a sheep from a goat, and rain is as essentially different from snow as water from earth, that abstract *idea* which is the essence of one being impossible to be communicated to the other. And thus any two abstract *ideas* that in any part vary one from an-other, with two distinct names annexed to them, constitute two distinct sorts or, if you please, *species*, as essentially different as any two the most remote or opposite in the world.
15. But since the *essences* of things are thought by some (and not without reason) to be wholly unknown, it may not be amiss to consider the *several significations of the word essence*.
First, Essence may be taken for the being of anything whereby it is what it is. And thus the real internal, but generally (in Substances) unknown, constitution of things, whereon their discoverable qualities depend, may be called their *essence*. This is the proper original signification of the word, as is evident

from the formation of it: *essentia*, in its primary notation, signifying properly *being*. And in this sense it is still used, when we speak of the *essence* of particular things, without giving them any name.

Secondly, The learning and disputes of the Schools having been much busied about *genus* and *species*, the word *essence* has almost lost its primary signification and, instead of the real constitution of things, has been almost wholly applied to the artificial constitution of *genus* and *species*. It is true, there is ordinarily supposed a real constitution of the sorts of things, and it is past doubt there must be some real constitution on which any collection of simple *ideas* co-existing must depend. But, it being evident that things are ranked under names into sorts or *species*, only as they agree to certain abstract *ideas* to which we have annexed those names, the *essence* of each *genus* or sort comes to be nothing but that abstract *idea* which the general or *sortal* (if I may have leave so to call it from *sort*, as I do *general* from *genus*) name stands for. And this we shall find to be that which the word *essence* imports in its most familiar use. These two sorts of *essences*, I suppose, may not unfitly be termed the one the *real*, the other the *nominal essence*.

16. *Between the nominal essence and the name* there is so *near a connexion* that the name of any sort of things cannot be attributed to any particular being but what has this *essence*, whereby it answers that abstract *idea* whereof that name is the sign.

17. Concerning the real essences of corporeal substances (to mention those only) there are, if I mistake not, two opinions. The one is of those who, using the word *essence* for they know not what, suppose a certain number of those essences, according to which all natural things are made and wherein they do exactly every one of them partake, and so become of this or that *species*. The other and more rational opinion is of those who look on all natural things to have a real, but unknown, constitution of their insensible parts, from which flow those sensible qualities which serve us to distinguish them one from another, according as we have occasion to rank them into sorts, under common denominations. The former of these opinions, which supposes these *essences* as a certain number of forms or moulds wherein all natural things that exist are cast and do equally partake, has, I imagine, very much perplexed the knowledge of natural things. The frequent productions of monsters in all the species of animals, and of changelings, and other strange issues of human birth carry with them difficulties not possible to con-

sist with this *hypothesis*, since it is as impossible that two things partaking exactly of the same real *essence* should have different properties, as that two figures partaking in the same real *essence* of a circle should have different properties. But were there no other reason against it, yet the *supposition of essences that cannot be known* and the making them, nevertheless, to be that which distinguishes the species of things *is* so *wholly useless* and unserviceable to any part of our knowledge that that alone were sufficient to make us lay it by and content ourselves with such *essences* of the sorts or species of things as come within the reach of our knowledge: which, when seriously considered, will be found, as I have said, to be nothing else but those abstract complex *ideas* to which we have annexed distinct general names.

18. *Essences* being thus distinguished into *nominal and real*, we may further observe that, *in* the species of *simple* ideas *and modes*, they *are always the same*, but *in substances always quite different*. Thus, a figure including a space between three lines is the real as well as nominal *essence* of a triangle, it being not only the abstract *idea* to which the general name is annexed, but the very *essentia* or being of the thing itself, that foundation from which all its properties flow, and to which they are all inseparably annexed. But it is far otherwise concerning that parcel of matter which makes the ring on my finger, wherein these two *essences* are apparently different. For it is the real constitution of its insensible parts, on which depend all those properties of colour, weight, fusibility, fixedness, etc., which makes it to be *gold* or gives it a right to that name which is therefore its nominal *essence*, since nothing can be called *gold* but what has a conformity of qualities to that abstract complex *idea* to which that name is annexed. But this distinction of *essences* belonging particularly to substances, we shall, when we come to consider their names, have an occasion to treat of more fully.

Chapter IV

OF THE NAMES OF SIMPLE IDEAS

1. Though all words, as I have shown, signify nothing immediately but the *ideas* in the mind of the speaker, yet upon a nearer survey we shall find that the *names of simple* ideas, *mixed*

modes (under which I comprise relations too) *and natural substances have each of them something peculiar* and different from the other. For example:

2.   *First,* The *names of simple* ideas *and substances,* with the abstract *ideas* in the mind which they immediately signify, *intimate* also *some real existence* from which was derived their original pattern. But the *names of mixed modes terminate in the* idea that is in the mind and lead not the thoughts any further, as we shall see more at large in the following chapter.

3.   *Secondly,* The *names of simple* ideas *and modes signify always the real as well as nominal essence of their species.* But *the names of natural substances signify* rarely, if ever, anything but *barely the nominal essences* of those species, as we shall show in the chapter that treats of the names of substances in particular.

4.   *Thirdly,* The *names of simple* ideas *are not capable of any definitions;* the names of all complex *ideas* are. It has not, that I know, hitherto been taken notice of, by anybody, what words are and what are not capable of being defined: the want whereof is (as I am apt to think) not seldom the occasion of great wrangling and obscurity in men's discourses, whilst some demand definitions of terms that cannot be defined, and others think they ought to rest satisfied in an explication made by a more general word and its restriction (or to speak in terms of art by a genus and difference), when, even after such definition made according to rule, those who hear it have often no more a clear conception of the meaning of the word than they had before. This at least I think, that the showing what words are and what are not capable of definitions and wherein consists a good definition is not wholly besides our present purpose, and perhaps will afford so much light to the nature of these signs and our *ideas* as to deserve a more particular consideration.

5.   I will not here trouble myself to prove that all terms are not definable from that progress *in infinitum* which it will visibly lead us into, if we should allow that all names could be defined. For if the terms of one definition were still to be defined by another, where at last should we stop? But I shall from the nature of our *ideas* and the signification of our words show *why some names can, and others cannot be defined,* and which they are.

6.   I think it is agreed that *a definition is* nothing else but *the showing the meaning of one word by several other not synonymous terms.* The meaning of words being only the *ideas* they are made to stand for by him that uses them, the meaning of any term is then shown or the word is defined when, by other words, the

idea it is made the sign of and annexed to, in the mind of the speaker, is as it were represented or set before the view of another, and thus its signification ascertained: this is the only use and end of definitions, and therefore the only measure of what is or is not a good definition.

7. This being premised, I say that *the names of simple ideas, and those only, are incapable of being defined.* The reason whereof is this, that the several terms of a definition signifying several *ideas*, they can all together by no means represent an *idea* which has no composition at all; and therefore a definition which is properly nothing but the showing the meaning of one word by several others, not signifying each the same thing, can in the names of simple *ideas* have no place.

8. The not observing this difference in our *ideas* and their names has produced that eminent trifling in the Schools, which is so easy to be observed in the definitions they give us of some few of these simple *ideas*. For, as to the greatest part of them, even those masters of definitions were fain to leave them untouched, merely by the impossibility they found in it. What more exquisite *jargon* could the wit of man invent than this definition, *The act of a being in power, as far forth as in power,* which would puzzle any rational man, to whom it was not already known by its famous absurdity, to guess what word it could ever be supposed to be the explication of. If *Tully,* asking a *Dutchman* what *beweging* was, should have received this explication in his own language, that it was *Actus entis in potentia quatenus in potentia,* I ask whether anyone can imagine he could thereby have understood what the word *beweging* signified or have guessed what *idea* a *Dutchman* ordinarily had in his mind and would signify to another when he used that sound.

9. Nor have the modern philosophers, who have endeavoured to throw off the *jargon* of the Schools and speak intelligibly, much better succeeded in defining simple *ideas*, whether by explaining their causes or any otherwise. The *atomists*, who define motion to be a *passage from one place to another*, what do they more than put one synonymous word for another? For what is *passage* other than *motion*? And if they were asked what passage was, how would they better define it than by *motion*? For is it not at least as proper and significant to say *passage is a motion from one place to another* as to say *motion is a passage*, etc. This is to translate and not to define, when we change two words of the same signification one for another; which, when one is better understood than the other, may serve to discover what

idea the unknown stands for, but is very far from a *definition*, unless we will say every English word in the dictionary is the definition of the Latin word it answers, and that motion is a definition of *motus*. *Nor will the successive application of the parts of the* superficies *of one body to those of another*, which the *Cartesians* give us, prove a much better definition of motion when well examined.

10.   *The act of perspicuous, as far forth as perspicuous* is another peripatetic definition of a simple *idea*, which, though not more absurd than the former of *motion*, yet betrays its uselessness and insignificancy more plainly, because experience will easily convince anyone that it cannot make the meaning of the word *light* (which it pretends to define) at all understood by a blind man; but the definition of *motion* appears not at first sight so useless, because it escapes this way of trial. For this simple *idea* entering by the touch as well as sight, it is impossible to show an example of anyone who has no other way to get the *idea* of *motion* but barely by the definition of that name. Those who tell us that *light* is a great number of little globules, striking briskly on the bottom of the eye, speak more intelligibly than the Schools; but yet these words never so well understood would make the *idea* the word *light* stands for no more known to a man that understands it not before, than if one should tell him that *light* was nothing but a company of little tennis-balls which fairies all day long struck with rackets against some men's foreheads, whilst they passed by others. For granting this explication of the thing to be true, yet the *idea* of the cause of *light*, if we had it never so exact, would no more give us the *idea* of *light* itself as it is such a particular perception in us than the *idea* of the figure and motion of a sharp piece of steel would give us the *idea* of that pain which it is able to cause in us. For the cause of any sensation and the sensation itself, in all the simple *ideas* of one sense, are two *ideas*, and two *ideas* so different and distant one from another that no two can be more so. And therefore should *Descartes's* globules strike never so long on the *retina* of a man who was blind by a *gutta serena*, he would thereby never have any *idea* of *light* or anything approaching to it, though he understood what little globules were and what striking on another body was never so well. And therefore the *Cartesians* very well distinguish between that light which is the cause of that sensation in us, and the *idea* which is produced in us by it and is that which is properly light.

CHAPTER V

OF THE NAMES OF MIXED MODES AND RELATIONS

1. THE names of mixed modes being general, they stand, as has been shown, for sorts or species of things, each of which has its peculiar essence. The essences of these species also, as has been shown, are nothing but the abstract *ideas* in the mind, to which the name is annexed. Thus far the names and essences of mixed modes have nothing but what is common to them with other *ideas*; but if we take a little nearer survey of them, we shall find that they have something peculiar, which perhaps may deserve our attention.

2. The first particularity I shall observe in them is that the abstract *ideas* or, if you please, the essences of the several species *of mixed modes are made by the understanding*, wherein they differ from those of simple *ideas*; in which sort the mind has no power to make any one, but only receives such as are presented to it by the real existence of things operating upon it.

3. In the next place, these *essences of the species of mixed modes are* not only *made* by the mind, but made *very arbitrarily*, made without patterns, or reference to any real existence. Wherein they differ from those of substances, which carry with them the supposition of some real being, from which they are taken, and to which they are conformable. But, in its complex *ideas* of mixed modes, the mind takes a liberty not to follow the existence of things exactly. It unites and retains certain collections, as so many distinct specific *ideas*; whilst others, that as often occur in nature and are as plainly suggested by outward things, pass neglected, without particular names or specifications. Nor does the mind, in these of mixed modes, as in the complex *ideas* of substances, examine them by the real existence of things, or verify them by patterns containing such peculiar compositions in nature. To know whether his *idea* of *adultery* or *incest* be right will a man seek it anywhere amongst things existing? Or is it true because anyone has been witness to such an action? No; but it suffices here that men have put together such a collection into one complex *idea* that makes the *archetype* and specific *idea*, whether ever any such action were committed *in rerum natura* or no.

4. To understand this aright, we must consider *wherein this making of these complex* ideas *consists*; and that is not in the

making any new *idea*, but putting together those which the mind had before. Wherein the mind does these three things: first, it chooses a certain number. Secondly, it gives them connexion, and makes them into one *idea*. Thirdly, it ties them together by a name. If we examine how the mind proceeds in these and what liberty it takes in them, we shall easily observe how these essences of the species of mixed modes are the workmanship of the mind and, consequently, that the species themselves are of men's making.

5. Nobody can doubt but that these *ideas* of mixed modes are made by a voluntary collection of *ideas* put together in the mind, independent from any original patterns in nature, who will but reflect that this sort of complex *ideas* may be made, abstracted, and have names given them, and so a species be constituted, before any one individual of that species ever existed. Who can doubt but the *ideas* of *sacrilege* or *adultery* might be framed in the minds of men, and have names given them, and so these species of mixed modes be constituted, before either of them was ever committed; and might be as well discoursed of and reasoned about, and as certain truths discovered of them, whilst yet they had no being but in the understanding, as well as now that they have but too frequently a real existence? Whereby it is plain how much *the sorts of mixed modes are the creatures of the understanding*, where they have a being as subservient to all the ends of real truth and knowledge as when they really exist; and we cannot doubt but law-makers have often made laws about species of actions which were only the creatures of their own understandings, beings that had no other existence but in their own minds. And I think nobody can deny but that the *resurrection* was a species of mixed modes in the mind, before it really existed.

6. To see *how arbitrarily these essences of mixed modes are made* by the mind, we need but take a view of almost any of them. A little looking into them will satisfy us that it is the mind that combines several scattered independent *ideas* into one complex one and, by the common name it gives them, makes them the essence of a certain species, without regulating itself by any connexion they have in nature. For what greater connexion in nature has the *idea* of a man, than the *idea* of a sheep, with killing, that this is made a particular species of action, signified by the word *murder*, and the other not? Or what union is there in nature between the *idea* of the relation of a father, with killing, than that of a son or neighbour, that those are combined into one complex *idea* and thereby made the essence of the distinct species *parricide*, whilst the other makes no distinct species at

all? But, though they have made killing a man's father or mother a distinct species from killing his son or daughter, yet, in some other cases, son and daughter are taken in too, as well as father and mother; and they are all equally comprehended in the same species, as in that of *incest*. Thus the mind in mixed modes arbitrarily unites into complex *ideas* such as it finds convenient; whilst others that have altogether as much union in nature are left loose, and never combined into one *idea*, because they have no need of one name. It is evident then that the mind, by its free choice, gives a connexion to a certain number of *ideas* which in nature have no more union with one another than others that it leaves out. Why else is the part of the weapon the beginning of the wound is made with taken notice of, to make the distinct species called *stabbing*, and the figure and matter of the weapon left out? I do not say this is done without reason, as we shall see more by and by; but this I say, that it is done by the free choice of the mind pursuing its own ends, and that therefore these species of mixed modes are the workmanship of the understanding; and there is nothing more evident than that for the most part, in the framing these *ideas*, the mind searches not its patterns in nature, nor refers the *ideas* it makes to the real existence of things, but puts such together as may best serve its own purposes, without tying itself to a precise imitation of anything that really exists.

7. But, though these complex *ideas* or *essences of mixed modes* depend on the mind and are made by it with great liberty, yet they *are not made at random* and jumbled together without any reason at all. Though these complex *ideas* be not always copied from nature, yet they are always suited to the end for which abstract *ideas* are made; and though they be combinations made of *ideas* that are loose enough, and have as little union in themselves as several others to which the mind never gives a connexion that combines them into one *idea*, yet they are always made for the convenience of communication, which is the chief end of language. The use of language is by short sounds to signify with ease and dispatch general conceptions, wherein not only abundance of particulars may be contained, but also a great variety of independent *ideas* collected into one complex one. In the making therefore of the species of mixed modes, men have had regard only to such combinations as they had occasion to mention one to another. Those they have combined into distinct complex *ideas* and given names to, whilst others that in nature have as near a union are left loose and unregarded. For to go no further than human actions themselves, if they

would make distinct abstract *ideas* of all the varieties might be observed in them, the number must be infinite, and the memory confounded with the plenty, as well as overcharged to little purpose. It suffices that men make and name so many complex *ideas* of these mixed modes as they find they have occasion to have names for in the ordinary occurrence of their affairs. If they join to the *idea* of killing the *idea* of father or mother and so make a distinct species from killing a man's son or neighbour, it is because of the different heinousness of the crime; and the distinct punishment is due to the murdering a man's father and mother, different from what ought to be inflicted on the murder of a son or neighbour; and therefore they find it necessary to mention it by a distinct name, which is the end of making that distinct combination. But though the *ideas* of mother and daughter are so differently treated in reference to the *idea* of killing that the one is joined with it to make a distinct abstract *idea* with a name, and so a distinct species, and the other not, yet in respect of carnal knowledge they are both taken in under *incest*, and that still for the same convenience of expressing under one name and reckoning of one species such unclean mixtures as have a peculiar turpitude beyond others; and this to avoid circumlocutions and tedious descriptions.

8. A moderate skill *in different languages* will easily satisfy one of the truth of this, it being so obvious to observe great store of *words in one* language *which have not any that answer them in another*. Which plainly shows that those of one country, by their customs and manner of life, have found occasion to make several complex *ideas* and give names to them, which others never collected into specific *ideas*. This could not have happened if these species were the steady workmanship of nature, and not collections made and abstracted by the mind, in order to naming, and for the convenience of communication. The terms of our law, which are not empty sounds, will hardly find words that answer them in the Spanish or Italian, no scanty languages; much less, I think, could anyone translate them into the *Caribbee* or *Westoe* tongues; and the *versura* of the *Romans* or *corban* of the *Jews* have no words in other languages to answer them, the reason whereof is plain from what has been said. Nay, if we will look a little more nearly into this matter and exactly compare different languages, we shall find that, though they have words which in translations and dictionaries are supposed to answer one another, yet there is scarce one of ten amongst the names of complex *ideas*, especially of mixed modes, that stands for the same precise *idea* which the word does that in

dictionaries it is rendered by. There are no *ideas* more common and less compounded than the measures of time, extension, and weight; and the Latin names, *hora, pes, libra,* are without difficulty rendered by the *English* names, *hour, foot,* and *pound*; but yet there is nothing more evident than that the *ideas* a *Roman* annexed to these Latin names were very far different from those which an *Englishman* expresses by those English ones. And if either of these should make use of the measures that those of the other language designed by their names, he would be quite out in his account. These are too sensible proofs to be doubted; and we shall find this much more so in the names of more abstract and compounded *ideas,* such as are the greatest part of those which make up moral discourses; whose names, when men come curiously to compare with those they are translated into in other languages, they will find very few of them exactly to correspond in the whole extent of their significations.

9. The reason why I take so particular notice of this is that we may not be mistaken about *genera* and *species* and their *essences,* as if they were things regularly and constantly made by nature and had a real existence in things, when they appear upon a more wary survey to be nothing else but an artifice of the understanding, for the easier signifying such collections of *ideas* as it should often have occasion to communicate by one general term; under which, divers particulars, as far forth as they agreed to that abstract *idea,* might be comprehended. And if the doubtful signification of the word *species* may make it sound harsh to some that I say that the species of mixed modes are made by the understanding, yet I think it can by nobody be denied that it is the mind makes those abstract complex *ideas* to which specific names are given. And if it be true, as it is, that the mind makes the patterns for sorting and naming of things, I leave it to be considered who makes the boundaries of the sort or *species,* since with me, *species* and *sort* have no other difference than that of a Latin and English *idiom.*

10. *The near relation* that there is *between species, essences, and* their *general name,* at least in *mixed modes,* will further appear when we consider that it is the name that seems to preserve those *essences* and give them their lasting duration. For, the connexion between the loose parts of those complex *ideas* being made by the mind, this union, which has no particular foundation in nature, would cease again, were there not something that did, as it were, hold it together and keep the parts from scattering. Though therefore it be the mind that makes the collection, it is the name which is as it were the knot that ties

them fast together. What a vast variety of different *ideas* does the word *triumphus* hold together and deliver to us as one *species*! Had this name been never made or quite lost, we might, no doubt, have had descriptions of what passed in that solemnity; but yet I think that which holds those different parts together in the unity of one complex *idea* is that very word annexed to it: without which, the several parts of that would no more be thought to make one thing than any other show which, having never been made but once, had never been united into one complex *idea*, under one denomination. How much, therefore, in mixed modes the unity necessary to any essence depends on the mind, and how much the continuation and fixing of that unity depends on the name in common use annexed to it, I leave to be considered by those who look upon *essences* and *species* as real established things in nature.

11.   Suitable to this, we find that *men speaking of mixed modes seldom* imagine *or take any other for species of them but such as are set out by name*: because they being of man's making only, in order to naming, no such *species* are taken notice of or supposed to be unless a *name* be joined to it, as the sign of man's having combined into one *idea* several loose ones, and by that *name* giving a lasting union to the parts which would otherwise cease to have any, as soon as the mind laid by that abstract *idea* and ceased actually to think on it. But when a name is once annexed to it, wherein the parts of that complex *idea* have a settled and permanent union, then is the *essence* as it were established and the *species* looked on as complete. For to what purpose should the memory charge itself with such compositions, unless it were by abstraction to make them general? And to what purpose make them general, unless it were that they might have general *names*, for the convenience of discourse and communication? Thus we see that killing a man with a sword or a hatchet are looked on as no distinct species of action; but if the point of the sword first enter the body, it passes for a distinct *species*, where it has a distinct *name*, as in *England*, in whose language it is called *stabbing*; but in another country where it has not happened to be specified under a peculiar *name*, it passes not for a distinct *species*. But in the *species* of corporeal substances, though it be the mind that makes the nominal essence, yet since those *ideas* which are combined in it are supposed to have an union in nature, whether the mind joins them or no, therefore those are looked on as distinct *species* without any operation of the mind, either abstracting or giving a *name* to that complex *idea*.

12. Conformable also to what has been said concerning the *essences* of the *species* of *mixed modes*, that they are the creatures of the understanding rather than the works of nature: conformable, I say, to this, we find that *their names lead our thoughts to the mind, and no further.* When we speak of *justice* or *gratitude,* we frame to ourselves no imagination of anything existing, which we would conceive, but our thoughts terminate in the abstract *ideas* of those virtues and look not further: as they do when we speak of a *horse,* or *iron,* whose specific *ideas* we consider not as barely in the mind, but as in things themselves, which afford the original patterns of those *ideas.* But in mixed modes, at least the most considerable parts of them, which are moral beings, we consider the original patterns as being in the mind; and to those we refer for the distinguishing of particular beings under names. And hence I think it is that these *essences* of the *species* of mixed modes are by a more particular name called *notions,* as by a peculiar right, appertaining to the understanding.

13. Hence likewise we may learn *why the complex* ideas *of mixed modes are commonly more compounded and decompounded than those of natural substances.* Because they being the workmanship of the understanding, pursuing only its own ends and the conveniency of expressing in short those *ideas* it would make known to another, it does with great liberty unite often into one abstract *idea* things that in their nature have no coherence, and so under one term bundle together a great variety of compounded and decompounded *ideas.* Thus the name of *procession,* what a great mixture of independent *ideas* of persons, habits, tapers, orders, motions, sounds does it contain in that complex one, which the mind of man has arbitrarily put together, to express by that one name! Whereas the complex *ideas* of the sorts of substances are usually made up of only a small number of simple ones; and in the *species* of animals, these two, viz. shape and voice, commonly make the whole nominal essence.

CHAPTER VI

OF THE NAMES OF SUBSTANCES

1. THE *common names of substances,* as well as other general terms, *stand for sorts*: which is nothing else but the being made signs of such complex *ideas* wherein several particular substances

do or might agree, by virtue of which they are capable of being comprehended in one common conception and be signified by one name. I say do or might agree: for, though there be but one sun existing in the world, yet the *idea* of it being abstracted so that more substances (if there were several) might each agree in it, it is as much a sort as if there were as many suns as there are stars. They want not their reasons who think there are, and that each fixed star would answer the *idea* the name *sun* stands for to one who were placed in a due distance; which, by the way, may show us how much the sorts or, if you please, *genera* and *species* of things (for those Latin terms signify to me no more than the English word *sort*) depend on such collections of *ideas* as men have made, and not on the real nature of things: since it is not impossible but that, in propriety of speech, that might be a sun to one which is a star to another.

2.   The measure and boundary of each sort or *species*, whereby it is constituted that particular sort and distinguished from others, is that we call its *essence*, which *is* nothing but that *abstract* idea *to which the name is annexed*; so that everything contained in that *idea* is essential to that sort. This, though it be all the *essence* of natural substances that we know or by which we distinguish them into sorts, yet I call it by a peculiar name, the *nominal essence*, to distinguish it from that real constitution of substances upon which depends this *nominal essence* and all the properties of that sort; which, therefore, as has been said, may be called the *real essence*: v.g. the *nominal essence* of *gold* is that complex *idea* the word *gold* stands for, let it be for instance a body yellow, of a certain weight, malleable, fusible, and fixed. But the *real essence* is the constitution of the insensible parts of that body on which those qualities and all the other properties of *gold* depend. How far these two are different, though they are both called *essence*, is obvious at first sight to discover.

3.   For, though perhaps voluntary motion, with sense and reason, joined to a body of a certain shape be the complex *idea* to which I and others annex the name *man* and so be the *nominal essence* of the *species* so called, yet nobody will say that that complex *idea* is the *real essence* and source of all those operations which are to be found in any individual of that sort. The foundation of all those qualities which are the ingredients of our complex *idea* is something quite different; and had we such a knowledge of that constitution of *man* from which his faculties of moving, sensation, and reasoning, and other powers flow and on which his so regular shape depends, as it is possible angels have and it is certain his Maker has, we should have a quite other *idea*

of his *essence* than what now is contained in our definition of that *species*, be it what it will. And our *idea* of any individual *man* would be as far different from what it now is, as is his who knows all the springs and wheels and other contrivances within of the famous clock at *Strasbourg* from that which a gazing countryman has of it, who barely sees the motion of the hand and hears the clock strike and observes only some of the outward appearances.

4. That *essence*, in the ordinary use of the word, relates to *sorts*, and that it is considered in particular beings no further than as they are ranked into *sorts* appears from hence: that, take but away the abstract *ideas* by which we sort individuals and rank them under common names, and then the thought of anything *essential* to any of them instantly vanishes: we have no notion of the one without the other, which plainly shows their relation. It is necessary for me to be as I am, GOD and nature has made me so; but there is nothing I have is essential to me. An accident or disease may very much alter my colour or shape; a fever or fall may take away my reason or memory, or both; and an apoplexy leave neither sense, nor understanding, no, nor life. Other creatures of my shape may be made with more and better, or fewer and worse faculties than I have; and others may have reason and sense in a shape and body very different from mine. None of these are essential to the one or the other, or to any individual whatsoever, till the mind refers it to some sort or *species* of things; and then presently, according to the abstract *idea* of that sort, something is found *essential*. Let anyone examine his own thoughts and he will find that, as soon as he supposes or speaks of *essential*, the consideration of some *species* or the complex *idea* signified by some general name comes into his mind: and it is in reference to that that this or that quality is said to be essential. So that, if it be asked whether it be *essential* to me or any other particular corporeal being to have reason, I say no, no more than it is *essential* to this white thing I write on to have words in it. But if that particular being be to be counted of the sort *man* and to have the name *man* given it, then reason is *essential* to it, supposing reason to be a part of the complex *idea* the name *man* stands for, · as it is *essential* to this thing I write on to contain words, if I will give it the name *treatise* and rank it under that *species*. So that *essential and not essential relate only to our abstract ideas and the names annexed to them*; which amounts to no more but this: that whatever particular thing has not in it those qualities which are contained in the abstract *idea* which any general term stands

for cannot be ranked under that *species* nor be called by that name, since that abstract *idea* is the very *essence* of that *species*.
5. Thus if the *idea* of *body*, with some people, be bare extension or space, then solidity is not *essential* to body. If others make the *idea* to which they give the name *body* to be solidity and extension, then solidity is essential to *body*. That therefore and *that alone is* considered as *essential which makes a part of the complex* idea *the name of a sort stands for*, without which no particular thing can be reckoned of that sort nor be entitled to that name. Should there be found a parcel of matter that had all the other qualities that are in *iron*, but wanted obedience to the loadstone and would neither be drawn by it nor receive direction from it, would anyone question whether it wanted anything *essential*? It would be absurd to ask whether a thing really existing wanted anything *essential* to it. Or could it be demanded whether this made an *essential* or *specific* difference or no, since we have no other measure of *essential* or *specific* but our abstract *ideas*? And to talk of specific differences in nature, without reference to general *ideas* and names, is to talk unintelligibly. For I would ask anyone: What is sufficient to make an *essential* difference in nature between any two particular beings, without any regard had to some abstract *idea*, which is looked upon as the essence and standard of a *species*? All such patterns and standards being quite laid aside, particular beings, considered barely in themselves, will be found to have all their qualities equally *essential*; and everything in each individual will be *essential* to it or, which is more, nothing at all. For, though it may be reasonable to ask whether obeying the magnet be *essential* to *iron*, yet I think it is very improper and insignificant to ask whether it be *essential* to the particular parcel of matter I cut my pen with, without considering it under the name *iron* or as being of a certain *species*. And if, as has been said, our abstract *ideas*, which have names annexed to them, are the boundaries of *species*, nothing can be *essential* but what is contained in those *ideas*.
6. It is true, I have often mentioned a *real essence*, distinct in substances from those abstract *ideas* of them, which I call their *nominal essence*. By this *real essence*, I mean that real constitution of anything, which is the foundation of all those properties that are combined in and are constantly found to co-exist with the *nominal essence*, that particular constitution which everything has within itself, without any relation to anything without it. But *essence*, even in this sense, *relates to a sort*, and supposes a *species*. For, being that real constitution on which the properties

depend, it necessarily supposes a sort of things, properties belonging only to *species*, and not to individuals: v.g. supposing the nominal essence of *gold* to be body of such a peculiar colour and weight, with malleability and fusibility, the real essence is that constitution of the parts of matter on which these qualities and their union depend, and is also the foundation of its solubility in *aqua regia*, and other properties accompanying that complex *idea*. Here are *essences* and *properties*, but all upon supposition of a sort or general abstract *idea*, which is considered as immutable; but there is no individual parcel of matter to which any of these qualities are so annexed as to be *essential* to it or inseparable from it. That which is *essential* belongs to it as a condition whereby it is of this or that sort; but take away the consideration of its being ranked under the name of some abstract *idea*, and then there is nothing necessary to it, nothing inseparable from it. Indeed, as to the *real essences* of substances, we only suppose their being, without precisely knowing what they are; but that which annexes them still to the *species* is the nominal essence, of which they are the supposed foundation and cause.

7. The next thing to be considered is by which of those essences it is that *substances are determined into* sorts or *species*; and that, it is evident, is *by the nominal essence*. For it is that alone that the name, which is the mark of the sort, signifies. It is impossible therefore that anything should determine the sorts of things which we rank under general names but that *idea* which that name is designed as a mark for; which is that, as has been shown, which we call the *nominal essence*. Why do we say, this is a *horse* and that a *mule*, this is an *animal*, that an *herb*? How comes any particular thing to be of this or that *sort* but because it has that nominal essence or, which is all one, agrees to that abstract *idea* that name is annexed to? And I desire anyone but to reflect on his own thoughts when he hears or speaks any of those or other names of substances, to know what sort of *essences* they stand for.

8. And that the *species of things to us are nothing but the ranking them under distinct names, according to the complex* ideas *in us*, and not according to precise, distinct, real *essences* in them, is plain from hence: that we find many of the individuals that are ranked into one sort, called by one common name, and so received as being of one *species*, have yet qualities depending on their real constitutions, as far different one from another as from others from which they are accounted to differ *specifically*. This, as it is easy to be observed by all who have to do with natural

bodies, so chemists especially are often, by sad experience, convinced of it, when they, sometimes in vain, seek for the same qualities in one parcel of sulphur, antimony, or vitriol which they have found in others. For, though they are bodies of the same *species*, having the same nominal *essence*, under the same name, yet do they often, upon severe ways of examination, betray qualities so different one from another as to frustrate the expectation and labour of very wary chemists. But if things were distinguished into *species*, according to their real essences, it would be as impossible to find different properties in any two individual substances of the same *species* as it is to find different properties in two circles, or two equilateral triangles. That is properly the *essence* to us which determines every particular to this or that *classis* or, which is the same thing, to this or that general name; and what can that be else but that abstract *idea* to which that name is annexed, and so has, in truth, a reference, not so much to the being of particular things, as to their general denominations?

9. Nor indeed *can we* rank and *sort things*, and consequently (which is the end of sorting) denominate them *by their real essences*, because we know them not. Our faculties carry us no further towards the knowledge and distinction of substances than a collection of those sensible *ideas* which we observe in them; which, however made with the greatest diligence and exactness we are capable of, yet is more remote from the true internal constitution from which those qualities flow than, as I said, a countryman's *idea* is from the inward contrivance of that famous clock at *Strasbourg*, whereof he only sees the outward figure and motions. There is not so contemptible a plant or animal that does not confound the most enlarged understanding. Though the familiar use of things about us take off our wonder, yet it cures not our ignorance. When we come to examine the stones we tread on or the iron we daily handle, we presently find we know not their make, and can give no reason of the different qualities we find in them. It is evident the internal constitution, whereon their properties depend, is unknown to us. For to go no further than the grossest and most obvious we can imagine amongst them, what is that texture of parts, that real *essence*, that makes lead and antimony fusible, wood and stones not? What makes lead and iron malleable, antimony and stones not? And yet how infinitely these come short of the fine contrivances and inconceivable *real essences* of plants or animals, everyone knows. The workmanship of the all-wise and powerful God in the great fabric of the universe and every part thereof further

exceeds the capacity and comprehension of the most inquisitive and intelligent man than the best contrivance of the most ingenious man doth the conceptions of the most ignorant of rational creatures. Therefore we in vain pretend to range things into sorts and dispose them into certain classes under names, by their *real essences* that are so far from our discovery or comprehension. A blind man may as soon sort things by their colours, and he that has lost his smell as well distinguish a lily and a rose by their odours as by those internal constitutions which he knows not. He that thinks he can distinguish sheep and goats by their real essences that are unknown to him may be pleased to try his skill in those *species* called *cassowary* and *querechinchio*, and by their internal real essences determine the boundaries of those *species*, without knowing the complex *idea* of sensible qualities that each of those names stand for in the countries where those animals are to be found.

14. To distinguish substantial beings into *species*, according to the usual supposition that there are certain precise *essences* or *forms* of things whereby all the individuals existing are by nature distinguished into *species*, these things are necessary:

15. *First*, To be assured that nature, in the production of things, always designs them to partake of certain regulated established *essences*, which are to be the models of all things to be produced. This, in that crude sense it is usually proposed, would need some better explication before it can fully be assented to.

16. *Secondly*, It would be necessary to know whether nature always attains that *essence* it designs in the production of things. The irregular and monstrous births, that in divers sorts of animals have been observed, will always give us reason to doubt of one or both of these.

17. *Thirdly*, It ought to be determined whether those we call *monsters* be really a distinct *species*, according to the scholastic notion of the word *species*, since it is certain that everything that exists has its particular constitution; and yet we find that some of these monstrous productions have few or none of those qualities which are supposed to result from and accompany the *essence* of that *species* from whence they derive their originals, and to which, by their descent, they seem to belong.

18. *Fourthly*, The *real essences* of those things which we distinguish into *species*, and as so distinguished we name, ought to be known: i.e. we ought to have *ideas* of them. But since we are ignorant in these four points, *the supposed real essences of things stand us not in stead for the distinguishing substances into species.*

19. *Fifthly*, The only imaginable help in this case would be

that, having framed perfect complex *ideas* of the *properties* of things flowing from their different real essences, we should thereby distinguish them into *species*. But neither can this be done; for, being ignorant of the real essence itself, it is impossible to know all those properties that flow from it and are so annexed to it that, any one of them being away, we may certainly conclude that that essence is not there, and so the thing is not of that *species*. We can never know what are the precise number of properties depending on the real essence of *gold*; any one of which failing, the real essence of gold, and consequently gold, would not be there, unless we knew the real essence of gold itself, and by that determined that *species*. By the word *gold* here, I must be understood to design a particular piece of matter: v.g. the last guinea that was coined. For if it should stand here in its ordinary signification for that complex *idea* which I or anyone else calls gold, i.e. for the nominal essence of gold, it would be *jargon*: so hard is it to show the various meaning and imperfection of words when we have nothing else but words to do it by.

21.   But since, as has been remarked, we have need of general words, though we know not the real essences of things, all we can do is to collect such a number of simple *ideas* as, by examination, we find to be united together in things existing, and thereof to make one complex *idea*. Which, though it be not the real essence of any substance that exists, is yet *the specific essence* to which our name belongs, and is convertible with it; by which we may at least try the truth of these nominal essences. For example: there be those that say that the essence of *body* is *extension*; if it be so, we can never mistake in putting the essence of anything for the thing itself. Let us then in discourse put *extension* for *body*; and when we would say that body moves, let us say that extension moves, and see how it will look. He that should say that one extension by impulse moves another extension would, by the bare expression, sufficiently show the absurdity of such a notion. The *essence* of anything, in respect of us, is the whole complex *idea* comprehended and marked by that name; and in substances, besides the several distinct simple *ideas* that make them up, the confused one of substance or of an unknown support and cause of their union is always a part; and therefore the essence of body is not bare extension, but an extended solid thing; and so to say an extended solid thing moves or impels another is all one, and as intelligible, as to say *body* moves or impels. Likewise, to say that a rational animal is capable of conversation is all one as to say a *man*. But no one will say that

rationality is capable of conversation, because it makes not the whole essence to which we give the name man.

22.   There are creatures in the world that have shapes like ours, but are hairy and want language and reason. There are naturals amongst us that have perfectly our shape, but want reason, and some of them language too. There are creatures, as it is said (*sit fides penes auctorem,* but there appears no contradiction that there should be such) that, with language and reason, and a shape in other things agreeing with ours, have hairy tails; others where the males have no beards, and others where the females have. If it be asked whether these be all *men* or no, all of human *species,* it is plain the question refers only to the nominal essence: for those of them to whom the definition of the word *man* or the complex *idea* signified by that name agrees are *men,* and the other not. But if the inquiry be made concerning the supposed real essence, and whether the internal constitution and frame of these several creatures be specifically different, it is wholly impossible for us to answer, no part of that going into our specific *idea:* only we have reason to think that, where the faculties or outward frame so much differs, the internal constitution is not exactly the same. But what difference in the internal real constitution makes a specific difference it is in vain to inquire, whilst *our measures of species* be, as they *are, only our abstract ideas,* which we know, and not that internal constitution which makes no part of them. Shall the difference of hair only on the skin be a mark of a different internal specific constitution between a changeling and a drill, when they agree in shape and want of reason and speech? And shall not the want of reason and speech be a sign to us of different real constitutions and *species* between a changeling and a reasonable man? And so of the rest, if we pretend that the distinction of *species* or sorts is fixedly established by the real frame and secret constitutions of things.

26.   Since then it is evident that we sort and name substances by their *nominal* and not by their real *essences,* the next thing to be considered is how and by whom these *essences* come to be made. As to the latter, it is evident they *are made by the mind,* and not by nature: for were they nature's workmanship, they could not be so various and different in several men as experience tells us they are. For if we will examine it, we shall not find the nominal essence of any one *species* of substances in all men the same: no, not of that which of all others we are the most intimately acquainted with. It could not possibly be that the abstract *idea* to which the name *man* is given should be different

in several men, if it were of nature's making, and that to one it should be *animal rationale*, and to another *animal implume bipes latis unguibus*. He that annexes the name *man* to a complex *idea*, made up of sense and spontaneous motion, joined to a body of such a shape, has thereby one essence of the *species man*; and he that, upon further examination, adds rationality has another essence of the *species* he calls *man*: by which means the same individual will be a true *man* to the one which is not so to the other. I think there is scarce anyone will allow this upright figure, so well known, to be the essential difference of the *species man*; and yet how far men determine of the sorts of animals, rather by their shape than descent, is very visible, since it has been more than once debated whether several human *foetus* should be preserved or received to baptism or no, only because of the difference of their outward configuration from the ordinary make of children, without knowing whether they were not as capable of reason as infants cast in another mould; some whereof, though of an approved shape, are never capable of as much appearance of reason all their lives as is to be found in an ape or an elephant, and never give any signs of being acted by a rational soul. Whereby it is evident that the outward figure, which only was found wanting, and not the faculty of reason, which nobody could know would be wanting in its due season, was made essential to the human *species*. The learned divine and lawyer must, on such occasions, renounce his sacred definition of *animal rationale* and substitute some other essence of the human *species*. Monsieur *Ménage* furnishes us with an example worth the taking notice of on this occasion. *When the Abbot of St. Martin,* says he, *was born, he had so little of the figure of a man that it bespake him rather a monster. It was for some time under deliberation whether he should be baptized or no. However, he was baptized and declared a man provisionally* (till time should show what he would prove). *Nature had moulded him so untowardly that he was called all his life the Abbot Malotru,* i.e. ill-shaped. *He was of* Caën.[1] This child we see was very near being excluded out of the *species* of *man,* barely by his shape. He escaped very narrowly as he was; and, it is certain, a figure a little more oddly turned had cast him, and he had been executed as a thing not to be allowed to pass for a man. And yet there can be no reason given why, if the lineaments of his face had been a little altered, a rational soul could not have been lodged in him; why a visage somewhat longer, or a nose flatter, or a wider mouth could not have consisted, as well as the rest of his ill

[1] *Ménagiana.* 2. éd. 1694. t. i, p. 278.

figure, with such a soul, such parts as made him, disfigured as he was, capable to be a dignitary in the church.

27. Wherein, then, would I gladly know, consist the precise and *unmovable boundaries of* that *species*? It is plain, if we examine, there is *no* such thing *made by nature* and established by her amongst men. The real essence of that or any other sort of substances, it is evident, we know not; and therefore are so undetermined in our nominal essences, which we make ourselves, that, if several men were to be asked concerning some oddly-shaped *foetus*, as soon as born, whether it were a *man* or no, it is past doubt one should meet with different answers. Which could not happen if the nominal essences, whereby we limit and distinguish the *species* of substances, were not made by man with some liberty, but were exactly copied from precise boundaries set by nature, whereby it distinguished all substances into certain *species*. Who would undertake to resolve what *species* that monster was of which is mentioned by *Licetus*,[1] with a man's head and hog's body? Or those other which to the bodies of men had the heads of beasts, as dogs, horses, etc. If any of these creatures had lived and could have spoke, it would have increased the difficulty. Had the upper part to the middle been of human shape, and all below swine, had it been murder to destroy it? Or must the bishop have been consulted whether it were man enough to be admitted to the font or no? As I have been told, it happened in *France* some years since, in somewhat a like case. So uncertain are the boundaries of *species* of animals to us, who have no other measures than the complex *ideas* of our own collecting, and so far are we from certainly knowing what a *man* is, though perhaps it will be judged great ignorance to make any doubt about it. And yet I think I may say that the certain boundaries of that *species* are so far from being determined, and the precise number of simple *ideas*, which make the nominal essence, so far from being settled and perfectly known, that very material doubts may still arise about it; and I imagine none of the definitions of the word *man* which we yet have, nor descriptions of that sort of animal are so perfect and exact as to satisfy a considerate inquisitive person, much less to obtain a general consent and to be that which men would everywhere stick by in the decision of cases and determining of life and death, baptism or no baptism, in productions that might happen.

28. But though these *nominal essences of substances* are made by the mind, they are *not* yet *made so arbitrarily as those of*

[1] Liceto, F. *De monstrorum causis* . . . 1616. lib. i, c. 3.

mixed modes. To the making of any nominal essence it is necessary, *first*, that the *ideas* whereof it consists have such an union as to make but one *idea*, how compounded soever. *Secondly*, that the particular *ideas* so united be exactly the same, neither more nor less. For if two abstract complex *ideas* differ either in number or sorts of their component parts, they make two different, and not one and the same essence. In the first of these, the mind, in making its complex *ideas* of substances, only follows nature and puts none together which are not supposed to have an union in nature. Nobody joins the voice of a sheep with the shape of a horse, nor the colour of lead with the weight and fixedness of gold, to be the complex *ideas* of any real substances, unless he has a mind to fill his head with *chimeras* and his discourse with unintelligible words. Men, observing certain qualities always joined and existing together, therein copied nature, and of *ideas* so united made their complex ones of substances. For though men may make what complex *ideas* they please and give what names to them they will, yet if they will be understood when they speak of things really existing, they must in some degree conform their *ideas* to the things they would speak of; or else men's language will be like that of *Babel*, and every man's words, being intelligible only to himself, would no longer serve to conversation and the ordinary affairs of life, if the ideas they stand for be not some way answering the common appearances and agreement of substances as they really exist.

29. *Secondly*, Though the mind of man, *in making* its *complex ideas of substances*, never puts any together that do not really, or are not supposed to, co-exist, and so it truly borrows that union from nature: yet *the number* it combines *depends upon the various care, industry, or fancy of him that makes it.* Men generally content themselves with some few sensible obvious qualities, and often, if not always, leave out others as material and as firmly united as those that they take. Of sensible substances there are two sorts: one of organized bodies, which are propagated by seed; and in these the shape is that which to us is the leading quality and most characteristical part that determines the *species*; and therefore in vegetables and animals, an extended solid substance of such a certain figure usually serves the turn. For however some men seem to prize their definition of *animal rationale*, yet, should there a creature be found that had language and reason but partaked not of the usual shape of a man, I believe it would hardly pass for a *man*, how much soever it were *animal rationale*. And if *Balaam's* ass had, all his

life, discoursed as rationally as he did once with his master, I doubt yet whether anyone would have thought him worthy the name *man* or allowed him to be of the same *species* with himself. As in vegetables and animals it is the shape, so in most other bodies not propagated by seed it is the colour we most fix on and are most led by. Thus, where we find the colour of gold, we are apt to imagine all the other qualities comprehended in our complex *idea* to be there also; and we commonly take these two obvious qualities, viz. shape and colour, for so presumptive *ideas* of several *species* that in a good picture we readily say, this is a lion, and that a rose; this is a gold, and that a silver goblet, only by the different figures and colours represented to the eye by the pencil.

30. But though this serves well enough for gross and confused conceptions and inaccurate ways of talking and thinking, yet *men are far enough from having agreed on the precise number of simple* ideas *or qualities belonging to any sort of things, signified by its name.* Nor is it a wonder, since it requires much time, pains and skill, strict inquiry, and long examination to find out what and how many those simple *ideas* are which are constantly and inseparably united in nature and are always to be found together in the same subject. Most men, wanting either time, inclination, or industry enough for this, even to some tolerable degree, content themselves with some few obvious and outward appearances of things, thereby readily to distinguish and sort them for the common affairs of life; and so, without further examination, give them names, or take up the names already in use. Which, though in common conversation they pass well enough for the signs of some few obvious qualities co-existing, are yet far enough from comprehending, in a settled signification, a precise number of simple *ideas*, much less all those which are united in nature. He that shall consider, after so much stir about *genus* and *species* and such a deal of talk of specific differences, how few words we have yet settled definitions of may, with reason, imagine that those *forms* which there hath been so much noise made about are only *chimeras*, which give us no light into the specific natures of things. And he that shall consider how far the names of substances are from having significations wherein all who use them do agree will have reason to conclude that, though the nominal essences of substances are all supposed to be copied from nature, yet they are all, or most of them, very imperfect: since the composition of those complex *ideas* are, in several men, very different; and therefore that these boundaries of *species* are as men, and not as nature, makes them, if at least there are in nature any such prefixed bounds. It is true that

many particular substances are so made by nature that they have agreement and likeness one with another, and so afford a foundation of being ranked into sorts. But the sorting of things by us or the making of determinate *species* being in order to naming and comprehending them under general terms, I cannot see how it can be properly said that nature sets the boundaries of the *species* of things; or, if it be so, our boundaries of *species* are not exactly conformable to those in nature. For we, having need of general names for present use, stay not for a perfect discovery of all those qualities which would best show us their most material differences and agreements; but we ourselves divide them by certain obvious appearances into *species*, that we may the easier, under general names, communicate our thoughts about them. For having no other knowledge of any substance but of the simple *ideas* that are united in it, and observing several particular things to agree with others in several of those simple *ideas*, we make that collection our specific *idea* and give it a general name, that in recording our own thoughts and in our discourse with others we may in one short word design all the individuals that agree in that complex *idea*, without enumerating the simple *ideas* that make it up, and so not waste our time and breath in tedious descriptions; which we see they are fain to do who would discourse of any new sort of things they have not yet a name for.

32.   If the *number of simple* ideas *that make the nominal essence* of the lowest *species* or first sorting of individuals *depends on the mind* of man variously collecting them, it is much more evident that they do so in the more comprehensive *classis* which, by the masters of logic, are called *genera*. These are complex *ideas* designedly imperfect; and it is visible at first sight that several of those qualities that are to be found in the things themselves are purposely left out of *generical ideas*. For as the mind, to make general *ideas* comprehending several particulars, leaves out those of time and place and such other that make them incommunicable to more than one individual, so to make other yet more general *ideas* that may comprehend different sorts, it leaves out those qualities that distinguish them and puts into its new collection only such *ideas* as are common to several sorts. The same convenience that made men express several parcels of yellow matter coming from *Guinea* and *Peru* under one name, sets them also upon making of one name that may comprehend both gold and silver and some other bodies of different sorts. This is done by leaving out those qualities which are peculiar to each sort and retaining a complex *idea* made up of those that

are common to them all. To which the name *metal* being annexed, there is a *genus* constituted; the essence whereof, being that abstract *idea* containing only malleableness and fusibility, with certain degrees of weight and fixedness wherein some bodies of several kinds agree, leaves out the colour and other qualities peculiar to gold and silver and the other sorts comprehended under the name *metal*. Whereby it is plain that men follow not exactly the patterns set them by nature, when they make their general *ideas* of substances, since there is no body to be found which has barely malleableness and fusibility in it, without other qualities as inseparable as those. But men, in making their general *ideas*, seeking more the convenience of language and quick dispatch by short and comprehensive signs than the true and precise nature of things as they exist, have in the framing their abstract *ideas* chiefly pursued that end which was to be furnished with store of general and variously comprehensive names. So that in this whole business of *genera* and *species*, the *genus* or more comprehensive is but a partial conception of what is in the *species*, and the *species* but a partial *idea* of what is to be found in each individual. If therefore anyone will think that a *man* and a *horse* and an animal and a plant, etc., are distinguished by real essences made by nature, he must think nature to be very liberal of these real essences, making one for body, another for an animal, and another for a horse; and all these essences liberally bestowed upon *Bucephalus*. But if we would rightly consider what is done in all these *genera* and *species* or sorts, we should find that there is no new thing made, but only more or less comprehensive signs whereby we may be enabled to express, in a few syllables, great numbers of particular things as they agree in more or less general conceptions, which we have framed to that purpose. In all which we may observe that the more general term is always the name of a less complex *idea*, and that each *genus* is but a partial conception of the *species* comprehended under it. So that if these abstract general *ideas* be thought to be complete, it can only be in respect of a certain established relation between them and certain names which are made use of to signify them, and not in respect of anything existing as made by nature.

33. *This* is *adjusted to the true end of speech*, which is to be the easiest and shortest way of communicating our notions. For thus he that would make and discourse of things as they agreed in the complex *idea* of extension and solidity, needed but use the word *body* to denote all such. He that to these would join others, signified by the words life, sense, and spontaneous

motion, needed but use the word *animal* to signify all which partaked of those *ideas*; and he that had made a complex *idea* of a body, with life, sense, and motion, with the faculty of reasoning and a certain shape joined to it, needed but use the short monosyllable *man* to express all particulars that correspond to that complex *idea*. This is the proper business of *genus* and *species*; and this men do without any consideration of *real essences*, or *substantial forms*, which come not within the reach of our knowledge when we think of those things, nor within the signification of our words when we discourse with others.

34.   Were I to talk with anyone of a sort of birds I lately saw in St. *James'* Park: about three- or four-foot high, with a covering of something between feathers and hair, of a dark brown colour, without wings, but in the place thereof two or three little branches coming down like sprigs of Spanish broom, long great legs, with feet only of three claws and without a tail: I must make this description of it and so may make others understand me; but when I am told that the name of it is *Cassuaris*, I may then use that word to stand in discourse for all my complex *idea* mentioned in that description, though by that word, which is now become a specific name, I know no more of the real essence or constitution of that sort of animals than I did before, and knew probably as much of the nature of that *species* of birds before I learned the name, as many *Englishmen* do of swans or herons, which are specific names very well known of sorts of birds common in *England*.

Chapter VII

OF PARTICLES

1.   BESIDES words which are names of *ideas* in the mind, there are a great many others that are made use of to signify the *connexion* that the mind gives to *ideas or propositions, one with another*. The mind, in communicating its thought to others, does not only need signs of the *ideas* it has then before it, but others also to show or intimate some particular action of its own at that time relating to those *ideas*. This it does several ways, as *is* and *is not* are the general marks of the mind, affirming or denying. But besides affirmation or negation, without which there is in words no truth or falsehood, the mind does, in declaring its sentiments to others, connect not only the parts of

propositions but whole sentences one to another, with their several relations and dependencies, to make a coherent discourse.

2. The words whereby it signifies what connexion it gives to the several affirmations and negations that it unites in one continued reasoning or narration, are generally called *particles*; and it is in the right use of these that more particularly consists the clearness and beauty of a good style. To think well, it is not enough that a man has *ideas* clear and distinct in his thoughts, nor that he observes the agreement or disagreement of some of them; but he must think in train and observe the dependence of his thoughts and reasonings one upon another; and to express well such methodical and rational thoughts, he must have words to *show* what *connexion, restriction, distinction, opposition, emphasis,* etc., he gives to each respective *part of his discourse.* To mistake in any of these is to puzzle, instead of informing his hearer; and therefore it is that those words which are not truly by themselves the names of any *ideas* are of such constant and indispensable use in language and do much contribute to men's well expressing themselves.

3. This part of grammar has been, perhaps, as much neglected as some others over-diligently cultivated. It is easy for men to write one after another of *cases* and *genders, moods* and *tenses, gerunds* and *supines.* In these and the like there has been great diligence used; and particles themselves, in some languages, have been, with great show of exactness, ranked into their several orders. But though *prepositions* and *conjunctions,* etc., are names well known in grammar, and the particles contained under them carefully ranked into their distinct subdivisions, yet he who would show the right use of particles, and what significancy and force they have, must take a little more pains, enter into his own thoughts, and observe nicely the several postures of his mind in discoursing.

4. Neither is it enough, for the explaining of these words, to render them, as is usually in dictionaries, by words of another tongue which come nearest to their signification; for what is meant by them is commonly as hard to be understood in one as another language. They are all *marks of some action or intimation of the mind*; and therefore to understand them rightly, the several views, postures, stands, turns, limitations, and exceptions, and several other thoughts of the mind, for which we have either none or very deficient names, are diligently to be studied. Of these, there are a great variety, much exceeding the number of particles that most languages have to express them by; and

therefore it is not to be wondered that most of these particles have divers and sometimes almost opposite significations. In the Hebrew tongue there is a particle consisting but of one single letter, of which there are reckoned up, as I remember, seventy, I am sure above fifty several significations.

5. 'BUT' is a particle, none more familiar in our language; and he that says it is a discretive conjunction, and that it answers *sed* in Latin or *mais* in French, thinks he has sufficiently explained it. But it seems to me to intimate several relations the mind gives to the several propositions, or parts of them, which it joins by this monosyllable.

First, *BUT to say no more*: here it intimates a stop of the mind, in the course it was going, before it came to the end of it.

Secondly, *I saw BUT two plants*: here it shows that the mind limits the sense to what is expressed, with a negation of all other.

Thirdly, *You pray; BUT it is not that GOD would bring you to the true religion.*

Fourthly, *BUT that he would confirm you in your own.* The first of these *BUTS* intimates a supposition in the mind of something otherwise than it should be; the latter shows that the mind makes a direct opposition between that and what goes before it.

Fifthly, *All animals have sense; BUT a dog is an animal*: here it signifies little more but that the latter proposition is joined to the former, as the *minor* of a syllogism.

6. To these, I doubt not, might be added a great many other significations of this particle, if it were my business to examine it in its full latitude and consider it in all the places it is to be found: which, if one should do, I doubt whether, in all those manners it is made use of, it would deserve the title of *discretive* which grammarians give to it. But I intend not here a full explication of this sort of signs. The instances I have given in this one may give occasion to reflect upon their use and force in language, and lead us into the contemplation of several actions of our minds in discoursing, which it has found a way to intimate to others by these particles, some whereof constantly, and others in certain constructions, have the sense of a whole sentence contained in them.

Chapter IX

OF THE IMPERFECTION OF WORDS

1. FROM what has been said in the foregoing chapters, it is easy
to perceive what imperfection there is in language and how the
very nature of words makes it almost unavoidable for many of
them to be doubtful and uncertain in their significations. To
examine the perfection or imperfection of words, it is necessary
first to consider their use and end: for as they are more or less
fitted to attain that, so are they more or less perfect. We have,
in the former part of this discourse, often upon occasion mentioned *a double use of words*.

First, One for the recording of our own thoughts.

Secondly, The other for the communicating of our thoughts
to others.

2. As to the first of these, *for the recording our own thoughts* for
the help of our own memories, whereby, as it were, we talk to
ourselves, any words will serve the turn. For since sounds are
voluntary and indifferent signs of any *ideas*, a man may use what
words he pleases to signify his own *ideas* to himself; and there
will be no imperfection in them if he constantly use the same
sign for the same *idea*, for then he cannot fail of having his
meaning understood; wherein consists the right use and perfection of language.

3. *Secondly*, as to *communication of words*, that too *has a
double use*.

   I. *Civil*.

  II. *Philosophical*.

First, By their *civil use*, I mean such a communication of
thoughts and *ideas* by words as may serve for the upholding
common conversation and commerce about the ordinary affairs
and conveniences of civil life in the societies of men one amongst
another.

Secondly, By the *philosophical use* of words, I mean such an
use of them as may serve to convey the precise notions of things,
and to express in general propositions certain and undoubted
truths which the mind may rest upon and be satisfied with in
its search after true knowledge. These two uses are very
distinct; and a great deal less exactness will serve in the one than
in the other, as we shall see in what follows.

4. The chief end of language in communication being to be
understood, words serve not well for that end, neither in civil

nor philosophical discourse, when any word does not excite in the hearer the same *idea* which it stands for in the mind of the speaker. Now, since sounds have no natural connexion with our *ideas*, but have all their signification from the arbitrary imposition of men, the *doubtfulness* and uncertainty *of their signification*, which *is the imperfection* we here are speaking of, has its cause more in the *ideas* they stand for than in any incapacity there is in one sound more than in another to signify any *idea*, for in that regard they are all equally perfect.

That, then, which makes doubtfulness and uncertainty in the signification of some more than other words, is the difference of *ideas* they stand for.

5. Words having naturally no signification, the *idea* which each stands for must be learned and retained by those who would exchange thoughts and hold intelligible discourse with others in any language. But this is hardest to be done where,

First, The *ideas* they stand for are very complex, and made up of a great number of *ideas* put together.

Secondly, Where the *ideas* they stand for have no certain connexion in nature, and so no settled standard anywhere in nature existing, to rectify and adjust them by.

Thirdly, Where the signification of the word is referred to a standard, which standard is not easy to be known.

Fourthly, Where the signification of the word and the real essence of the thing are not exactly the same.

These are difficulties that attend the signification of several words that are intelligible. Those which are not intelligible at all, such as names standing for any simple *ideas* which another has not organs or faculties to attain, as the names of colours to a blind man or sounds to a deaf man, need not here be mentioned.

In all these cases, we shall find an imperfection in words, which I shall more at large explain in their particular application to our several sorts of *ideas*; for, if we examine them, we shall find that the *names of mixed modes are most liable to doubtfulness and imperfection, for the two first of these reasons, and the names of substances chiefly for the two latter*.

6. *First*, The names of *mixed modes* are, many of them, liable to great uncertainty and obscurity in their signification.

I. *Because of* that *great composition* these complex *ideas* are often made up of. To make words serviceable to the end of communication, it is necessary (as has been said) that they excite in the hearer exactly the same *idea* they stand for in the mind of the speaker. Without this, men fill one another's heads with noise and sounds, but convey not thereby their thoughts, and lay not before one another their *ideas*, which is the end of discourse and language. But when a word stands for a very complex *idea* that is compounded and decompounded, it is not easy for men to form and retain that *idea* so exactly as to make the name in common use stand for the same precise *idea*, without any the least variation. Hence it comes to pass that men's names of very compound *ideas*, such as for the most part are moral words, have seldom in two different men the same precise signification, since one man's complex *idea* seldom agrees with another's, and often differs from his own, from that which he had yesterday or will have tomorrow.

7. II. *Because the names of mixed modes* for the most part *want standards* in nature whereby men may rectify and adjust their significations; therefore they are very various and doubtful. They are assemblages of *ideas* put together at the pleasure of the mind, pursuing its own ends of discourse and suited to its own notions, whereby it designs not to copy anything really existing, but to denominate and rank things as they come to agree with those archetypes or forms it has made. He that first brought the word *sham*, *wheedle*, or *banter* in use, put together as he thought fit those *ideas* he made it stand for; and as it is with any new names of modes that are now brought into any language, so was it with the old ones when they were first made use of. Names, therefore, that stand for collections of *ideas* which the mind makes at pleasure must needs be of doubtful signification, when such collections are nowhere to be found constantly united in nature, nor any patterns to be shown whereby men may adjust them. What the word *murder* or *sacrilege*, etc., signifies can never be known from things themselves: there be many of the parts of those complex *ideas* which are not visible in the action itself; the intention of the mind, or the relation of holy things, which make a part of *murder* or *sacrilege*, have no necessary connexion with the outward and visible action of him that commits either; and the pulling the trigger of the gun with which the murder is committed and is all the action that perhaps is visible, has no natural connexion with those other *ideas* that make up the complex one named *murder*. They have their union and combination only from the understanding which unites them under one name; but, uniting them without any rule or pattern, it cannot be but that the signification of the name that stands for such voluntary collections should be often various in the minds of different men, who have scarce any standing rule to regulate themselves and their notions by in such arbitrary *ideas*.

8.   It is true, *common use*, that is, the rule of propriety, may be
supposed here to afford some aid, to settle the signification of
language; and it cannot be denied but that in some measure it
does. Common use *regulates the meaning of words* pretty well
for common conversation; but, nobody having an authority to
establish the precise signification of words, nor determine to
what *ideas* anyone shall annex them, common use is not sufficient to adjust them to philosophical discourses: there being
scarce any name of any very complex *idea* (to say nothing of
others) which, in common use, has not a great latitude and which,
keeping within the bounds of propriety, may not be made the
sign of far different *ideas*. Besides, the rule and measure of
propriety itself being nowhere established, it is often matter of
dispute whether this or that way of using a word be propriety
of speech or no. From all which it is evident that the names of
such kind of very complex *ideas* are naturally liable to this
imperfection, to be of doubtful and uncertain signification, and,
even in men that have a mind to understand one another, do not
always stand for the same *idea* in speaker and hearer. Though
the names *glory* and *gratitude* be the same in every man's
mouth, through a whole country, yet the complex collective
idea which everyone thinks on or intends by that name is
apparently very different in men using the same language.

9.   *The way* also *wherein the names of mixed modes are ordinarily learned does* not a little *contribute to the doubtfulness of their
signification*. For, if we will observe how children learn languages, we shall find that, to make them understand what the
names of simple *ideas* or substances stand for, people ordinarily
show them the thing whereof they would have them have the
idea, and then repeat to them the name that stands for it: as
white, sweet, milk, sugar, cat, dog. But as for mixed modes,
especially the most material of them, moral words, the sounds
are usually learned first; and then, to know what complex *ideas*
they stand for, they are either beholden to the explication of
others or (which happens for the most part) are left to their own
observation and industry; which being little laid out in the
search of the true and precise meaning of names, these moral
words are in most men's mouths little more than bare sounds; or
when they have any, it is for the most part but a very loose, and
undetermined, and, consequently, obscure and confused signification.   And even those themselves who have with more
attention settled their notions, do yet hardly avoid the inconvenience to have them stand for complex *ideas* different from
those which other, even intelligent and studious men make them

the signs of. Where shall one find any either *controversial debate* or *familiar discourse* concerning *honour, faith, grace, religion, church*, etc., wherein it is not easy to observe the different notions men have of them; which is nothing but this: that they are not agreed in the signification of those words nor have in their minds the same complex *ideas* which they make them stand for, and so all the contests that follow thereupon are only about the meaning of a sound. And hence we see that, in the interpretation of laws, whether divine or human, there is no end: comments beget comments, and explications make new matter for explications; and of limiting, distinguishing, varying the signification of these moral words, there is no end. These *ideas* of men's making are, by men still having the same power, multiplied *in infinitum*. Many a man who was pretty well satisfied of the meaning of a text of scripture or clause in the code, at first reading has, by consulting commentators, quite lost the sense of it, and by those elucidations given rise or increase to his doubts, and drawn obscurity upon the place. I say not this that I think commentaries needless, but to show how uncertain the names of mixed modes naturally are, even in the mouths of those who had both the intention and the faculty of speaking as clearly as language was capable to express their thoughts.

10. What obscurity this has unavoidably brought upon the writings of men who have lived in remote ages and different countries, it will be needless to take notice: since the numerous volumes of learned men, employing their thoughts that way, are proofs more than enough to show what attention, study, sagacity, and reasoning is required to find out the true meaning *of ancient authors*. But there being no writings we have any great concernment to be very solicitous about the meaning of, but those that contain either truths we are required to believe, or laws we are to obey and draw inconveniences on us when we mistake or transgress, we may be less anxious about the sense of other authors; who writing but their own opinions, we are under no greater necessity to know them than they to know ours. Our good or evil depending not on their decrees, we may safely be ignorant of their notions; and therefore in the reading of them, if they do not use their words with a due clearness and perspicuity, we may lay them aside and, without any injury done them, resolve thus with ourselves,

Si non vis intelligi, debes negligi.

CHAPTER X

OF THE ABUSE OF WORDS

1.   BESIDES the imperfection that is naturally in language, and the obscurity and confusion that is so hard to be avōided in the use of words, there are several *wilful faults and neglects* which men are guilty of in this way of communication, whereby they render these signs less clear and distinct in their signification than naturally they need to be.

2.   *First*, In this kind, the first and most palpable abuse is the using of words without clear and distinct *ideas*, or, which is worse, signs without anything signified. Of these there are two sorts:

I.   One may observe, in all languages, certain words that, if they be examined, will be found, in their first original and their appropriated use, not to stand for any clear and distinct *ideas*. These, for the most part, the several *sects* of philosophy and religion have introduced. For their authors or promoters, either affecting something singular and out of the way of common apprehensions, or to support some strange opinions or cover some weakness of their hypothesis, seldom fail to *coin* new words and such as, when they come to be examined, may justly be called *insignificant terms*. For having either had no determinate collection of *ideas* annexed to them when they were first invented or at least such as, if well examined, will be found inconsistent, it is no wonder if afterwards, in the vulgar use of the same party, they remain empty sounds with little or no signification amongst those who think it enough to have them often in their mouths, as the distinguishing characters of their church or school, without much troubling their heads to examine what are the precise *ideas* they stand for. I shall not need here to heap up instances, everyone's reading and conversation will sufficiently furnish him; or, if he wants to be better stored, the great mint-masters of these kind of terms, I mean the schoolmen and metaphysicians (under which, I think, the disputing natural and moral philosophers of these latter ages may be comprehended) have wherewithal abundantly to content him.

3.   II. Others there be who extend this abuse yet further, who take so little care to lay by words which, in their primary notation, have scarce any clear and distinct *ideas* which they are annexed to, that, by an unpardonable negligence, they familiarly *use words* which the propriety of language has affixed to

very important *ideas, without any distinct meaning* at all. *Wisdom, glory, grace,* etc., are words frequent enough in every man's mouth; but, if a great many of these who use them should be asked what they mean by them, they would be at a stand and not know what to answer: a plain proof that, though they have learned those sounds and have them ready at their tongues' end, yet there are no determined *ideas* laid up in their minds which are to be expressed to others by them.

4. *Men* having been *accustomed* from their cradles *to learn words* which are easily got and retained *before they knew* or had framed *the complex ideas* to which they were annexed, or which were to be found in the things *they* were thought to *stand* for, they *usually continue to do so* all their lives; and without taking the pains necessary to settle in their minds determined *ideas,* they use their words for such unsteady and confused notions as they have, contenting themselves with the same words other people use, as if their very sound necessarily carried with it constantly the same meaning. This, though men make a shift with in the ordinary occurrences of life, where they find it necessary to be understood, and therefore they make signs till they are so: yet this insignificancy in their words, when they come to reason concerning either their tenets or interest, manifestly fills their discourse with abundance of empty unintelligible noise and jargon, especially in moral matters, where the words for the most part standing for arbitrary and numerous collections of *ideas* not regularly and permanently united in nature, their bare sounds are often only thought on, or at least very obscure and uncertain notions annexed to them. Men take the words they find in use amongst their neighbours, and that they may not seem ignorant what they stand for, use them confidently without much troubling their heads about a certain fixed meaning, whereby, besides the ease of it, they obtain this advantage: that as in such discourses they seldom are in the right, so they are as seldom to be convinced that they are in the wrong, it being all one to go about to draw those men out of their mistakes, who have no settled notions, as to dispossess a vagrant of his habitation who has no settled abode. This I guess to be so, and everyone may observe in himself and others whether it be or no.

5. *Secondly,* Another great abuse of words is *inconstancy* in the use of them. It is hard to find a discourse written of any subject, especially of controversy, whereon one shall not observe, if he read with attention, the same words (and those commonly the most material in the discourse and upon which the argument

turns) used sometimes for one collection of simple *ideas* and sometimes for another, which is a perfect abuse of language. Words being intended for signs of my *ideas* to make them known to others, not by any natural signification but by a voluntary imposition, it is plain cheat and abuse when I make them stand sometimes for one thing and sometimes for another, the wilful doing whereof can be imputed to nothing but great folly or greater dishonesty. And a man in his accounts with another may, with as much fairness, make the characters of numbers stand sometimes for one and sometimes for another collection of tunis: v.g., this character 3 stand sometimes for three, sometimes for four, and sometimes for eight, as in his discourse or reasoning make the same words stand for different collections of simple *ideas*. If men should do so in their reckonings, I wonder who would have to do with them? One who would speak thus in the affairs and business of the world, and call 8 sometimes seven and sometimes nine, as best served his advantage, would presently have clapped upon him one of the two names men constantly are disgusted with. And yet in arguings and learned contests, the same sort of proceeding passes commonly for wit and learning; but to me it appears a greater dishonesty than the misplacing of counters in the casting up a debt, and the cheat the greater, by how much truth is of greater concernment and value than money.

6. *Thirdly*, Another abuse of language is an *affected obscurity* by either applying old words to new and unusual significations, or introducing new and ambiguous terms without defining either, or else putting them so together as may confound their ordinary meaning. Though the peripatetic philosophy has been most eminent in this way, yet other sects have not been wholly clear of it. There is scarce any of them that are not cumbered with some difficulties (such is the imperfection of human knowledge), which they have been fain to cover with obscurity of terms and to confound the signification of words which, like a mist before people's eyes, might hinder their weak parts from being discovered. That *body* and *extension*, in common use, stand for two distinct *ideas* is plain to anyone that will but reflect a little. For were their signification precisely the same, it would be proper, and as intelligible, to say the *body of an extension*, as *the extension of a body*; and yet there are those who find it necessary to confound their signification. To this abuse and the mischiefs of confounding the signification of words, logic and the liberal sciences, as they have been handled in the Schools, have given reputation; and the admired art of

disputing hath added much to the natural imperfection of languages, whilst it has been made use of and fitted to perplex the signification of words more than to discover the knowledge and truth of things. And he that will look into that sort of learned writings will find the words there much more obscure, uncertain, and undetermined in their meaning than they are in ordinary conversation.

7. This is unavoidably to be so, where men's parts and learning are estimated by their skill in *disputing*. And if reputation and reward shall attend these conquests, which depend mostly on the fineness and niceties of words, it is no wonder if the wit of man so employed should perplex, involve, and subtilize the signification of sounds, so as never to want something to say in opposing or defending any question, the victory being adjudged not to him who had truth on his side but the last word in the dispute.

14. *Fourthly*, Another great *abuse of words is the taking them for things*. This, though it in some degree concerns all names in general, yet more particularly affects those of substances. To this abuse those men are most subject who confine their thoughts to any one system and give themselves up into a firm belief of the perfection of any received hypothesis: whereby they come to be persuaded that the terms of that sect are so suited to the nature of things that they perfectly correspond with their real existence. Who is there, that has been bred up in the peripatetic philosophy, who does not think the ten names, under which are ranked the ten predicaments, to be exactly conformable to the nature of things? Who is there of that school that is not persuaded that *substantial forms, vegetative souls, abhorrence of a vacuum, intentional species*, etc., are something real? These words men have learned from their very entrance upon knowledge and have found their masters and systems lay great stress upon them, and therefore they cannot quit the opinion that they are conformable to nature and are the representations of something that really exists. The *Platonists* have their *soul of the world*, and the *Epicureans* their *endeavour towards motion* in their atoms when at rest. There is scarce any sect in philosophy has not a distinct set of terms that others understand not. But yet this gibberish, which in the weakness of human understanding serves so well to palliate men's ignorance and cover their errors, comes by familiar use amongst those of the same tribe to seem the most important part of language, and of all other the terms the most significant; and should *aerial* and *aetherial vehicles* come once by the prevalency of that doctrine to be generally received anywhere, no doubt those terms would

make impressions on men's minds so as to establish them in the persuasion of the reality of such things, as much as *peripatetic forms* and *intentional species* have heretofore done.

15. How much *names taken for things* are apt to *mislead the understanding*, the attentive reading of philosophical writers would abundantly discover, and that, perhaps, in words little suspected of any such misuse. I shall instance in one only, and that a very familiar one. How many intricate disputes have there been about *matter*, as if there were some such thing really in nature, distinct from *body*, as it is evident the word *matter* stands for an *idea* distinct from the *idea* of body? For if the *ideas* these two terms stood for were precisely the same, they might indifferently in all places be put one for another. But we see that, though it be proper to say, There is *one matter of all bodies*, one cannot say, There is *one body of all matters*; we familiarly say: one *body* is bigger than another, but it sounds harsh (and I think is never used) to say: one *matter* is bigger than another. Whence comes this then? Viz. from hence: that though *matter* and *body* be not really distinct, but wherever there is the one, there is the other, yet *matter* and *body* stand for two different conceptions, whereof the one is incomplete and but a part of the other. For *body* stands for a solid extended figured substance, whereof *matter* is but a partial and more confused conception, it seeming to me to be used for the substance and solidity of body without taking in its extension and figure; and therefore it is that, speaking of *matter*, we speak of it always as one, because in truth it expressly contains nothing but the *idea* of a solid substance which is everywhere the same, everywhere uniform. This being our *idea* of *matter*, we no more conceive or speak of different *matters* in the world than we do of different solidities, though we both conceive and speak of different bodies because extension and figure are capable of variation. But since solidity cannot exist without extension and figure, the taking *matter* to be the name of something really existing under that precision has no doubt produced those obscure and unintelligible discourses and disputes which have filled the heads and books of philosophers concerning *materia prima*; which imperfection or abuse, how far it may concern a great many other general terms, I leave to be considered. This, I think, I may at least say, that we should have a great many fewer disputes in the world if words were taken for what they are, the signs of our *ideas* only and not for things themselves. For when we argue about *matter* or any the like term, we truly argue only about the *idea* we express by that sound, whether that precise

idea agree to anything really existing in nature or no. And if men would tell what *ideas* they make their words stand for, there could not be half that obscurity or wrangling in the search or support of truth that there is.

CHAPTER XI

OF THE REMEDIES OF THE FOREGOING IMPERFECTIONS AND ABUSES

1. THE natural and improved imperfections of languages we have seen above at large; and speech being the great bond that holds society together, and the common conduit whereby the improvements of knowledge are conveyed from one man and one generation to another, it would well deserve our most serious thoughts to consider what *remedies* are to be found *for these inconveniences* above-mentioned.

2. I am not so vain to think that anyone can pretend to attempt the perfect *reforming* the *languages* of the world, no, not so much as of his own country, without rendering himself ridiculous. To require that men should use their words constantly in the same sense and for none but determined and uniform *ideas*, would be to think that all men should have the same notions and should talk of nothing but what they have clear and distinct *ideas* of. Which is not to be expected by anyone who hath not vanity enough to imagine he can prevail with men to be very knowing or very silent. And he must be very little skilled in the world who thinks that a voluble tongue shall accompany only a good understanding, or that men's talking much or little shall hold proportion only to their knowledge.

3. But though the market and exchange must be left to their own ways of talking and gossipings not be robbed of their ancient privilege; though the Schools and men of argument would perhaps take it amiss to have anything offered to abate the length or lessen the number of their disputes, yet methinks those *who* pretend *seriously* to *search after* or maintain *truth*, should think themselves obliged to study how they might deliver themselves without obscurity, doubtfulness, or equivocation; to which men's words are naturally liable, if care be not taken.

4. For he that shall well consider the *errors* and obscurity, the mistakes and confusion that is *spread in the world by an ill use of words*, will find some reason to doubt whether language, as it

has been employed, has contributed more to the improvement or hindrance of knowledge amongst mankind. How many are there that, when they would think on things, fix their thoughts only on words, especially when they would apply their minds to moral matters? And who then can wonder if the result of such contemplations and reasonings about little more than sounds, whilst the *ideas* they annexed to them are very confused or very unsteady, or perhaps none at all: who can wonder, I say, that such thoughts and reasonings end in nothing but obscurity and mistake, without any clear judgment or knowledge?

5. This inconvenience in an ill use of words men suffer in their own private meditations; but much more manifest are the disorders which follow from it in conversation, discourse, and arguings with others. For language being the great conduit whereby men convey their discoveries, reasonings, and knowledge from one to another, he that makes an ill use of it, though he does not corrupt the fountains of knowledge which are in things themselves, yet he does, as much as in him lies, break or stop the pipes whereby it is distributed to the public use and advantage of mankind. He that uses words without any clear and steady meaning, what does he but lead himself and others into errors? And he that designedly does it ought to be looked on as an enemy to truth and knowledge. And yet who can wonder that all the sciences and parts of knowledge have been so overcharged with obscure and equivocal terms and insignificant and doubtful expressions, capable to make the most attentive or quick-sighted very little or not at all the more knowing or orthodox, since subtilty, in those who make profession to teach or defend truth, hath passed so much for a virtue: a virtue indeed which, consisting for the most part in nothing but the fallacious and illusory use of *obscure* or *deceitful terms*, is only fit to *make* men more *conceited* in their ignorance and *obstinate* in their errors.

6. Let us look into the books of controversy of any kind, there we shall see that the effect of obscure, unsteady, or equivocal terms is nothing but noise and wrangling about sounds, without convincing or bettering a man's understanding. For if the *idea* be not agreed on betwixt the speaker and hearer for which the words stand, the argument is not about things but names. As often as such a word whose signification is not ascertained betwixt them comes in use, their understandings have no other object wherein they agree but barely the sound, the things that they think on at that time as expressed by that word being quite different.

10. In the names of *substances*, for a right use of them, some-

thing more is required than barely *determined ideas*: in these *the names must also be conformable to things* as they exist; but of this I shall have occasion to speak more at large by and by. This exactness is absolutely necessary in inquiries after philosophical knowledge and in controversies about truth. And though it would be well too if it extended itself to common conversation and the ordinary affairs of life, yet I think that is scarce to be expected. Vulgar notions suit vulgar discourses; and both, though confused enough, yet serve pretty well the market and the wake. Merchants and lovers, cooks and tailors have words wherewithal to dispatch their ordinary affairs; and so, I think, might philosophers and disputants too, if they had a mind to understand and to be clearly understood.

11.   *Thirdly,* It is not enough that men have *ideas,* determined *ideas,* for which they make these signs stand; but they *must* also take care to *apply their words* as near as may be *to such* ideas *as common use has annexed them to.* For words, especially of languages already framed, being no man's private possession but the common measure of commerce and communication, it is not for anyone at pleasure to change the stamp they are current in, nor alter the *ideas* they are affixed to; or at least, when there is a necessity to do so, he is bound to give notice of it. Men's intentions in speaking are, or at least should be, to be understood; which cannot be without frequent explanations, demands, and other the like incommodious interruptions, where men do not follow common use. Propriety of speech is that which gives our thoughts entrance into other men's minds with the greatest ease and advantage, and therefore deserves some part of our care and study, especially in the names of moral words. The proper signification and use of terms is best to be learned from those who in their writings and discourses appear to have had the clearest notions and applied to them their terms with the exactest choice and fitness. This way of using a man's words according to the propriety of the language, though it have not always the good fortune to be understood, yet most commonly leaves the blame of it on him who is so unskilful in the language he speaks as not to understand it, when made use of as it ought to be.

12.   *Fourthly,* But because common use has not so visibly annexed any signification to words as to make men know always certainly what they precisely stand for; and because men in the improvement of their knowledge come to have *ideas* different from the vulgar and ordinary received ones, for which they must either make new words (which men seldom venture to do, for fear of being thought guilty of affectation or novelty) or else

must use old ones in a new signification. Therefore after the observation of the foregoing rules, it is sometimes necessary, for the ascertaining the signification of words, to *declare their meaning* where either common use has left it uncertain and loose (as it has in most names of very complex *ideas*) or where the term, being very material in the discourse and that upon which it chiefly turns, is liable to any doubtfulness or mistake.

15. *Secondly, Mixed modes,* especially those belonging to morality, being most of them such combinations of *ideas* as the mind puts together of its own choice and whereof there are not always standing patterns to be found existing, the signification of their names cannot be made known, as those of simple *ideas,* by any showing, but, in recompense thereof, may be perfectly and exactly *defined*. For they being combinations of several *ideas* that the mind of man has arbitrarily put together, without reference to any archetypes, men may, if they please, exactly know the *ideas* that go to each composition, and so both use these words in a certain and undoubted signification, and perfectly declare, when there is occasion, what they stand for. This, if well considered, would lay great blame on those who make not their discourses about moral things very clear and distinct. For since the precise signification of the names of mixed modes or, which is all one, the real essence of each species is to be known, they being not of nature's but man's making, it is a great negligence and perverseness to discourse of moral things with uncertainty and obscurity; which is more pardonable in treating of natural substances, where doubtful terms are hardly to be avoided, for a quite contrary reason, as we shall see by and by.

16. Upon this ground it is that I am bold to think that *morality is capable of demonstration,* as well as mathematics: since the precise real essence of the things moral words stand for may be perfectly known, and so the congruity or incongruity of the things themselves be certainly discovered, in which consists perfect knowledge. Nor let anyone object that the names of substances are often to be made use of in morality, as well as those of modes, from which will arise obscurity. For as to substances, when concerned in moral discourses, their divers natures are not so much inquired into as supposed: v.g. when we say that *man is subject to law,* we mean nothing by *man* but a corporeal rational creature; what the real essence or other qualities of that creature are in this case is no way considered. And therefore, whether a child or changeling be a *man* in a physical sense may amongst the naturalists be as disputable as it will, it concerns not at all the *moral man,* as I may call him, which is this immove-

able unchangeable *idea, a corporeal rational being.* For were there a monkey or any other creature to be found that had the use of reason to such a degree as to be able to understand general signs and to deduce consequences about general *ideas,* he would no doubt be subject to law and, in that sense, be a *man,* how much soever he differed in shape from others of that name. The names of substances, if they be used in them as they should, can no more disturb moral than they do mathematical discourses: where, if the mathematicians speak of a *cube* or *globe* of *gold,* or any other body, he has his clear settled *idea,* which varies not, though it may by mistake be applied to a particular body to which it belongs not.

17. This I have here mentioned by the by, to show of what consequence it is for men in their names of mixed modes and, consequently, in all their moral discourses to define their words when there is occasion, since thereby moral knowledge may be brought to so great clearness and certainty. And it must be great want of ingenuity (to say no worse of it) to refuse to do it, since a *definition is the only way whereby the precise meaning of moral words can be known,* and yet a way whereby their meaning may be known *certainly* and without leaving any room for any contest about it. And therefore the negligence or perverseness of mankind cannot be excused, if their discourses in morality be not much more clear than those in natural philosophy, since they are about *ideas* in the mind which are none of them false or disproportionate, they having no external beings for *archetypes* which they are referred to and must correspond with. It is far easier for men to frame in their minds an *idea* which shall be the standard to which they will give the name *justice,* with which pattern so made, all actions that agree shall pass under that denomination, than, having seen *Aristides,* to frame an *idea* that shall, in all things, be exactly like him who is as he is, let men make what *idea* they please of him. For the one, they need but know the combination of *ideas* that are put together within in their own minds; for the other, they must inquire into the whole nature and abstruse hidden constitution and various qualities of a thing existing without them.

18. Another reason that makes the *defining of mixed modes* so necessary, *especially of moral words,* is what I mentioned a little before, viz. that it is *the only way whereby the signification of the most of* them can be known with certainty. For the *ideas* they stand for being for the most part such whose component parts nowhere exist together, but scattered and mingled with others, it is the mind alone that collects them and gives them the union

of one *idea*; and it is only by words, enumerating the several simple *ideas* which the mind has united, that we can make known to others what their names stand for: the assistance of the senses in this case not helping us, by the proposal of sensible objects, to show the *ideas* which our names of this kind stand for, as it does often in the names of sensible simple *ideas* and also to some degree in those of substances.

19.   *Thirdly, For the explaining* the signification of *the names of substances*, as they stand for the *ideas* we have of their distinct species, both the fore-mentioned ways, viz. of *showing and defining, are requisite* in many cases to be made use of. For, there being ordinarily in each sort some leading qualities, to which we suppose the other *ideas* which make up our complex *idea* of that species annexed, we forwardly give the specific name to that thing wherein that characteristical mark is found, which we take to be the most distinguishing *idea* of that species. These leading or characteristical (as I may so call them) *ideas*, in the sorts of animals and vegetables are (as has been before remarked, ch. vi, § 29, and ch. ix, § 15) mostly figure, and in inanimate bodies colour, and in some both together. Now,

20.   These *leading sensible qualities* are those wh'ch make *the chief ingredients of our specific ideas*, and consequently the most observable and invariable part in the definitions of our specific names, as attributed to sorts *of substances* coming under our knowledge. For though the sound *man*, in its own nature, be as apt to signify a complex *idea* made up of animality and rationality, united in the same subject, as to signify any other combination: yet, used as a mark to stand for a sort of creatures we count of our own kind, perhaps the outward shape is as necessary to be taken into our complex *idea*, signified by the word *man*, as any other we find in it; and therefore, why *Plato's animal implume bipes latis unguibus* should not be as good a definition of the name *man*, standing for that sort of creatures, will not be easy to show: for it is the shape, as the leading quality, that seems more to determine that species than a faculty of reasoning, which appears not at first and in some never. And if this be not allowed to be so, I do not know how they can be excused from murder who kill monstrous births (as we call them) because of an unordinary shape, without knowing whether they have a rational soul or no, which can be no more discerned in a well-formed than ill-shaped infant as soon as born. And who is it has informed us that a rational soul can inhabit no tenement, unless it has just such a sort of frontispiece or can join itself to and inform no sort of body but one that is just of such an outward

structure.

21.   Now *these leading qualities are best made known by showing* and can hardly be made known otherwise. For the shape of a *horse* or *cassowary* will be but rudely and imperfectly imprinted on the mind by words, the sight of the animals doth it a thousand times better; and the *idea* of the particular colour of *gold* is not to be got by any description of it, but only by the frequent exercise of the eyes about it; as is evident in those who are used to this metal, who will frequently distinguish true from counterfeit, pure from adulterate, by the sight, where others (who have as good eyes but yet by use have not got the precise nice *idea* of that peculiar yellow) shall not perceive any difference. The like may be said of those other simple *ideas*, peculiar in their kind to any substance; for which precise *ideas* there are no peculiar names. The particular ringing sound there is in *gold*, distinct from the sound of other bodies, has no particular name annexed to it, no more than the particular yellow that belongs to that metal.

22.   But because many of the simple *ideas* that make up our specific *ideas* of substances are powers, which lie not obvious to our senses in the things as they ordinarily appear: therefore, *in* the signification of our *names of substances, some part of the signification will be better made known by enumerating those simple* ideas *than in showing the substance itself.* For he that, to the yellow shining colour of *gold* got by sight, shall from my enumerating them have the *ideas* of great ductility, fusibility, fixedness, and solubility in *aqua regia* will have a perfecter *idea* of *gold* than he can have by seeing a piece of *gold* and thereby imprinting in his mind only its obvious qualities. But if the formal constitution of this shining, heavy, ductile thing (from whence all these its properties flow) lay open to our senses, as the formal constitution or essence of a triangle does, the signification of the word *gold* might as easily be ascertained as that of *triangle.*

23.   Hence we may take notice how much the foundation of all *our knowledge of corporeal things lies in our senses.* For how spirits, separate from bodies, (whose knowledge and *ideas* of these things is certainly much more perfect than ours) know them we have no notion, no *idea* at all. The whole extent of our knowledge or imagination reaches not beyond our own *ideas*, limited to our ways of perception. Though yet it be not to be doubted that spirits of a higher rank than those immersed in flesh may have as clear *ideas* of the radical constitution of substances as we have of a triangle, and so perceive how all their properties and operations flow from thence: but the manner

how they come by that knowledge exceeds our conceptions.

24.   But though definitions will serve to explain the names of substances as they stand for our *ideas*, yet they leave them not without great imperfection as they stand for things.   For our names of substances being not put barely for our *ideas*, but being made use of ultimately to represent things, and so are put in their place, their signification must agree with the truth of things as well as with men's *ideas*.   And therefore in substances, we are not always to rest in the ordinary complex *idea* commonly received as the signification of that word, but must go a little further and inquire into the nature and properties of the things themselves, and thereby perfect, as much as we can, our *ideas* of their distinct species, or else learn them from such as are used to that sort of things and are experienced in them.   For since it is intended their names should stand for such collections of simple *ideas* as do really exist in things themselves, as well as for the complex *idea* in other men's minds which in their ordinary acceptation they stand for, therefore *to define their names right, natural history is to be inquired into,* and their properties are, with care and examination, to be found out.   For it is not enough, for the avoiding inconveniencies in discourses and arguings about natural bodies and substantial things, to have learned, from the propriety of the language, the common but confused or very imperfect *idea* to which each word is applied, and to keep them to that *idea* in our use of them; but we must, by acquainting ourselves with the history of that sort of things, rectify and settle our complex *idea* belonging to each specific name; and in discourse with others (if we find them mistake us) we ought to tell what the complex *idea* is that we make such a name stand for.   This is the more necessary to be done by all those who search after knowledge and philosophical verity in that children, being taught words whilst they have but imperfect notions of things, apply them at random and without much thinking and seldom frame determined *ideas* to be signified by them.   Which custom (it being easy and serving well enough for the ordinary affairs of life and conversation) they are apt to continue when they are men, and so begin at the wrong end, learning words first and perfectly, but make the notions, to which they apply those words afterwards, very overtly.   By this means it comes to pass that men speaking the proper language of their country, i.e. according to grammar-rules of that language, do yet speak very improperly of things themselves and, by their arguing one with another, make but small progress in the discoveries of useful truths and the knowledge of things as

they are to be found in themselves, and not in our imaginations; and it matters not much, for the improvement of our knowledge, how they are called.

25.   It were therefore to be wished that men, versed in physical inquiries and acquainted with the several sorts of natural bodies, would set down those simple *ideas* wherein they observe the individuals of each sort constantly to agree. This would remedy a great deal of that confusion which comes from several persons applying the same name to a collection of a smaller or greater number of sensible qualities, proportionably as they have been more or less acquainted with or accurate in examining the qualities of any sort of things which come under one denomination. But a dictionary of this sort, containing, as it were, a natural history, requires too many hands as well as too much time, cost, pains, and sagacity ever to be hoped for; and till that be done, we must content ourselves with such definitions of the names of substances as explain the sense men use them in. And it would be well, where there is occasion, if they would afford us so much. This yet is not usually done; but men talk to one another and dispute in words whose meaning is not agreed between them, out of a mistake that the signification of common words are certainly established and the precise *ideas* they stand for perfectly known, and that it is a shame to be ignorant of them. Both which suppositions are false: no names of complex *ideas* having so settled determined significations that they are constantly used for the same precise *ideas*. Nor is it a shame for a man not to have a certain knowledge of anything but by the necessary ways of attaining it; and so it is no discredit not to know what precise *idea* any sound stands for in another man's mind, without he declare it to me by some other way than barely using that sound, there being no other way without such a declaration certainly to know it. Indeed, the necessity of communication by language brings men to an agreement in the signification of common words, within some tolerable latitude, that may serve for ordinary conversation; and so a man cannot be supposed wholly ignorant of the *ideas* which are annexed to words by common use, in a language familiar to him. But common use, being but a very uncertain rule, which reduces itself at last to the *ideas* of particular men, proves often but a very variable standard. But though such a dictionary as I have above mentioned will require too much time, cost, and pains to be hoped for in this age, yet methinks it is not unreasonable to propose that words standing for things which are known and distinguished by their outward shapes should be expressed by

little draughts and prints made of them. A vocabulary made after this fashion would perhaps, with more ease and in less time, teach the true signification of many terms, especially in languages of remote countries or ages, and settle truer *ideas* in men's minds of several things, whereof we read the names in ancient authors, than all the large and laborious comments of learned critics. Naturalists that treat of plants and animals have found the benefit of this way; and he that has had occasion to consult them will have reason to confess that he has a clear *idea* of *apium* or *ibex*, from a little print of that herb or beast, than he could have from a long definition of the names of either of them. And so, no doubt, he would have of *strigil* and *sistrum* if, instead of a *currycomb* and *cymbal*, which are the English names dictionaries render them by, he could see stamped in the margin small pictures of these instruments as they were in use amongst the ancients. *Toga, tunica, pallium* are words easily translated by *gown, coat,* and *cloak*; but we have thereby no more true *ideas* of the fashion of those habits amongst the *Romans* than we have of the faces of the tailors who made them. Such things as these, which the eye distinguishes by their shapes, would be best let into the mind by draughts made of them, and more determine the signification of such words than any other words set for them or made use of to define them. But this only by the by.

BOOK IV

OF KNOWLEDGE AND OPINION

CHAPTER I

OF KNOWLEDGE IN GENERAL

1. SINCE *the mind,* in all its thoughts and reasonings, hath no other immediate object but its own *ideas,* which it alone does or can contemplate, it is evident that our knowledge is only conversant about them.

2. *Knowledge* then seems to me to be nothing but *the perception of the connexion and agreement, or disagreement and repugnancy, of any of our ideas.* In this alone it consists. Where this perception is, there is knowledge; and where it is not, there, though we may fancy, guess, or believe, yet we always come short of knowledge. For when we know that *white is not black,* what do we else but perceive that these two *ideas* do not agree? When we possess ourselves with the utmost security of the demonstration that *the three angles of a triangle are equal to two right ones,* what do we more but perceive that equality to two right ones does necessarily agree to and is inseparable from the three angles of a triangle?

3. But to understand a little more distinctly wherein this agreement or disagreement consists, I think we may reduce it all to these four sorts:

    1. *Identity,* or *diversity.*
    2. *Relation.*
    3. *Co-existence,* or *necessary connexion.*
    4. *Real existence.*

4. *First,* As to the first sort of agreement or disagreement, viz. *identity* or *diversity.* It is the first act of the mind, when it has any sentiments or *ideas* at all, to perceive its *ideas,* and so far as it perceives them, to know each what it is, and thereby also to perceive their difference and that one is not another. This is so absolutely necessary that without it there could be no knowledge, no reasoning, no imagination, no distinct thoughts at all. By this the mind clearly and infallibly perceives each *idea* to

agree with itself and to be what it is, and all distinct *ideas* to disagree, i.e. the one not to be the other; and this it does without pains, labour, or deduction, but at first view, by its natural power of perception and distinction. And though men of art have reduced this into those general rules, *What is, is*, and *It is impossible for the same thing to be and not to be*, for ready application in all cases wherein there may be occasion to reflect on it: yet it is certain that the first exercise of this faculty is about particular *ideas*. A man infallibly knows, as soon as ever he has them in his mind, that the *ideas* he calls *white* and *round* are the very *ideas* they are, and that they are not other *ideas* which he calls *red* or *square*. Nor can any maxim or proposition in the world make him know it clearer or surer than he did before, and without any such general rule. This then is the first agreement or disagreement which the mind perceives in its *ideas*, which it always perceives at first sight; and if there ever happen any doubt about it, it will always be found to be about the names and not the *ideas* themselves, whose identity and diversity will always be perceived as soon and as clearly as the *ideas* themselves are; nor can it possibly be otherwise.

5. *Secondly*, The next sort of agreement or disagreement the mind perceives in any of its *ideas* may, I think, be called *relative*, and is nothing but *the perception of the relation between any two ideas*, of what kind soever, whether substances, modes, or any other. For, since all distinct *ideas* must eternally be known not to be the same, and so be universally and constantly denied one of another, there could be no room for any positive knowledge at all if we could not perceive any relation between our *ideas* and find out the agreement or disagreement they have one with another, in several ways the mind takes of comparing them.

6. *Thirdly*, The third sort of agreement or disagreement to be found in our *ideas*, which the perception of the mind is employed about, is *co-existence* or *non-co-existence* in the same subject; and this belongs particularly to substances. Thus when we pronounce, concerning *gold*, that it is fixed, our knowledge of this truth amounts to no more but this: that fixedness, or a power to remain in the fire unconsumed, is an *idea* that always accompanies and is joined with that particular sort of yellowness, weight, fusibility, malleableness, and solubility in *aqua regia*, which make our complex *idea* signified by the word *gold*.

7. *Fourthly*, The fourth and last sort is that of *actual real existence* agreeing to any *idea*. Within these four sorts of agreement or disagreement is, I suppose, contained all the knowledge we have or are capable of; for all the inquiries that we can make

concerning any of our *ideas*, all that we know or can affirm concerning any of them is that it is or is not the same with some other; that it does or does not always co-exist with some other *idea* in the same subject; that it has this or that relation to some other *idea*; or that it has a real existence without the mind. Thus, *Blue is not yellow* is of identity. *Two triangles upon equal bases between two parallels are equal* is of relation. *Iron is susceptible of magnetical impressions* is of co-existence. GOD *is* is of real existence. Though identity and co-existence are truly nothing but relations, yet they are so peculiar ways of agreement or disagreement of our *ideas* that they deserve well to be considered as distinct heads and not under relation in general, since they are so different grounds of affirmation and negation; as will easily appear to anyone who will but reflect on what is said in several places of this Essay. I should now proceed to examine the several degrees of our knowledge, but that it is necessary first to consider the different acceptations of the word *knowledge.*

8. There are several ways wherein the mind is possessed of truth, each of which is called *knowledge.*

(1) There is *actual knowledge*, which is the present view the mind has of the agreement or disagreement of any of its *ideas*, or of the relation they have one to another.

(2) A man is said to know any proposition, which having been once laid before his thoughts, he evidently perceived the agreement or disagreement of the *ideas* whereof it consists, and so lodged it in his memory that, whenever that proposition comes again to be reflected on, he, without doubt or hesitation, embraces the right side, assents to, and is certain of the truth of it. This, I think, one may call *habitual knowledge*; and thus a man may be said to know all those truths which are lodged in his memory, by a foregoing clear and full perception, whereof the mind is assured past doubt as often as it has occasion to reflect on them. For our finite understandings being able to think clearly and distinctly but on one thing at once, if men had no knowledge of any more than what they actually thought on, they would all be very ignorant, and he that knew most would know but one truth, that being all he was able to think on at one time.

9. Of habitual knowledge there are, also, vulgarly speaking, two degrees:

First, The one is of *such truths laid up in the memory as, whenever they occur to the mind, it actually perceives the relation is between those* ideas. And this is in all those truths whereof we have an *intuitive knowledge*, where the *ideas* themselves, by an immediate view, discover their agreement or disagreement one with another.

Secondly, The other is of *such truths whereof the mind having been convinced, it retains the memory of the conviction, without the proofs*. Thus a man, that remembers certainly that he once perceived the demonstration that the three angles of a triangle are equal to two right ones, is certain that he knows it, because he cannot doubt of the truth of it. In his adherence to a truth where the demonstration by which it was at first known is forgot, though a man may be thought rather to believe his memory than really to know (and this way of entertaining a truth seemed formerly to me like something between opinion and knowledge, a sort of assurance which exceeds bare belief, for that relies on the testimony of another), yet upon a due examination I find it comes not short of perfect certainty and is in effect true knowledge. That which is apt to mislead our first thoughts into a mistake in this matter is that the agreement or disagreement of the *ideas* in this case is not perceived, as it was at first, by an actual view of all the intermediate *ideas* whereby the agreement or disagreement of those in the proposition was at first perceived, but by other intermediate *ideas* that show the agreement or disagreement of the *ideas* contained in the proposition whose certainty we remember. For example, in this proposition that the three angles of a triangle are equal to two right ones, one who has seen and clearly perceived the demonstration of this truth knows it to be true when that demonstration is gone out of his mind, so that at present it is not actually in view and possibly cannot be recollected; but he knows it in a different way from what he did before. The agreement of the two *ideas* joined in that proposition is perceived, but it is by the intervention of other *ideas* than those which at first produced that perception. He remembers, i.e. he knows (for remembrance is but the reviving of some past knowledge) that he was once certain of the truth of this proposition, that the three angles of a triangle are equal to two right ones. The immutability of the same relations between the same immutable things is now the *idea* that shows him that, if the three angles of a triangle were once equal to two right ones, they will always be equal to two right ones. And hence he comes to be certain that what was once true in the case is always true, what *ideas* once agreed will always agree, and consequently what he once knew to be true he will always know to be true, as long as he can remember that he once knew it. Upon this ground it is that particular demonstrations in mathematics afford general knowledge. If then the perception that the same *ideas* will eternally have the same habitudes and relations be not a sufficient ground of knowledge, there could be no knowledge of general propositions in mathematics: for no mathematical demonstration would be any other than particular, and when a man had demonstrated any proposition concerning one triangle or circle, his knowledge would not reach beyond that particular diagram. If he would extend it further, he must renew his demonstration in another instance before he could know it to be true in another like triangle, and so on; by which means one could never come to the knowledge of any general propositions. Nobody, I think, can deny that Mr. *Newton* certainly knows any proposition that he now at any time reads in his book to be true, though he has not in actual view that admirable chain of intermediate *ideas* whereby he at first discovered it to be true. Such a memory as that, able to retain such a train of particulars, may be well thought beyond the reach of human faculties, when the very discovery, perception, and laying together that wonderful connexion of *ideas* is found to surpass most readers' comprehension. But yet it is evident the author himself knows the proposition to be true, remembering he once saw the connexion of those *ideas*: as certainly as he knows such a man wounded another, remembering that he saw him run him through. But because the memory is not always so clear as actual perception and does in all men more or less decay in length of time, this amongst other differences is one which shows that *demonstrative knowledge* is much more imperfect than *intuitive*, as we shall see in the following chapter.

Chapter II

OF THE DEGREES OF OUR KNOWLEDGE

1. ALL our knowledge consisting, as I have said, in the view the mind has of its own *ideas*, which is the utmost light and greatest certainty we, with our faculties and in our way of knowledge, are capable of, it may not be amiss to consider a little the degrees of its evidence. The different clearness of our knowledge seems to me to lie in the different way of perception the mind has of the agreement or disagreement of any of its *ideas*. For if we will reflect on our own ways of thinking, we shall find that sometimes the mind perceives the agreement or disagreement of two

ideas immediately by themselves, without the intervention of any other; and this I think we may call *intuitive knowledge*. For in this the mind is at no pains of proving or examining but perceives the truth, as the eye doth light, only by being directed toward it. Thus the mind perceives that *white* is not *black*, that a *circle* is not a *triangle*, that *three* are more than *two* and equal to *one* and *two*. Such kind of truths the mind perceives at the first sight of the *ideas* together, by bare *intuition*, without the intervention of any other *idea*; and this kind of knowledge is the clearest and most certain that human frailty is capable of. This part of knowledge is irresistible and, like bright sunshine, forces itself immediately to be perceived, as soon as ever the mind turns its view that way; and leaves no room for hesitation, doubt, or examination, but the mind is presently filled with the clear light of it. It is on this *intuition* that depends all the certainty and evidence of all our knowledge, which certainty everyone finds to be so great that he cannot imagine, and therefore not require, a greater; for a man cannot conceive himself capable of a greater certainty than to know that any *idea* in his mind is such as he perceives it to be, and that two *ideas* wherein he perceives a difference are different and not precisely the same. He that demands a greater certainty than this demands he knows not what, and shows only that he has a mind to be a sceptic without being able to be so. Certainty depends so wholly on this intuition that in the next degree of *knowledge*, which I call *demonstrative*, this intuition is necessary in all the connexions of the intermediate *ideas*, without which we cannot attain knowledge and certainty.

2. The next degree of knowledge is where the mind perceives the agreement or disagreement of any *ideas*, but not immediately. Though, wherever the mind perceives the agreement or disagreement of any of its *ideas*, there be certain knowledge: yet it does not always happen that the mind sees that agreement or disagreement which there is between them, even where it is discoverable; and in that case, remains in ignorance, and at most gets no further than a probable conjecture. The reason why the mind cannot always perceive presently the agreement or disagreement of two *ideas* is because those *ideas*, concerning whose agreement or disagreement the inquiry is made, cannot by the mind be so put together as to show it. In this case then, when the mind cannot so bring its *ideas* together as by their immediate comparison and as it were juxtaposition or application one to another, to perceive their agreement or disagreement, it is fain, by the intervention of other *ideas* (one or more, as it happens) to

discover the agreement or disagreement which it searches; and this is that which we call *reasoning*. Thus the mind, being willing to know the agreement or disagreement in bigness between the three angles of a triangle and two right ones, cannot by an immediate view and comparing them do it, because the three angles of a triangle cannot be brought at once and be compared with any one or two angles; and so of this the mind has no immediate, no intuitive knowledge. In this case the mind is fain to find out some other angles to which the three angles of a triangle have an equality, and finding those equal to two right ones, comes to know their equality to two right ones.

3. Those intervening *ideas* which serve to show the agreement of any two others are called *proofs*; and where the agreement or disagreement is by this means plainly and clearly perceived, it is called *demonstration*: it being *shown* to the understanding, and the mind made see that it is so. A quickness in the mind to find out these intermediate *ideas* (that shall discover the agreement or disagreement of any other) and to apply them right is, I suppose, that which is called *sagacity*.

4. *This knowledge by intervening proofs*, though it be certain, yet the evidence of it is *not* altogether *so clear* and bright, nor the assent so ready, *as* in *intuitive* knowledge. For, though in *demonstration* the mind does at last perceive the agreement or disagreement of the *ideas* it considers, yet it is not without pains and attention: there must be more than one transient view to find it. A steady application and pursuit is required to this discovery, and there must be a progression by steps and degrees, before the mind can in this way arrive at certainty and come to perceive the agreement or repugnancy between two *ideas* that need proofs and the use of reason to show it.

5. *Another difference between intuitive and demonstrative knowledge* is that, though in the latter all doubt be removed when, by the intervention of the intermediate *ideas*, the agreement or disagreement is perceived, yet before the demonstration there was a doubt; which in intuitive knowledge cannot happen to the mind that has its faculty of perception left to a degree capable of distinct *ideas*, no more than it can be a doubt to the eye (that can distinctly see white and black) whether this ink and this paper be all of a colour. If there be sight in the eyes, it will at first glimpse, without hesitation, perceive the words printed on this paper, different from the colour of the paper; and so if the mind have the faculty of distinct perception, it will perceive the agreement or disagreement of those *ideas* that produce intuitive knowledge. If the eyes have lost the faculty of seeing, or the mind of

perceiving, we in vain inquire after the quickness of sight in one or clearness of perception in the other.

6.   It is true, the perception produced by *demonstration* is also very clear, yet it is often with a great abatement of that evident lustre and full assurance that always accompany that which I call *intuitive*: like a face reflected by several mirrors one to another, where, as long as it retains the similitude and agreement with the object, it produces a knowledge; but it is still in every successive reflection, with a lessening of that perfect clearness and distinctness which is in the first; till at last, after many removes, it has a great mixture of dimness and is not at first sight so knowable, especially to weak eyes. Thus it is with knowledge made out by a long train of proofs.

7.   Now, *in every step reason makes in demonstrative knowledge, there is an intuitive knowledge* of that agreement or disagreement it seeks with the next intermediate *idea* which it uses as a proof; for if it were not so, that yet would need a proof, since without the perception of such agreement or disagreement, there is no knowledge produced. If it be perceived by itself, it is intuitive knowledge; if it cannot be perceived by itself, there is need of some intervening *idea*, as a common measure to show their agreement or disagreement. By which it is plain that every step in reasoning that produces knowledge has intuitive certainty; which when the mind perceives, there is no more required but to remember it to make the agreement or disagreement of the *ideas*, concerning which we inquire, visible and certain. So that to make anything a *demonstration*, it is necessary to perceive the immediate agreement of the intervening *ideas* whereby the agreement or disagreement of the two *ideas* under examination (whereof the one is always the first, and the other the last in the account) is found. This intuitive perception of the agreement or disagreement of the intermediate *ideas*, in each step and progression of the *demonstration*, must also be carried exactly in the mind, and a man must be sure that no part is left out; which because, in long deductions and the use of many proofs, the memory does not always so readily and exactly retain, therefore it comes to pass that this is more imperfect than intuitive knowledge, and men embrace often falsehood for demonstrations.

8.   The necessity of this intuitive knowledge in each step of scientifical or demonstrative reasoning gave occasion, I imagine, to that *mistaken axiom, that all reasoning was ex praecognitis et praeconcessis*; which, how far it is mistaken, I shall have occasion to show more at large, where I come to consider propositions, and particularly those propositions which are called maxims, and

to show that it is by a mistake that they are supposed to be the foundations of all our knowledge and reasonings.

9. It has been generally taken for granted that mathematics alone are capable of demonstrative certainty; but to have such an agreement or disagreement as may intuitively be perceived being, as I imagine, not the privilege of the *ideas* of *number*, *extension*, and *figure* alone, it may possibly be the want of due method and application in us, and not of sufficient evidence in things, that demonstration has been thought to have so little to do in other parts of knowledge, and been scarce so much as aimed at by any but mathematicians. For whatever *ideas* we have wherein the mind can perceive the immediate agreement or disagreement that is between them, there the mind is capable of intuitive knowledge; and where it can perceive the agreement or disagreement of any two *ideas*, by an intuitive perception of the agreement or disagreement they have with any intermediate *ideas*, there the mind is capable of demonstration, which is not limited to *ideas* of extension, figure, number, and their modes.

10. The reason why it has been generally sought for and supposed to be only in those, I imagine, has been not only the general usefulness of those sciences, but because, in comparing their equality or excess, the modes of numbers have every the least difference very clear and perceivable; and though in extension every the least excess is not so perceptible, yet the mind has found out ways to examine and discover demonstratively the just equality of two angles, or extensions, or figures; and both these, i.e. numbers and figures, can be set down by visible and lasting marks wherein the *ideas* under consideration are perfectly determined, which for the most part they are not where they are marked only by names and words.

11. But in other simple *ideas*, whose modes and differences are made and counted by degrees and not quantity, we have not so nice and accurate a distinction of their differences as to perceive or find ways to measure their just equality or the least differences. For those other simple *ideas* being appearances or sensations produced in us by the size, figure, number, and motion of minute corpuscles singly insensible, their different degrees also depend upon the variation of some or all of those causes: which, since it cannot be observed by us in particles of matter whereof each is too subtle to be perceived, it is impossible for us to have any exact measures of the different degrees of these simple *ideas*. For supposing the sensation or *idea* we name *whiteness* be produced in us by a certain number of globules which, having a verticity about their own centres, strike

upon the *retina* of the eye with a certain degree of rotation as well as progressive swiftness: it will hence easily follow that the more the superficial parts of any body are so ordered as to reflect the greater number of globules of light and to give them that proper rotation which is fit to produce this sensation of white in us, the more white will that body appear that, from an equal space, sends to the *retina* the greater number of such corpuscles with that peculiar sort of motion. I do not say that the nature of light consists in very small round globules, nor of whiteness in such a texture of parts as gives a certain rotation to these globules when it reflects them, for I am not now treating physically of light or colours; but this, I think I may say: that I cannot (and I would be glad anyone would make intelligible that he did) conceive how bodies without us can anyways affect our senses but by the immediate contact of the sensible bodies themselves, as in tasting and feeling, or the impulse of some insensible particles coming from them, as in seeing, hearing, and smelling; by the different impulse of which parts, caused by their different size, figure, and motion, the variety of sensations is produced in us.

12.   Whether then they be globules or no, or whether they have a verticity about their own centres that produce the *idea* of *whiteness* in us, this is certain: that the more particles of light are reflected from a body, fitted to give them that peculiar motion which produces the sensation of whiteness in us, and possibly too, the quicker that peculiar motion is, the whiter does the body appear from which the greater number are reflected; as is evident in the same piece of paper put in the sunbeams, in the shade, and in a dark hole, in each of which it will produce in us the *idea* of whiteness in far different degrees.

13.   Not knowing, therefore, what number of particles nor what motion of them is fit to produce any precise degree of *whiteness*, we cannot demonstrate the certain equality of any two degrees of *whiteness*, because we have no certain standard to measure them by, nor means to distinguish every the least real difference, the only help we have being from our senses, which in this point fail us. But where the difference is so great as to produce in the mind clearly distinct *ideas* whose differences can be perfectly retained, there these *ideas* of colours, as we see in different kinds, as blue and red, are as capable of demonstration as *ideas* of number and extension. What I have here said of *whiteness* and colours I think holds true in all secondary qualities and their modes.

14.   These two, viz. intuition and demonstration, are the degrees of our knowledge; whatever comes short of one of these,

with what assurance soever embraced, is but faith or opinion, but not knowledge, at least in all general truths. There is, indeed, another *perception* of the mind, employed about *the particular existence of finite beings* without us, which, going beyond bare probability and yet not reaching perfectly to either of the foregoing degrees of certainty, passes under the name of knowledge. There can be nothing more certain than that the *idea* we receive from an external object is in our minds: this is intuitive knowledge. But whether there be anything more than barely that *idea* in our minds, whether we can thence certainly infer the existence of anything without us which corresponds to that *idea* is that whereof some men think there may be a question made: because men may have such *ideas* in their minds, when no such thing exists, no such object affects their senses. But yet here I think we are provided with an evidence that puts us past doubting: for I ask anyone whether he be not invincibly conscious to himself of a different perception, when he looks on the sun by day and thinks on it by night, when he actually tastes wormwood or smells a rose or only thinks on that savour or odour? We as plainly find the difference there is between any *idea* revived in our minds by our own memory and actually coming into our minds by our senses, as we do between any two distinct *ideas*. If anyone say a dream may do the same thing, and all these *ideas* may be produced in us without any external objects, he may please to dream that I make him this answer: (1) That it is no great matter whether I remove his scruple or no: where all is but dream, reasoning and arguments are of no use, truth and knowledge nothing. (2) That I believe he will allow a very manifest difference between dreaming of being in the fire and being actually in it. But yet if he be resolved to appear so sceptical as to maintain that what I call being actually in the fire is nothing but a dream, and that we cannot thereby certainly know that any such thing as fire actually exists without us, I answer: that we certainly finding that pleasure or pain follows upon the application of certain objects to us whose existence we perceive or dream that we perceive by our senses, this certainty is as great as our happiness or misery, beyond which we have no concernment to know or to be. So that, I think, we may add to the two former sorts of *knowledge* this also of the existence of particular external objects, by that perception and consciousness we have of the actual entrance of *ideas* from them, and allow these *three degrees of knowledge*, viz. *intuitive, demonstrative, and sensitive*, in each of which there are different degrees and ways of evidence and certainty.

15. But since our knowledge is founded on and employed about our *ideas* only, will it not follow from thence that it is conformable to our *ideas*; and that where our *ideas* are clear and distinct, or obscure and confused, our knowledge will be so too? To which I answer, No: for our knowledge consisting in the perception of the agreement or disagreement of any two *ideas*, its clearness or obscurity consists in the clearness or obscurity of that perception, and not in the clearness or obscurity of the *ideas* themselves: v.g. a man that has as clear *ideas* of the angles of a triangle, and of equality to two right ones, as any mathematician in the world may yet have but a very obscure perception of their agreement, and so have but a very obscure knowledge of it. But *ideas* which, by reason of their obscurity or otherwise, are confused cannot produce any clear or distinct knowledge: because, as far as any *ideas* are confused, so far the mind cannot perceive clearly whether they agree or disagree.   Or to express the same thing in a way less apt to be misunderstood: he that hath not determined the *ideas* to the words he uses cannot make propositions of them of whose truth he can be certain.

CHAPTER III

OF THE EXTENT OF HUMAN KNOWLEDGE

1. KNOWLEDGE, as has been said, lying in the perception of the agreement or disagreement of any of our *ideas*, it follows from hence that:

First, We can have *knowledge* no further than we have *ideas*.

2. *Secondly*, That we can have no *knowledge* further than we can have perception of that agreement or disagreement; which perception being: (1) either by *intuition*, or the immediate comparing any two *ideas*; or (2) by *reason*, examining the agreement or disagreement of two *ideas* by the intervention of some others; or (3) by *sensation*, perceiving the existence of particular things. Hence it also follows:

3. *Thirdly*, That we cannot have an *intuitive knowledge* that shall extend itself to all our *ideas* and all that we would know about them; because we cannot examine and perceive all the relations they have one to another, by juxtaposition or an immediate comparison one with another.   Thus having the *ideas* of an obtuse and an acute angled triangle, both drawn from equal bases and between parallels, I can by intuitive knowledge perceive the one not to be the other, but cannot that way know whether they be equal or no, because their agreement or disagreement in equality can never be perceived by an immediate comparing them; the difference of figure makes their parts incapable of an exact immediate application, and therefore there is need of some intervening quantities to measure them by, which is demonstration or rational knowledge.

4.   *Fourthly*, It follows, also, from what is above observed that our *rational knowledge* cannot reach to the whole extent of our *ideas*: because between two different *ideas* we would examine, we cannot always find such *mediums* as we can connect one to another with an intuitive knowledge in all the parts of the deduction; and wherever that fails, we come short of knowledge and demonstration.

5.   *Fifthly*, Sensitive *knowledge*, reaching no further than the existence of things actually present to our senses, is yet much narrower than either of the former.

6.   From all which it is evident that *the extent of our knowledge* comes not only short of the reality of things, but even of the extent of our own *ideas*. Though our knowledge be limited to our *ideas* and cannot exceed them either in extent or perfection; and though these be very narrow bounds in respect of the extent of all-being, and far short of what we may justly imagine to be in some even created understandings, not tied down to the dull and narrow information that is to be received from some few and not very acute ways of perception, such as are our senses: yet it would be well with us if our knowledge were but as large as our *ideas*, and there were not many doubts and inquiries concerning the *ideas* we have, whereof we are not nor, I believe, ever shall be in this world resolved. Nevertheless, I do not question but that human knowledge, under the present circumstances of our beings and constitutions, may be carried much further than it hitherto has been, if men would sincerely and with freedom of mind employ all that industry and labour of thought in improving the means of discovering truth, which they do for the colouring or support of falsehood, to maintain a system, interest, or party they are once engaged in. But yet after all I think I may, without injury to human perfection, be confident that our knowledge would never reach to all we might desire to know concerning those *ideas* we have, nor be able to surmount all the difficulties and resolve all the questions that might arise concerning any of them. We have the *ideas* of a *square*, a *circle*, and *equality*, and yet, perhaps, shall never be able to find a circle equal to a square, and certainly know that it

is so. We have the *ideas* of *matter* and *thinking*, but possibly shall never be able to know whether any mere material being thinks or no: it being impossible for us, by the contemplation of our own *ideas*, without revelation, to discover whether Omnipotency has not given to some systems of matter, fitly disposed, a power to perceive and think, or else joined and fixed to matter, so disposed, a thinking immaterial substance: it being, in respect of our notions, not much m re remote from our comprehension to conceive that GOD can, if he pleases, superadd to matter a faculty of thinking, than th t he should superadd to it another substance with a faculty of thinking, since we know not wherein thinking consists, nor to what sort of substances the Almighty has been pleased to give that power, which cannot be in any created being but merely by the good pleasure and bounty of the Creator. For I see no contradiction in it that the first eternal thinking Being should, if he pleased, give to certain systems of created senseless matter, put together as he thinks fit, some degrees of sense, perception, and thought: though, as I think I have proved, *lib. IV, ch. x*, it is no less than a contradiction to suppose matter (which is evidently in its own nature void of sense and thought) should be that eternal first thinking being. What certainty of knowledge can anyone have that some perceptions, such as, v.g. pleasure and pain, should not be in some bodies themselves, after a certain manner modified and moved, as well as that they should be in an immaterial substance upon the motion of the parts of body: body, as far as we can conceive, being able only to strike and affect body; and motion, according to the utmost reach of our *ideas*, being able to produce nothing but motion; so that when we allow it to produce pleasure or pain, or the *idea* of a colour or sound, we are fain to quit our reason, go beyond our *ideas*, and attribute it wholly to the good pleasure of our Maker. For since we must allow he has annexed effects to motion, which we can no way conceive motion able to produce, what reason have we to conclude that he could not order them as well to be produced in a subject we cannot conceive capable of them, as well as in a subject we cannot conceive the motion of matter can any way operate upon? I say not this that I would any way lessen the belief of the soul's immateriality; I am not here speaking of probability but knowledge, and I think not only that it becomes the modesty of philosophy not to pronounce mag'sterially where we want that evidence that can produce knowledge, but also that it is of use to us to discern how far our knowledge does reach; for the state we are at present in not being that of vision, we must, in many things, content ourselves with faith and probability; and in the present question about the immateriality of the soul, if our faculties cannot arrive at demonstrative certainty, we need not think it strange. All the great ends of morality and religion are well enough secured without philosophical proofs of the soul's immateriality, since it is evident that he who made us at first begin to subsist here, sensible intelligent beings, and for several years continued us in such a state, can and will restore us to the like state of sensibility in another world and make us capable there to receive the retribution he has designed to men, according to their doings in this life. And therefore it is not of such mighty necessity to determine one way or the other, as some, over zealous for or against the immateriality of the soul, have been forward to make the world believe: who, either on the one side, indulging too much their thoughts immersed altogether in matter, can allow no existence to what is not material; or who, on the other side, finding not *cogitation* within the natural powers of matter examined over and over again by the utmost intention of mind, have the confidence to conclude that omnipotency itself cannot give perception and thought to a substance which has the modification of solidity. He that considers how hardly sensation is, in our thoughts, reconcilable to extended matter, or existence to anything that has no extension at all, will confess that he is very far from certainly knowing what his soul is. It is a point which seems to me to be put out of the reach of our knowledge; and he who will give himself leave to consider freely and look into the dark and intricate part of each hypothesis, will scarce find his reason able to determine him fixedly for or against the soul's materiality: since, on which side soever he views it, either as an unextended substance or as a thinking extended matter, the difficulty to conceive either will, whilst either alone is in his thoughts, still drive him to the contrary side. An unfair way which some men take with themselves, who, because of the unconceivableness of something they find in one, throw themselves violently into the contrary hypothesis, though altogether as unintelligible to an unbiassed understanding. This serves not only to show the weakness and the scantiness of our knowledge, but the insignificant triumph of such sort of arguments, which, drawn from our own views, may satisfy us that we can find no certainty on one side of the question, but do not at all thereby help us to truth by running into the opposite opinion, which on examination will be found clogged with equal difficulties. For what safety, what advantage to anyone is it, for the avoiding the seeming absurdities and, to him, unsurmountable rubs he meets with in one opinion, to take refuge in the contrary, which is built on something altogether as inexplicable and as far remote from his comprehension? It is past controversy that we have in us something that thinks: our very doubts about what it is confirm the certainty of its being, though we must content ourselves in the ignorance of what kind of *being* it is; and it is in vain to go about to be sceptical in this, as it is unreasonable in most other cases to be positive against the being of anything because we cannot comprehend its nature. For I would fain know what substance exists that has not something in it which manifestly baffles our understandings. Other spirits, who see and know the nature and inward constitution of things, how much must they exceed us in knowledge? To which if we add larger comprehension, which enables them at one glance to see the connexion and agreement of very many *ideas* and readily supplies to them the intermediate proofs which we, by single and slow steps and long poring in the dark, hardly at last find out and are often ready to forget one before we have hunted out another, we may guess at some part of the happiness of superior ranks of spirits, who have a quicker and more penetrating sight, as well as a larger field of knowledge. But to return to the argument in hand: our *knowledge*, I say, is not only limited to the paucity and imperfections of the *ideas* we have and which we employ it about, but even comes short of that too; but how far it reaches let us now inquire.

7. The affirmations or negations we make concerning the *ideas* we have may, as I have before intimated in general, be reduced to these four sorts, viz. identity, co-existence, relation, and real existence. I shall examine how far our knowledge extends in each of these:

8. *First, As to identity and diversity*: in this way of the agreement or disagreement of our *ideas, our intuitive knowledge is as far extended as our ideas* themselves; and there can be no *idea* in the mind which it does not presently, by an intuitive knowledge, perceive to be what it is, and to be different from any other.

9. *Secondly, As to* the second sort, which is the *agreement or disagreement* of our *ideas in co-existence*: in this our knowledge is very short, though in this consists the greatest and most material part of our knowledge concerning substances. For our *ideas* of the species of substances being, as I have shown, nothing but certain collections of simple *ideas* united in one subject, and so co-existing together: v.g. our *idea* of *flame* is a body hot, luminous, and moving upward; of *gold*, a body heavy to a certain degree, yellow, malleable, and fusible: these, or some

such complex *ideas* as these, in men's minds, do these two names of the different substances, *flame* and *gold*, stand for. When we would know anything further concerning these or any other sort of substances, what do we inquire but what other qualities or powers these substances have or have not? Which is nothing else but to know what other simple *ideas* do or do not co-exist with those that make up that complex *idea*.

10.   This, how weighty and considerable a part soever of human science, is yet very narrow, and scarce any at all.   The reason whereof is that the simple *ideas* whereof our complex *ideas* of substances are made up are, for the most part, such as carry with them, in their own nature, no visible necessary connexion or inconsistency with any other simple *ideas*, whose *co-existence* with them we would inform ourselves about.

11.   The *ideas* that our complex ones of substances are made up of, and about which our knowledge concerning substances is most employed, are those of their *secondary qualities*; which depending all (as has been shown) upon the primary qualities of their minute and insensible parts or, if not upon them, upon something yet more remote from our comprehension, it is impossible we should know which have a necessary union or inconsistency one with another; for, not knowing the root they spring from, not knowing what size, figure, and texture of parts they are on which depend and from which result those qualities which make our complex *idea* of gold, it is impossible we should know what other qualities result from or are incompatible with the same constitution of the insensible parts of *gold*, and so consequently must always *co-exist* with that complex *idea* we have of it, or else are *inconsistent* with it.

12.   Besides this ignorance of the primary qualities of the insensible parts of bodies, on which depend all their secondary qualities, there is yet another and more incurable part of ignorance, which sets us more remote from a certain knowledge of the *co-existence* or *in-co-existence* (if I may so say) of different *ideas* in the same subject; and that is that there is no discoverable connexion between any *secondary quality and those primary qualities* that it depends on.

13.   That the size, figure, and motion of one body should cause a change in the size, figure, and motion of another body is not beyond our conception; the separation of the parts of one body upon the intrusion of another, and the change from rest to motion upon impulse: these, and the like, seem to us to have some *connexion* one with another.   And if we knew these primary qualities of bodies, we might have reason to hope we

might be able to know a great deal more of these operations of them one upon another; but our minds not being able to discover any *connexion* betwixt these primary qualities of bodies and the sensations that are produced in us by them, we can never be able to establish certain and undoubted rules of the consequence or *co-existence* of any secondary qualities, though we could discover the size, figure, or motion of those invisible parts which immediately produce them. We are so far from knowing what figure, size, or motion of parts produce a yellow colour, a sweet taste, or a sharp sound that we can by no means conceive how any *size, figure, or motion* of any particles can possibly produce in us the *idea* of any *colour, taste,* or *sound* whatsoever: there is no conceivable *connexion* betwixt the one and the other.

14. In vain, therefore, shall we endeavour to discover by our *ideas* (the only true way of certain and universal knowledge) what other *ideas* are to be found constantly joined with that of our complex *idea* of any substance: since we neither know the real constitution of the minute parts on which their qualities do depend; nor, did we know them, could we discover any necessary *connexion* between them and any of the *secondary qualities*; which is necessary to be done before we can certainly know their *necessary co-existence*. So that, let our complex *idea* of any species of substances be what it will, we can hardly, from the simple *ideas* contained in it, certainly determine the *necessary co-existence* of any other quality whatsoever. Our knowledge in all these inquiries reaches very little further than our experience. Indeed some few of the primary qualities have a necessary dependence and visible connexion one with another, as figure necessarily supposes extension, receiving or communicating motion by impulse supposes solidity. But though these and perhaps some others of our *ideas* have, yet there are so *few* of them that have a *visible connexion* one with another, that we can by intuition or demonstration discover the co-existence of very few of the qualities that are to be found united in substances; and we are left only to the assistance of our senses to make known to us what qualities they contain. For of all the qualities that are *co-existent* in any subject, without this dependence and evident connexion of their *ideas* one with another, we cannot know certainly any two to *co-exist* any further than experience by our senses informs us. Thus though we see the yellow colour and upon trial find the weight, malleableness, fusibility, and fixedness that are united in a piece of gold: yet, because no one of these *ideas* has any evident *dependence* or necessary connexion

with the other, we cannot certainly know that where any four of these are, the fifth will be there also, how highly probable soever it may be: because the highest probability amounts not to certainty, without which there can be no true knowledge. For this *co-existence* can be no further known than it is perceived; and it cannot be perceived but either in particular subjects, by the observation of our senses, or in general, by the necessary *connexion* of the *ideas* themselves.

15. *As to incompatibility or repugnancy to co-existence,* we may know that any subject can have of each sort of primary qualities but one particular at once: v.g. each particular extension, figure, number of parts, motion, excludes all other of each kind. The like also is certain of all sensible *ideas* peculiar to each sense; for whatever of each kind is present in any subject excludes all other of that sort: v.g. no one subject can have two smells or two colours at the same time. To this, perhaps, will be said, Has not an *opal,* or the infusion of *lignum nephriticum,* two colours at the same time? To which I answer that these bodies, to eyes differently placed, may at the same time afford different colours; but I take liberty also to say that, to eyes differently placed, it is different parts of the object that reflect the particles of light, and therefore it is not the same part of the object, and so not the very same subject which at the same time appears both yellow and azure. For it is as impossible that the very same particle of any body should at the same time differently modify or reflect the rays of light, as that it should have two different figures and textures at the same time.

16. But *as to the powers of substances* to change the sensible qualities of other bodies, which make a great part of our inquiries about them and is no inconsiderable branch of our knowledge: I doubt, as to these, whether *our knowledge reaches* much further than our experience, or whether we can come to the discovery of most of these powers and be certain that they are in any subject by the connexion with any of those *ideas* which to us make its essence. Because the active and passive powers of bodies and their ways of operating consisting in a texture and motion of parts which we cannot by any means come to discover, it is but in very few cases we can be able to perceive their dependence on or repugnance to any of those *ideas* which make our complex one of that sort of things. I have here instanced in the corpuscularian hypothesis, as that which is thought to go furthest in an intelligible explication of the qualities of bodies; and I fear the weakness of human understanding is scarce able to substitute another which will afford us a fuller and clearer

discovery of the necessary connexion and *co-existence* of the powers which are to be observed united in several sorts of them. This at least is certain: that whichever hypothesis be clearest and truest (for of that it is not my business to determine), our knowledge concerning corporeal substances will be very little advanced by any of them, till we are made to see what qualities and powers of bodies have a *necessary connexion or repugnancy* one with another; which in the present state of philosophy I think we know but to a very small degree. And I doubt whether, with those faculties we have, we shall ever be able to carry our general knowledge (I say not particular experience) in this part much further. Experience is that which in this part we must depend on. And it were to be wished that it were more improved. We find the advantages some men's generous pains have this way brought to the stock of natural knowledge. And if others, especially the philosophers by fire, who pretend to it, had been so wary in their observations and sincere in their reports as those who call themselves philosophers ought to have been, our acquaintance with the bodies here about us and our insight into their powers and operations had been yet much greater.

17. If we are at a loss in respect of the powers and operations of bodies, I think it is easy to conclude *we are much more in the dark in reference to spirits*; whereof we naturally have no *ideas* but what we draw from that of our own, by reflecting on the operations of our own souls within us as far as they can come within our observation. But how inconsiderable a rank the spirits that inhabit our bodies hold amongst those various and possibly innumerable kinds of nobler beings, and how far short they come of the endowments and perfections of cherubims and seraphims and infinite sorts of spirits above us is what, by a transient hint, in another place, I have offered to my reader's consideration.

18. As to the third sort of our knowledge, viz. the *agreement or disagreement of any of our* ideas *in any other relation*; this, as it is the largest field of our knowledge, so it is hard to determine how far it may extend: because the advances that are made in this part of knowledge depending on our sagacity in finding intermediate *ideas* that may show the *relations* and *habitudes* of *ideas* whose co-existence is not considered, it is a hard matter to tell when we are at an end of such discoveries, and when reason has all the helps it is capable of, for the finding of proofs or examining the agreement or disagreement of remote *ideas*. They that are ignorant of *algebra* cannot imagine the wonders in this

kind that are to be done by it; and what further improvements and helps, advantageous to other parts of knowledge, the sagacious mind of man may yet find out, it is not easy to determine. This at least I believe: that the *ideas* of quantity are not those alone that are capable of demonstration and knowledge; and that other and perhaps more useful parts of contemplation would afford us certainty, if vices, passions, and domineering interest did not oppose or menace such endeavours.

The *idea* of a supreme Being, infinite in power, goodness, and wisdom, whose workmanship we are and on whom we depend, and the *idea* of ourselves as understanding rational beings, being such as are clear in us, would, I suppose, if duly considered and pursued, afford such foundations of our duty and rules of action as might place *morality amongst the sciences capable of demonstration*: wherein I doubt not but from self-evident propositions, by necessary consequences as incontestable as those in mathematics, the measures of right and wrong might be made out to anyone that will apply himself with the same indifferency and attention to the one as he does to the other of these sciences. The *relation* of other *modes* may certainly be perceived, as well as those of number and extension; and I cannot see why they should not also be capable of demonstration, if due methods were thought on to examine or pursue their agreement or disagreement. *Where there is no property there is no injustice* is a proposition as certain as any demonstration in *Euclid*: for the *idea* of *property* being a right to anything, and the idea to which the name *injustice* is given being the invasion or violation of that right, it is evident that, these *ideas* being thus established, and these names annexed to them, I can as certainly know this proposition to be true as that a triangle has three angles equal to two right ones. Again, *No government allows absolute liberty*: the *idea* of government being the establishment of society upon certain rules or laws which require conformity to them, and the *idea* of absolute liberty being for anyone to do whatever he pleases, I am as capable of being certain of the truth of this proposition as of any in mathematics.

19. That which in this respect has given the advantage to the *ideas* of quantity and made them thought more capable of certainty and demonstration is,

First, That they can be set down and represented by sensible marks, which have a greater and nearer correspondence with them than any words or sounds whatsoever. Diagrams drawn on paper are copies of the *ideas* in the mind, and not liable to the uncertainty that words carry in their signification. An angle, circle, or square, drawn in lines, lies open to the view and cannot be mistaken: it remains unchangeable and may at leisure be considered and examined, and the demonstration be revised, and all the parts of it may be gone over more than once, without any danger of the least change in the *ideas*. This cannot be thus done in *moral ideas*: we have no sensible marks that resemble them whereby we can set them down, we have nothing but words to express them by; which, though when written they remain the same, yet the *ideas* they stand for may change in the same man; and it is very seldom that they are not different in different persons.

Secondly, Another thing that makes the greater difficulty in *ethics* is that *moral ideas* are commonly more complex than those of the figures ordinarily considered in mathematics. From whence these two inconveniences follow: *First*, that their names are of more uncertain signification, the precise collection of simple *ideas* they stand for not being so easily agreed on; and so the sign that is used for them in communication always, and in thinking often, does not steadily carry with it the same *idea*. Upon which the same disorder, confusion, and error follows as would if a man, going to demonstrate something of an *heptagon*, should, in the diagram he took to do it, leave out one of the angles or by oversight make the figure with one angle more than the name ordinarily imported or he intended it should, when at first he thought of his demonstration. This often happens and is hardly avoidable in very complex moral *ideas* where, the same name being retained, one angle, i.e. one simple *idea*, is left out or put in in the complex one (still called by the same name), more at one time than another. *Secondly*, from the complexedness of these moral *ideas* there follows another inconvenience, (viz.) that the mind cannot easily retain those precise combinations so exact and perfectly as is necessary in the examination of the habitudes and correspondences, agreements or disagreements, of several of them one with another, especially where it is to be judged of, by long deductions and the intervention of several other complex *ideas*, to show the agreement or disagreement of two remote ones.

The great help against this which mathematicians find in diagrams and figures, which remain unalterable in their draughts, is very apparent, and the memory would often have great difficulty otherwise to retain them so exactly, whilst the mind went over the parts of them step by step to examine their several correspondences. And though, in casting up a long sum, either in *addition, multiplication,* or *division,* every part be only a progression of the mind, taking a view of its own *ideas* and considering their agreement or disagreement; and the resolution of the question be nothing but the result of the whole, made up of such particulars whereof the mind has a clear perception: yet without setting down the several parts by marks whose precise significations are known, and by marks that last and remain in view when the memory had let them go, it would be almost impossible to carry so many different *ideas* in mind without confounding or letting slip some parts of the reckoning, and thereby making all our reasonings about it useless. In which case, the cyphers or marks help not the mind at all to perceive the agreement of any two or more numbers, their equalities, or proportions: that the mind has only by intuition of its own *ideas* of the numbers themselves. But the numerical characters are helps to the memory to record and retain the several *ideas* about which the demonstration is made, whereby a man may know how far his intuitive knowledge in surveying several of the particulars has proceeded, that so he may without confusion go on to what is yet unknown, and at last have in one view before him the result of all his perceptions and reasonings.

20. One part of *these disadvantages* in moral *ideas*, which has made them be thought not capable of demonstration, may in a good measure be *remedied* by definitions, setting down that collection of simple *ideas* which every term shall stand for, and then using the terms steadily and constantly for that precise collection. And what methods *algebra*, or something of that kind, may hereafter suggest to remove the other difficulties is not easy to foretell. Confident I am that, if men would, in the same method and with the same indifferency, search after moral as they do mathematical truths, they would find them to have a stronger connexion one with another and a more necessary consequence from our clear and distinct *ideas*, and to come nearer perfect demonstration than is commonly imagined. But much of this is not to be expected, whilst the desire of esteem, riches, or power makes men espouse the well-endowed opinions in fashion, and then seek arguments either to make good their beauty, or varnish over and cover their deformity. Nothing being so beautiful to the eye as truth is to the mind; nothing so deformed and irreconcilable to the understanding as a lie. For though many a man can with satisfaction enough own a not very handsome wife in his bosom, yet who is bold enough openly to avow that he has espoused a falsehood and received into his breast so ugly a thing as a lie? Whilst the parties of men cram their tenets down all men's throats whom they can get into

their power, without permitting them to examine their truth or falsehood, and will not let truth have fair play in the world nor men the liberty to search after it: what improvements can be expected of this kind? What greater light can be hoped for in the moral sciences? The subject part of mankind in most places might instead thereof, with *Egyptian* bondage, expect *Egyptian* darkness, were not the candle of the Lord set up by himself in men's minds, which it is impossible for the breath or power of man wholly to extinguish.

21. As to the fourth sort of our knowledge, viz. *of* the *real actual existence* of things: we have an intuitive knowledge of our own *existence*, a demonstrative knowledge of the *existence* of a god; of the *existence* of anything else, we have no other but a sensitive knowledge, which extends not beyond the objects present to our senses.

22. Our knowledge being so narrow, as I have shown, it will perhaps give us some light into the present state of our minds if we look a little into the dark side, and take a view of *our ignorance*; which, being infinitely larger than our knowledge, may serve much to the quieting of disputes and improvement of useful knowledge, if, discovering how far we have clear and distinct *ideas*, we confine our thoughts within the contemplation of those things that are within the reach of our understandings and launch not out into that abyss of darkness (where we have not eyes to see, nor faculties to perceive anything) out of a presumption that nothing is beyond our comprehension. But to be satisfied of the folly of such a conceit, we need not go far. He that knows anything knows this in the first place: that he need not seek long for instances of his ignorance. The meanest and most obvious things that come in our way have dark sides that the quickest sight cannot penetrate into. The clearest and most enlarged understandings of thinking men find themselves puzzled and at a loss in every particle of matter. We shall the less wonder to find it so, when we consider the *causes of our ignorance* which, from what has been said, I suppose will be found to be chiefly these three:

First, Want of *ideas*.

Secondly, Want of a discoverable connexion between the *ideas* we have.

Thirdly, Want of tracing and examining our *ideas*.

23. *First*, There are some things, and those not a few, that we are ignorant of for *want of ideas*.

First, All the simple *ideas* we have are confined (as I have shown) to those we receive from corporeal objects by *sensation*, and from the operations of our own minds as the objects of *reflection*. But how much these few and narrow inlets are disproportionate to the vast whole extent of all beings, will not be hard to persuade those who are not so foolish as to think their span the measure of all things. What other simple *ideas* it is possible the creatures in other parts of the universe may have, by the assistance of senses and faculties more or perfecter than we have or different from ours, it is not for us to determine. But to say or think there are no such, because we conceive nothing of them, is no better an argument than if a blind man should be positive in it, that there was no such thing as sight and colours, because he had no manner of *idea* of any such thing nor could by any means frame to himself any notions about seeing. The ignorance and darkness that is in us no more hinders nor confines the knowledge that is in others, than the blindness of a mole is an argument against the quick-sightedness of an eagle. He that will consider the infinite power, wisdom, and goodness of the Creator of all things will find reason to think it was not all laid out upon so inconsiderable, mean, and impotent a creature as he will find man to be, who in all probability is one of the lowest of all intellectual beings. What faculties therefore other species of creatures have to penetrate into the nature and inmost constitutions of things, what *ideas* they may receive of them, far different from ours, we know not. This we know and certainly find, that we want several other views of them, besides those we have, to make discoveries of them more perfect. And we may be convinced that the *ideas* we can attain to by our faculties are very disproportionate to things themselves, when a positive clear distinct one of substance itself, which is the foundation of all the rest, is concealed from us. But want of *ideas* of this kind, being a part as well as cause of our ignorance, cannot be described. Only this, I think, I may confidently say of it: that the intellectual and sensible world are in this perfectly alike; that that part, which we see of either of them, holds no proportion with what we see not; and whatsoever we can reach, with our eyes or our thoughts, of either of them is but a point, almost nothing, in comparison of the rest.

24. *Secondly,* Another great cause of ignorance is the *want of* ideas *we are capable of.* As the want of *ideas*, which our faculties are not able to give us, shuts us wholly from those views of things which it is reasonable to think other beings, perfecter than we, have, of which we know nothing, so the want of *ideas* I now speak of keeps us in ignorance of things we conceive capable of being known to us. *Bulk, figure,* and *motion* we have

ideas of. But though we are not without *ideas* of these primary qualities of bodies in general, yet not knowing what is the particular *bulk, figure,* and *motion* of the greatest part of the bodies of the universe, we are ignorant of the several powers, efficacies, and ways of operation whereby the effects which we daily see are produced. These are hid from us, in some things by being *too remote, and* in others by being too *minute.* When we consider the vast distance of the known and visible parts of the world, and the reasons we have to think that what lies within our ken is but a small part of the immense universe, we shall then discover an huge abyss of ignorance. What are the particular fabrics of the great masses of matter which make up the whole stupendous frame of corporeal beings; how far they are extended; what is their motion, and how continued, or communicated; and what influence they have one upon another are contemplations that, at first glimpse, our thoughts lose themselves in. If we narrow our contemplation and confine our thoughts to this little canton, I mean this system of our sun and the grosser masses of matter that visibly move about it, what several sorts of vegetables, animals, and intellectual corporeal beings, infinitely different from those of our little spot of earth, may there probably be in the other planets, to the knowledge of which even of their outward figures and parts we can no way attain whilst we are confined to this earth, there being no natural means either by sensation or reflection to convey their certain *ideas* into our minds? They are out of the reach of those inlets of all our knowledge; and what sorts of furniture and inhabitants those mansions contain in them we cannot so much as guess, much less have clear and distinct *ideas* of them.

25. If a great, nay, far the greatest part of the several ranks of *bodies* in the universe escape our notice by their remoteness, there are others that are no less concealed from us by their *minuteness.* These insensible corpuscles being the active parts of matter and the great instruments of nature on which depend not only all their secondary qualities but also most of their natural operations, our want of precise distinct *ideas* of their primary qualities keeps us in an incurable ignorance of what we desire to know about them. I doubt not but, if we could discover the figure, size, texture, and motion of the minute constituent parts of any two bodies, we should know without trial several of their operations one upon another, as we do now the properties of a square or a triangle. Did we know the mechanical affections of the particles of *rhubarb, hemlock, opium,* and a *man,* as a watchmaker does those of a watch, whereby it performs its

operations, and of a file, which by rubbing on them will alter the figure of any of the wheels, we should be able to tell beforehand that *rhubarb* will purge, *hemlock* kill, and *opium* make a man sleep: as well as a watchmaker can that a little piece of paper laid on the balance will keep the watch from going till it be removed; or that some small part of it being rubbed by a file, the machine would quite lose its motion, and the watch go no more. The dissolving of silver in *aqua fortis* and gold in *aqua regia*, and not *vice versa*, would be then perhaps no more difficult to know than it is to a smith to understand why the turning of one key will open a lock and not the turning of another. But whilst we are destitute of senses acute enough to discover the minute particles of bodies and to give us *ideas* of their mechanical affections, we must be content to be ignorant of their properties and ways of operation; nor can we be assured about them any further than some few trials we make are able to reach. But whether they will succeed again another time, we cannot be certain. This hinders our certain knowledge of universal truths concerning natural bodies, and our reason carries us herein very little beyond particular matter of fact.

26. And therefore I am apt to doubt that, how far soever human industry may advance useful and *experimental* philosophy *in physical things*, *scientifical* will still be out of our reach: because we want perfect and adequate *ideas* of those very bodies which are nearest to us and most under our command. Those which we have ranked into classes under names and we think ourselves best acquainted with, we have but very imperfect and incomplete *ideas* of. Distinct *ideas* of the several sorts of bodies that fall under the examination of our senses perhaps we may have; but adequate *ideas*, I suspect, we have not of any one amongst them. And though the former of these will serve us for common use and discourse, yet, whilst we want the latter, we are not capable of *scientifical knowledge*, nor shall ever be able to discover general, instructive, unquestionable truths concerning them. *Certainty* and *demonstration* are things we must not, in these matters, pretend to. By the colour, figure, taste, and smell and other sensible qualities, we have as clear and distinct *ideas* of sage and hemlock as we have of a circle and a triangle; but having no *ideas* of the particular primary qualities of the minute parts of either of these plants, nor of other bodies which we would apply them to, we cannot tell what effects they will produce nor, when we see those effects, can we so much as guess, much less know, their manner of production. Thus having no *ideas* of the particular mechanical affections of the

minute parts of bodies that are within our view and reach, we are ignorant of their constitutions, powers, and operations; and of bodies more remote, we are yet more ignorant, not knowing so much as their very outward shapes or the sensible and grosser parts of their constitutions.

27.   This at first sight will show us how disproportionate our knowledge is to the whole extent even of material beings; to which if we add the consideration of that infinite number of *spirits* that may be, and probably are, which are yet more remote from our knowledge, whereof we have no cognizance nor can frame to ourselves any distinct *ideas* of their several ranks and sorts, we shall find this cause of ignorance conceal from us, in an impenetrable obscurity, almost the whole intellectual world: a greater, certainly, and more beautiful world than the material. For bating some very few and those, if I may so call them, superficial *ideas* of spirit, which by reflection we get of our own, and from thence the best we can collect of the Father of all spirits, the eternal independent Author of them and us and all things, we have no certain information so much as of the existence of other spirits but by revelation.   Angels of all sorts are naturally beyond our discovery; and all those intelligences, whereof it is likely there are more orders than of corporeal substances, are things whereof our natural faculties give us no certain account at all.   That there are minds and thinking beings in other men as well as himself, every man has a reason, from their words and actions, to be satisfied; and the knowledge of his own mind cannot suffer a man, that considers, to be ignorant that there is a GOD.   But that there are degrees of spiritual beings between us and the great GOD, who is there that by his own search and ability can come to know?   Much less have we distinct *ideas* of their different natures, conditions, states, powers, and several constitutions wherein they agree or differ from one another and from us.   And therefore in what concerns their different species and properties, we are under an absolute ignorance.

28.   *Secondly,* What a small part of the substantial beings that are in the universe the want of *ideas* leave open to our knowledge, we have seen.   In the next place, another cause of ignorance, of no less moment, is a want of *a discoverable connexion* between those *ideas* which we have.   For wherever we want that, we are utterly incapable of universal and certain knowledge and are, as in the former case, left only to observation and experiment: which, how narrow and confined it is, how far from general knowledge, we need not be told.   I shall give some few instances

of this cause of our ignorance and so leave it. It is evident that the bulk, figure, and motion of several bodies about us produce in us several sensations, as of colours, sounds, tastes, smells, pleasure and pain, etc. These mechanical affections of bodies having no affinity at all with those *ideas* they produce in us (there being no conceivable connexion between any impulse of any sort of body and any perception of a colour or smell which we find in our minds), we can have no distinct knowledge of such operations beyond our experience and can reason no otherwise about them than as effects produced by the appointment of an infinitely wise agent, which perfectly surpass our comprehensions. As the *ideas* of sensible secondary qualities, which we have in our minds, can by us be no way deduced from bodily causes, nor any correspondence or connexion be found between them and those primary qualities which (experience shows us) produce them in us: so, on the other side, the operation of our minds upon our bodies is as inconceivable. How any thought should produce a motion in body is as remote from the nature of our *ideas*, as how any body should produce any thought in the mind. That it is so, if experience did not convince us, the consideration of the things themselves would never be able in the least to discover to us. These, and the like, though they have a constant and regular connexion in the ordinary course of things: yet, that connexion being not discoverable in the *ideas* themselves, which appearing to have no necessary dependence one on another, we can attribute their connexion to nothing else but the arbitrary determination of that all-wise Agent who has made them to be and to operate as they do, in a way wholly above our weak understandings to conceive.

29. In some of our *ideas* there are certain relations, habitudes, and connexions so visibly included in the nature of the *ideas* themselves, that we cannot conceive them separable from them by any power whatsoever. And in these only, we are capable of certain and universal knowledge. Thus the *idea* of a right-lined triangle necessarily carries with it an equality of its angles to two right ones. Nor can we conceive this relation, this connexion of these two *ideas*, to be possibly mutable or to depend on any arbitrary power, which of choice made it thus or could make it otherwise. But the coherence and continuity of the parts of matter, the production of sensation in us of colours and sounds, etc., by impulse and motion, nay, the original rules and communication of motion being such wherein we can discover no natural connexion with any *ideas* we have, we cannot but ascribe them to the arbitrary will and good pleasure of the wise Architect.

I need not, I think, here mention the resurrection of the dead, the future state of this globe of earth, and such other things, which are by everyone acknowledged to depend wholly on the determination of a free agent. The things that, as far as our observation reaches, we constantly find to proceed regularly, we may conclude do act by a law set them, but yet by a law that we know not: whereby, though causes work steadily and effects constantly flow from them, yet their *connexions* and *dependencies* being not discoverable in our *ideas*, we can have but an experimental knowledge of them. From all which it is easy to perceive what a darkness we are involved in, how little it is of being and the things that are that we are capable to know. And therefore we shall do no injury to our knowledge, when we modestly think with ourselves, that we are so far from being able to comprehend the whole nature of the universe and all the things contained in it that we are not capable of a philosophical *knowledge* of the bodies that are about us and make a part of us; concerning their secondary qualities, powers, and operations, we can have no universal certainty. Several effects come every day within the notice of our senses, of which we have so far *sensitive knowledge*; but the causes, manner, and certainty of their production, for the two foregoing reasons, we must be content to be ignorant of. In these we can go no further than particular experience informs us of matter of fact, and by analogy to guess what effects the like bodies are, upon other trials, like to produce. But as to a perfect *science* of natural bodies (not to mention spiritual beings), we are, I think, so far from being capable of any such thing that I conclude it lost labour to seek after it.

30. *Thirdly*, Where we have adequate *ideas*, and where there is a certain and discoverable connexion between them, yet we are often ignorant for want of *tracing* those *ideas* which we have or may have, and for want of finding out those intermediate *ideas* which may show us what habitude of agreement or disagreement they have one with another. And thus many are ignorant of mathematical truths, not out of any imperfection of their faculties or uncertainty in the things themselves, but for want of application in acquiring, examining, and by due ways comparing those *ideas*. That which has most contributed to hinder the due *tracing* of our *ideas* and finding out their relations and agreements or disagreements one with another, has been, I suppose, the ill use of *words*. It is impossible that men should ever truly seek or certainly discover the agreement or disagreement of *ideas* themselves, whilst their thoughts flutter

about or stick only in sounds of doubtful and uncertain significations. Mathematicians, abstracting their thoughts from names and accustoming themselves to set before their minds the *ideas* themselves that they would consider, and not sounds instead of them, have avoided thereby a great part of that perplexity, puddering, and confusion which has so much hindered men's progress in other parts of knowledge. For, whilst they stick in words of undetermined and uncertain signification, they are unable to distinguish true from false, certain from probable, consistent from inconsistent, in their own opinions. This having been the fate or misfortune of a great part of the men of letters, the increase brought into the stock of real knowledge has been very little in proportion to the schools, disputes, and writings the world has been filled with: whilst students, being lost in the great wood of words, knew not whereabout they were, how far their discoveries were advanced, or what was wanting in their own or the general stock of knowledge. Had men in the discoveries of the material done as they have in those of the intellectual world, involved all in the obscurity of uncertain and doubtful ways of talking: volumes writ of navigation and voyages, theories and stories of zones and tides multiplied and disputed, nay, ships built and fleets set out would never have taught us the way beyond the line; and the antipodes would be still as much unknown as when it was declared heresy to hold there were any. But having spoken sufficiently of words and the ill or careless use that is commonly made of them, I shall not say anything more of it here.

Chapter IV

OF THE REALITY OF KNOWLEDGE

1. I DOUBT not but my reader, by this time, may be apt to think that I have been all this while only building a castle in the air and be ready to say to me: To what purpose all this stir? Knowledge, say you, is only the perception of the agreement or disagreement of our own *ideas*; but who knows what those *ideas* may be? Is there anything so extravagant as the imaginations of men's brains? Where is the head that has no *chimeras* in it? Or if there be a sober and a wise man, what difference will there be by your rules between his knowledge and that of the most extravagant fancy in the world? They both have their *ideas* and perceive their agreement and disagreement one with

another. If there be any difference between them, the advantage will be on the warm-headed man's side, as having the more *ideas* and the more lively. And so, by your rules, he will be the more knowing. If it be true that all knowledge lies only in the perception of the agreement or disagreement of our own *ideas*, the visions of an enthusiast and the reasonings of a sober man will be equally certain. It is no matter how things are: so a man observe but the agreement of his own imaginations and talk conformably, it is all truth, all certainty. Such castles in the air will be as strongholds of truth as the demonstrations of *Euclid.* That an harpy is not a centaur is by this way as certain knowledge, and as much a truth, as that a square is not a circle.

But *of what use is all this* fine *knowledge of men's own imaginations* to a man that inquires after the reality of things? It matters not what men's fancies are, it is the knowledge of things that is only to be prized: it is this alone gives a value to our reasonings and preference to one man's knowledge over another's, that it is of things as they really are and not of dreams and fancies.

2. To which I answer that, if our knowledge of our *ideas* terminate in them and reach no further where there is something further intended, our most serious thoughts will be of little more use than the reveries of a crazy brain, and the truths built thereon of no more weight than the discourses of a man who sees things clearly in a dream and with great assurance utters them. But I hope, before I have done, to make it evident that this way of certainty, by the knowledge of our own *ideas*, goes a little further than bare imagination; and I believe it will appear that all the certainty of general truths a man has lies in nothing else.

3. It is evident the mind knows not things immediately, but only by the intervention of the *ideas* it has of them. *Our knowledge,* therefore, is *real* only so far as there is a conformity between our *ideas* and the reality of things. But what shall be here the criterion? How shall the mind, when it perceives nothing but its own *ideas,* know that they agree with things themselves? This, though it seems not to want difficulty, yet, I think, there be two sorts of *ideas* that we may be assured agree with things.

4. *First,* The first are simple *ideas* which, since the mind, as has been shown, can by no means make to itself, must necessarily be the product of things operating on the mind in a natural way and producing therein those perceptions which by the wisdom and will of our Maker they are ordained and adapted to. From whence it follows that *simple* ideas *are not fictions* of

our fancies, but the natural and regular productions of things without us, really operating upon us, and so carry with them all the conformity which is intended or which our state requires; for they represent to us things under those appearances which they are fitted to produce in us: whereby we are enabled to distinguish the sorts of particular substances, to discern the states they are in, and so to take them for our necessities and apply them to our uses. Thus the *idea* of whiteness or bitterness, as it is in the mind, exactly answering that power which is in any body to produce it there, has all the real conformity it can or ought to have with things without us. And this conformity between our simple *ideas* and the existence of things is sufficient for real knowledge.

5. *Secondly, All our complex* ideas, *except those of substances,* being *archetypes* of the mind's own making, not intended to be the copies of anything nor referred to the existence of anything as to their originals, *cannot want any conformity necessary to real knowledge.* For that which is not designed to represent anything but itself can never be capable of a wrong representation nor mislead us from the true apprehension of anything by its dislikeness to it; and such, excepting those of substances, are all our complex *ideas.* Which, as I have shown in another place, are combinations of *ideas* which the mind, by its free choice, puts together, without considering any connexion they have in nature. And hence it is that in all these sorts the *ideas* themselves are considered as the *archetypes,* and things no otherwise regarded but as they are conformable to them. So that we cannot but be infallibly certain that all the knowledge we attain concerning these *ideas* is real and reaches things themselves. Because in all our thoughts, reasonings, and discourses of this kind, we intend things no further than as they are conformable to our *ideas.* So that in these we cannot miss of a certain undoubted reality.

6. I doubt not but it will be easily granted that the *knowledge* we have *of mathematical truths is* not only certain, but *real knowledge,* and not the bare empty vision of vain, insignificant *chimeras* of the brain; and yet, if we will consider, we shall find that it is only of our own *ideas.* The mathematician considers the truth and properties belonging to a rectangle or circle only as they are in *idea* in his own mind. For it is possible he never found either of them existing mathematically, i.e. precisely true, in his life. But yet the knowledge he has of any truths or properties belonging to a circle, or any other mathematical figure, are nevertheless true and certain, even of real things existing:

because real things are no further concerned, nor intended to be meant by any such propositions, than as things really agree to those *archetypes* in his mind. Is it true of the *idea* of a *triangle*, that its three angles are equal to two right ones? It is true also of a *triangle*, wherever it really exists. Whatever other figure exists, that is not exactly answerable to that *idea* of a *triangle* in his mind, is not at all concerned in that proposition. And therefore he is certain all his knowledge concerning such *ideas* is real knowledge: because, intending things no further than they agree with those his *ideas*, he is sure what he knows concerning those figures, when they have barely *an ideal existence* in his mind, will hold true of them also when they have a real existence in matter: his consideration being barely of those figures which are the same wherever or however they exist.

7. And hence it follows that *moral knowledge* is as *capable of real certainty* as mathematics. For certainty being but the perception of the agreement or disagreement of our *ideas*, and demonstration nothing but the perception of such agreement by the intervention of other *ideas* or mediums, our *moral ideas*, as well as mathematical, being *archetypes* themselves and so adequate and complete *ideas*, all the agreement or disagreement which we shall find in them will produce real knowledge, as well as in mathematical figures.

8. For the attaining of *knowledge* and certainty, it is requisite that we have determined *ideas*; and, to make our knowledge *real*, it is requisite that the *ideas* answer their *archetypes*. Nor let it be wondered that I place the certainty of our knowledge in the consideration of our *ideas*, with so little care and regard (as it may seem) to the real existence of things: since most of those discourses which take up the thoughts and engage the disputes of those who pretend to make it their business to inquire after truth and certainty will, I presume, upon examination, be found to be *general propositions* and notions in which existence is not at all concerned. All the discourses of the mathematicians about the squaring of a circle, conic sections, or any other part of mathematics *concern not* the *existence* of any of those figures; but their demonstrations, which depend on their *ideas*, are the same, whether there be any square or circle existing in the world or no. In the same manner, the truth and certainty of *moral* discourses abstracts from the lives of men and the existence of those virtues in the world whereof they treat; nor are *Tully's* Offices less true, because there is nobody in the world that exactly practises his rules and lives up to that pattern of a virtuous man which he has given us, and which existed nowhere

when he writ but in *idea*. If it be true in speculation, i.e. in *idea*, that *murder deserves death*, it will also be true in reality of any action that exists conformable to that *idea* of *murder*. As for other actions, the truth of that proposition concerns them not. And thus it is of all other species of things which have no other essences but those *ideas* which are in the minds of men.

9. But it will here be said that, if *moral knowledge* be placed in the contemplation of our own *moral ideas*, and those, as other modes, be of our own making, what strange notions will there be of *justice* and *temperance*? What confusion of virtues and vices, if everyone may make what *ideas* of them he pleases? No confusion or disorder in the things themselves, nor the reasonings about them; no more than (in mathematics) there would be a disturbance in the demonstration, or a change in the properties of figures and their relations one to another, if a man should make a triangle with four corners, or a *trapezium* with four right angles: that is in plain *English*, change the names of the figures and call that by one name which mathematicians called ordinarily by another. For let a man make to himself the *idea* of a figure with three angles whereof one is a right one, and call it, if he please, *equilaterum* or *trapezium* or anything else, the properties of and demonstrations about that *idea* will be the same as if he called it a *rectangular-triangle*. I confess, the change of the name, by the impropriety of speech, will at first disturb him who knows not what *idea* it stands for; but as soon as the figure is drawn, the consequences and demonstrations are plain and clear. Just the same is it in *moral* knowledge: let a man have the *idea* of taking from others, without their consent, what their honest industry has possessed them of, and call this *justice* if he please. He that takes the name here without the *idea* put to it will be mistaken, by joining another *idea* of his own to that name; but strip the *idea* of that name or take it such as it is in the speaker's mind, and the same things will agree to it as if you called it *injustice*. Indeed, wrong names in moral discourses breed usually more disorder, because they are not so easily rectified as in mathematics, where the figure once drawn and seen makes the name useless and of no force. For what need of a sign, when the thing signified is present and in view? But in moral names, that cannot be so easily and shortly done, because of the many decompositions that go to the making up the complex *ideas* of those modes. But yet for all this, the *miscalling of* any of those *ideas*, contrary to the usual signification of the words of that language, hinders not but that we may have certain and demonstrative knowledge of their several agree-

ments and disagreements, if we will carefully, as in mathematics, keep to the same precise *ideas* and trace them in their several relations one to another, without being led away by their names. If we but separate the *idea* under consideration from the sign that stands for it, our knowledge goes equally on in the discovery of real truth and certainty, whatever sounds we make use of.

10.   One thing more we are to take notice of: that where GOD or any other law-maker hath defined any moral names, there they have made the essence of that species to which that name belongs, and there it is not safe to apply or use them otherwise; but in other cases it is bare impropriety of speech to apply them contrary to the common usage of the country. But yet even this too disturbs not the certainty of that knowledge, which is still to be had by a due contemplation and comparing of those even nicknamed *ideas*.

11.   *Thirdly,* There is another sort of *complex ideas* which, being referred to *archetypes* without us, may differ from them, and so our knowledge about them may come short of being real. Such are our *ideas* of substances, which, consisting of a collection of simple *ideas*, supposed taken from the works of nature, may yet vary from them by having more or different *ideas* united in them than are to be found united in the things themselves; from whence it comes to pass that they may, and often do, fail of being exactly conformable to things themselves.

12.   I say then that, to have *ideas* of *substances* which, by being conformable to things, may afford us *real* knowledge, it is not enough, as in modes, to put together such *ideas* as have no inconsistency, though they did never before so exist: v.g., the *ideas* of *sacrilege* or *perjury,* etc., were as real and true *ideas* before, as after, the existence of any such fact. But *our ideas of substances,* being supposed copies and referred to *archetypes* without us, must still be taken from something that does or has existed: they must not consist of *ideas* put together at the pleasure of our thoughts, without any real pattern they were taken from, though we can perceive no inconsistency in such a combination. The reason whereof is because, we knowing not what real constitution it is of substances whereon our simple *ideas* depend, and which really is the cause of the strict union of some of them one with another and the exclusion of others, there are very few of them that we can be sure are or are not inconsistent in nature, any further than experience and sensible observation reaches. Herein, therefore, is founded the *reality* of our knowledge concerning *substances*: that all our complex *ideas* of them

must be such, and such only, as are made up of such simple ones as have been discovered to co-exist in nature. And our *ideas*, being thus true though not perhaps very exact copies, are yet the subjects of *real* (as far as we have any) *knowledge* of them. Which (as has been already shown) will not be found to reach very far; but so far as it does, it will still be *real knowledge*. Whatever *ideas* we have, the agreement we find they have with others will still be knowledge. If those *ideas* be abstract, it will be general knowledge. But to make it *real* concerning substances, the *ideas* must be taken from the real existence of things. Whatever simple *ideas* have been found to co-exist in any substance, these we may with confidence join together again and so make abstract *ideas* of substances. For whatever have once had an union in nature may be united again.

Chapter V

OF TRUTH IN GENERAL

1. WHAT is *truth* was an inquiry many ages since; and it being that which all mankind either do or pretend to search after, it cannot but be worth our while carefully to examine wherein it consists, and so acquaint ourselves with the nature of it, as to observe how the mind distinguishes it from falsehood.

2. *Truth* then seems to me, in the proper import of the word, to signify nothing but *the joining or separating of signs, as the things signified by them do agree or disagree one with another*. The *joining* or *separating* of signs here meant is what by another name we call proposition. So that truth properly belongs only to propositions; whereof there are two sorts, viz. mental and verbal, as there are two sorts of signs commonly made use of, viz. *ideas* and words.

3. To form a clear notion of *truth*, it is very necessary to consider *truth* of thought and *truth* of words, distinctly one from another; but yet it is very difficult to treat of them asunder. Because it is unavoidable, in treating of mental propositions, to make use of words, and then the instances given of *mental propositions* cease immediately to be barely mental *and* become *verbal*. For a *mental proposition* being nothing but a bare consideration of the *ideas* as they are in our minds stripped of names, they lose the nature of purely *mental propositions* as soon as they are put into words.

4.   And that which makes it yet *harder to treat of mental* and verbal *propositions separately* is that most men, if not all, in their thinking and reasonings within themselves, make use of words instead of *ideas*, at least when the subject of their meditation contains in it complex *ideas*. Which is a great evidence of the imperfection and uncertainty of our *ideas* of that kind and may, if attentively made use of, serve for a mark to show us what are those things we have clear and perfect established *ideas* of, and what not. For if we will curiously observe the way our mind takes in thinking and reasoning, we shall find, I suppose, that when we make any propositions within our own thoughts about *white* or *black*, *sweet* or *bitter*, a *triangle* or a *circle*, we can and often do frame in our minds the *ideas* themselves, without reflecting on the names. But when we would consider or make propositions about the more complex *ideas*, as of a *man, vitriol, fortitude, glory*, we usually put the name for the *idea*: because the *ideas* these names stand for being for the most part imperfect, confused, and undetermined, we reflect on the *names* themselves because they are more clear, certain, and distinct, and readier occur to our thoughts than the pure *ideas*; and so we make use of these words instead of the *ideas* themselves, even when we would meditate and reason within ourselves and make tacit mental propositions. In *substances*, as has been already noted, this is occasioned by the imperfection of our *ideas*: we making the name stand for the real essence of which we have no *idea* at all. In *modes*, it is occasioned by the great number of simple *ideas* that go to the making them up. For many of them being compounded, the *name* occurs much easier than the complex *idea* itself, which requires time and attention to be recollected and exactly represented to the mind, even in those men who have formerly been at the pains to do it, and is utterly impossible to be done by those who, though they have ready in their memory the greatest part of the common words of their language, yet perhaps never troubled themselves in all their lives to consider what precise *ideas* the most of them stood for. Some confused or obscure notions have served their turns; and many who talk very much of *religion* and *conscience*, of *church* and *faith*, of *power* and *right*, of *obstructions* and *humours*, *melancholy* and *choler* would perhaps have little left in their thoughts and meditations if one should desire them to think only of the things themselves and lay by those words with which they so often confound others, and not seldom themselves also.

5.   But to return to the consideration of truth. We must, I say,

observe two sorts of propositions that we are capable of making.

First, mental, wherein the *ideas* in our understandings *are,* without the use of words, *put together or separated* by the mind perceiving or judging of their agreement or disagreement.

Secondly, verbal propositions, which *are words* the signs of our *ideas put together or separated in affirmative or negative sentences.* By which way of affirming or denying, these signs made by sounds are, as it were, put together or separated one from another. So that: proposition consists in joining or separating signs, and truth consists in the putting together or separating these signs according as the things which they stand for agree or disagree.

6. Everyone's experience will satisfy him that the mind, either by perceiving or supposing the agreement or disagreement of any of its *ideas,* does tacitly within itself put them into a kind of proposition affirmative or negative; which I have endeavoured to express by the terms *putting together* and *separating.* But this action of the mind, which is so familiar to every thinking and reasoning man, is easier to be conceived by reflecting on what passes in us when we affirm or deny, than to be explained by words. When a man has in his mind the *idea* of two lines, viz. the *side* and *diagonal* of a square, whereof the diagonal is an inch long, he may have the *idea* also of the division of that line into a certain number of equal parts: v.g. into five, ten, an hundred, a thousand, or any other number, and may have the *idea* of that inch line being divisible or not divisible, into such equal parts as a certain number of them will be equal to the side line. Now whenever he perceives, believes, or supposes such a kind of divisibility to agree or disagree to his *idea* of that line, he as it were *joins* or *separates* those two *ideas,* viz. the *idea* of that line and the *idea* of that kind of divisibility, and so makes a mental proposition, which is true or false according as such a kind of divisibility, a divisibility into such *aliquot* parts, does really agree to that line or no. When *ideas* are so put together or separated in the mind as they or the things they stand for do agree or not, that is, as I may call it, *mental truth.* But *truth of words* is something more: and that is the affirming or denying of words one of another, as the *ideas* they stand for agree or disagree; and this again is twofold: either *purely verbal* and trifling, which I shall speak of, *chap. x; or real* and instructive, which is the object of that real knowledge which we have spoken of already.

7. But here again will be apt to occur the same doubt about truth that did about knowledge; and it will be objected that, if

truth be nothing but the joining or separating of words in propositions as the *ideas* they stand for agree or disagree in men's minds, the knowledge of *truth is not so valuable a thing* as it is taken to be, nor worth the pains and time men employ in the search of it: since *by this account* it amounts to no more than the conformity of words to the *chimeras* of men's brains. Who knows not what odd notions many men's heads are filled with, and what strange *ideas* all men's brains are capable of? But if we rest here, we know the truth of nothing by this rule but of the visionary world in our own imaginations, nor have other truth but what as much concerns *harpies* and *centaurs* as men and horses. For those and the like may be *ideas* in our heads and have their agreement and disagreement there, as well as the *ideas* of real beings, and so have as true propositions made about them. And it will be altogether as true a proposition to say all *centaurs are animals*, as that *all men are animals*; and the certainty of one as great as the other. For in both the propositions, the words are put together according to the agreement of the *ideas* in our minds, and the agreement of the *idea* of *animal* with that of *centaur* is as clear and visible to the mind as the agreement of the *idea* of *animal* with that of *man*; and so these two propositions are equally true, equally certain. But of what use is all such truth to us?

8. Though what has been said in the foregoing chapter, to distinguish real from imaginary knowledge, might suffice here in answer to this doubt, to distinguish *real truth* from *chimerical* or (if you please) *barely nominal*, they depending both on the same foundation: yet it may not be amiss here again to consider that, though our words signify nothing but our *ideas*, yet being designed by them to signify things, the *truth* they contain when put into propositions will be only *verbal* when they stand for *ideas* in the mind that have not an agreement with the reality of things. And therefore truth as well as knowledge may well come under the distinction of *verbal* and *real*: that being only *verbal truth* wherein terms are joined according to the agreement or disagreement of the *ideas* they stand for, without regarding whether our *ideas* are such as really have or are capable of having an existence in nature. But then it is they contain *real truth*: when these signs are joined as our *ideas* agree, and when our *ideas* are such as we know are capable of having an existence in nature; which in substances we cannot know but by knowing that such have existed.

9. *Truth* is the marking down in words the agreement or disagreement of *ideas* as it is. *Falsehood* is the marking down in

words the agreement or disagreement of *ideas* otherwise than it is. And so far as these *ideas*, thus marked by sounds, agree to their archetypes, so far only is the *truth real*. The knowledge of this truth consists in knowing what *ideas* the words stand for and the perception of the agreement or disagreement of those *ideas*, according as it is marked by those words.

10. But because words are looked on as the great conduits of truth and knowledge, and that in conveying and receiving of truth and commonly in reasoning about it we make use of words and propositions, I shall more at large inquire wherein the certainty of real truths contained in propositions consists, and where it is to be had, and endeavour to show in what sort of universal propositions we are capable of being *certain* of their real truth or falsehood.

I shall begin with general propositions, as those which most employ our thoughts and exercise our contemplation. *General truths* are most looked after by the mind as those that most enlarge our knowledge and, by their comprehensiveness satisfying us at once of many particulars, enlarge our view and shorten our way to knowledge.

11. Besides truth taken in the strict sense before-mentioned, there are other sorts of truths: As (1) *Moral truth*, which is speaking things according to the persuasion of our own minds, though the proposition we speak agree not to the reality of things. (2) *Metaphysical truth*, which is nothing but the real existence of things, conformable to the *ideas* to which we have annexed their names. This, though it seems to consist in the very beings of things, yet when considered a little nearly, will appear to include a tacit proposition whereby the mind joins that particular thing to the *idea* it had before settled with a name to it. But these considerations of truth either having been before taken notice of or not being much to our present purpose, it may suffice here only to have mentioned them.

CHAPTER VI

OF UNIVERSAL PROPOSITIONS, THEIR TRUTH AND CERTAINTY

1. THOUGH the examining and judging of *ideas* by themselves, their names being quite laid aside, be the best and surest way to clear and distinct knowledge: yet, through the prevailing custom of using sounds for *ideas*, I think it is very seldom practised. Everyone may observe how common it is for names to be made

use of, instead of the *ideas* themselves, even when men think and reason within their own breasts, especially if the *ideas* be very complex and made up of a great collection of simple ones. This makes *the consideration of words and propositions* so *necessary a part of the treatise of knowledge* that it is very hard to speak intelligibly of the one without explaining the other.

2. All the knowledge we have being only of particular or *general truths*, it is evident that whatever may be done in the former of these, the latter, which is that which with reason is most sought after, can never be well made known and is very *seldom apprehended but as conceived and expressed in words.* It is not therefore out of our way, in the examination of our knowledge, to inquire into the truth and certainty of universal propositions.

3. But that we may not be misled in this case by that which is the danger everywhere, I mean by the doubtfulness of terms, it is fit to observe that certainty is twofold: *certainty of truth* and *certainty of knowledge.* *Certainty of truth* is when words are so put together in propositions as exactly to express the agreement or disagreement of the *ideas* they stand for as really it is. *Certainty of knowledge* is to perceive the agreement or disagreement of *ideas* as expressed in any proposition. This we usually call knowing, or being certain of the truth of any proposition.

4. Now, because *we cannot be certain of the truth of any general proposition unless we know the precise bounds and extent of the species its terms stand for*, it is necessary we should know the essence of each *species*, which is that which constitutes and bounds it. This, in all simple *ideas* and modes, is not hard to do. For in these, the real and nominal essence being the same or, which is all one, the abstract *idea* which the general term stands for being the sole essence and boundary that is or can be supposed of the *species*, there can be no doubt how far the *species* extends or what things are comprehended under each term: which, it is evident, are all that have an exact conformity with the *idea* it stands for, and no other. But in substances, wherein a real essence, distinct from the nominal, is supposed to constitute, determine, and bound the species, the extent of the general word is very uncertain; because, not knowing this real essence, we cannot know what is or is not of that *species*, and, consequently, what may or may not with certainty be affirmed of it. And thus speaking of a *man* or *gold* or any other *species* of natural substances, as supposed constituted by a precise real essence which nature regularly imparts to every individual of that kind whereby it is made to be of that species,

we cannot be certain of the truth of any affirmation or negation made of it. For *man* or *gold*, taken in this sense and used for *species* of things constituted by real essences, different from the complex *idea* in the mind of the speaker, stand for we know not what; and the extent of these species with such boundaries are so unknown and undetermined that it is impossible with any certainty to affirm that all men are rational, or that all gold is yellow. But where the nominal essence is kept to, as the boundary of each species, and men extend the application of any general term no further than to the particular things in which the complex *idea* it stands for is to be found, there they are in no danger to mistake the bounds of each *species* nor can be in doubt, on this account, whether any propositions be true or no. I have chosen to explain this uncertainty of propositions in this scholastic way, and have made use of the terms of *essences* and *species* on purpose, to show the absurdity and inconvenience there is to think of them as of any other sort of realities than barely abstract *ideas* with names to them. To suppose that the *species* of things are anything but the sorting of them under general names, according as they agree to several abstract *ideas* of which we make those names the signs, is to confound truth and introduce uncertainty into all general propositions that can be made about them. Though therefore these things might, to people not possessed with scholastic learning, be perhaps treated of in a better and clearer way: yet those wrong notions of *essences* or *species*, having got root in most people's minds who have received any tincture from the learning which has prevailed in this part of the world, are to be discovered and removed, to make way for that use of words which should convey certainty with it.

5. *The names of substances*, then, *whenever made to stand for species which are supposed to be constituted by real essences which we know not, are not capable to convey certainty to the understanding*: of the truth of general propositions made up of such terms we cannot be sure. The reason whereof is plain. For how can we be sure that this or that quality is in *gold*, when we know not what is or is not *gold*? Since in this way of speaking, nothing is *gold* but what partakes of an essence, which we, not knowing, cannot know where it is or is not and so cannot be sure that any parcel of matter in the world is or is not in this sense *gold*: being incurably ignorant whether it has or has not that which makes anything to be called *gold*, i.e. that real essence of *gold* whereof we have no *idea* at all. This being as impossible for us to know as it is for a blind man to tell in what flower the

colour of a *pansy* is or is not to be found, whilst he has no *idea* of the colour of a *pansy* at all. Or if we could (which is impossible) certainly know where a real essence, which we know not, is, v.g. in what parcels of matter the real essence of *gold* is, yet could we not be sure that this or that quality could with truth be affirmed of *gold*: since it is impossible for us to know that this or that quality or *idea* has a necessary connexion with a real essence of which we have no *idea* at all, whatever species that supposed real essence may be imagined to constitute.

6. On the other side, the *names of substances*, when made use of as they should be, for the *ideas* men have in their minds, though they carry a clear and determinate signification with them, *will not* yet *serve us to make many universal propositions of whose truth we can be certain*. Not because in this use of them we are uncertain what things are signified by them, but because the complex *ideas* they stand for are such combinations of simple ones as carry not with them any discoverable connexion or repugnancy but with a very few other *ideas*.

7. The complex *ideas* that our names of the species of substances properly stand for are collections of such qualities as have been observed to co-exist in an unknown *substratum*, which we call *substance*; but what other qualities necessarily co-exist with such combinations we cannot certainly know, unless we can discover their natural dependence: which, in their primary qualities, we can go but a very little way in; and in all their secondary qualities we can discover no connexion at all, for the reasons mentioned, *chap. iii*: viz. (1) Because we know not the real constitutions of substances on which each *secondary quality* particularly depends. (2) Did we know that, it would serve us only for experimental (not universal) knowledge, and reach with certainty no further than that bare instance. Because our understandings can discover no conceivable connexion between any *secondary quality* and any modification whatsoever of any of the *primary* ones. And therefore there are very few general propositions to be made concerning substances which can carry with them *undoubted certainty*.

8. *All gold is fixed* is a proposition whose truth we cannot be certain of, how universally soever it be believed. For if, according to the useless imagination of the Schools, anyone supposes the term *gold* to stand for a species of things set out by nature by a real essence belonging to it, it is evident he knows not what particular substances are of that species, and so cannot with certainty affirm anything universally of *gold*. But if he makes

gold stand for a species determined by its nominal essence, let the nominal essence, for example, be the complex *idea* of a *body* of a certain *yellow* colour, *malleable, fusible,* and *heavier* than any other known: in this proper use of the word *gold,* there is no difficulty to know what is or is not *gold.* But yet no other quality can with certainty be universally affirmed or denied of *gold* but what hath a discoverable connexion or inconsistency with that nominal essence. *Fixedness,* for example, having no necessary connexion that we can discover with the colour, weight, or any other simple *idea* of our complex one, or with the whole combination together: it is impossible that we should certainly know the truth of this proposition, that *all gold is fixed.*

9. As there is no discoverable connexion between *fixedness* and the colour, weight, and other simple *ideas* of that nominal essence of *gold*: so, if we make our complex *idea* of *gold* a *body yellow, fusible, ductile, weighty,* and *fixed,* we shall be at the same uncertainty concerning *solubility* in *aqua regia,* and for the same reason; since we can never, from consideration of the *ideas* themselves, with certainty affirm or deny, of a body whose complex *idea* is made up of yellow, very weighty, ductile, fusible, and fixed, that it is soluble in *aqua regia;* and so on of the rest of its qualities. I would gladly meet with one general affirmation concerning any quality of *gold* that anyone can certainly know is true. It will, no doubt, be presently objected, Is not this an universal certain proposition, *All gold is malleable?* To which I answer: It is a very certain proposition, if *malleableness* be a part of the complex *idea* the word *gold* stands for. But then here is nothing affirmed of *gold* but that that sound stands for an *idea* in which *malleableness* is contained, and such a sort of truth and certainty as this it is to say *a centaur is four-footed.* But if *malleableness* makes not a part of the specific essence the name *gold* stands for, it is plain, *All gold is malleable* is not a certain proposition. Because let the complex *idea* of *gold* be made up of which soever of its other qualities you please, *malleableness* will not appear to depend on that complex *idea* nor follow from any simple one contained in it. The connexion that *malleableness* has (if it has any) with those other qualities, being only by the intervention of the real constitution of its insensible parts, which since we know not, it is impossible we should perceive that connexion, unless we could discover that which ties them together.

10. The more, indeed, of these co-existing qualities we unite into one complex *idea* under one name, the more precise and

determinate we make the signification of that word; but yet never make it thereby more capable of *universal certainty* in respect of other qualities not contained in our complex *idea*, since we perceive not their connexion or dependence one on another, being ignorant both of that real constitution in which they are all founded, and also how they flow from it. For the chief part of our knowledge concerning substances is not, as in other things, barely of the relation of two *ideas* that may exist separately, but is of the necessary connexion and co-exist-ence of several distinct *ideas* in the same subject, or of their repugnancy so to co-exist. Could we begin at the other end and discover what it was wherein that colour consisted, what made a body lighter or heavier, what texture of parts made it malle-able, fusible and fixed, and fit to be dissolved in this sort of liquor and not in another: if (I say) we had such an *idea* as this of bodies and could perceive wherein all sensible qualities originally consist and how they are produced, we might frame such abstract *ideas* of them as would furnish us with matter of more general knowledge and enable us to make universal pro-positions that should carry *general truth* and *certainty* with them. But whilst our complex *ideas* of the sorts of substances are so remote from that internal real constitution on which their sensible qualities depend, and are made up of nothing but an imperfect collection of those apparent qualities our senses can discover, there can be very few general propositions concerning substances of whose real truth we can be *certainly* assured, since there are but few simple *ideas* of whose connexion and neces-sary co-existence we can have certain and undoubted know-ledge. I imagine, amongst all the *secondary qualities* of sub-stances and the powers relating to them, there cannot any two be named whose necessary co-existence or repugnance to co-exist can certainly be known, unless in those of the same sense, which necessarily exclude one another, as I have elsewhere shown. No one, I think, by the colour that is in any body, can certainly know what smell, taste, sound, or tangible qualities it has, nor what alterations it is capable to make or receive, on or from other bodies. The same may be said of the sound or taste, etc. Our specific names of substances standing for any collec-tions of such *ideas*, it is not to be wondered that we can, with them, make very few general propositions of *undoubted real certainty*. But yet so far as any complex *idea* of any sort of substances contains in it any simple *idea* whose necessary co-existence with any other may be discovered, so far *universal propositions* may *with certainty* be made concerning it: v.g.

could anyone discover a necessary connexion between *malleableness* and the *colour* or *weight* of *gold* or any other part of the complex *idea* signified by that name, he might make a *certain* universal proposition concerning *gold* in this respect; and the real truth of this proposition, that *all gold is malleable*, would be as *certain* as of this, *the three angles of all right-lined triangles are equal to two right ones*.

11.   Had we such *ideas* of substances as to know what real constitutions produce those sensible qualities we find in them and how those qualities flowed from thence, we could, by the specific *ideas* of their real essences in our own minds, more certainly find out their properties and discover what qualities they had or had not, than we can now by our senses; and to know the properties of *gold*, it would be no more necessary that *gold* should exist and that we should make experiments upon it than it is necessary, for the knowing the properties of a triangle, that a triangle should exist in any matter: the *idea* in our minds would serve for the one as well as the other.   But we are so far from being admitted into the secrets of nature that we scarce so much as ever approach the first entrance towards them.   For we are wont to consider the substances we meet with, each of them, as an entire thing by itself, having all its qualities in itself and independent of other things, overlooking, for the most part, the operations of those invisible fluids they are encompassed with and upon whose motions and operations depend the greatest part of those qualities which are taken notice of in them and are made by us the inherent marks of distinction whereby we know and denominate them.   Put a piece of *gold* anywhere by itself, separate from the reach and influence of all other bodies, it will immediately lose all its colour and weight, and perhaps malleableness too, which, for aught I know, would be changed into a perfect friability.   *Water*, in which to us *fluidity* is an essential quality, left to itself, would cease to be fluid.   But if inanimate bodies owe so much of their present state to other bodies without them that they would not be what they appear to us were those bodies that environ them removed, it is yet more so in *vegetables*, which are nourished, grow, and produce leaves, flowers, and seeds in a constant succession.   And if we look a little nearer into the state of *animals*, we shall find that their dependence as to life, motion, and the most considerable qualities to be observed in them is so wholly on extrinsical causes and qualities of other bodies that make no part of them, that they cannot subsist a moment without them: though yet those bodies on which they depend are little taken notice of, and

make no part of the complex *ideas* we frame of those animals. Take the air but a minute from the greatest part of living creatures, and they presently lose sense, life, and motion. This the necessity of breathing has forced into our knowledge. But how many other extrinsical and possibly very remote bodies do the springs of those admirable machines depend on, which are not vulgarly observed or so much as thought on; and how many are there which the severest inquiry can never discover? The inhabitants of this spot of the universe, though removed so many millions of miles from the sun, yet depend so much on the duly tempered motion of particles coming from or agitated by it that, were this earth removed but a small part of that distance, out of its present situation, and placed a little further or nearer that source of heat, it is more than probable that the greatest part of the animals in it would immediately perish: since we find them so often destroyed by an excess or defect of the sun's warmth, which an accidental position, in some parts of this our little globe, exposes them to. The qualities observed in a *loadstone* must needs have their source far beyond the confines of that body; and the ravage made often on several sorts of animals by invisible causes, the certain death (as we are told) of some of them by barely passing the line or, as it is certain of others, by being removed into a neighbouring country, evidently show that the concurrence and operation of several bodies, with which they are seldom thought to have anything to do, is absolutely necessary to make them be what they appear to us and to preserve those qualities by which we know and distinguish them. We are then quite out of the way when we think that things contain within themselves the qualities that appear to us in them; and we in vain search for that constitution within the body of a fly or an elephant upon which depend those qualities and powers we observe in them. For which perhaps, to understand them aright, we ought to look not only beyond this our earth and atmosphere, but even beyond the sun or remotest star our eyes have yet discovered. For how much the being and operation of particular substances in this our globe depend on causes utterly beyond our view is impossible for us to determine. We see and perceive some of the motions and grosser operations of things here about us, but whence the streams come that keep all these curious machines in motion and repair, how conveyed and modified, is beyond our notice and apprehension; and the great parts and wheels, as I may so say, of this stupendous structure of the universe, may, for aught we know, have such a connexion and dependence in their influences and operations one upon another, that perhaps things in this our mansion would put on quite another face and cease to be what they are, if some one of the stars or great bodies incomprehensibly remote from us should cease to be or move as it does. This is certain: things, however absolute and entire they seem in themselves, are but retainers to other parts of nature for that which they are most taken notice of by us. Their observable qualities, actions, and powers are owing to something without them; and there is not so complete and perfect a part that we know of nature which does not owe the being it has, and the excellencies of it, to its neighbours; and we must not confine our thoughts within the surface of any body, but look a great deal further, to comprehend perfectly those qualities that are in it.

12. If this be so, it is not to be wondered that *we have very imperfect* ideas *of substances*, and that the real essences, on which depend their properties and operations, are unknown to us. We cannot discover so much as that *size*, *figure*, and *texture* of their minute and active parts, which is really in them: much less the different motions and impulses made in and upon them by bodies from without, upon which depends and by which is formed the greatest and most remarkable part of those qualities we observe in them, and of which our complex *ideas* of them are made up. This consideration alone is enough to put an end to all our hopes of ever having the *ideas* of their real essences; which whilst we want, the nominal essences we make use of instead of them will be able to furnish us but very sparingly with any *general knowledge* or universal propositions capable of real *certainty*.

13. We are not therefore to wonder if *certainty* be to be found in very few general propositions made concerning substances: our knowledge of their qualities and properties go very seldom further than our senses reach and inform us. Possibly, inquisitive and observing men may by strength of *judgment* penetrate further and, on probabilities taken from wary observation and hints well laid together, often guess right at what experience has not yet discovered to them. But this is but guessing still: it amounts only to opinion and has not that *certainty* which is requisite to knowledge. For all *general knowledge* lies only in our own thoughts and consists barely in the contemplation of our own abstract *ideas*. Wherever we perceive any agreement or disagreement amongst them, there we have *general knowledge* and, by putting the names of those *ideas* together accordingly in propositions, can with certainty pronounce *general truths*. But because the abstract *ideas* of substances, for which their specific

names stand, whenever they have any distinct and determinate signification, have a discoverable connexion or inconsistency with but a very few other *ideas*: the *certainty of universal propositions concerning substances* is very narrow and scanty in that part, which is our principal inquiry concerning them; and there is scarce any of the names of substances, let the *idea* it is applied to be what it will, of which we can generally and with certainty pronounce that it has or has not this or that other quality belonging to it and constantly co-existing or inconsistent with that *idea*, wherever it is to be found.

14.   Before we can have any tolerable knowledge of this kind, we must first know what changes the *primary qualities* of one body do regularly produce in the *primary qualities* of another, and how. Secondly, we must know what *primary qualities* of any body produce certain sensations or *ideas* in us. This is, in truth, no less than to know all the effects of matter under its divers modifications of bulk, figure, cohesion of parts, motion and rest. Which, I think, everybody will allow is utterly impossible to be known by us without revelation. Nor, if it were revealed to us what sort of figure, bulk, and motion of corpuscles would produce in us the sensation of a *yellow* colour; and what sort of figure, bulk, and texture of parts in the superficies of any body were fit to give such corpuscles their due motion to produce that colour: would that be enough to make *universal* propositions with *certainty* concerning the several sorts of them, unless we had faculties acute enough to perceive the precise bulk, figure, texture, and motion of bodies in those minute parts, by which they operate on our senses, that so we might by those frame our abstract *ideas* of them? I have mentioned here only *corporeal* substances, whose operations seem to lie more level to our understandings; for, as to the *operations of spirits*, both their thinking and moving of bodies, we at first sight find ourselves at a loss: though perhaps, when we have applied our thoughts a little nearer to the consideration of bodies and their operations and examined how far our notions, even in these, reach with any clearness beyond sensible matter of fact, we shall be bound to confess that, even in these too, our discoveries amount to very little beyond perfect ignorance and incapacity.

15.   This is evident: *the abstract complex* ideas *of substances*, for which their general names stand, not comprehending their real constitutions, *can afford us but very little universal certainty*. Because our *ideas* of them are not made up of that on which those qualities we observe in them and would inform ourselves about do depend, or with which they have any certain connex-

ion. V.g., let the *idea* to which we give the name *man* be, as it commonly is, a body of the ordinary shape, with sense, voluntary motion, and reason joined to it. This being the abstract *idea* and consequently the essence of our species *man*, we can make but very few general certain propositions concerning *man*, standing for such an *idea*. Because, not knowing the real constitution on which sensation, power of motion, and reasoning, with that peculiar shape, depend, and whereby they are united together in the same subject, there are very few other qualities with which we can perceive them to have a necessary connexion; and therefore we cannot with certainty affirm that *all men sleep by intervals*, that *no man can be nourished by wood or stones*, that *all men will be poisoned by hemlock*: because these *ideas* have no connexion nor repugnancy with this our nominal essence of *man*, with this abstract *idea* that name stands for. We must, in these and the like, appeal to trial in particular subjects, which can reach but a little way. We must content ourselves with probability in the rest; but can have no general certainty, whilst our specific *idea* of *man* contains not that real constitution which is the root wherein all his inseparable qualities are united, and from whence they flow. Whilst our *idea* the word *man* stands for is only an imperfect collection of some sensible qualities and powers in him, there is no discernible connexion or repugnance between our specific *idea* and the operation of either the parts of hemlock or stones upon his constitution. There are animals that safely eat hemlock, and others that are nourished by wood and stones; but as long as we want *ideas* of those real constitutions of different sorts of animals, whereon these and the like qualities and powers depend, we must not hope to reach *certainty* in universal propositions concerning them. Those few *ideas* only, which have a discernible connexion with our nominal essence or any part of it, can afford us such propositions. But these are so few, and of so little moment, that we may justly look on our certain *general knowledge of substances* as almost none at all.

16. To conclude: *General propositions*, of what kind soever, are then only capable of *certainty* when the terms used in them stand for such *ideas* whose agreement or disagreement, as there expressed, is capable to be discovered by us. And we are then certain of their truth or falsehood, when we perceive the *ideas* the terms stand for to agree or not agree, according as they are affirmed or denied one of another. Whence we may take notice that *general certainty* is never to be found but in our *ideas*. Whenever we go to seek it elsewhere, in experiment or observa-

tions without us, our knowledge goes not beyond particulars. It is the contemplation of our own abstract *ideas* that alone is able to afford us *general knowledge*.

CHAPTER VII

OF MAXIMS

1. THERE are a sort of propositions which, under the name of *maxims* and *axioms*, have passed for principles of science and, because they are *self-evident*, have been supposed innate, without that anybody (that I know) ever went about to show the reason and foundation of their clearness or cogency. It may, however, be worthwhile to inquire into the reason of their evidence and see whether it be peculiar to them alone, and also examine how far they influence and govern our other knowledge.

2. *Knowledge*, as has been shown, consists in the perception of the agreement or disagreement of *ideas*; now where that agreement or disagreement is perceived immediately by itself, without the intervention or help of any other, there our *knowledge is self-evident*. This will appear to be so to anyone who will but consider any of those propositions which, without any proof, he assents to at first sight: for, in all of them, he will find that the reason of his assent is from that agreement or disagreement which the mind by an immediate comparing them, finds in those *ideas* answering the affirmation or negation in the proposition.

3. This being so, in the next place let us consider whether this *self-evidence* be peculiar only to those propositions which commonly pass under the name of maxims and have the dignity of axioms allowed them. And here it is plain that several other truths, not allowed to be axioms, partake equally with them in this *self-evidence*. This we shall see, if we go over these several sorts of agreement or disagreement of *ideas* which I have above mentioned, viz. identity, relation, co-existence, and real existence; which will discover to us that not only those few propositions which have had the credit of *maxims* are self-evident, but a great many, even almost an infinite number of *other propositions* are such.

4. For, *First*, the immediate perception of the agreement or disagreement of *identity* being founded in the mind's having

distinct *ideas*, this affords us as many *self-evident* propositions as we have distinct *ideas*. Everyone that has any knowledge at all has, as the foundation of it, various and distinct *ideas*; and it is the first act of the mind (without which it can never be capable of any knowledge) to know every one of its *ideas* by itself, and distinguish it from others. Everyone finds in himself that he knows the *ideas* he has; that he knows also, when any one is in his understanding and what it is; and that, when more than one are there, he knows them distinctly and unconfusedly one from another. Which always being so (it being impossible but that he should perceive what he perceives) he can never be in doubt, when any *idea* is in his mind, that it is there and is that *idea* it is; and that two distinct *ideas*, when they are in his mind, are there and are not one and the same *idea*. So that all such affirmations and negations are made without any possibility of doubt, uncertainty, or hesitation, and must necessarily be assented to as soon as understood: that is, as soon as we have in our minds determined *ideas*, which the terms in the proposition stand for. And therefore wherever the mind with attention considers any proposition, so as to perceive the two *ideas* signified by the terms and affirmed or denied one of the other, to be the same or different, it is presently and infallibly certain of the truth of such a proposition, and this equally whether these propositions be in terms standing for more general *ideas*, or such as are less so, v.g. whether the general *idea* of *being* be affirmed of itself, as in this proposition, *Whatsoever is, is*; or a more particular *idea* be affirmed of itself, as *A man is a man*, or *Whatsoever is white is white*. Or whether the *idea* of *being* in general be denied of *not being*, which is the only (if I may so call it) *idea* different from it, as in this other proposition: *It is impossible for the same to be and not to be*; or any *idea* of any particular being be denied of another different from it, as *A man is not a horse, Red is not blue*. The difference of the *ideas*, as soon as the terms are understood, makes the truth of the proposition presently visible, and that with an equal certainty and easiness, in the less as well as the more general propositions, and all for the same reason, viz. because the mind perceives in any *ideas* that it has the same *idea* to be the same with itself, and two different *ideas* to be different and not the same. And this it is equally certain of: whether these *ideas* be more or less general, abstract, and comprehensive. It is not therefore alone to these two general propositions, *Whatsoever is, is*, and *It is impossible for the same thing to be and not to be*, that this self-evidence belongs by any peculiar right. The perception of being or not being belongs no more to these vague *ideas*, signified by the terms *whatsoever* and *thing*, than it does to any other *ideas*. These two general maxims, amounting to no more in short but this, that *The same is the same* and *The same is not different*, are truths known in more particular instances as well as in these general maxims, and known also in particular instances before these general maxims are ever thought on; and draw all their force from the discernment of the mind employed about particular *ideas*. There is nothing more visible than that the mind, without the help of any proof or reflection on either of these general propositions, perceives so clearly and knows so certainly that the *idea* of *white* is the *idea* of white and not the *idea* of blue, and that the *idea* of white, when it is in the mind, is there and is not absent, that the consideration of these axioms can add nothing to the evidence or certainty of its knowledge. Just so it is (as everyone may experiment in himself) in all the *ideas* a man has in his mind: he knows each to be itself and not to be another, and to be in his mind and not away when it is there, with a certainty that cannot be greater; and therefore the truth of no general proposition can be known with a greater certainty, nor add anything to this. So that, in respect of identity, our intuitive knowledge reaches as far as our *ideas*. And we are capable of making as many self-evident propositions as we have names for distinct *ideas*. And I appeal to everyone's own mind whether this proposition, *A circle is a circle*, be not as self-evident a proposition as that consisting of more general terms, *Whatsoever is, is*; and again, whether this proposition, *Blue is not red*, be not a proposition that the mind can no more doubt of, as soon as it understands the words, than it does of that axiom, *It is impossible for the same thing to be and not to be*? And so of all the like.

5.   *Secondly*, As to *co-existence*, or such necessary connexion between two *ideas* that, in the subject where one of them is supposed, there the other must necessarily be also: of such agreement or disagreement as this, the mind has an immediate perception but in very few of them. And therefore in this sort we have but very little intuitive knowledge; nor are there to be found very many propositions that are self-evident, though some there are: v.g. the *idea* of filling a place equal to the contents of its superficies being annexed to our *idea* of body, I think it is a self-evident proposition *that two bodies cannot be in the same place*.

6.   *Thirdly*, As to the *relations* of modes, mathematicians have framed many axioms concerning that one relation of equality. As, *Equals taken from equals, the remainder will be equals*; which,

with the rest of that kind, however they are received for maxims by the mathematicians and are unquestionable truths, yet I think that anyone who considers them will not find that they have a clearer self-evidence than these: that *One and one are equal to two*; that *If you take from the five fingers of one hand two, and from the five fingers of the other hand two, the remaining numbers will be equal*. These and a thousand other such propositions may be found in numbers, which at very first hearing force the assent and carry with them an equal, if not greater clearness than those mathematical axioms.

7. *Fourthly*, As to *real existence*, since that has no connexion with any other of our *ideas* but that of ourselves and of a First Being, we have, in that concerning the real existence of all other beings, not so much as demonstrative, much less a self-evident knowledge; and, therefore, concerning those there are no maxims.

Chapter VIII

OF TRIFLING PROPOSITIONS

1. WHETHER the maxims treated of in the foregoing chapter be of that use to real knowledge as is generally supposed, I leave to be considered. This, I think, may confidently be affirmed, that there are universal propositions; that, though they be certainly true, yet they add no light to our understandings, bring no increase to our knowledge. Such are,

2. *First, All purely identical propositions*. These obviously and at first blush appear to contain no instruction in them; for when we affirm the said term of itself, whether it be barely verbal, or whether it contains any clear and real *idea*, it shows us nothing but what we must certainly know before, whether such a proposition be either made by or proposed to us. Indeed, that most general one, *What is, is*, may serve sometimes to show a man the absurdity he is guilty of when, by circumlocution or equivocal terms, he would in particular instances deny the same thing of itself; because nobody will so openly bid defiance to common sense as to affirm visible and direct contradictions in plain words, or, if he does, a man is excused if he breaks off any further discourse with him. But yet, I think I may say that neither that received maxim nor any other identical proposition teaches us anything; and, though in such kind of propositions

this great and magnified maxim, boasted to be the foundation of demonstration, may be and often is made use of to confirm them, yet all it proves amounts to no more than this: that the same word may with great certainty be affirmed of itself, without any doubt of the truth of any such proposition and, let me add also, without any real knowledge.

3. For at this rate, any very ignorant person, who can but make a proposition and knows what he means when he says *aye* or *no*, may make a million of propositions of whose truths he may be infallibly certain, and yet not know one thing in the world thereby: v.g. What is a soul, is a soul; or, *a soul is a soul*; *a spirit is a spirit*; *a fetiche is a fetiche*, etc. These all being equivalent to this proposition, viz. *What is, is*; i.e. *What hath existence, hath existence*; or *Who hath a soul, hath a soul.* What is this more than trifling with words? It is but like a monkey shifting his oyster from one hand to the other; and had he had but words, might no doubt have said: Oyster in right hand is *subject*, and oyster in left hand is *predicate*; and so might have made a self-evident proposition of oyster, i.e. *Oyster is oyster*, and yet, with all this, not have been one whit the wiser or more knowing; and that way of handling the matter would much at one have satisfied the monkey's hunger or a man's understanding, and they two would have improved in knowledge and bulk together.

I know there are some who, because *identical propositions* are self-evident, show a great concern for them and think they do great service to philosophy by crying them up, as if in them was contained all knowledge, and the understanding were led into all truth by them only. I grant as forwardly as anyone that they are all true and self-evident. I grant further that the foundation of all our knowledge lies in the faculty we have of perceiving the same *idea* to be the same, and of discerning it from those that are different, as I have shown in the foregoing chapter. But how that vindicates the making use of *identical propositions* for the improvement of knowledge from the imputation of trifling, I do not see. Let anyone repeat as often as he pleases that *The will is the will*, or lay what stress on it he thinks fit: of what use is this, and an infinite the like propositions, for the enlarging our knowledge? Let a man abound as much as the plenty of words which he has will permit him in such propositions as these, *A law is a law*, and *Obligation is obligation, Right is right*, and *Wrong is wrong*: will these and the like ever help him to an acquaintance with *ethics*, or instruct him or others in the knowledge of *morality*? Those who know not, nor perhaps ever will know what is *right* and what is *wrong*, nor the measures of them, can with as much assurance make and infallibly know the truth of these and all such propositions as he that is best instructed in *morality* can do. But what advance do such propositions give in the knowledge of anything necessary or useful for their conduct?

He would be thought to do little less than trifle who, for the enlightening the understanding in any part of knowledge, should be busy with *identical propositions*, and insist on such maxims as these: *Substance is substance* and *Body is body*, *A vacuum is a vacuum* and *A vortex is a vortex*, *A centaur is a centaur* and *A chimera is a chimera*, etc. For these and all such are equally true, equally certain, and equally self-evident. But yet they cannot but be counted trifling, when made use of as principles of instruction, and stress laid on them as helps to knowledge, since they teach nothing but what everyone who is capable of discourse knows without being told: viz. that the same term is the same term, and the same idea the same idea. And upon this account it was that I formerly did and do still think the offering and inculcating such propositions, in order to give the understanding any new light or inlet into the knowledge of things, no better than trifling.

Instruction lies in something very different, and he that would enlarge his own or another's mind to truths he does not yet know must find out intermediate *ideas*, and then lay them in such order one by another that the understanding may see the agreement or disagreement of those in question. Propositions that do this are instructive; but they are far from such as affirm the same term of itself, which is no way to advance one's self or others in any sort of knowledge. It no more helps to that than it would help anyone, in his learning to read, to have such propositions as these inculcated to him, *an A is an A*, and *a B is a B*; which a man may know as well as any schoolmaster, and yet never be able to read a word as long as he lives. Nor do these or any such identical propositions help him one jot forwards in the skill of reading, let him make what use of them he can.

If those who blame my calling them *trifling propositions* had but read and been at the pains to understand what I had above writ in very plain *English*, they could not but have seen that by *identical propositions* I mean only such wherein the same term importing the same *idea* is affirmed of itself: which I take to be the proper signification of *identical proposition*; and concerning all such, I think I may continue safely to say that to propose them as instructive is no better than trifling. For no one who has the use of reason can miss them, where it is necessary they should be taken notice of, nor doubt of their truth when he does take notice of them.

But if men will call propositions *identical* wherein the same term is not affirmed of itself, whether they speak more properly than I, others must judge; this is certain: all that they say of propositions that are not *identical*, in my sense, concerns not me nor what I have said, all that I have said, relating to those propositions wherein the same term is affirmed of itself. And I would fain see an instance wherein any such can be made use of, to the advantage and improvement of anyone's knowledge. Instances of other kinds, whatever use may be made of them, concern not me, as not being such as I call *identical*.

4.   *Secondly*, Another sort of trifling propositions is *when a part of the complex* idea *is predicated of the name of the whole*: a part of the definition of the word defined. Such are all propositions wherein the *genus* is predicated of the *species*, or more comprehensive of less comprehensive terms; for what information, what knowledge carries this proposition in it, viz. *Lead is a metal*, to a man who knows the complex *idea* the name *lead* stands for? All the simple *ideas* that go to the complex one signified by the term *metal* being nothing but what he before comprehended and signified by the name *lead*. Indeed, to a man that knows the signification of the word *metal*, and not of the word *lead*, it is a shorter way to explain the signification of the word *lead*, by saying it is a *metal*, which at once expresses several of its simple *ideas*, than to enumerate them one by one, telling him it is a body very *heavy, fusible*, and *malleable*.

5.   A like trifling it is *to predicate any other part of the definition of the term defined*, or to affirm any one of the simple *ideas* of a complex one, of the name of the whole complex *idea*, as *All gold is fusible*. For *fusibility* being one of the simple *ideas* that goes to the making up the complex one the sound *gold* stands for, what can it be but playing with sounds, to affirm that of the name *gold* which is comprehended in its received signification? It would be thought little better than ridiculous to affirm gravely, as a truth of moment, that *gold is yellow*; and I see not how it is any jot more material to say *it is fusible*, unless that quality be left out of the complex *idea* of which the sound *gold* is the mark in ordinary speech. What instruction can it carry with it, to tell one that which he hath been told already or he is supposed to know before? For I am supposed to know the signification of the word another uses to me, or else he is to tell me. And if I know that the name *gold* stands for this complex *idea* of *body, yellow, heavy, fusible, malleable*, it will not much

instruct me to put it solemnly afterwards in a proposition and gravely say *All gold is fusible*. Such propositions can only serve to show the disingenuity of one who will go from the definition of his own terms, by reminding him sometimes of it; but carry no knowledge with them but of the signification of words, however certain they be.

6. *Every* man *is an animal* or living body, is as certain a proposition as can be; but no more conducing to the knowledge of things than to say *A palfrey is an ambling horse*, or a neighing, ambling *animal*: both being only about the signification of words, and make me know but this, that *body*, *sense*, and *motion* or power of sensation and moving, are three of those *ideas* that I always comprehend and signify by the word *man*; and where they are not to be found together, the name *man* belongs not to that thing; and so of the other, that *body*, *sense*, and *a certain way of going*, with *a certain kind of voice*, are some of those *ideas* which I always comprehend and signify by the word *palfrey*, and when they are not to be found together, the name *palfrey* belongs not to that thing. It is just the same, and to the same purpose, when any term, standing for any one or more of the simple *ideas* that altogether make up that complex *idea* which is called a *man*, is affirmed of the term *man*: v.g. suppose a *Roman* signified by the word *homo* all these distinct *ideas* united in one subject, *corporietas, sensibilitas, potentia se movendi, rationalitas, risibilitas*, he might no doubt with great certainty universally affirm one, more, or all of these together of the word *homo*, but did no more than say that the word *homo* in his country comprehended in its signification all these *ideas*. Much like a *Romance* knight, who by the word *palfrey* signified these *ideas, body of a certain figure, four-legged, with sense, motion, ambling, neighing, white, used to have a woman on his back*, might with the same certainty universally affirm also any or all of these of the word *palfrey*; but did thereby teach no more but that the word *palfrey*, in his or Romance language, stood for all these, and was not to be applied to anything where any of these was wanting. But he that shall tell me that, in whatever thing *sense, motion, reason*, and *laughter* were united, that thing had actually a notion of God or would be cast into a sleep by *opium*, made indeed an instructive proposition: because, neither *having the notion of* God nor *being cast into sleep by opium* being contained in the *idea* signified by the word *man*, we are by such propositions taught something more than barely what the word *man* stands for; and therefore the knowledge contained in it is more than *verbal*.

7. Before a man makes any proposition, he is supposed to

understand the terms he uses in it; or else he talks like a parrot, only making a noise by imitation and framing certain sounds which he has learnt of others, but not, as a rational creature, using them for signs of *ideas* which he has in his mind. The hearer also is supposed to understand the terms as the speaker uses them, or else he talks jargon and makes an unintelligible noise. And therefore he trifles with words who makes such a proposition which, when it is made, contains no more than one of the terms does, and which a man was supposed to know before: v.g. *A triangle hath three sides*, or *Saffron is yellow*. And this is no further tolerable than where a man goes to explain his terms to one who is supposed or declares himself not to understand him; and then *it teaches only the signification of that word* and the use of that sign.

8. We can know then the truth of two sorts of propositions with perfect *certainty*: the one is of those trifling propositions which have a certainty in them, but it is but a *verbal certainty*, but not instructive. And, secondly, we can know the truth and so may be *certain* in propositions which affirm something of another, which is a necessary consequence of its precise complex *idea*, but not contained in it: as that *the external angle of all triangles is bigger than either of the opposite internal angles*; which relation of the outward angle to either of the opposite internal angles making no part of the complex *idea* signified by the name triangle, this is a real truth and conveys with it instructive *real knowledge*.

9. We having little or no knowledge of what combinations there be of simple *ideas* existing together in substances but by our senses, we cannot make any universal *certain* propositions concerning them, any further than our nominal essences lead us; which being to a very few and inconsiderable truths, in respect of those which depend on their real constitutions, the general *propositions* that are made *about substances, if they are certain, are for the most part but trifling*; and if they are instructive, are uncertain, and such as we can have no knowledge of their real truth, how much soever constant observation and analogy may assist our judgments in guessing. Hence it comes to pass that one may often meet with very clear and coherent discourses that amount yet to nothing. For it is plain that names of substantial beings, as well as others as far as they have relative significations affixed to them, may, with great truth, be joined negatively and affirmatively in propositions, as their relative definitions make them fit to be so joined; and propositions consisting of such terms may, with the same clearness, be deduced one from an-

other as those that convey the most real truths, and all this without any knowledge of the nature or reality of things existing without us. By this method one may make demonstrations and undoubted propositions in words, and yet thereby advance not one jot in the knowledge of the truth of things: v.g. he that, having learnt these following words with their ordinary mutually relative acceptations annexed to them, v.g. *substance, man, animal, form, soul, vegetative, sensitive, rational,* may make several undoubted propositions about the soul without knowing at all what the soul really is; and of this sort a man may find an infinite number of propositions, reasonings, and conclusions, in books of metaphysics, school-divinity, and some sort of natural philosophy, and, after all, know as little of God, *spirits,* or *bodies* as he did before he set out.

10. He that hath liberty to define, i.e. determine, the signification of his names of substances (as certainly everyone does in effect, who makes them stand for his own *ideas*) and makes their significations at a venture, taking them from his own or other men's fancies and not from an examination or inquiry into the nature of things themselves, may with little trouble demonstrate them one of another, according to those several respects and mutual relations he has given them one to another wherein, however things agree or disagree in their own nature, he needs mind nothing but his own notions, with the names he hath bestowed upon them; but thereby no more increases his own knowledge than he does his riches who, taking a bag of counters, calls one in a certain place a *pound*, another in another place a *shilling*, and a third in a third place a *penny*, and so proceeding, may undoubtedly reckon right and cast up a great sum, according to his counters so placed and standing for more or less as he pleases, without being one jot the richer or without even knowing how much a pound, shilling, or penny is, but only that one is contained in the other twenty times, and contains the other twelve; which a man may also do in the signification of words, by making them, in respect of one another, more or less or equally comprehensive.

11. Though yet, concerning most words used in discourses, especially argumentative and controversial, there is this more to be complained of, which is the worst sort of *trifling* and which sets us yet further from the certainty of knowledge we hope to attain by them or find in them, viz. that most writers are so far from instructing us in the nature and knowledge of things that they *use their words loosely* and uncertainly, and do not, by using them constantly and steadily in the same significations,

make plain and clear deductions of words one from another and make their discourses coherent and clear (how little soever it were instructive), which were not difficult to do, did they not find it convenient to shelter their ignorance or obstinacy under the obscurity and perplexedness of their terms; to which perhaps inadvertency and ill custom does in many men much contribute.

12.   To conclude, *Barely verbal propositions* may be known by these following *marks*:

First, All propositions wherein two abstract terms are affirmed one of another are barely about the signification of sounds. For since no abstract *idea* can be the same with any other but itself, when its abstract name is affirmed of any other term, it can signify no more but this: that it may or ought to be called by that name, or that these two names signify the same *idea*. Thus, should anyone say that *Parsimony is frugality*, that *Gratitude is justice*, that this or that action is or is not *temperance*: however specious these and the like propositions may at first sight seem, yet when we come to press them and examine nicely what they contain, we shall find that it all amounts to nothing but the signification of those terms.

13.   *Secondly*, All *propositions wherein a part of the complex* idea which any term stands for *is predicated of that term, are only* verbal, v.g. to say *that gold is a metal*, or *heavy*. And thus all propositions wherein more comprehensive words, called *genera*, are *affirmed* of subordinate or less comprehensive, called *species or individuals*, are barely verbal.

When by these two rules we have examined the propositions that make up the discourses we ordinarily meet with, both in and out of books, we shall perhaps find that a greater part of them than is usually suspected are purely about the signification of words, and contain nothing in them but the use and application of these signs.

This I think I may lay down for an infallible rule: that wherever the distinct *idea* any word stands for is not known and considered, and something not contained in the *idea* is not affirmed or denied of it, there our thoughts stick wholly in sounds and are able to attain no real truth or falsehood. This, perhaps, if well heeded, might save us a great deal of useless amusement and dispute, and very much shorten our trouble and wandering in the search of real and true knowledge.

CHAPTER IX

OF OUR KNOWLEDGE OF EXISTENCE

1.   HITHERTO we have only considered the essences of things; which, being only abstract *ideas* and thereby removed in our thoughts from particular existence (that being the proper operation of the mind in abstraction, to consider an *idea* under no other existence but what it has in the understanding) give us no knowledge of real existence at all.   Where, by the way, we may take notice that *universal propositions* of whose truth or falsehood we can have certain knowledge concern not *existence*; and further, that all *particular affirmations or negations* that would not be certain if they were made general are only concerning *existence*: they declaring only the accidental union or separation of *ideas* in things existing, which, in their abstract natures, have no known necessary union or repugnancy.

2.   But, leaving the nature of propositions and different ways of predication to be considered more at large in another place, let us proceed now to inquire concerning our knowledge of the *existence* of things, and how we come by it.   I say, then, that we have the knowledge of *our own existence* by intuition, of the *existence of* GOD by demonstration, and of other things by sensation.

3.   As for *our own existence*, we perceive it so plainly and so certainly that it neither needs nor is capable of any proof.   For nothing can be more evident to us than our own existence.   *I think, I reason, I feel pleasure and pain*: can any of these be more evident to me than my own existence?   If I doubt of all other things, that very doubt makes me perceive my own *existence*, and will not suffer me to doubt of that.   For if I know *I feel pain*, it is evident I have as certain perception of my own existence as of the existence of the pain I feel; or, if I know *I doubt*, I have as certain perception of the existence of the thing doubting, as of that thought which I call *doubt*.   Experience then convinces us that *we have an intuitive knowledge of our own existence* and an internal infallible perception that we are.   In every act of sensation, reasoning, or thinking, we are conscious to ourselves of our own being and, in this matter, come not short of the highest degree of *certainty*.

CHAPTER X

OF OUR KNOWLEDGE OF THE EXISTENCE OF A GOD

1. THOUGH GOD has given us no innate *ideas* of himself,
though he has stamped no original characters on our minds
wherein we may read his being: yet, having furnished us with
those faculties our minds are endowed with, he hath not left
himself without witness, since we have sense, perception, and
reason and cannot want a clear proof of him, as long as we carry
ourselves about us. Nor can we justly complain of our ignorance in this great point, since he has so plentifully provided us
with the means to discover and know him, so far as is necessary
to the end of our being and the great concernment of our
happiness. But, though this be the most obvious truth that
reason discovers, and though its evidence be (if I mistake not)
equal to mathematical certainty: yet it requires thought and
attention, and the mind must apply itself to a regular deduction
of it from some part of our intuitive knowledge, or else we shall
be as uncertain and ignorant of this as of other propositions
which are in themselves capable of clear demonstration. To
show, therefore, that we are capable of *knowing*, i.e. *being certain*,
that there is a GOD and how we may come by this certainty, I
think we need go no further than ourselves and that undoubted
knowledge we have of our own existence.

2. I think it is beyond question that *man has a clear perception
of his own being*: he knows certainly that he exists and that he is
something. He that can doubt whether he be anything or no, I
speak not to, no more than I would argue with pure nothing, or
endeavour to convince nonentity that it were something. If
anyone pretends to be so sceptical as to deny his own existence
(for really to doubt of it is manifestly impossible), let him for me
enjoy his beloved happiness of being nothing, until hunger or
some other pain convince him of the contrary. This, then, I
think I may take for a truth, which everyone's certain knowledge assures him of, beyond the liberty of doubting, viz. that
he is something that actually exists.

3. In the next place, man knows, by an intuitive certainty,
that bare *nothing can no more produce any real being than it can
be equal to two right angles*. If a man knows not that nonentity,
or the absence of all being, cannot be equal to two right angles,
it is impossible he should know any demonstration in *Euclid*.
If, therefore, we know there is some real being, and that non-

entity cannot produce any real being, it is an evident demonstration that from eternity there has been something, since what was not from eternity had a beginning, and what had a beginning must be produced by something else.

4. Next, it is evident that what had its being and beginning from another must also have all that which is in and belongs to its being from another too. All the powers it has must be owing to and received from the same source. This eternal source, then, of all being must also be the source and original of all power: and so *this eternal being must be also the most powerful*.

5. Again, a man finds in himself *perception* and *knowledge*. We have then got one step further, and we are certain now that there is not only some being, but some knowing, intelligent being in the world.

There was a time, then, when there was no knowing being, and when knowledge began to be; or else there has been also *a knowing being from eternity*. If it be said there was a time when no being had any knowledge, when that eternal being was void of all understanding, I reply that then it was impossible there should ever have been any knowledge: it being as impossible that things wholly void of knowledge, and operating blindly and without any perception, should produce a knowing being, as it is impossible that a triangle should make itself three angles bigger than two right ones . For it is as repugnant to the *idea* of senseless matter that it should put into itself sense, perception, and knowledge, as it is repugnant to the *idea* of a triangle that it should put into itself greater angles than two right ones.

6. Thus, from the consideration of ourselves and what we infallibly find in our own constitutions, our reason leads us to the knowledge of this certain and evident truth: that *there is an eternal, most powerful, and most knowing being*, which whether anyone will please to call *God*, it matters not. The thing is evident, and, from this *idea* duly considered, will easily be deduced all those other attributes which we ought to ascribe to this eternal being. If nevertheless anyone should be found so senselessly arrogant as to suppose man alone knowing and wise, but yet the product of mere ignorance and chance; and that all the rest of the universe acted only by that blind haphazard: I shall leave with him that very rational and emphatical rebuke of *Tully, lib. ii, De Leg.*, to be considered at his leisure. 'What can be more sillily arrogant and misbecoming than for a man to think that he has a mind and understanding in him, but yet in

all the universe beside there is no such thing? Or that those things, which with the utmost stretch of his reason he can scarce comprehend, should be moved and managed without any reason at all?' *Quid est enim verius quam neminem esse oportere tam stulte arrogantem, ut in se mentem & rationem putet inesse, in caelo mundoque non putet? Aut ea quae vix summa ingenii ratione comprehendat nulla ratione moveri putet?*

From what has been said, it is plain to me we have a more certain knowledge of the existence of a GOD than of anything our senses have not immediately discovered to us. Nay, I presume I may say that we more certainly know that there is a GOD than that there is anything else without us. When I say we *know*, I mean there is such a knowledge within our reach, which we cannot miss if we will but apply our minds to that, as we do to several other inquiries.

7. *How far the* idea *of a most perfect being*, which a man may frame in his mind, does or does not prove the *existence of a* GOD, I will not here examine. For in the different make of men's tempers and application of their thoughts, some arguments prevail more on one, and some on another, for the confirmation of the same truth. But yet I think this I may say, that it is an ill way of establishing this truth and silencing atheists: to lay the whole stress of so important a point as this upon that sole foundation; and take some men's having that *idea* of GOD in their minds (for it is evident some men have none, and some worse than none, and the most very different) for the only proof of a deity; and, out of an overfondness of that darling invention, cashier or at least endeavour to invalidate all other arguments and forbid us to hearken to those proofs as being weak or fallacious, which our own existence and the sensible parts of the universe offer so clearly and cogently to our thoughts, that I deem it impossible for a considering man to withstand them. For I judge it as certain and clear a truth as can anywhere be delivered, that *the invisible things of* GOD *are clearly seen from the creation of the world, being understood, by the things that are made, even his eternal power and godhead*. Though our own being furnishes us, as I have shown, with an evident and incontestable proof of a deity, and I believe nobody can avoid the cogency of it who will but as carefully attend to it as to any other demonstration of so many parts: yet, this being so fundamental a truth and of that consequence that all religion and genuine morality depend thereon, I doubt not but I shall be forgiven by my reader if I go over some parts of this argument again and enlarge a little more upon them.

8.   There is no truth more evident than that *something* must be *from eternity*. I never yet heard of anyone so unreasonable, or that could suppose so manifest a contradiction, as a time wherein there was perfectly nothing: this being of all absurdities the greatest, to imagine that pure nothing, the perfect negation and absence of all beings, should ever produce any real existence.

It being then unavoidable for all rational creatures to conclude that something has existed from eternity, let us next see what kind of thing that must be.

9.   There are but two sorts of beings in the world that man knows or conceives.

First, Such as are purely material, without sense, perception, or thought, as the clippings of our beards, and parings of our nails.

Secondly, Sensible, thinking, perceiving beings, such as we find ourselves to be. Which, if you please, we will hereafter call *cogitative and incogitative* beings; which to our present purpose, if for nothing else, are perhaps better terms than material and immaterial.

10.   If, then, there must be something eternal, let us see what sort of being it must be. And to that, it is very obvious to reason that it must necessarily be a *cogitative* being. For it is as impossible to conceive that ever bare incogitative matter should produce a thinking intelligent being, as that nothing should of itself produce matter. Let us suppose any parcel of matter eternal, great or small; we shall find it, in itself, able to produce nothing. For example: let us suppose the matter of the next pebble we meet with eternal, closely united, and the parts firmly at rest together; if there were no other being in the world, must it not eternally remain so, a dead inactive lump? Is it possible to conceive it can add motion to itself, being purely matter, or produce anything? Matter, then, by its own strength, cannot produce in itself so much as motion; the motion it has must also be from eternity, or else be produced and added to matter by some other being more powerful than matter: matter, as is evident, having not power to produce motion in itself. But let us suppose motion eternal too, yet matter, *incogitative matter* and motion, whatever changes it might produce of figure and bulk, *could never produce thought*: knowledge will still be as far beyond the power of motion and matter to produce, as matter is beyond the power of *nothing* or *nonentity* to produce. And I appeal to everyone's own thoughts whether he cannot as easily conceive matter produced by *nothing* as thought to be produced by pure matter, when before there was no such thing as thought

or an intelligent being existing. Divide matter into as minute parts as you will (which we are apt to imagine a sort of spiritualizing, or making a thinking thing of it), vary the figure and motion of it as much as you please: a globe, cube, cone, prism, cylinder, etc., whose diameters are but 1,000,000th part of a *gry*[1], will operate no otherwise upon other bodies of proportionable bulk than those of an inch or foot diameter; and you may as rationally expect to produce sense, thought, and knowledge by putting together in a certain figure and motion gross particles of matter, as by those that are the very minutest that do anywhere exist. They knock, impel, and resist one another just as the greater do, and that is all they can do. So that if we will suppose nothing first or eternal, *matter* can never begin to be; if we suppose bare matter without motion eternal, *motion* can never begin to be; if we suppose only matter and motion first or eternal, *thought* can never begin to be. For it is impossible to conceive that matter either with or without motion could have originally, in and from itself, sense, perception, and knowledge: as is evident from hence, that then sense, perception, and knowledge must be a property eternally inseparable from matter and every particle of it. Not to add that, though our general or specific conception of matter makes us speak of it as one thing, yet really all matter is not one individual thing, neither is there any such thing existing as one material being or one single body that we know or can conceive. And therefore if matter were the eternal first cogitative being, there would not be one eternal infinite cogitative being, but an infinite number of eternal finite cogitative beings, independent one of another, of limited force and distinct thoughts, which could never produce that order, harmony, and beauty which is to be found in nature. Since therefore whatsoever is the first eternal *being* must necessarily be cogitative; and whatsoever is first of all things must necessarily contain in it and actually have, at least, all the perfections that can ever after exist; nor can it ever give to another any perfection that it hath not, either actually in itself or at least in a higher degree: it necessarily follows that the first eternal being cannot be matter.

11.   If, therefore, it be evident that *something* necessarily must *exist from eternity*, it is also as evident that *that something must*

[1] A gry is one-tenth of a line, a line one-tenth of an inch, an inch one-tenth of a philosophical foot, a philosophical foot one-third of a pendulum whose diadroms, in the latitude of 45 degrees, are each equal to one second of time or one-sixtieth of a minute. I have affectedly made use of this measure here, and the parts of it under a decimal division with names to them, because I think it would be of general convenience that this should be the common measure in the commonwealth of letters.

necessarily *be a cogitative being*: for it is as impossible that incogitative matter should produce a cogitative being as that nothing, or the negation of all being, should produce a positive being or matter.

12. Though this discovery of the *necessary existence of an eternal mind* does sufficiently lead us into the knowledge of GOD, since it will hence follow that all other knowing beings that have a beginning must depend on him, and have no other ways of knowledge or extent of power than what he gives them; and therefore, if he made those, he made also the less excellent pieces of this universe, all inanimate beings: whereby his *omniscience, power*, and *providence* will be established, and all his other attributes necessarily follow; yet, to clear up this a little further, we will see what doubts can be raised against it.

13. *First*, Perhaps it will be said that, though it be as clear as demonstration can make it that there must be an eternal being, and that being must also be knowing, yet it does not follow but that thinking being may also be material. Let it be so; it equally still follows that there is a GOD. For if there be an eternal, omniscient, omnipotent being, it is certain that there is a GOD, whether you imagine that being to be material or no. But herein I suppose lies the danger and deceit of that supposition: there being no way to avoid the demonstration that there is an eternal knowing being, men, devoted to matter, would willingly have it granted that this knowing being is material; and then, letting slide out of their minds or the discourse the demonstration whereby an eternal knowing being was proved necessarily to exist, would argue all to be matter and so deny a GOD, that is, an eternal cogitative being: whereby they are so far from establishing, that they destroy their own hypothesis. For if there can be, in their opinion, eternal matter without any eternal cogitative being, they manifestly separate matter and thinking and suppose no necessary connexion of the one with the other, and so establish the necessity of an eternal spirit, but not of matter: since it has been proved already that an eternal cogitative being is unavoidably to be granted. Now if thinking and matter may be separated, *the eternal existence of matter will not follow from the eternal existence of a cogitative being*, and they suppose it to no purpose.

14. But now let us see how they can satisfy themselves, or others, that this *eternal thinking being is material*.

First, I would ask them whether they imagine that all matter, *every particle of matter*, *thinks*? This, I suppose, they will scarce say, since then there would be as many eternal thinking beings as there are particles of matter, and so an infinity of gods. And yet, if they will not allow matter as matter, that is, every particle of matter, to be as well cogitative as extended, they will have as hard a task to make out to their own reasons a cogitative being out of incogitative particles, as an extended being out of unextended parts, if I may so speak.

15.   *Secondly*, if all matter does not think, I next ask whether it be *only one atom that does so*? This has as many absurdities as the other, for then this atom of matter must be alone eternal or not. If this alone be eternal, then this alone, by its powerful thought or will, made all the rest of matter. And so we have the creation of matter by a powerful thought, which is that the materialists stick at. For if they suppose one single thinking atom to have produced all the rest of matter, they cannot ascribe that pre-eminency to it upon any other account than that of its thinking, the only supposed difference. But allow it to be by some other way which is above our conception, it must be still creation, and these men must give up their great maxim, *Ex nihilo nil fit*. If it be said that all the rest of matter is equally eternal as that thinking atom, it will be to say anything at pleasure, though never so absurd; for to suppose all matter eternal, and yet one small particle in knowledge and power infinitely above all the rest, is without any the least appearance of reason to frame any hypothesis. Every particle of matter, as matter, is capable of all the same figures and motions of any other; and I challenge anyone, in his thoughts, to add anything else to one above another.

16.   *Thirdly*, if then neither one peculiar atom alone can be this eternal thinking being; nor all matter, as matter, i.e. every particle of matter, can be it: it only remains that it is *some certain system of matter*, duly put together, that is this *thinking eternal being*. This is that which, I imagine, is that notion which men are aptest to have of GOD, who would have him a material being, as most readily suggested to them by the ordinary conceit they have of themselves and other men, which they take to be material thinking beings. But this imagination, however more natural, is no less absurd than the other: for to suppose the eternal thinking being to be nothing else but a composition of particles of matter, each whereof is incogitative, is to ascribe all the wisdom and knowledge of that eternal being only to the *juxta-position* of parts, than which nothing can be more absurd. For unthinking particles of matter, however put together, can have nothing thereby added to them but a new relation of position, which it is impossible should give thought and knowledge to

them.

17. But further, this *corporeal system* either has all its parts at rest, or it is a certain motion of the parts wherein its thinking consists. If it be perfectly at rest, it is but one lump, and so can have no privileges above one atom.

If it be the motion of its parts on which its thinking depends, all the thoughts there must be unavoidably accidental and limited: since all the particles that by motion cause thought, being each of them in itself without any thought, cannot regulate its own motions, much less be regulated by the thought of the whole: since that thought is not the cause of motion (for then it must be antecedent to it and so without it), but the consequence of it whereby freedom, power, choice, and all rational and wise thinking or acting will be quite taken away; so that such a thinking being will be no better nor wiser than pure blind matter, since to resolve all into the accidental unguided motions of blind matter, or into thought depending on unguided motions of blind matter, is the same thing, not to mention the narrowness of such thoughts and knowledge that must depend on the motion of such parts. But there needs no enumeration of any more absurdities and impossibilities in this hypothesis (however full of them it be) than that before-mentioned: since, let this thinking system be all or a part of the matter of the universe, it is impossible that any one particle should either know its own or the motion of any other particle, or the whole know the motion of every particular, and so regulate its own thoughts or motions, or indeed have any thought resulting from such motion.

18. Others would have *matter* to be *eternal*, notwithstanding that they allow an eternal, cogitative, immaterial being. This, though it take not away the being of a GOD, yet since it denies one and the first great piece of his workmanship, the creation, let us consider it a little. *Matter* must be allowed eternal; why? Because you cannot conceive how it can be made out of nothing; why do you not also think yourself eternal? You will answer, perhaps, because about twenty or forty years since, you began to be. But if I ask you what that *you* is which began then to be, you can scarce tell me. The matter whereof you are made began not then to be, for if it did, then it is not eternal: but it began to be put together in such a fashion and frame as makes up your body; but yet that frame of particles is not you, it makes not that thinking thing you are (for I have now to do with one who allows an eternal, immaterial, thinking being, but would have unthinking matter eternal too): therefore, when did that thinking thing begin to be? If it did never begin to be, then have you

always been a thinking thing from eternity: the absurdity whereof I need not confute till I meet with one who is so void of understanding as to own it. If, therefore, you can allow a thinking thing to be made out of nothing (as all things that are not eternal must be), why also can you not allow it possible for a material being to be made out of nothing by an equal power, but that you have the experience of the one in view, and not of the other? Though, when well considered, creation of a spirit will be found to require no less power than the creation of matter. Nay possibly, if we would emancipate ourselves from vulgar notions and raise our thoughts as far as they would reach to a closer contemplation of things, we might be able to aim at some dim and seeming conception how matter might at first be made and begin to exist by the power of that eternal first being; but to give beginning and being to a spirit would be found a more inconceivable effect of omnipotent power. But this being what would perhaps lead us too far from the notions on which the philosophy now in the world is built, it would not be pardonable to deviate so far from them or to inquire, so far as grammar itself would authorize, if the common settled opinion opposes it, especially in this place where the received doctrine serves well enough to our present purpose and leaves this past doubt: that the creation or beginning of any one SUBSTANCE out of nothing being once admitted, the creation of all other but the CREATOR himself may, with the same ease, be supposed.

19. But you will say, Is it not impossible to admit of the *making anything out of nothing*, since we cannot possibly conceive it? I answer, No, because it is not reasonable to deny the power of an infinite being because we cannot comprehend its operations. We do not deny other effects upon this ground, because we cannot possibly conceive the manner of their production. We cannot conceive how anything but impulse of body can move body; and yet that is not a reason sufficient to make us deny it possible, against the constant experience we have of it in ourselves, in all our voluntary motions, which are produced in us only by the free action or thought of our own minds, and are not, nor can be the effects of the impulse or determination of the motion of blind matter in or upon our bodies: for then it could not be in our power or choice to alter it. For example, my right hand writes whilst my left hand is still. What causes rest in one and motion in the other? Nothing but my will, a thought of my mind; my thought only changing, the right hand rests, and the left hand moves. This is matter of fact which cannot be denied.

Explain this and make it intelligible, and then the next step will be to understand creation. For the giving a new determination to the motion of the animal spirits (which some make use of to explain voluntary motion) clears not the difficulty one jot, to alter the determination of motion being in this case no easier nor less than to give motion itself, since the new determination given to the animal spirits must be either immediately by thought, or by some other body put in their way by thought which was not in their way before, and so must owe its motion to thought: either of which leaves voluntary motion as unintelligible as it was before. In the meantime, it is an overvaluing ourselves to reduce all to the narrow measure of our capacities, and to conclude all things impossible to be done whose manner of doing exceeds our comprehension. This is to make our comprehension infinite or God finite, when what he can do is limited to what we can conceive of it. If you do not understand the operations of your own finite mind, that thinking thing within you, do not deem it strange that you cannot comprehend the operations of that eternal infinite mind who made and governs all things and whom the heaven of heavens cannot contain.

Chapter XI

OF OUR KNOWLEDGE OF THE EXISTENCE OF OTHER THINGS

1. The knowledge of our own being we have by intuition. The existence of a God, reason clearly makes known to us, as has been shown.

The *knowledge of the existence* of any other thing we can have only by *sensation*: for, there being no necessary connexion of *real existence* with any *idea* a man hath in his memory, nor of any other existence but that of God with the existence of any particular man, no particular man can know the *existence* of any other being but only when, by actual operating upon him, it makes itself perceived by him. For the having the *idea* of anything in our mind no more proves the existence of that thing, than the picture of a man evidences his being in the world, or the visions of a dream make thereby a true history.

2. It is therefore the actual receiving of *ideas* from without that gives us notice of the *existence* of other things and makes us know that something doth exist at that time without us which causes that *idea* in us, though perhaps we neither know nor consider how it does it; for it takes not, from the certainty of our

senses and the *ideas* we receive by them, that we know not the manner wherein they are produced: v.g. whilst I write this, I have, by the paper affecting my eyes, that *idea* produced in my mind which, whatever object causes, I call *white*, by which I know that that quality or accident (i.e. whose appearance before my eyes always causes that *idea*) doth really exist and hath a being without me. And of this, the greatest assurance I can possibly have and to which my faculties can attain is the testimony of my eyes, which are the proper and sole judges of this thing whose testimony I have reason to rely on, as so certain that I can no more doubt whilst I write this that I see white and black, and that something really exists that causes that sensation in me, than that I write or move my hand: which is a certainty as great as human nature is capable of concerning the existence of anything but a man's self alone and of GOD.

3.   *The notice we have by our senses of the existing of things without us*, though it be not altogether so certain as our intuitive knowledge or the deductions of our reason employed about the clear abstract *ideas* of our own minds, yet it is an assurance that *deserves the name of knowledge*. If we persuade ourselves that our faculties act and inform us right concerning the existence of those objects that affect them, it cannot pass for an ill-grounded confidence: for I think nobody can, in earnest, be so sceptical as to be uncertain of the existence of those things which he sees and feels. At least, he that can doubt so far (whatever he may have with his own thoughts) will never have any controversy with me, since he can never be sure I say anything contrary to his opinion. As to myself, I think GOD has given me assurance enough of the existence of things without me, since, by their different application, I can produce in myself both pleasure and pain, which is one great concernment of my present state. This is certain: the confidence that our faculties do not herein deceive us is the greatest assurance we are capable of concerning the existence of material beings. For we cannot act anything but by our faculties, nor talk of knowledge itself but by the help of those faculties which are fitted to apprehend even what knowledge is. But besides the assurance we have from our senses themselves, that they do not err in the information they give us of the existence of things without us when they are affected by them, we are further confirmed in this assurance by other concurrent reasons.

4.   *First,* It is plain those perceptions are produced in us by exterior causes affecting our senses, because *those that want the organs of any sense never can have the* ideas *belonging to that*

sense produced in their minds. This is too evident to be doubted, and therefore we cannot but be assured that they come in by the organs of that sense, and no other way. The organs themselves, it is plain, do not produce them: for then the eyes of a man in the dark would produce colours, and his nose smell roses in the winter; but we see nobody gets the relish of a pineapple till he goes to the *Indies*, where it is, and tastes it.

5. *Secondly*, Because *sometimes I find that I cannot avoid the having those* ideas *produced in my mind.* For though, when my eyes are shut, or windows fast, I can at pleasure recall to my mind the *ideas* of *light*, or the *sun*, which former sensations had lodged in my memory: so I can at pleasure lay by that *idea*, and take into my view that of the *smell* of a rose, or *taste* of sugar. But, if I turn my eyes at noon towards the sun, I cannot avoid the *ideas* which the light or sun then produces in me. So that there is a manifest difference between the *ideas* laid up in my memory (over which, if they were there only, I should have constantly the same power to dispose of them and lay them by at pleasure) and those which force themselves upon me and I cannot avoid having. And therefore it must needs be some exterior cause and the brisk acting of some objects without me, whose efficacy I cannot resist, that produces those *ideas* in my mind, whether I will or no. Besides, there is nobody who doth not perceive the difference in himself between contemplating the sun as he hath the *idea* of it in his memory, and actually looking upon it: of which two, his perception is so distinct that few of his *ideas* are more distinguishable one from another, and therefore he hath certain knowledge that they are not both memory or the actions of his mind and fancies only within him, but that actual seeing hath a cause without.

6. *Thirdly*, Add to this, that *many of those* ideas *are produced in us with pain, which afterwards we remember without the least offence.* Thus, the pain of heat or cold, when the *idea* of it is revived in our minds, gives us no disturbance, which when felt was very troublesome, and is again when actually repeated: which is occasioned by the disorder the external object causes in our bodies when applied to it; and we remember the pain of *hunger*, *thirst*, or the *headache* without any pain at all: which would either never disturb us, or else constantly do it as often as we thought of it, were there nothing more but *ideas* floating in our minds and appearances entertaining our fancies, without the real existence of things affecting us from abroad. The same may be said of pleasure accompanying several actual sensations; and though mathematical demonstration depends not upon

sense, yet the examining them by diagrams gives great credit to the evidence of our sight and seems to give it a certainty approaching to that of the demonstration itself. For it would be very strange that a man should allow it for an undeniable truth that two angles of a figure, which he measures by lines and angles of a diagram, should be bigger one than the other, and yet doubt of the existence of those lines and angles which, by looking on, he makes use of to measure that by.

7. *Fourthly*, Our *senses* in many cases bear *witness* to the truth of each other's report concerning the existence of sensible things without us. He that sees a *fire* may, if he doubt whether it be anything more than a bare fancy, feel it too and be convinced by putting his hand in it. Which certainly could never be put into such exquisite pain by a bare *idea* or phantom, unless that the pain be a fancy too: which yet he cannot, when the burn is well, by raising the *idea* of it, bring upon himself again.

Thus I see, whilst I write this, I can change the appearance of the paper and, by designing the letters, tell beforehand what new *idea* it shall exhibit the very next moment, barely by drawing my pen over it: which will neither appear (let me fancy as much as I will) if my hand stands still or, though I move my pen, if my eyes be shut; nor, when those characters are once made on the paper, can I choose afterwards but see them as they are, that is, have the *ideas* of such letters as I have made. Whence it is manifest that they are not barely the sport and play of my own imagination, when I find that the characters that were made at the pleasure of my own thoughts do not obey them, nor yet cease to be whenever I shall fancy it, but continue to affect my senses constantly and regularly, according to the figures I made them. To which if we will add that the sight of those shall, from another man, draw such sounds as I beforehand design they shall stand for, there will be little reason left to doubt that those words I write do really exist without me, when they cause a long series of regular sounds to affect my ears, which could not be the effect of my imagination, nor could my memory retain them in that order.

8. But yet, if after all this anyone will be so sceptical as to distrust his senses and to affirm that all we see and hear, feel and taste, think and do during our whole being is but the series and deluding appearances of a long dream, whereof there is no reality, and therefore will question the existence of all things or our knowledge of anything: I must desire him to consider that, if all be a dream, then he doth but dream that he makes the

question, and so it is not much matter that a waking man should answer him. But yet if he pleases he may dream that I make him this answer, that *the certainty of* things existing *in rerum natura*, when we have *the testimony of our senses* for it, is not only *as great* as our frame can attain to, but *as our condition needs*. For our faculties being suited not to the full extent of being, nor to a perfect, clear, comprehensive knowledge of things free from all doubt and scruple, but to the preservation of us in whom they are, and accommodated to the use of life: they serve to our purpose well enough if they will but give us certain notice of those things which are convenient or inconvenient to us. For he that sees a candle burning and hath experimented the force of its flame by putting his finger in it will little doubt that this is something existing without him which does him harm and puts him to great pain: which is assurance enough, when no man requires greater certainty to govern his actions by than what is as certain as his actions themselves. And if our dreamer pleases to try whether the glowing heat of a glass furnace be barely a wandering imagination in a drowsy man's fancy, by putting his hand into it, he may perhaps be wakened into a certainty greater than he could wish that it is something more than bare imagination. So that this evidence is as great as we can desire, being as certain to us as our pleasure or pain, i.e. happiness or misery, beyond which we have no concernment, either of knowing or being. Such an assurance of the existence of things without us is sufficient to direct us in the attaining the good and avoiding the evil which is caused by them, which is the important concernment we have of being made acquainted with them.

9. In fine then, when our senses do actually convey into our understandings any *idea*, we cannot but be satisfied that there doth something at that time really exist without us which doth affect our senses, and by them give notice of itself to our apprehensive faculties, and actually produce that *idea* which we then perceive; and we cannot so far distrust their testimony as to doubt that such collections of simple *ideas*, as we have observed by our senses to be united together, do really exist together. But *this knowledge extends as far as the present testimony of our senses*, employed about particular objects that do then affect them, *and no further*. For if I saw such a collection of simple *ideas* as is wont to be called *man*, existing together one minute since, and am now alone, I cannot be certain that the same man exists now, since there is no necessary connexion of his existence a minute since with his existence now: by a thousand

ways he may cease to be since I had the testimony of my senses
for his existence. And if I cannot be certain that the man I saw
last today is now in being, I can less be certain that he is so who
hath been longer removed from my senses and I have not seen
since yesterday or since the last year; and much less can I be
certain of the existence of men that I never saw. And, therefore,
though it be highly probable that millions of men do now exist,
yet, whilst I am alone, writing this, I have not that certainty of
it which we strictly call knowledge: though the great likelihood
of it puts me past doubt, and it be reasonable for me to do
several things upon the confidence that there are men (and men
also of my acquaintance, with whom I have to do) now in the
world; but this is but probability, not knowledge.

10. Whereby yet we may observe how foolish and vain a thing
it is for a man of a narrow knowledge who, having reason given
him to judge of the different evidence and probability of things
and to be swayed accordingly, how *vain*, I say, it is *to expect
demonstration* and certainty *in things not capable of it*, and
refuse assent to very rational propositions and act contrary to
very plain and clear truths because they cannot be made out so
evident as to surmount every the least (I will not say reason, but)
pretence of doubting. He that, in the ordinary affairs of life,
would admit of nothing but direct plain demonstration would
be sure of nothing in this world but of perishing quickly.
The wholesomeness of his meat or drink would not give him
reason to venture on it, and I would fain know what it is he
could do upon such grounds as were capable of no doubt, no
objection.

11. As, when our senses are actually employed about any
object, we do know that it does exist, so *by our memory* we may
be assured that heretofore things that affected our senses have
existed. And thus *we have knowledge of the past existence* of
several things whereof, our senses having informed us, our
memories still retain the *ideas*; and of this we are past all doubt,
so long as we remember well. But this knowledge also reaches
no further than our senses have formerly assured us. Thus,
seeing water at this instant, it is an unquestionable truth to me
that water doth exist; and remembering that I saw it yesterday,
it will also be always true and, as long as my memory retains it,
always an undoubted proposition to me that water did exist
10th *July*, 1688; as it will also be equally true that a certain
number of very fine colours did exist, which at the same time
I saw upon a bubble of that water; but, being now quite out of
the sight both of the water and bubbles too, it is no more certainly

known to me that the water doth now exist than that the bubbles or colours therein do so: it being no more necessary that water should exist today because it existed yesterday, than that the colours or bubbles exist today because they existed yesterday, though it be exceedingly much more probable: because water hath been observed to continue long in existence, but bubbles, and the colours on them, quickly cease to be.

12. What *ideas* we have of spirits, and how we come by them, I have already shown. But though we have those *ideas* in our minds and know we have them there, the having the *ideas* of spirits does not make us *know* that any such things do exist without us, or *that there are any finite spirits* or any other spiritual beings but the eternal GOD. We have ground from revelation, and several other reasons, to believe with assurance that there are such creatures; but our senses not being able to discover them, we want the means of knowing their particular existences. For we can no more know that there are finite spirits really existing, by the *idea* we have of such beings in our minds, than by the *ideas* anyone has of fairies or centaurs he can come to know that things answering those *ideas* do really exist.

And therefore, concerning the existence of finite spirits as well as several other things, we must content ourselves with the evidence of faith: but universal certain propositions concerning this matter are beyond our reach. For however true it may be, v.g. that all the intelligent spirits that GOD ever created do still exist, yet it can never make a part of our certain knowledge. These and the like propositions we may assent to, as highly probable, but are not, I fear, in this state capable of knowing. We are not, then, to put others upon demonstrating, nor ourselves upon search of universal certainty in all those matters wherein we are not capable of any other knowledge but what our senses give us in this or that particular.

13. By which it appears that there are two sorts of *propositions*: (1) There is one sort of propositions *concerning* the *existence* of anything answerable to such an *idea*: as having the *idea* of an *elephant, phoenix, motion,* or an *angel* in my mind, the first and natural inquiry is whether such a thing does anywhere exist? And this knowledge is only of *particulars*. No existence of anything without us, but only of GOD, can certainly be known further than our senses inform us. (2) There is another sort of *propositions*, wherein is expressed the agreement or disagreement of our abstract *ideas* and their dependence one on another.

Such propositions may be *universal* and certain. So, having the *idea* of GOD and myself, of fear and obedience, I cannot but be sure that GOD is to be feared and obeyed by me; and this proposition will be certain concerning *man* in general, if I have made an abstract *idea* of such a species whereof I am one particular. But yet this proposition, how certain soever, that men ought to fear and obey GOD, proves not to me the existence of men in the world, but will be true of all such creatures whenever they do exist: which *certainty* of such general propositions depends on the agreement or disagreement to be discovered in those abstract *ideas*.

14. In the former case, our knowledge is the consequence of the existence of things producing *ideas* in our minds by our senses; in the latter, knowledge is the consequence of the *ideas* (be they what they will) that are in our minds producing there general certain propositions. Many of these are called *aeternae veritates*, and all of them indeed are so: not from being written, all or any of them, in the minds of all men, or that they were any of them propositions in anyone's mind till he, having got the abstract *ideas*, joined or separated them by affirmation or negation. But wheresoever we can suppose such a creature as *man* is, endowed with such faculties and thereby furnished with such *ideas* as we have, we must conclude he must needs, when he applies his thoughts to the consideration of his *ideas*, know the truth of certain propositions that will arise from the agreement or disagreement which he will perceive in his own *ideas*. Such propositions are therefore called *eternal truths*: not because they are eternal propositions actually formed, and antecedent to the understanding that at any time makes them; nor because they are imprinted on the mind from any patterns that are anywhere out of the mind, and existed before: but because, being once made about abstract *ideas* so as to be true, they will, whenever they can be supposed to be made again at any time, past or to come, by a mind having those *ideas*, always actually be true. For names being supposed to stand perpetually for the same *ideas*, and the same *ideas* having immutably the same habitudes one to another, propositions concerning any abstract *ideas* that are once true must needs be *eternal verities*.

1.   IT having been the common received opinion amongst men of letters that *maxims* were the foundation of all knowledge, and that the sciences were each of them built upon certain *praecognita*, from whence the understanding was to take its rise and by which it was to conduct itself in its inquiries into the matters belonging to that science, the beaten road of the Schools has been to lay down in the beginning one or more general propositions as foundations whereon to build the knowledge that was to be had of that subject. These doctrines, thus laid down for foundations of any science, were called *principles*, as the beginnings from which we must set out and look no further backwards in our inquiries, as we have already observed.

2.   One thing which might probably give an occasion to this way of proceeding in other sciences was (as I suppose) the good success it seemed to have in *mathematics*, wherein men being observed to attain a great certainty of knowledge, these sciences came by pre-eminence to be called μαθήματα and μάθησις, learning, or things learned, thoroughly learned, as having of all others the greatest certainty, clearness, and evidence in them.

3.   But if anyone will consider, he will (I guess) find that *the great advancement* and certainty of *real knowledge*, which men arrived to in these sciences, was not owing to the influence of these principles nor derived from any peculiar advantage they received from two or three general maxims laid down in the beginning, but *from* the *clear, distinct, complete ideas* their thoughts were employed about and the relation of equality and excess, so clear between some of them that they had an intuitive knowledge, and by that a way to discover it in others, and this without the help of those *maxims*. For I ask, Is it not possible for a young lad to know that his whole body is bigger than his little finger, but by virtue of this axiom, that *The whole is bigger than a part*, nor be assured of it until he has learned that *maxim*? Or cannot a country-wench know that, having received a shilling from one that owes her three, and a shilling also from another that owes her three, that the remaining debts in each of their hands are equal? Cannot she know this, I say, without she fetch

the certainty of it from this maxim, that *If you take equals from equals, the remainder will be equals*, a maxim which possibly she never heard or thought of? I desire anyone to consider, from what has been elsewhere said, which is known first and clearest by most people: the particular instance or the general rule; and which it is that gives life and birth to the other. These general rules are but the comparing our more general and abstract *ideas*, which are the workmanship of the mind, made and names given to them for the easier dispatch in its reasonings, and drawing into comprehensive terms and short rules its various and multiplied observations. But knowledge began in the mind and was founded on particulars, though afterwards, perhaps, no notice be taken thereof: it being natural for the mind (forward still to enlarge its knowledge) most attentively to lay up those general notions and make the proper use of them, which is to disburden the memory of the cumbersome load of particulars. For I desire it may be considered what more certainty there is to a child or anyone that his body, little finger and all, is bigger than his little finger alone, after you have given to his body the name *whole* and to his little finger the name *part*, than he could have had before; or what new knowledge concerning his body can these two relative terms give him which he could not have without them? Could he not know that his body was bigger than his little finger if his language were yet so imperfect that he had no such relative terms as *whole* and *part*? I ask further, when he has got these names, how is he more certain that his body is a *whole* and his little finger a *part* than he was or might be certain, before he learnt those terms, that his body was bigger than his little finger? Anyone may as reasonably doubt or deny that his little finger is a part of his body as that it is less than his body. And he that can doubt whether it be less will as certainly doubt whether it be a part. So that the maxim, *The whole is bigger than a part*, can never be made use of, to prove the little finger less than the body, but when it is useless, by being brought to convince one of a truth which he knows already. For he that does not certainly know that any parcel of matter, with another parcel of matter joined to it, is bigger than either of them alone will never be able to know it by the help of these two relative terms *whole* and *part*, make of them what maxim you please.

4. But be it in the mathematics as it will, whether it be clearer that, taking an inch from a black line of two inches and an inch from a red line of two inches, the remaining parts of the two lines will be equal, or that *if you take equals from equals, the*

remainder will be equals: which, I say, of these two is the clearer and first known I leave to anyone to determine, it not being material to my present occasion. That which I have here to do is to inquire whether, if it be the readiest way to knowledge to begin with general maxims and build upon them, it be yet a safe way to take the *principles* which are laid down in any other science as unquestionable truths, and so receive them without examination and adhere to them without suffering them to be doubted of, because mathematicians have been so happy, or so fair, to use none but self-evident and undeniable. If this be so, I know not what may not pass for truth in morality, what may not be introduced and proved in natural philosophy.

Let that principle of some of the philosophers, that all is matter and that there is nothing else, be received for certain and indubitable, and it will be easy to be seen, by the writings of some that have revived it again in our days, what consequences it will lead us into. Let anyone, with *Polemo*, take the world; or, with the *Stoics*, the *aether* or the sun; or with *Anaximenes*, the air, to be *God*: and what a divinity, religion, and worship must we needs have! *Nothing* can be *so dangerous as principles* thus *taken up without questioning or examination*, especially if they be such as concern morality, which influence men's lives and give a bias to all their actions. Who might not justly expect another kind of life in *Aristippus*, who placed happiness in bodily pleasure; and in *Antisthenes*, who made virtue sufficient to felicity? And he, who with *Plato* shall place beatitude in the knowledge of GOD, will have his thoughts raised to other contemplations than those who look not beyond this spot of earth and those perishing things which are to be had in it. He that, with *Archelaus*, shall lay it down as a principle that right and wrong, honest and dishonest, are defined only by laws, and not by nature, will have other measures of moral rectitude and pravity than those who take it for granted that we are under obligations antecedent to all human constitutions.

5. If, therefore, those that pass for *principles* are *not certain* (which we must have some way to know, that we may be able to distinguish them from those that are doubtful) but are only made so to us by our blind assent, we are liable to be misled by them and, instead of being guided into truth, we shall, by principles, be only confirmed in mistake and error.

6. But since the knowledge of the certainty of principles, as well as of all other truths, depends only upon the perception we have of the agreement or disagreement of our *ideas, the way to improve our knowledge* is not, I am sure, blindly and with an

implicit faith, to receive and swallow principles; but is, I think, to get and *fix in our minds clear, distinct, and complete* ideas, as far as they are to be had, *and annex to them proper and constant names.* And thus, perhaps, without any other principles, but barely considering those *ideas* and, by *comparing them one with another*, finding their agreement and disagreement and their several relations and habitudes, we shall get more true and clear knowledge by the conduct of this one rule, than by taking up principles and thereby putting our minds into the disposal of others.

7. *We must*, therefore, if we will proceed as reason advises, *adapt our methods of inquiry to the nature of the* ideas *we examine* and the truth we search after. General and certain truths are only founded in the habitudes and relations of abstract *ideas*. A sagacious and methodical application of our thoughts, for the finding out these relations, is the only way to discover all that can be put with truth and certainty concerning them into general propositions. By what steps we are to proceed in these is to be learned in the schools of the mathematicians who, from very plain and easy beginnings, by gentle degrees and a continued chain of reasonings, proceed to the discovery and demonstration of truths that appear at first sight beyond human capacity. The art of finding proofs, and the admirable methods they have invented for the singling out and laying in order those inter- mediate *ideas* that demonstratively show the equality or in- equality of inapplicable quantities, is that which has carried them so far and produced such wonderful and unexpected dis- coveries; but whether something like this, in respect of other *ideas*, as well as those of magnitude, may not in time be found out, I will not determine. This, I think, I may say: that, if other *ideas* that are the real as well as nominal essences of their species were pursued in the way familiar to mathematicians, they would carry our thoughts further and with greater evidence and clear- ness than possibly we are apt to imagine.

8. This gave me the confidence to advance that conjecture which I suggest, Chap. iii, viz. that *morality is capable of demon- stration*, as well as mathematics. For the *ideas* that ethics are conversant about being all real essences, and such as I imagine have a discoverable connexion and agreement one with another: so far as we can find their habitudes and relations, so far we shall be possessed of certain, real, and general truths; and I doubt not but, if a right method were taken, a great part of morality might be made out with that clearness that could leave, to a considering man, no more reason to doubt, than he could have to doubt of

the truth of propositions in mathematics which have been demonstrated to him.

9.   In our search after the knowledge of *substances*, our want of *ideas* that are suitable to such a way of proceeding obliges us to a quite different method. We advance not here as in the other (where our abstract *ideas* are real as well as nominal essences), by contemplating our *ideas* and considering their relations and correspondences: that helps us very little, for the reasons that in another place we have at large set down. By which I think it is evident that substances afford matter of very little general knowledge; and the bare contemplation of their abstract *ideas* will carry us but a very little way in the search of truth and certainty. What, then, are we to do for the improvement of our *knowledge in substantial beings*? Here we are to take a quite contrary course, the want of *ideas* of their real *essences* sends us from our own thoughts to the things themselves as they exist. *Experience here must teach me* what reason cannot; and it is by trying alone that I can certainly know what other qualities co-exist with those of my complex *idea*, v.g. whether that *yellow, heavy, fusible* body I call *gold* be *malleable* or no; which experi-ence (which way ever it prove, in that particular body I examine) makes me not certain that it is so in all or any other *yellow, heavy, fusible* bodies but that which I have tried. Because it is no consequence one way or the other from my complex *idea*: the necessity or inconsistency of *malleability* hath no visible con-nexion with the combination of that *colour, weight*, and *fusibility* in any body. What I have said here of the nominal essence of *gold*, supposed to consist of a body of such a determinate *colour, weight*, and *fusibility*, will hold true if *malleableness, fixedness*, and *solubility* in *aqua regia* be added to it. Our reasonings from these *ideas* will carry us but a little way in the certain discovery of the other properties in those masses of matter wherein all these are to be found. Because the other properties of such bodies depending not on these, but on that unknown real essence on which these also depend, we cannot by them discover the rest: we can go no further than the simple *ideas* of our nominal essence will carry us, which is very little beyond themselves and so afford us but very sparingly any certain, universal, and useful truths. For upon trial, having found that particular piece (and all others of that colour, weight, and fusibility that I ever tried) *malleable*, that also makes now perhaps a part of my complex *idea*, part of my nominal essence of *gold*; whereby though I make my complex *idea* to which I affix the name *gold* to consist of more simple *ideas* than before: yet still, it not containing the

real essence of any species of bodies, it helps me not certainly to know (I say to know, perhaps it may to conjecture) the other remaining properties of that body, further than they have a visible connexion with some or all of the simple *ideas* that make up my nominal essence. For example, I cannot be certain from this complex *idea* whether *gold* be fixed or no: because, as before, there is no necessary connexion or inconsistency to be discovered betwixt a complex *idea* of a body *yellow, heavy, fusible, malleable*, betwixt these, I say, and *fixedness*, so that I may certainly know that in whatsoever body these are found, there *fixedness* is sure to be. Here again for assurance I must apply myself to *experience*: as far as that reaches I may have certain knowledge, but no further.

10. I deny not but a man, accustomed to rational and regular experiments, shall be able to see further into the nature of bodies and guess righter at their yet unknown properties than one that is a stranger to them; but yet, as I have said, this is but judgment and opinion, not knowledge and certainty. This *way of* getting and *improving our knowledge in substances only by experience* and history, which is all that the weakness of our faculties in this state of *mediocrity* which we are in in this world can attain to, makes me suspect that natural philosophy is not capable of being made a science. We are able, I imagine, to reach very little general knowledge concerning the species of bodies and their several properties. Experiments and historical observations we may have, from which we may draw advantages of ease and health, and thereby increase our stock of conveniences for this life; but beyond this I fear our talents reach not, nor are our faculties, as I guess, able to advance.

11. From whence it is obvious to conclude that, since our faculties are not fitted to penetrate into the internal fabric and real essences of bodies, but yet plainly discover to us the being of a GOD and the knowledge of ourselves, enough to lead us into a full and clear discovery of our duty and great concernment, it will become us, as rational creatures, to employ those faculties we have about what they are most adapted to, and follow the direction of nature where it seems to point us out the way. For it is rational to conclude that our proper employment lies in those inquiries, and in that sort of knowledge which is most suited to our natural capacities and carries in it our greatest interest, i.e. the condition of our eternal estate. Hence I think I may conclude that *morality* is *the proper science and business of mankind in general* (who are both concerned and fitted to search out their *summum bonum*) as several arts, conversant about several parts

of nature, are the lot and private talent of particular men, for the common use of human life and their own particular subsistence in this world. Of what consequence the discovery of one natural body and its properties may be to human life, the whole great continent of *America* is a convincing instance: whose ignorance in useful arts and want of the greatest part of the conveniences of life, in a country that abounded with all sorts of natural plenty, I think may be attributed to their ignorance of what was to be found in a very ordinary, despicable stone, I mean the mineral of *iron*. And whatever we think of our parts or improvements in this part of the world, where knowledge and plenty seem to vie with each other, yet to anyone that will seriously reflect on it, I suppose it will appear past doubt that, were the use of *iron* lost among us, we should in a few ages be unavoidably reduced to the wants and ignorance of the ancient savage *Americans*, whose natural endowments and provisions come no way short of those of the most flourishing and polite nations. So that he who first made known the use of that one contemptible mineral may be truly styled the father of arts and author of plenty.

12. I would *not therefore* be thought to disesteem or *dissuade the study of nature*. I readily agree the contemplation of his works gives us occasion to admire, revere, and glorify their Author and, if rightly directed, may be of greater benefit to mankind than the monuments of exemplary charity that have at so great charge been raised by the founders of hospitals and almshouses. He that first invented printing, discovered the use of the compass, or made public the virtue and right use of *quinquina*, did more for the propagation of knowledge, for the supplying and increase of useful commodities, and saved more from the grave than those who built colleges, workhouses, and hospitals. All that I would say is that we should not be too forwardly possessed with the opinion or expectation of knowledge where it is not to be had, or by ways that will not attain it; that we should not take doubtful systems for complete sciences, nor unintelligible notions for scientifical demonstrations. In the knowledge of bodies, we must be content to glean what we can from particular experiments, since we cannot from a discovery of their real essences grasp at a time whole sheaves, and in bundles comprehend the nature and properties of whole species together. Where our inquiry is concerning co-existence or repugnancy to co-exist, which by contemplation of our *ideas* we cannot discover, there experience, observation, and natural history must give us by our senses and by retail an insight into corporeal substances. The knowledge of bodies we must get by our senses

warily employed in taking notice of their qualities and operations on one another; and what we hope to know of separate spirits in this world we must, I think, expect only from revelation. He that shall consider *how little general maxims, precarious principles, and hypotheses laid down at pleasure have promoted true knowledge* or helped to satisfy the inquiries of rational men after real improvements, how little, I say, the setting out at that end has for many ages together advanced men's progress towards the knowledge of natural philosophy, will think we have reason to thank those who in this latter age have taken another course and have trod out to us, though not an easier way to learned ignorance, yet a surer way to profitable knowledge.

13. Not that we may not, to explain any *phenomena* of nature, make use of any probable *hypothesis* whatsoever: *hypotheses*, if they are well made, are at least great helps to the memory and often direct us to new discoveries. But my meaning is that we should *not take up any one too hastily* (which the mind, that would always penetrate into the causes of things and have principles to rest on, is very apt to do) till we have very well examined particulars and made several experiments in that thing which we would explain by our hypothesis and see whether it will agree to them all, whether our principles will carry us quite through and not be as inconsistent with one *phenomenon* of nature, as they seem to accommodate and explain another. And at least that we take care that the name of *principles* deceive us not, nor impose on us, by making us receive that for an unquestionable truth which is really at best but a very doubtful conjecture, such as are most (I had almost said all) of the *hypotheses* in natural philosophy.

14. But whether natural philosophy be capable of certainty or no, the *ways to enlarge our knowledge*, as far as we are capable, seem to me, in short, to be these two:

First, The *first* is *to get and settle in our minds* determined *ideas* of those things whereof we have general or specific names, at least, of so many of them as we would consider and improve our knowledge in or reason about. And if they be *specific* ideas of *substances*, we should endeavour also to make them as complete as we can, whereby I mean that we should put together as many simple *ideas* as, being constantly observed to co-exist, may perfectly determine the *species*; and each of those simple *ideas* which are the ingredients of our complex one should be clear and distinct in our minds. For it being evident that our knowledge cannot exceed our *ideas*: as far as they are either imperfect, confused, or obscure, we cannot expect to have certain, perfect, or clear knowledge.

Secondly, The other is the art of *finding out* those *intermediate ideas*, which may show us the agreement or repugnancy of other *ideas* which cannot be immediately compared.

CHAPTER XV

OF PROBABILITY

1. As demonstration is the showing the agreement or disagreement of two *ideas* by the intervention of one or more proofs which have a constant, immutable, and visible connexion one with another, so *probability* is nothing but the appearance of such an agreement or disagreement by the intervention of proofs whose connexion is not constant and immutable, or at least is not perceived to be so, but is or appears for the most part to be so, and is enough to induce the mind to *judge* the proposition to be true or false, rather than the contrary. For example: In the demonstration of it a man perceives the certain, immutable connexion there is of equality between the three angles of a *triangle* and those intermediate ones which are made use of to show their equality to two right ones; and so, by an intuitive knowledge of the agreement or disagreement of the intermediate *ideas* in each step of the progress, the whole series is continued with an evidence which clearly shows the agreement or disagreement of those three angles in equality to two right ones; and thus he has certain knowledge that it is so. But another man, who never took the pains to observe the demonstration, hearing a mathematician, a man of credit, affirm the three angles of a triangle to be equal to two right ones, *assents* to it, i.e. receives it for true. In which case the foundation of his assent is the probability of the thing: the proof being such as for the most part carries truth with it, the man on whose testimony he receives it not being wont to affirm anything contrary to or besides his knowledge, especially in matters of this kind. So that that which causes his assent to this proposition, that the three angles of a triangle are equal to two right ones, that which makes him take these *ideas* to agree, without knowing them to do so, is the wonted veracity of the speaker in other cases, or his supposed veracity in this.

2. Our knowledge, as has been shown, being very narrow, and we not happy enough to find certain truth in everything which we have occasion to consider: most of the propositions we think, reason, discourse, nay, act upon, are such as we cannot have undoubted knowledge of their truth; yet some of them border so near upon certainty that we make no doubt at all about them, but *assent* to them as firmly and act according to that assent as resolutely as if they were infallibly demonstrated, and that our knowledge of them was perfect and certain. But there being degrees herein, from the very neighbourhood of certainty and demonstration quite down to improbability and unlikeliness, even to the confines of impossibility, and also degrees of *assent* from full *assurance* and confidence quite down to *conjecture, doubt,* and *distrust,* I shall come now (having, as I think, found out the bounds of human knowledge and certainty) in the next place to consider *the several degrees and grounds of probability, and assent or faith.*

3. *Probability* is likeliness to be true, the very notation of the word signifying such a proposition for which there be arguments or proofs to make it pass or be received for true. The entertainment the mind gives this sort of propositions is called *belief, assent,* or *opinion,* which is the admitting or receiving any proposition for true, upon arguments or proofs that are found to persuade us to receive it as true, without certain knowledge that it is so. And herein lies the *difference between probability* and *certainty, faith* and *knowledge,* that in all the parts of knowledge there is intuition; each immediate *idea,* each step has its visible and certain connexion: in belief, not so. That which makes me believe is something extraneous to the thing I believe, something not evidently joined on both sides to, and so not manifestly showing the agreement or disagreement of, those *ideas* that are under consideration.

4. *Probability,* then, being to supply the defect of our knowledge and to guide us where that fails, is always conversant about propositions whereof we have no certainty, but only some inducements to receive them for true. The *grounds of it* are, in short, these *two* following:

First, The conformity of anything with our own knowledge, observation, and experience.

Secondly, The testimony of others, vouching their observation and experience. In the testimony of others is to be considered: (1) The number. (2) The integrity. (3) The skill of the witnesses. (4) The design of the author, where it is a testimony out of a book cited. (5) The consistency of the parts, and circumstances of the relation. (6) Contrary testimonies.

5. Probability wanting that intuitive evidence which infallibly determines the understanding and produces certain knowledge, *the mind, if it will proceed rationally, ought to examine all the*

grounds of probability and see how they make more or less *for or against* any probable proposition, before it assents to or dissents from it; and, upon a due balancing the whole, reject or receive it, with a more or less firm assent, proportionably to the preponderancy of the greater grounds of probability on one side or the other. For example:

If I myself see a man walk on the ice, it is past *probability*, it is knowledge; but if another tells me he saw a man in *England* in the midst of a sharp winter walk upon water hardened with cold, this has so great conformity with what is usually observed to happen that I am disposed by the nature of the thing itself to assent to it, unless some manifest suspicion attend the relation of that matter of fact. But if the same thing be told to one born between the tropics, who never saw nor heard of any such thing before, there the whole probability relies on testimony; and as the relators are more in number and of more credit and have no interest to speak contrary to the truth, so that matter of fact is like to find more or less belief. Though to a man whose experience has been always quite contrary, and has never heard of anything like it, the most untainted credit of a witness will scarce be able to find belief. And as it happened to a *Dutch* ambassador who, entertaining the King of *Siam* with the particularities of *Holland*, which he was inquisitive after, amongst other things told him that the water in his country would sometimes, in cold weather, be so hard that men walked upon it and that it would bear an elephant, if he were there. To which the King replied, *Hitherto I have believed the strange things you have told me because I look upon you as a sober fair man, but now I am sure you lie.*

6.   Upon these grounds depends the *probability* of any proposition; and as the conformity of our knowledge, as the certainty of observations, as the frequency and constancy of experience and the number and credibility of testimonies do more or less agree or disagree with it, so is any proposition in itself more or less probable. There is another, I confess, which, though by itself it be no true ground of *probability*, yet is often made use of for one, by which men most commonly regulate their assent and upon which they pin their faith more than anything else, and that is *the opinion of others*, though there cannot be a more dangerous thing to rely on, nor more likely to mislead one, since there is much more falsehood and error among men than truth and knowledge. And if the opinions and persuasions of others whom we know and think well of be a ground of assent, men have reason to be Heathens in *Japan*, Mahometans in *Turkey*,

Papists in *Spain*, Protestants in *England*, and Lutherans in *Sweden*. But of this wrong ground of assent, I shall have occasion to speak more at large in another place.

CHAPTER XVI

OF THE DEGREES OF ASSENT

1. THE grounds of probability we have laid down in the foregoing chapter, as they are the foundations on which our *assent* is built: so are they also the measure whereby its several degrees are or ought to be *regulated*; only we are to take notice that, whatever grounds of probability there may be, they yet operate no further on the mind, which searches after truth and endeavours to judge right, than they appear, at least in the first judgment or search that the mind makes. I confess, in the opinions men have and firmly stick to in the world, their *assent* is not always from an actual view of the reasons that at first prevailed with them: it being in many cases almost impossible, and in most very hard, even for those who have very admirable memories, to retain all the proofs which upon a due examination made them embrace that side of the question. It suffices that they have once with care and fairness sifted the matter as far as they could; and that they have searched into all the particulars that they could imagine to give any light to the question; and with the best of their skill cast up the account upon the whole evidence; and thus, having once found on which side the probability appeared to them, after as full and exact an inquiry as they can make, they lay up the conclusion in their memories as a truth they have discovered; and for the future they remain satisfied with the testimony of their memories that this is the opinion that, by the proofs they have once seen of it, deserves such a *degree* of their *assent* as they afford it.

2. This is all that the greatest part of men are capable of doing, in regulating their *opinions* and judgments, unless a man will exact of them either to retain distinctly in their memories all the proofs concerning any probable truth, and that too in the same order and regular deduction of consequences in which they have formerly placed or seen them (which sometimes is enough to fill a large volume upon one single question), or else they must require a man, for every opinion that he embraces, every day to examine the proofs: both which are impossible. It is unavoidable therefore that the memory be relied on in the case, and that *men*

be persuaded of several opinions whereof the proofs are not actually in their thoughts, nay, which perhaps they are not able actually to recall. Without this, the greatest part of men must be either very sceptics, or change every moment and yield themselves up to whoever, having lately studied the question, offers them arguments which, for want of memory, they are not able presently to answer.

3. I cannot but own that men's *sticking* to their *past judgment* and adhering firmly to conclusions formerly made is often the cause of great obstinacy in error and mistake. But the fault is not that they rely on their memories for what they have before well judged, but because they judged before they had well examined. May we not find a great number (not to say the greatest part) of men that think they have formed right judgments of several matters, and that for no other reason but because they never thought otherwise? That imagine themselves to have judged right only because they never questioned, never examined their own opinions? Which is indeed to think they judged right because they never judged at all; and yet these of all men hold their opinions with the greatest stiffness, those being generally the most fierce and firm in their tenets who have least examined them. What we once know, we are certain is so; and we may be secure that there are no latent proofs undiscovered which may overturn our knowledge or bring it in doubt. But, in matters of probability, it is not in every case we can be sure that we have all the particulars before us that any way concern the question, and that there is no evidence behind and yet unseen, which may cast the probability on the other side and outweigh all that at present seems to preponderate with us. Who almost is there that hath the leisure, patience, and means to collect together all the proofs concerning most of the opinions he has, so as safely to conclude that he hath a clear and full view, and that there is no more to be alleged for his better information? And yet we are forced to determine ourselves on the one side or other. The conduct of our lives and the management of our great concerns will not bear delay: for those depend, for the most part, on the determination of our judgment in points wherein we are not capable of certain and demonstrative knowledge, and wherein it is necessary for us to embrace the one side or the other.

4. Since, therefore, it is unavoidable to the greatest part of men, if not all, to have several *opinions* without certain and indubitable proofs of their truth; and it carries too great an imputation of ignorance, lightness, or folly for men to quit and renounce their former tenets presently upon the offer of an

argument which they cannot immediately answer and show the insufficiency of: it would, methinks, become all men to maintain *peace*, and the common offices of humanity, *and friendship*, *in the diversity of opinions*, since we cannot reasonably expect that anyone should readily and obsequiously quit his own opinion and embrace ours, with a blind resignation to an authority which the understanding of man acknowledges not. For however it may often mistake, it can own no other guide but reason, nor blindly submit to the will and dictates of another. If he you would bring over to your sentiments be one that examines before he assents, you must give him leave at his leisure to go over the account again and, recalling what is out of his mind, examine all the particulars to see on which side the advantage lies; and if he will not think our arguments of weight enough to engage him anew in so much pains, it is but what we do often ourselves in the like case, and we should take it amiss if others should prescribe to us what points we should study. And if he be one who takes his opinions upon trust, how can we imagine that he should renounce those tenets, which time and custom have so settled in his mind, that he thinks them self-evident and of an unquestionable certainty, or which he takes to be impressions he has received from GOD himself or from men sent by Him? How can we expect, I say, that opinions thus settled should be given up to the arguments of authority of a stranger or adversary, especially if there be any suspicion of interest or design, as there never fails to be where men find themselves ill-treated? We should do well to commiserate our mutual ignorance and endeavour to remove it in all the gentle and fair ways of information, and not instantly treat others ill, as obstinate and perverse, because they will not renounce their own and receive our opinions, or at least those we would force upon them, when it is more than probable that we are no less obstinate in not embracing some of theirs. For where is the man that has incontestable evidence of the truth of all that he holds, or of the falsehood of all he condemns, or can say that he has examined to the bottom all his own or other men's opinions? The necessity of believing without knowledge, nay, often upon very slight grounds, in this fleeting state of action and blindness we are in, should make us more busy and careful to inform ourselves than constrain others. At least, those who have not thoroughly examined to the bottom all their own tenets must confess they are unfit to prescribe to others, and are unreasonable in imposing that as truth on other men's belief which they themselves have not searched into nor weighed the arguments of probability on which they should receive or reject it. Those who have fairly and truly examined, and are thereby got past doubt in all the doctrines they profess and govern themselves by, would have a juster pretence to require others to follow them; but these are so few in number and find so little reason to be magisterial in their opinions that nothing insolent and imperious is to be expected from them; and there is reason to think that, if men were better instructed themselves, they would be less imposing on others.

5. But, to return to the grounds of assent and the several degrees of it, we are to take notice that the propositions we receive upon inducements of *probability* are *of two sorts*: either concerning some particular existence or, as it is usually termed, matter of fact which, falling under observation, is capable of human testimony; or else concerning things which, being beyond the discovery of our senses, are not capable of any such testimony.

6. Concerning the *first* of these, viz. *particular matter of fact.*

First, Where any particular thing, consonant to the constant observation of ourselves and others in the like case, comes attested by the concurrent reports of all that mention it, we receive it as easily and build as firmly upon it as if it were certain knowledge; and we reason and act thereupon with as little doubt as if it were perfect demonstration. Thus, if all *Englishmen*, who have occasion to mention it, should affirm that it froze in *England* the last winter, or that there were swallows seen there in the summer, I think a man could almost as little doubt of it as that seven and four are eleven. The first, therefore, and *highest degree of probability* is when the general consent of all men in all ages, as far as it can be known, concurs with a man's constant and never-failing experience, in like cases, to confirm the truth of any particular matter of fact attested by fair witnesses: such are all the stated constitutions and properties of bodies, and the regular proceedings of causes and effects in the ordinary course of nature. This we call an argument from the nature of things themselves. For what our own and other men's constant observation has found always to be after the same manner, that we with reason conclude to be the effects of steady and regular causes, though they come not within the reach of our knowledge. Thus, that fire warmed a man, made lead fluid, and changed the colour or consistency in wood or charcoal, that iron sunk in water and swam in quicksilver: these and the like propositions about particular facts, being agreeable to our constant experience as often as we have to do with these matters, and being generally spoke of (when mentioned by others) as things found constantly to be so and therefore not so much as controverted by anybody, we are put past doubt that a relation affirming any such thing to have been or any predication that it will happen again in the same manner is very true. These *probabilities* rise so near to *certainty* that they govern our thoughts as absolutely and influence all our actions as fully as the most evident demonstration; and in what concerns us we make little or no difference between them and certain knowledge; our belief, thus grounded, rises to *assurance*.

7. *Secondly, The next degree of probability* is when I find, by my own experience and the agreement of all others that mention it, a thing to be for the most part so, and that the particular instance of it is attested by many and undoubted witnesses: v.g. history giving us such an account of men in all ages, and my own experience, as far as I had an opportunity to observe, confirming it, that most men prefer their private advantage to the public. If all historians that write of *Tiberius* say that *Tiberius* did so, it is extremely probable. And in this case, our assent has a sufficient foundation to raise itself to a degree which we may call *confidence*.

8. *Thirdly*, In things that happen indifferently, as that a bird should fly this or that way, that it should thunder on a man's right or left hand, etc., when any particular matter of fact is vouched by the concurrent testimony of unsuspected witnesses, there our assent is also unavoidable. Thus: that there is such a city in *Italy* as *Rome*; that about 1700 years ago, there lived in it a man called *Julius Caesar*; that he was a general, and that he won a battle against another called *Pompey*. This, though in the nature of the thing there be nothing for nor against it, yet being related by historians of credit and contradicted by no one writer, a man cannot avoid believing it and can as little doubt of it as he does of the being and actions of his own acquaintance, whereof he himself is a witness.

9. Thus far the matter goes easy enough. Probability upon such grounds carries so much evidence with it that it naturally determines the judgment and leaves us as little liberty to believe or disbelieve, as a demonstration does, whether we will know or be ignorant. The difficulty is when testimonies contradict common experience, and the reports of history and witnesses clash with the ordinary course of nature or with one another: there it is where diligence, attention, and exactness is required, to form a right judgment and to proportion the *assent* to the different evidence and probability of the thing, which rises and falls according as those two foundations of credibility, viz.

common observation in like cases and particular testimonies in that particular instance, favour or contradict it. These are liable to so great variety of contrary observations, circumstances, reports, different qualifications, tempers, designs, oversights, etc., of the reporters, that it is impossible to reduce to precise rules the various degrees wherein men give their assent. This only may be said in general, that as the arguments and proofs *pro* and *con*, upon due examination, nicely weighing every particular circumstance, shall to anyone appear upon the whole matter in a greater or less degree to preponderate on either side, so they are fitted to produce in the mind such different entertainment as we call *belief, conjecture, guess, doubt, wavering, distrust, disbelief*, etc.

10. This is what concerns *assent* in matters wherein testimony is made use of: concerning which, I think, it may not be amiss to take notice of a rule observed in the law of *England*, which is that, though the attested copy of a record be good proof, yet the copy of a copy, never so well attested and by never so credible witnesses, will not be admitted as a proof in judicature. This is so generally approved as reasonable and suited to the wisdom and caution to be used in our inquiry after material truths that I never yet heard of anyone that blamed it. This practice, if it be allowable in the decisions of right and wrong, carries this observation along with it, viz. that any testimony, the further off it is from the original truth, the less force and proof it has. The being and existence of the thing itself is what I call the original truth. A credible man vouching his knowledge of it is a good proof; but if another, equally credible, do witness it from his report, the testimony is weaker; and a third, that attests the hearsay of an hearsay, is yet less considerable. So that *in traditional truths, each remove weakens the force of the proof*; and the more hands the tradition has successively passed through, the less strength and evidence does it receive from them. This I thought necessary to be taken notice of, because I find amongst some men the quite contrary commonly practised, who look on opinions to gain force by growing older; and what a thousand years since would not, to a rational man contemporary with the first voucher, have appeared at all probable, is now urged as certain beyond all question, only because several have since, from him, said it one after another. Upon this ground propositions, evidently false or doubtful enough in their first beginning, come by an inverted rule of probability, to pass for authentic truths; and those which found or deserved little credit from the mouths of their first authors are thought to grow venerable by

age and are urged as undeniable.

11. I would not be thought here to lessen the credit and use of *history*: it is all the light we have in many cases, and we receive from it a great part of the useful truths we have, with a convincing evidence. I think nothing more valuable than the records of antiquity: I wish we had more of them and more uncorrupted. But this truth itself forces me to say that no *probability* can rise higher than its first original. What has no other evidence than the single testimony of one only witness must stand or fall by his only testimony, whether good, bad, or indifferent; and though cited afterwards by hundreds of others, one after another, is so far from receiving any strength thereby, that it is only the weaker. Passion, interest, inadvertency, mistake of his meaning, and a thousand odd reasons or capriccios men's minds are acted by (impossible to be discovered) may make one man quote another man's words or meaning wrong. He that has but ever so little examined the citations of writers cannot doubt how little credit the quotations deserve where the originals are wanting, and consequently how much less quotations of quotations can be relied on. This is certain, that what in one age was affirmed upon slight grounds can never after come to be more valid in future ages by being often repeated. But the further still it is from the original, the less valid it is, and has always less force in the mouth or writing of him that last made use of it than in his from whom he received it.

12. The probabilities we have hitherto mentioned are only such as concern matter of fact, and such things as are capable of observation and testimony. There remains that other sort *concerning* which men entertain opinions with variety of assent, though the *things* be such *that, falling not under the reach of our senses, they are not capable of testimony*. Such are: (1) The existence, nature, and operations of finite immaterial beings without us; as spirits, angels, devils, etc. Or the existence of material beings which, either for their smallness in themselves or remoteness from us, our senses cannot take notice of, as whether there be any plants, animals, and intelligent inhabitants in the planets and other mansions of the vast universe. (2) Concerning the manner of operation in most parts of the works of nature wherein, though we see the sensible effects, yet their causes are unknown, and we perceive not the ways and manner how they are produced. We see animals are generated, nourished, and move; the loadstone draws iron; and the parts of a candle, successively melting, turn into flame and give us both light and heat. These and the like effects we see and know; but the

causes that operate, and the manner they are produced in, we can only guess and probably conjecture. For these and the like, coming not within the scrutiny of human senses, cannot be examined by them or be attested by anybody, and therefore can appear more or less probable only as they more or less agree to truths that are established in our minds and as they hold proportion to other parts of our knowledge and observation. *Analogy* in these matters is the only help we have, and it is from that alone we draw all our grounds of probability. Thus, observing that the bare rubbing of two bodies violently one upon another produces heat, and very often fire itself, we have reason to think that what we call heat and fire consists in a violent agitation of the imperceptible minute parts of the burning matter; observing likewise that the different refractions of pellucid bodies produce in our eyes the different appearances of several colours, and also that the different ranging and laying the superficial parts of several bodies, as of velvet, watered silk, etc., does the like, we think it probable that the colour and shining of bodies is in them nothing but the different arrangement and refraction of their minute and insensible parts. Thus, finding in all parts of the creation that fall under human observation that there is a gradual connexion of one with another, without any great or discernible gaps between, in all that great variety of things we see in the world, which are so closely linked together that, in the several ranks of beings, it is not easy to discover the bounds betwixt them: we have reason to be persuaded that, by such gentle steps, things ascend upwards in degrees of perfection. It is an hard matter to say where sensible and rational begin, and where insensible and irrational end; and who is there quick-sighted enough to determine precisely which is the lowest species of living things, and which the first of those which have no life? Things, as far as we can observe, lessen and augment as the quantity does in a regular cone where, though there be a manifest odds betwixt the bigness of the diameter at remote distance, yet the difference between the upper and under, where they touch one another, is hardly discernible. The difference is exceeding great between some men and some animals; but, if we will compare the understanding and abilities of some men and some brutes, we shall find so little difference that it will be hard to say that that of the man is either clearer or larger. Observing, I say, such gradual and gentle descents downwards in those parts of the creation that are beneath man, the rule of analogy may make it probable that it is so also in things above us and beyond our observation, and that there are several ranks of intelligent beings, excelling us in several degrees of perfection, ascending upwards towards the infinite perfection of the creator by gentle steps and differences that are every one at no great distance from the next to it. This sort of probability, which is the best conduct of rational experiments, and the rise of hypothesis has also its use and influence; and a wary reasoning from analogy leads us often into the discovery of truths and useful productions, which would otherwise lie concealed.

CHAPTER XVII

OF REASON

1. THE *word reason* in the *English* language *has different significations*: sometimes it is taken for true and clear principles; sometimes for clear and fair deductions from those principles; and sometimes for the cause, and particularly the final cause. But the consideration I shall have of it here is in a signification different from all these, and that is as it stands for a faculty in man, that faculty whereby man is supposed to be distinguished from beasts, and wherein it is evident he much surpasses them.

2. If general knowledge, as has been shown, consists in a perception of the agreement or disagreement of our own *ideas*, and the knowledge of the existence of all things without us (except only of a GOD, whose existence every man may certainly know and demonstrate to himself from his own existence) be had only by our senses, what room then is there for the exercise of any other faculty but outward sense and inward perception? What need is there of reason? Very much: both for the enlargement of our knowledge and regulating our assent; for it hath to do both in knowledge and opinion, and is necessary and assisting to all our other intellectual faculties, and indeed contains two of them, viz. *sagacity and illation*. By the one, it finds out; and by the other, it so orders the intermediate *ideas* as to discover what connexion there is in each link of the chain whereby the extremes are held together, and thereby, as it were, to draw into view the truth sought for: which is that we call *illation* or *inference*, and consists in nothing but the perception of the connexion there is between the *ideas* in each step of the deduction, whereby the mind comes to see either the certain agreement or disagreement of any two *ideas*, as in demonstration, in which it arrives at knowledge, or their probable connexion on which it

gives or withholds its assent, as in opinion. Sense and intuition reach but a very little way. The greatest part of our knowledge depends upon deductions and intermediate *ideas*; and in those cases where we are fain to substitute assent instead of knowledge, and take propositions for true without being certain they are so, we have need to find out, examine, and compare the grounds of their probability. In both these cases, the faculty which finds out the means and rightly applies them, to discover certainty in the one and probability in the other, is that which we call reason. For as reason perceives the necessary and indubitable connexion of all the *ideas* or proofs one to another, in each step of any demonstration that produces knowledge: so it likewise perceives the probable connexion of all the *ideas* or proofs one to another, in every step of a discourse to which it will think assent due. This is the lowest degree of that which can be truly called reason. For where the mind does not perceive this probable connexion, where it does not discern whether there be any such connexion or no, there men's opinions are not the product of judgment or the consequence of reason, but the effects of chance and hazard, of a mind floating at all adventures, without choice and without direction.

3. So that we may in *reason* consider these *four degrees*: the first and highest is the discovering and finding out of proofs; the second, the regular and methodical disposition of them and laying them in a clear and fit order, to make their connexion and force be plainly and easily perceived; the third is the perceiving their connexion; and the fourth, a making a right conclusion. These several degrees may be observed in any mathematical demonstration: it being one thing to perceive the connexion of each part as the demonstration is made by another; another to perceive the dependence of the conclusion on all the parts; a third to make out a demonstration clearly and neatly one's self and, something different from all these, to have first found out those intermediate *ideas* or proofs by which it is made.

4. There is one thing more which I shall desire to be considered concerning reason, and that is whether *syllogism*, as is generally thought, be the proper instrument of it and the usefullest way of exercising this faculty. The causes I have to doubt are these:

First, Because syllogism serves our reason but in one only of the forementioned parts of it, and that is to show the connexion of the proofs in any one instance, and no more; but in this it is of no great use, since the mind can perceive such connexion where it really is as easily, nay, perhaps better, without it.

If we will observe the actings of our own minds, we shall find that we reason best and clearest when we only observe the connexion of the proof, without reducing our thoughts to any rule of syllogism. And therefore we may take notice that there are many men, that reason exceeding clear and rightly, who know not how to make a syllogism. He that will look into many parts of *Asia* and *America* will find men reason there perhaps as acutely as himself, who yet never heard of a syllogism nor can reduce any one argument to those forms; and I believe scarce anyone ever makes syllogisms in reasoning within himself. Indeed syllogism is made use of on occasion to discover a fallacy hid in a rhetorical flourish or cunningly wrapped up in a smooth period and, stripping an absurdity of the cover of wit and good language, show it in its naked deformity. But the weakness or fallacy of such a loose discourse it shows, by the artificial form it is put into, only to those who have thoroughly studied *mode and figure* and have so examined the many ways that three propositions may be put together as to know which of them does certainly conclude right and which not, and upon what grounds it is that they do so. All who have so far considered *syllogism* as to see the reason why, in three propositions laid together in one form, the conclusion will be certainly right but in another not certainly so, I grant, are certain of the conclusion they draw from the premisses in the allowed *modes* and *figures*; but they who have not so far looked into those forms are not sure by virtue of syllogism that the conclusion certainly follows from the premisses: they only take it to be so by an implicit faith in their teachers and a confidence in those forms of argumentation; but this is still but believing, not being certain. Now if of all mankind those who can make syllogisms are extremely few in comparison of those who cannot; and if of those few who have been taught logic there is but a very small number who do any more than believe that syllogisms in the allowed *modes* and *figures* do conclude right, without knowing certainly that they do so; if syllogisms must be taken for the only proper instrument of reason and means of knowledge, it will follow that before *Aristotle* there was not one man that did or could know anything by reason, and that since the invention of syllogisms there is not one of ten thousand that doth.

But God has not been so sparing to men, to make them barely two-legged creatures, and left it to *Aristotle* to make them rational, i.e. those few of them that he could get so to examine the grounds of syllogisms as to see that, in above threescore ways that three propositions may be laid together, there are but about fourteen wherein one may be sure that the conclusion is right, and upon what ground it is that in these few the conclusion is certain and in the other not. God has been more bountiful to mankind than so. He has given them a mind that can reason without being instructed in methods of syllogizing; the understanding is not taught to reason by these rules, it has a native faculty to perceive the coherence or incoherence of its *ideas*, and can range them right without any such perplexing repetitions. I say not this any way to lessen *Aristotle*, whom I look on as one of the greatest men amongst the ancients; whose large views, acuteness, and penetration of thought and strength of judgment, few have equalled; and who, in this very invention of forms of argumentation wherein the conclusion may be shown to be rightly inferred, did great service against those who were not ashamed to deny anything. And I readily own that all right reasoning may be reduced to his forms of syllogism. But yet I think, without any diminution to him, I may truly say that they are not the only nor the best way of reasoning, for the leading of those into truth who are willing to find it and desire to make the best use they may of their reason for the attainment of knowledge. And he himself, it is plain, found out some forms to be conclusive and others not, not by the forms themselves but by the original way of knowledge, i.e. by the visible agreement of *ideas*. Tell a country gentlewoman that the wind is south-west, and the weather louring, and like to rain, and she will easily understand it is not safe for her to go abroad thin clad in such a day after a fever: she clearly sees the probable connexion of all these, viz. south-west wind and clouds, rain, wetting, taking cold, relapse, and danger of death, without tying them together in those artificial and cumbersome fetters of several syllogisms that clog and hinder the mind, which proceeds from one part to another quicker and clearer without them; and the probability which she easily perceives in things thus in their native state would be quite lost, if this argument were managed learnedly and proposed in mode and figure. For it very often confounds the connexion; and, I think, everyone will perceive in mathematical demonstrations that the knowledge gained thereby comes shortest and clearest without syllogism.

Inference is looked on as the great act of the rational faculty, and so it is when it is rightly made; but the mind, either very desirous to enlarge its knowledge, or very apt to favour the sentiments it has once imbibed, is very forward to make inferences, and therefore often makes too much haste before it perceives the connexion of the *ideas* that must hold the extremes together.

To infer is nothing but, by virtue of one proposition laid down as true, to draw in another as true, i.e. to see or suppose such a connexion of the two *ideas* of the inferred proposition. V.g., Let this be the proposition laid down, *Men shall be punished in another world*, and from thence be inferred this other, *Then men can determine themselves*. The question now is to know whether the mind has made this inference right or no; if it has made it by finding out the intermediate *ideas* and taking a view of the connexion of them placed in a due order, it has proceeded rationally and made a right inference. If it has done it without such a view, it has not so much made an inference that will hold or an inference of right reason as shown a willingness to have it be, or be taken for such. But in neither case is it *syllogism* that discovered those *ideas* or showed the connexion of them, for they must be both found out and the connexion everywhere perceived before they can rationally be made use of in *syllogism*: unless it can be said that any *idea*, without considering what connexion it hath with the two other whose agreement should be shown by it, will do well enough in a *syllogism* and may be taken at a venture for the *medius terminus*, to prove any conclusion. But this nobody will say, because it is by virtue of the perceived agreement of the intermediate *idea* with the extremes that the extremes are concluded to agree; and therefore each intermediate *idea* must be such as in the whole chain hath a visible connexion with those two it is placed between, or else thereby the conclusion cannot be inferred or drawn in; for wherever any link of the chain is loose and without connexion, there the whole strength of it is lost, and it hath no force to infer or draw in anything. In the instance above-mentioned, what is it shows the force of the inference and, consequently, the reasonableness of it, but a view of the connexion of all the intermediate *ideas* that draw in the conclusion or proposition inferred? V.g., *Men shall be punished*, — *God the punisher*, — *just punishment*, — *the punished guilty* — *could have done otherwise* — *freedom* — *self-determination*: by which chain of *ideas* thus visibly linked together in train, i.e. each intermediate *idea* agreeing on each side with those two it is immediately placed between, the *ideas* of men and self-determination appear to be connected: i.e. this proposition, *Men can determine themselves*, is drawn in or inferred from this, *that they shall be punished in the other world*. For here the mind, seeing the connexion there is between the *idea of men's punishment in the other world* and the *idea of God punishing*, between *God punishing* and *the justice of the punishment*, between *justice of punishment* and *guilt*, between *guilt* and a *power to do otherwise*, between a *power to do otherwise* and *freedom*, and between *freedom* and *self-determination*, sees the connexion between *men* and *self-determination*.

Now I ask whether the connexion of the extremes be not more clearly seen in this simple and natural disposition than in the perplexed repetitions and jumble of five or six *syllogisms*. I must beg pardon for calling it jumble, till somebody shall put these *ideas* into so many *syllogisms* and then say that they are less jumbled and their connexion more visible when they are transposed and repeated and spun out to a greater length in artificial forms, than in that short natural plain order they are laid down in here, wherein everyone may see it, and wherein they must be seen before they can be put into a train of *syllogisms*. For the natural order of the connecting *ideas* must direct the order of the *syllogisms*, and a man must see the connexion of each intermediate *idea* with those that it connects, before he can with reason make use of it in a *syllogism*. And when all those syllogisms are made, neither those that are nor those that are not logicians will see the force of the argumentation, i.e. the connexion of the extremes, one jot the better. [For those that are not men of art, not knowing the true forms of *syllogism*, nor the reasons of them, cannot know whether they are made in right and conclusive *modes* and *figures* or no, and so are not at all helped by the forms they are put into, though by them the natural order, wherein the mind could judge of their respective connexion, being disturbed renders the illation much more uncertain than without them.] And as for logicians themselves, they see the connexion of each intermediate *idea* with those it stands between (on which the force of the inference depends) as well before as after the *syllogism* is made, or else they do not see it at all. For a *syllogism* neither shows nor strengthens the connexion of any two *ideas* immediately put together, but, only by the connexion seen in them, shows what connexion the extremes have one with another. But what connexion the intermediate has with either of the extremes in that syllogism, that no syllogism does or can show. That the mind only doth or can perceive, as they stand there in that *juxtaposition*, only by its own view, to which the syllogistical form it happens to be in gives no help or light at all: it only shows that, if the intermediate *idea* agrees with those it is on both sides immediately applied to, then those two remote ones or, as they are called, *extremes* do certainly agree; and therefore the immediate connexion of each *idea* to that which it is applied to on each side, on which the force of the reasoning depends, is as well seen before as after the *syllogism* is made, or else he that makes the syllogism could never see it at all. This, as has been already observed, is seen only by the eye, or the perceptive faculty of the mind, taking a view of them laid together, in a *juxtaposition*: which view of any two it has equally, whenever they are laid together in any proposition, whether that proposition be placed as a *major* or a *minor*, in a *syllogism* or no.

Of what use, then, are *syllogisms*? I answer, Their chief and main use is in the Schools, where men are allowed without shame to deny the agreement of *ideas* that do manifestly agree; or out of the Schools, to those who from thence have learned without shame to deny the connexion of *ideas*, which even to themselves is visible. But to an ingenuous searcher after truth, who has no other aim but to find it, there is no need of any such form to force the allowing of the inference: the truth and reasonableness of it is better seen in ranging of the *ideas* in a simple and plain order; and hence it is that men, in their own inquiries after truth, never use *syllogisms* to convince themselves [or in teaching others to instruct willing learners]. Because, before they can put them into a *syllogism*, they must see the connexion that is between the intermediate *idea* and the two other *ideas* it is set between and applied to, to show their agreement; and when they see that, they see whether the inference be good or no; and so *syllogism* comes too late to settle it. For to make use again of the former instance, I ask whether the mind considering the *idea* of justice placed as an intermediate *idea* between the *punishment* of men and the guilt of the punished (and till it does so consider it, the mind cannot make use of it as a *medius terminus*) does not as plainly see the force and strength of the inference, as when it is formed into syllogism. To show it in a very plain and easy example, let *animal* be the intermediate *idea* or *medius terminus* that the mind makes use of to show the connexion of *homo* and *vivens*; I ask whether the mind does not more readily and plainly see that connexion in the simple and proper position of the connecting *idea* in the middle, thus:

> *Homo* — *Animal* — *vivens*,

than in this perplexed one,

> *Animal* — *vivens* — *Homo* — *Animal*;

which is the position these *ideas* have in a syllogism, to show the connexion between *homo* and *vivens* by the intervention of *animal*.

Indeed syllogism is thought to be of necessary use, even to the lovers of truth, to show them the fallacies that are often concealed in florid, witty, or involved discourses. But that this is a

mistake will appear, if we consider that the reason why sometimes men, who sincerely aim at truth, are imposed upon by
such loose and, as they are called, rhetorical discourses is that,
their fancies being struck with some lively metaphorical representations, they neglect to observe or do not easily perceive what
are the true *ideas* upon which the inference depends. Now to
show such men the weakness of such an argumentation, there
needs no more but to strip it of the superfluous *ideas* which,
blended and confounded with those on which the inference
depends, seem to show a connexion where there is none or, at
least, do hinder the discovery of the want of it, and then to lay
the naked *ideas* on which the force of the argumentation depends
in their due order; in which position the mind, taking a view of
them, sees what connexion they have, and so is able to judge of
the inference without any need of a syllogism at all.

I grant that *mode* and *figure* is commonly made use of in such
cases, as if the detection of the incoherence of such loose discourses were wholly owing to the syllogistical form; and so I
myself formerly thought, till upon a stricter examination I now
find that laying the intermediate *ideas* naked in their due order
shows the incoherence of the argumentation better than syllogism: not only as subjecting each link of the chain to the immediate view of the mind in its proper place, whereby its connexion
is best observed, but also because syllogism shows the incoherence only to those (who are not one of ten thousand) who perfectly understand *mode* and *figure* and the reason upon which
those forms are established; whereas a due and orderly placing
of the *ideas* upon which the inference is made makes everyone,
both logician or not logician, who understands the terms and
hath the faculty to perceive the agreement or disagreement of
such *ideas* (without which, in or out of syllogism, he cannot
perceive the strength or weakness, coherence or incoherence of
the discourse) see the want of connexion in the argumentation
and the absurdity of the inference.

And thus I have known a man, unskilful in syllogism, who at
first hearing could perceive the weakness and inconclusiveness of
a long artificial and plausible discourse, wherewith others better
skilled in syllogism have been misled. And I believe there are
few of my readers who do not know such. And indeed, if it were
not so, the debates of most princes' councils and the business of
assemblies would be in danger to be mismanaged, since those
who are relied upon and have usually a great stroke in them are
not always such who have the good luck to be perfectly knowing
in the forms of *syllogism* or expert in *mode* and *figure*. And if

syllogism were the only or so much as the surest way to detect the fallacies of artificial discourses, I do not think that all mankind, even princes in matters that concern their crowns and dignities, are so much in love with falsehood and mistake that they would everywhere have neglected to bring syllogism into the debates of moment, or thought it ridiculous so much as to offer them in affairs of consequence: a plain evidence to me that men of parts and penetration, who were not idly to dispute at their ease, but were to act according to the result of their debates and often pay for their mistakes with their heads or fortunes, found those scholastic forms were of little use to discover truth or fallacy, whilst both the one and the other might be shown, and better shown without them, to those who would not refuse to see what was visibly shown them.

Secondly, Another reason that makes me doubt whether syllogism be the only proper instrument of reason, in the discovery of truth, is that, of whatever use *mode* and *figure* is pretended to be in the laying open of fallacy (which has been above considered), those scholastic forms of discourse are not less liable to fallacies than the plainer ways of argumentation; and for this I appeal to common observation, which has always found these artificial methods of reasoning more adapted to catch and entangle the mind than to instruct and inform the understanding. And hence it is that men, even when they are baffled and silenced in this scholastic way, are seldom or never convinced, and so brought over to the conquering side: they perhaps acknowledge their adversary to be the more skilful disputant, but rest nevertheless persuaded of the truth on their side, and go away, worsted as they are, with the same opinion they brought with them: which they could not do if this way of argumentation carried light and conviction with it, and made men see where the truth lay. And therefore syllogism has been thought more proper for the attaining victory in dispute, than for the discovery or confirmation of truth in fair inquiries. And if it be certain that fallacies can be couched in syllogisms, as it cannot be denied, it must be something else and not syllogism that must discover them.

I have had experience how ready some men are, when all the use which they have been wont to ascribe to anything is not allowed, to cry out that I am for laying it wholly aside. But to prevent such unjust and groundless imputations, I tell them that I am not for taking away any helps to the understanding in the attainment of knowledge. And if men skilled in and used to syllogisms find them assisting to their reason in the discovery of

truth, I think they ought to make use of them. All that I aim at
is that they should not ascribe more to these forms than belongs
to them, and think that men have no use, or not so full a use, of
their reasoning faculty without them. Some eyes want spectacles
to see things clearly and distinctly: but let not those that use them
therefore say nobody can see clearly without them; those who
do so will be thought in favour with art (which perhaps they are
beholding to) a little too much to depress and discredit nature.
Reason, by its own penetration where it is strong and exercised,
usually sees quicker and clearer without syllogism. If use of
those spectacles has so dimmed its sight that it cannot without
them see consequences or inconsequences in argumentation, I
am not so unreasonable as to be against the using them. Everyone knows what best fits his own sight. But let him not thence
conclude all in the dark, who use not just the same helps that he
finds a need of.

5. But however it be in knowledge, I think I may truly say it is
of *far* less or *no use* at all *in probabilities*. For the assent there
being to be determined by the preponderancy, after a due
weighing of all the proofs, with all circumstances on both sides,
nothing is so unfit to assist the mind in that as syllogism: which,
running away with one assumed probability or one topical
argument, pursues that till it has led the mind quite out of
sight of the thing under consideration; and forcing it upon some
remote difficulty, holds it fast there, entangled perhaps and as it
were manacled in the chain of syllogisms, without allowing it
that liberty, much less affording it the helps requisite to
show on which side, all things considered, is the greater
probability.

6. But let it help us (as perhaps may be said) in convincing
men of their errors and mistakes (and yet I would fain see the
man that was forced out of his opinion by dint of *syllogism*):
yet still it fails *our reason* in that part which, if not its highest
perfection, is yet certainly its hardest task, and that which we
most need its help in, and that is *the finding out of proofs and
making new discoveries*. The rules of *syllogism* serve not to
furnish the mind with those intermediate *ideas* that may show the
connexion of remote ones. This way of reasoning discovers no
new proofs, but is the art of marshalling and ranging the old
ones we have already. The 47th proposition of the First Book of
Euclid is very true, but the discovery of it, I think, not owing to
any rules of common logic. A man knows first, and then he is
able to prove syllogistically. So that *syllogism* comes after
nowledge, and then a man has little or no need of it. But it is

chiefly by the finding out those *ideas* that show the connexion
of distant ones that our stock of knowledge is increased, and
that useful arts and sciences are advanced. *Syllogism*, at best, is
but the art of fencing with the little knowledge we have, without
making any addition to it. And if a man should employ his
reason all this way, he will not do much otherwise than he who,
having got some iron out of the bowels of the earth, should have
it beaten up all into swords and put it into his servants' hands to
fence with and bang one another. Had the king of *Spain*
employed the hands of his people and his *Spanish* iron so, he
had brought to light but little of that treasure that lay so long hid
in the dark entrails of *America*. And I am apt to think that he
who shall employ all the force of his reason only in brandishing of
syllogisms will discover very little of that mass of knowledge
which lies yet concealed in the secret recesses of nature, and
which, I am apt to think, native rustic reason (as it formerly has
done) is likelier to open a way to and add to the common stock
of mankind, rather than any scholastic proceeding by the strict
rules of mode and figure.

7. I doubt not nevertheless but there are ways to be found to
assist our reason in this most useful part; and this the judicious
Hooker encourages me to say who, in his *Eccl. Pol. lib.* I, §6,
speaks thus: *If there might be added the right helps of true art
and learning (which helps, I must plainly confess, this age of the
world, carrying the name of a learned age, doth neither much
know nor generally regard), there would undoubtedly be almost as
much difference in maturity of judgment between men therewith
inured, and that which now men are, as between men that are
now, and innocents.* I do not pretend to have found or discovered here any of those *right helps of art* this great man of deep
thought mentions; but this is plain, that *syllogism* and the logic
now in use, which were as well known in his days, can be none of
those he means. It is sufficient for me if by a discourse, perhaps
something out of the way (I am sure as to me wholly new and
unborrowed), I shall have given occasion to others to cast about
for new discoveries and to seek in their own thoughts for those
right helps of art which will scarce be found, I fear, by those who
servilely confine themselves to the rules and dictates of others.
For beaten tracks lead this sort of cattle (as an observing *Roman*
calls them) whose thoughts reach only to imitation, *non quo
eundem est, sed quo itur.* But I can be bold to say that this age is
adorned with some men of that strength of judgment and largeness of comprehension that, if they would employ their thoughts
on this subject, could open new and undiscovered ways to the

advancement of knowledge.

8. Having here had an occasion to speak of *syllogism* in general and the use of it in reasoning, and the improvement of our knowledge, it is fit, before I leave this subject, to take notice of one manifest mistake in the rules of *syllogism*: viz. that no syllogistical reasoning can be right and conclusive, but what has at least one general proposition in it. As if we could not *reason* and have knowledge *about particulars*. Whereas, in truth, the matter rightly considered, the immediate object of all our reasoning and knowledge is nothing but particulars. Every man's reasoning and knowledge is only about the *ideas* existing in his own mind, which are truly, every one of them, particular existences; and our knowledge and reasoning about other things is only as they correspond with those our particular *ideas*. So that the perception of the agreement or disagreement of our particular *ideas* is the whole and utmost of all our knowledge. Universality is but accidental to it and consists only in this, that the particular *ideas* about which it is are such as more than one particular thing can correspond with and be represented by. But the perception of the agreement or disagreement of any two *ideas*, and consequently our knowledge, is equally clear and certain whether either or both or neither of those *ideas* be capable of representing more real beings than one or no. One thing more I crave leave to offer about syllogism, before I leave it, viz. may one not upon just ground inquire whether the form syllogism now has is that which in reason it ought to have? For the *medius terminus* being to join the extremes, i.e. the intermediate *ideas* by its intervention, to show the agreement or disagreement of the two in question, would not the position of the *medius terminus* be more natural and show the agreement or disagreement of the extremes clearer and better if it were placed in the middle between them? Which might be easily done by transposing the propositions and making the *medius terminus* the predicate of the first, and the subject of the second. As thus:

> *Omnis homo est animal,*
> *Omne animal est vivens,*
> *Ergo omnis homo est vivens.*

> *Omne corpus est extensum & solidum,*
> *Nullum extensum & solidum est pura extensio,*
> *Ergo corpus non est pura extensio.*

I need not trouble my reader with instances in *syllogisms*, whose conclusions are particular. The same reason holds for the same form in them as well as in the general.

CHAPTER XVIII

OF FAITH AND REASON, AND THEIR DISTINCT PROVINCES

1. IT has been above shown: (1) That we are of necessity ignorant and want knowledge of all sorts where we want *ideas*. (2) That we are ignorant and want rational knowledge where we want proofs. (3) That we want general knowledge and certainty, as far as we want clear and determined specific *ideas*. (4) That we want probability to direct our assent in matters where we have neither knowledge of our own nor testimony of other men to bottom our reason upon.

From these things thus premised, I think we may come to lay down the measures and *boundaries between faith and reason*: the want whereof may possibly have been the cause, if not of great disorders, yet at least of great disputes, and perhaps mistakes, in the world. For till it be resolved how far we are to be guided by reason, and how far by faith, we shall in vain dispute and endeavour to convince one another in matters of religion.

2. I find every sect, as far as reason will help them, make use of it gladly; and where it fails them, they cry out, *It is matter of faith, and above reason.* And I do not see how they can argue with anyone, or ever convince a gainsayer who makes use of the same plea, without setting down strict boundaries between *faith* and *reason*, which ought to be the first point established in all questions where *faith* has anything to do.

Reason, therefore, here, as contradistinguished to *faith*, I take to be the discovery of the certainty or probability of such propositions or truths, which the mind arrives at by deduction made from such *ideas* which it has got by the use of its natural faculties, viz. by sensation or reflection.

Faith, on the other side, is the assent to any proposition, not thus made out by the deductions of reason, but upon the credit of the proposer as coming from GOD, in some extraordinary way of communication. This way of discovering truths to men we call *revelation*.

3. First, then, I say that *no man inspired by* GOD *can by any revelation communicate to others any new simple ideas* which they had not before from sensation or reflection. For, whatsoever

impressions he himself may have from the immediate hand of GOD, this revelation, if it be of new simple *ideas*, cannot be conveyed to another, either by words or any other signs. Because words, by their immediate operation on us, cause no other *ideas* but of their natural sounds; and it is by the custom of using them for signs that they excite and revive in our minds latent *ideas*, but yet only such *ideas* as were there before. For words seen or heard recall to our thoughts those *ideas* only which to us they have been wont to be signs of, but cannot introduce any perfectly new and formerly unknown simple *ideas*. The same holds in all other signs, which cannot signify to us things of which we have before never had any *idea* at all.

Thus whatever things were discovered to St. *Paul*, when he was rapt up into the third heaven, whatever new *ideas* his mind there received, all the description he can make to others of that place is only this, that there are such things *as eye hath not seen, nor ear heard, nor hath it entered into the heart of man to conceive*. And supposing GOD should discover to anyone supernaturally, a species of creatures inhabiting, for example, *Jupiter* or *Saturn* (for that it is possible there may be such, nobody can deny) which had six senses, and imprint on his mind the *ideas* conveyed to theirs by that sixth sense: he could no more, by words, produce in the minds of other men those *ideas* imprinted by that sixth sense, than one of us could convey the *idea* of any colour, by the sounds of words, into a man who, having the other four senses perfect, had always totally wanted the fifth, of seeing. For our simple *ideas*, then, which are the foundation and sole matter of all our notions and knowledge, we must depend wholly on our reason, I mean, our natural faculties; and can by no means receive them, or any of them, from *traditional revelation*, I say *traditional revelation* in distinction to *original revelation*. By the one, I mean that first impression which is made immediately by GOD on the mind of any man, to which we cannot set any bounds; and by the other, those impressions delivered over to others in words and the ordinary ways of conveying our conceptions one to another.

4. *Secondly*, I say that *the same truths may be discovered and conveyed down from revelation, which are discoverable to us by reason*, and by those *ideas* we naturally may have. So GOD might, by revelation, discover the truth of any proposition in *Euclid*; as well as men, by the natural use of their faculties, come to make the discovery themselves. In all things of this kind there is little need or use of *revelation*, GOD having furnished us with natural and surer means to arrive at the know-

ledge of them. For whatsoever truth we come to the clear discovery of, from the knowledge and contemplation of our own *ideas*, will always be certainer to us than those which are conveyed to us by *traditional revelation*. For the knowledge we have that this *revelation* came at first from GOD can never be so sure as the knowledge we have from the clear and distinct perception of the agreement or disagreement of our own *ideas*: v.g. if it were revealed, some ages since, that the three angles of a triangle were equal to two right ones, I might assent to the truth of that proposition upon the credit of the tradition that it was revealed; but that would never amount to so great a certainty as the knowledge of it upon the comparing and measuring my own *ideas* of two right angles and the three angles of a triangle. The like holds in matter of fact knowable by our senses: v.g. the history of the deluge is conveyed to us by writings which had their original from revelation; and yet nobody, I think, will say he has as certain and clear a knowledge of the flood as *Noah*, that saw it, or that he himself would have had, had he then been alive and seen it. For he has no greater an assurance than that of his senses, that it is writ in the book supposed writ by *Moses* inspired; but he has not so great an assurance that *Moses* wrote that book as if he had seen *Moses* write it. So that the assurance of its being a revelation is less still than the assurance of his senses.

5. In propositions, then, whose certainty is built upon the clear perception of the agreement or disagreement of our *ideas*, attained either by immediate intuition, as in self-evident propositions, or by evident deductions of reason in demonstrations, we need not the assistance of *revelation*, as necessary to gain our assent and introduce them into our minds. Because the natural ways of knowledge could settle them there, or had done it already; which is the greatest assurance we can possibly have of anything, unless where GOD immediately reveals it to us; and there too our assurance can be no greater than our knowledge is, that it is a *revelation* from GOD. But yet nothing, I think, can under that title shake or overrule plain knowledge, or rationally prevail with any man to admit it for true in a direct contradiction to the clear evidence of his own understanding. For since no evidence of our faculties, by which we receive such *revelations*, can exceed, if equal, the certainty of our intuitive knowledge, we can never receive for a truth anything that is directly contrary to our clear and distinct knowledge: v.g. the *ideas* of one body and one place do so clearly agree, and the mind has so evident a perception of their agreement, that we can never assent to a

proposition that affirms the same body to be in two distant places at once, however it should pretend to the authority of a divine *revelation*: since the evidence, *first*, that we deceive not ourselves in ascribing it to GOD; *secondly*, that we understand it right, can never be so great as the evidence of our own intuitive knowledge whereby we discern it impossible for the same body to be in two places at once. And therefore *no proposition can be received for divine revelation* or obtain the assent due to all such, *if it be contradictory to our clear intuitive knowledge.* Because this would be to subvert the principles and foundations of all knowledge, evidence, and assent whatsoever; and there would be left no difference between truth and falsehood, no measures of credible and incredible in the world, if doubtful propositions shall take place before self-evident, and what we certainly know give way to what we may possibly be mistaken in. In propositions therefore contrary to the clear perception of the agreement or disagreement of any of our *ideas*, it will be in vain to urge them as matters of *faith*. They cannot move our assent under that or any other title whatsoever. For *faith* can never convince us of anything that contradicts our knowledge. Because, though *faith* be founded on the testimony of GOD (who cannot lie) revealing any proposition to us: yet we cannot have an assurance of the truth of its being a divine revelation greater than our own knowledge: since the whole strength of the certainty depends upon our knowledge that GOD revealed it; which, in this case, where the proposition supposed revealed contradicts our knowledge or reason, will always have this objection hanging to it, (viz.) that we cannot tell how to conceive that to come from GOD, the bountiful Author of our being, which, if received for true, must overturn all the principles and foundations of knowledge he has given us; render all our faculties useless; wholly destroy the most excellent part of his workmanship, our understandings; and put a man in a condition wherein he will have less light, less conduct than the beast that perisheth. For if the mind of man can never have a clearer (and, perhaps, not so clear) evidence of anything to be a divine *revelation*, as it has of the principles of its own reason, it can never have a ground to quit the clear evidence of its reason, to give place to a proposition whose *revelation* has not a greater evidence than those principles have.

6.   Thus far a man has use of reason and ought to hearken to it, even in immediate and original *revelation*, where it is supposed to be made to himself. But to all those who pretend not to immediate *revelation*, but are required to pay obedience and to

receive the truths revealed to others which, by the tradition of writings or word of mouth, are conveyed down to them, reason has a great deal more to do, and is that only which can induce us to receive them. For matter of faith being only divine revelation and nothing else, *faith*, as we use the word (called commonly, *divine faith*) has to do with no propositions but those which are supposed to be divinely revealed. So that I do not see how those who make revelation alone the sole object of *faith* can say that it is a matter of *faith*, and not of *reason*, to believe that such or such a proposition, to be found in such or such a book, is of divine inspiration, unless it be revealed that that proposition, or all in that book, was communicated by divine inspiration. Without such a *revelation*, the believing or not believing that proposition or book to be of divine authority can never be matter of *faith*, but matter of reason, and such as I must come to an assent to only by the use of my reason, which can never require or enable me to believe that which is contrary to itself: it being impossible for reason ever to procure any assent to that which to itself appears unreasonable.

In all things, therefore, where we have clear evidence from our *ideas* and those principles of knowledge I have above mentioned, *reason* is the proper judge; and *revelation*, though it may, in consenting with it, confirm its dictates, yet cannot in such cases invalidate its decrees; *nor can we be obliged, where we have the clear and evident sentence of reason, to quit it for the contrary opinion, under a pretence that it is matter of faith*, which can have no authority against the plain and clear dictates of *reason*.

7. But, *thirdly*, there being many things wherein we have very imperfect notions, or none at all; and other things, of whose past, present, or future existence, by the natural use of our faculties, we can have no knowledge at all: these, as being beyond the discovery of our natural faculties and above *reason*, are, when revealed, *the proper matter of faith*. Thus, that part of the angels rebelled against GOD and thereby lost their first happy state, and that the dead shall rise and live again: these and the like, being beyond the discovery of *reason*, are purely matters of *faith*, with which *reason* has, directly, nothing to do.

8. But since GOD, in giving us the light of *reason*, has not thereby tied up his own hands from affording us, when he thinks fit, the light of *revelation* in any of those matters wherein our natural faculties are able to give a probable determination: *revelation*, where God has been pleased to give it, *must carry it*

against the probable conjectures of reason. Because the mind, not being certain of the truth of that it does not evidently know, but only yielding to the probability that appears in it, is bound to give up its assent to such a testimony which, it is satisfied, comes from one who cannot err and will not deceive. But yet, it still belongs to *reason* to judge of the truth of its being a revelation and of the signification of the words wherein it is delivered. Indeed, if anything shall be thought *revelation* which is contrary to the plain principles of reason and the evident knowledge the mind has of its own clear and distinct *ideas*, there *reason* must be hearkened to, as to a matter within its province: since a man can never have so certain a knowledge that a proposition which contradicts the clear principles and evidence of his own knowledge was divinely revealed, or that he understands the words rightly wherein it is delivered, as he has that the contrary is true; and so is bound to consider and judge of it as a matter of reason and not swallow it, without examination, as a matter of *faith*.

9. *First*, Whatever proposition is revealed of whose truth our mind, by its natural faculties and notions, cannot judge, that is purely *matter of faith*, and above reason.

Secondly, All propositions whereof the mind, by the use of its natural faculties, can come to determine and judge, from naturally acquired *ideas*, are *matter of reason*, with this difference still: that, in those concerning which it has but an uncertain evidence and so is persuaded of their truth only upon probable grounds, which still admit a possibility of the contrary to be true without doing violence to the certain evidence of its own knowledge and overturning the principles of all reason, in such probable propositions, I say, an evident *revelation* ought to determine our assent, even against probability. For where the principles of reason have not evidenced a proposition to be certainly true or false, there clear *revelation*, as another principle of truth and ground of assent, may determine; and so it may be matter of *faith* and be also above *reason*. Because *reason*, in that particular matter, being able to reach no higher than probability, *faith* gave the determination where *reason* came short, and *revelation* discovered on which side the truth lay.

10. Thus far the dominion of *faith* reaches, and that without any violence or hindrance to *reason*, which is not injured or disturbed, but assisted and improved by new discoveries of truth coming from the eternal fountain of all knowledge. Whatever GOD hath revealed is certainly true: no doubt can be made of it. This is the proper object of *faith*; but whether it be a divine

revelation or no, *reason* must judge, which can never permit the mind to reject a greater evidence to embrace what is less evident, nor allow it to entertain probability in opposition to knowledge and certainty. There can be no evidence that any traditional revelation is of divine original, in the words we receive it and in the sense we understand it, so clear and so certain as that of the principles of reason; and therefore *nothing that is contrary to, and inconsistent with, the clear and self-evident dictates of reason has a right to be urged or assented to as a matter of faith, wherein reason hath nothing to do.* Whatsoever is divine *revelation*, ought to overrule all our opinions, prejudices, and interests, and hath a right to be received with full assent; such a submission as this, of our *reason* to *faith*, takes not away the landmarks of knowledge: this shakes not the foundations of reason, but leaves us that use of our faculties for which they were given us.

11. *If the provinces of faith and reason are not kept distinct by these boundaries*, there will, in matter of religion, be no room for *reason* at all, and those extravagant opinions and ceremonies that are to be found in the several religions of the world will not deserve to be blamed. For, to this crying up of *faith* in opposition to *reason*, we may, I think, in good measure ascribe those absurdities that fill almost all the religions which possess and divide mankind. For men, having been principled with an opinion that they must not consult *reason* in the things of religion, however apparently contradictory to common sense and the very principles of all their knowledge, have let loose their fancies and natural superstition, and have been by them led into so strange opinions and extravagant practices in religion that a considerate man cannot but stand amazed at their follies and judge them so far from being acceptable to the great and wise GOD, that he cannot avoid thinking them ridiculous and offensive to a sober, good man. So that in effect religion, which should most distinguish us from beasts and ought most peculiarly to elevate us as rational creatures above brutes, is that wherein men often appear most irrational and more senseless than beasts themselves. *Credo, quia impossibile est: I believe, because it is impossible*, might, in a good man, pass for a sally of zeal, but would prove a very ill rule for men to choose their opinions or religion by.

CHAPTER XXI

OF THE DIVISION OF THE SCIENCES

1. ALL that can fall within the compass of human understanding being either, *first*, the nature of things, as they are in themselves, their relations, and their manner of operation; or, *secondly*, that which man himself ought to do, as a rational and voluntary agent, for the attainment of any end, especially happiness; or, *thirdly*, the ways and means whereby the knowledge of both the one and the other of these are attained and communicated: I think *science* may be divided properly into these *three sorts*:

2. *First*, The knowledge of things as they are in their own proper beings, their constitutions, properties, and operations; whereby I mean not only matter and body, but spirits also, which have their proper natures, constitutions, and operations, as well as bodies. This, in a little more enlarged sense of the word, I call φυσική, or *natural philosophy*. The end of this is bare speculative truth; and whatsoever can afford the mind of man any such, falls under this branch, whether it be God himself, angels, spirits, bodies, or any of their affections, as number, and figure, etc.

3. *Secondly*, Πρακτική, the skill of right applying our own powers and actions, for the attainment of things good and useful. The most considerable under this head is *ethics*, which is the seeking out those rules and measures of human actions which lead to happiness, and the means to practise them. The end of this is not bare speculation and the knowledge of truth, but right, and a conduct suitable to it.

4. *Thirdly*, The third branch may be called σημειωτική, or *the doctrine of signs*; the most usual whereof being words, it is aptly enough termed also λογική, *logic*: the business whereof is to consider the nature of signs the mind makes use of for the understanding of things, or conveying its knowledge to others. For, since the things the mind contemplates are none of them, besides itself, present to the understanding, it is necessary that something else, as a sign or representation of the thing it considers, should be present to it: and these are *ideas*. And because the scene of *ideas* that makes one man's thoughts cannot be laid open to the immediate view of another, nor laid up anywhere but in the memory, a no very sure repository: therefore to communicate our thoughts to one another, as well as record them

for our own use, signs of our *ideas* are also necessary. Those which men have found most convenient, and therefore generally make use of, are articulate sounds. The consideration, then, of *ideas* and *words* as the great instruments of knowledge makes no despicable part of their contemplation who would take a view of human knowledge in the whole extent of it. And perhaps if they were distinctly weighed and duly considered, they would afford us another sort of logic and critique than what we have been hitherto acquainted with.

5.   *This* seems to me *the first and most general, as well as natural, division* of the objects of our understanding. For a man can employ his thoughts about nothing but either the contemplation of *things* themselves, for the discovery of truth; or about the things in his own power, which are his own *actions*, for the attainment of his own ends; or the *signs* the mind makes use of, both in the one and the other, and the right ordering of them, for its clearer information. All which three, viz. *things* as they are in themselves knowable; *actions* as they depend on us, in order to happiness; and the right use of *signs* in order to knowledge, being *toto coelo* different: they seemed to me to be the three great provinces of the intellectual world, wholly separate and distinct one from another.

FINIS

INDEX